Palestine, Imperialism and the Struggle for Freedom

Philip Marfleet

Bookmarks
Publications

About the author

Philip Marfleet is Emeritus Professor of Social Science at the University of East London, UK. He is the author of *Revolution and Counter-revolution in Iran* (1988), *Intifada: Zionism, Imperialism and Palestinian Resistance* (1989), *Refugees in a Global Era* (2006), and *Egypt – Contested Revolution* (2016). He is editor with Rabab El Mahdi of *Egypt – the Moment of Change* (2009) and with Keiko Sakai of *Iraq Since the Invasion* (2020). He is a member of the editorial board of *International Socialism*.

Palestine, Imperialism and the Struggle for Freedom
by Philip Marfleet

Published 2025 by Bookmarks Publications
c/o 1 Bloomsbury Street, London WC1B 3QE

Cover design by Esther Nelsen
Typeset in Adobe Caslon and Whitney by Ben Windsor
Printed by Halstan, Amersham HP6 6HJ

ISBN paperback 978-1-917020-37-4
Kindle 978-1-917020-38-1
ePub 978-1-917020-39-8
PDF 978-1-917020-40-4

Contents

This book is dedicated to

THE SAMIDIN

– those who exist, resist,
and will return

and to
Tony Cliff,
Chanie Rosenberg
and John Rose

– Jewish revolutionaries
resolute in the struggle for
a free Palestine

Preface

Many thanks to comrades and friends who made possible the writing of this book. It draws extensively on first-hand experiences in Palestine, Lebanon, Syria, Jordan and Egypt, and on many discussions with those in the front line of struggle with the Israeli state and with Arab regimes that have helped to sustain it.

I finally understood the reality – and the contradictions – of Israeli repression when standing outside the *muqata'a* near Ramallah in 2002. The building was first constructed as a British fort in the Mandate era and had been converted to headquarters for Yasser Arafat's Palestine Authority. Furious at the Al-Aqsa Intifada, which had begun two years earlier, Israeli leaders ordered its demolition – not merely destruction of the concrete hulk but its reduction to dust. All that remained after the work done by explosives, bulldozers and crushers were a few rooms for the sickly Arafat, surrounded by piles of sand and gravel.

The scene was theatrical. Did the demolition give satisfaction to Israeli leaders? Was it meant to demonstrate the futility of resistance? If so, it was a striking failure, for in villages, towns and cities across the West Bank and Gaza millions of people continued actively to defy military rule.

For the next two decades Israel launched wave after wave of assaults, with Gaza the key target. In 2023 its leaders deployed their army, navy and air force in savage attacks rightly seen as a sustained genocidal offensive. Much of Gaza too was reduced to rubble, but Israel failed to destroy armed resistance or to quell *sumud* – the steadfastness or fortitude that has long characterised Palestinian lives under occupation.

This book addresses resistance from the earliest years of British rule to the Gaza war that began in 2023. It sets Palestinian agency in the context of wider struggles against colonialism and the specific problems presented by the Zionist settler movement with its ambition to control historic Palestine 'from the river [Jordan] to the [Mediterranean] sea'. It views Palestinian resistance as part of struggles against imperialist networks across the Middle East – and in particular as a catalyst for movements that have contested regimes in neighbouring states, most importantly in Egypt. It contends that the liberation of Palestine is intimately associated with revolutionary struggles across the region.

....

Thanks to those who patiently read drafts of this book and responded with comments, criticisms and ideas for improvement, especially to: Anne Alexander, Rob Ferguson, Lynne Hubbard, Lee Marfleet, Angela Sibley and Mark Thomas. Thanks to Palestinian and Egyptian activists, especially Aisha, Daoud, Hossam, Laila, Mohammed, Musa, Mustafa, Wael and Wassim, whom it would be unwise to name in full for reasons of security. Thanks to Carol Williams for her expertise in editing, to Esther Neslen for her fine design of the book cover, and to Ben Windsor for internal design and layout.

Thanks to those with whom I have been privileged to share discussions and initiatives in Cairo between 1976 and 2025, and whose insights inform my understanding of change in the Arab world. It is safe to name some of those no longer with us: I did not always agree with Ahmad Abdalla, Yusuf Darwish, Hisham Mubarak, Ibrahim Shukrallah and Hani Shukrallah but benefited greatly from our discussions. Special thanks and acknowledgment to Talal Asad for his encouragement, many years ago, of critical thinking about Palestine.

With appreciation and love to Lynne Hubbard, Lee Marfleet and Harry Hubbard.

....

This book was written during the assault on Gaza that began in October 2023. It was completed in February 2025 as US President Donald Trump asserted that he would 'clean out' Gaza, removing its millions of Palestinian residents. The declaration was greeted enthusiastically by politicians of the Israeli Right: Cabinet Minister Miki Zohar declared: 'Thank God for this miracle He performed for the people of Israel.'[1] In a volatile and dangerous situation, solidarity with the Palestinians and with those in Arab states who support their struggles is of profound importance. In the UK, this is co-ordinated by the Palestine Solidarity Campaign: palestinecampaign.org

Glossary

(Unless a proper name, A = Arabic, H = Hebrew)

AHC
Arab Higher Committee

ALA
Arab Liberation Army

ALF
Arab Liberation Front, Palestinian Iraqi-backed militia

Amal
Lebanese militia

ANM
Arab Nationalist Movement

Aramco
Arabian–American Oil Company (later Saudi Arabian Oil Company)

Avoda Ivrit (H)
Hebrew Labour

AWA
Arab Women's Association of Palestine

Ba'th
Arab nationalist current

BDS
Boycott, Divestment and Sanctions

Betar
Revisionist Zionist Party

Black and Tans
British auxiliary police

B'Tselem
Israeli Information Centre for Human Rights in the Occupied Territories

Comintern
Communist International

Cosatu
Congress of South African Trade Unions

Deuxième Bureau
Lebanese security agency

DFLP
Popular Democratic Front for the Liberation of Palestine

ECP
Egyptian Communist Party

Egyptian Labour Corps
Labour force conscripted by Britain, First World War

EPCSI
Egyptian Popular Committee in Solidarity with the Intifada

Eretz Israel (H)
Land of Israel

Fatah
Palestinian National Liberation Movement

Fedayeen (A)
Sacrificers, guerrilla fighters

FLN
Front de libération nationale (Algeria)

Freedom and Justice Party
Electoral organisation of the Muslim Brotherhood, Egypt

Green Hand
Palestinian guerrilla group

Gush Emunim
Bloc of the Faithful, Israeli settler movement

Haganah
Zionist militia

Hamas
Islamic Resistance Movement

Hasbara (H)
Propaganda

Histadrut
Israeli trade union federation

ICC
International Criminal Court

ICJ
International Court of Justice

IDF
Israeli Defence Forces

IMF
International Monetary Fund

Infitah (A)
Neoliberal economic policy (Egypt)

Intifada (A)
Uprising

Irgun
Revisionist Zionist militia

Istiqlal
Syrian/Palestinian nationalist party

Izz al-Din al-Qassam Brigades
Palestinian Islamist militia (Hamas)

Jewish Brigades
Jewish sections of British forces, First World War

Jihad (A)
Striving/exertion/struggle

JNF
Jewish National Fund

Kach
Extreme right Israeli party

Kataeb
Lebanese Maronite militia

Kibbutz (H)
Communal settlement

Kufiyya (A)
Headscarf

Lehi
Stern Group, Revisionist Zionist militia

Likud
Right-wing Israeli party

Minstanenim (H)
Infiltrators

Moshav (H)
Agricultural settlement

Nachala
Israeli settler organisation

Nakba (A)
Catastrophe, ethnic cleansing of Palestinians, 1948

Naksa (A)
Setback, war of 1967

NFLP
National Front for the Liberation of Palestine

NLF
National Liberation Front (Vietnam)

NRP
National Religious Party, right-wing Israeli party

Opec
Organisation of Petroleum Exporting Countries

Otzma Jehudit
Jewish Power, right-wing Israeli Party

PA
Palestinian Authority

Palmach
Elite Zionist militia

PAWS
Palestine Arab Workers Society

PCP
Palestine Communist Party

PLL
Palestine Labour League

PFLP
Popular Front for the Liberation of Palestine

PLDC
Palestine Land Development Company

PLA
Palestine Liberation Army

PLO
Palestine Liberation Organisation

PNC
Palestine National Council

QIZ
Qualified Industrial Zone

QME
Qualitative Military Edge

RAF
Royal Air Force

Saiqa
Syrian-backed Palestinian militia

Salaf (A)
Founding fathers of Islam

SNS
Special Night Squads

Society of the Muslim Brothers
Muslim Brotherhood, Islamist organisation

SOE
Special Operations Executive, undercover British unit

Sumud (A)
Steadfastness/fortitude (samidin – those who are steadfast)

Tathir (A)
Cleansing/purification

Thawra (A)
Revolution (The Revolution, sometimes The Resistance)

UAR
United Arab Republic

Umma (A)
Community of Muslims

UNLU
Unified National Leadership of the Uprising

UNDRP
United Nations Disaster Relief Project

UNHCR
Office of the United Nations High Commissioner for Refugees

UNRPR
United Nations Relief for Palestinian Refugees

UNRRA
United Nations Relief and Rehabilitation Administration

UNRWA
United Nations Relief and Works Agency

VWC
Voluntary Work Committee

Wafd
Egyptian nationalist party

Yishuv (H)
Jewish community in Palestine

Yisrael Beitanu
Israel Our Home, right-wing Israeli party

YMMA
Young Men's Muslim Association

Zakat (A)
Islamic alms tax

Timeline

1916 Sykes–Picot Agreement.
Britain and France divide the Arab East

1917 Britain invades Palestine. Balfour Declaration

1920 Arab Executive established by traditional Palestinian leaders

1921 Conflicts in Jaffa, British military intervention

1923 British Mandate comes into force

1929 'Western Wall'/'al-Buraq' conflicts.
Palestinian Youth Congress calls for independence.
Arab Women's Association of Palestine founded

1930 Shaw Commission and Passfield White Paper – British reports on Palestine. General strike of Palestinian Arabs

1931 MacDonald Letter to Zionist leaders

1933 Mass protests in Jaffa attacked by British

1935 Palestinian general strike. Al-Qassam uprising

1936 Indefinite general strike.
Guerrilla resistance initiated.
Arab Executive formed

1937 Palestine Royal Commission (Peel Commission) recommends partition

1938 Palestine Partition Commission (Woodhead Commission)

1939 MacDonald Paper repudiates partition

1946 Anglo-American Committee of Enquiry

1947 United Nations Commission proposes partition

1948 Zionist militias launch Nakba.
Arab armies enter Palestine.
Zionist leaders declare state of Israel

1950 Unrwa established

1956 Israel invades Gaza

1959 Fatah established

1964 PLO formed

1965 First guerrilla attacks on Israel

1967 June War, Israel occupies West Bank, Gaza, Sinai, Golan.
PFLP established

1968 Battle of Karama, solidarity movement in Egypt

1970 Black September offensive in Jordan

1973 October War

1974 First Israeli settlements in Occupied Territories

1982 Israel invades Lebanon, Beirut massacres

1987 Intifada begins in Gaza, solidarity in Arab states,
Hamas established

1991 US attacks Iraq, Palestinians evicted from Gulf states.
Madrid 'peace talks'

1993 Oslo Accords, PLO accepts Israel as a sovereign state

1994 Palestinian Authority (PA) established

1996 Arafat elected president of Palestinian ministate

2000 Al-Aqsa Intifada begins

2001 US invasion of Iraq, initiation of 'War on Terror'

2006 Hamas wins Palestinian elections, takes control in Gaza. Israel imposes blockade

2008 Invasion of Gaza, Israel launches Operation Cast Lead

2012 Further invasion of Gaza, Israel launches Operation Pillar of Defence

2014 Further Invasion of Gaza, Israel launches Operation Protective Edge

2021 Palestinian Unity Intifada

2023 Hamas launches Al-Aqsa Flood offensive, Israel launches Iron Swords invasion

2025 'Ceasefire' in Gaza

Introduction

This book is a contribution to the movement of solidarity with Palestine and to the struggle for a single, democratic unitary state from the river to the sea. It addresses pressing questions that arise from recent events in the Middle East:

- What accounts for the savagery of continuous Israeli assaults on the Palestinian people?
- Why have Israel's allies allowed its rulers to act with impunity?
- How have Palestinians maintained resistance against overwhelmingly powerful forces?
- What forms of solidarity can assist the Palestinians in their struggle for freedom?
- How can Palestinian liberation be achieved?

The answers lie in histories that began over 100 years ago. These are contested – shaped on the one hand by powerful institutions in Israel and among its allies and, on the other hand, by Palestinian accounts that rely upon memory and individual testimony. For decades, most Israeli historians practised 'memoricide', setting out records of the past in Palestine from which Arab society had been discarded. In this account Palestinians had never existed as a people or, if they had a shadowy presence, it ceased to have meaning when they were said to have abandoned their homes, providing the settler movement of European immigrants with sovereign rights in a new state. These falsehoods, established in the years after mass displacement of Palestinians in 1948, provided a template for decades of fabrication and outright deceit. Allies of Israel abroad embellished narratives of an admirable state struggling against the odds as a home for the Jewish people and a friend of liberal democracies in North America and Western Europe. The Palestinians were at best a footnote in these stories of high achievement. Sometimes they appeared as 'collateral damage', often they did not appear at all: 'memoricide' was a practice of denial, removing millions of people from history just as in 1948 they had been removed from towns, cities and villages of Palestine.

But Palestinians have been among the most active agents of change in the long history of colonialism. This book addresses Palestinian resistance as a continuous feature of politics in the Arab region and as a catalyst for movements of solidarity and emulation across the Arab East and the states of North Africa. Palestine has finally become 'Global Palestine', featuring centrally in world media and stimulating mass movements of support that challenge the agendas of powerful states. The book views Palestinian resistance from the perspectives of internationalism, anti-racism and anti-imperialism. It recognises the reality of antisemitism and the historic crises of European society that prompted migrations to Palestine of Jewish victims of racist hostility. It highlights the racist agendas of European colonial powers, including Islamophobia and systematic negation of the cultures and political interests of people of the Middle East. It addresses the exclusionary strategies of the Zionist movement and the increasingly open racism of the Israel state. It sees struggles against imperialism past and present as the basis for social justice across the region. It anticipates revolutionary change as the means for the liberation of Palestine.

'Miracles'

Israel came into existence formally in May 1948 – the outcome, according to widely held Zionist accounts, of 'a history of miracles'.[1] Israeli historian Alon Confino writes of a 'sense of marvel' among the Jewish population of Palestine following events in 1948 – 'at having the country largely to themselves'.[2] Most of the Palestinian Arab population had gone, leaving Jewish communities in possession of the land and enabled to create a new state.[3] Chaim Weizmann, first president of Israel, declared 'a miraculous clearing of the land: the miraculous simplification of Israel's task'.[4] A few years later, Emmanuel Rackman could write that establishment of the state was seen by many as a miracle from heaven: 'The least that anyone can say is that the achievement was well-nigh wondrous.'[5] The theme was persistent:

for celebrated Israeli novelist Amos Oz, speaking over 50 years later, the story of Israel was 'stunning...a brilliant success', a 'miracle' and 'a dream come true'.[6]

Avi Shlaim writes of miracles and myths perpetuated in much Israeli historical writing. Official and semi-official accounts of the 1948 conflict, he says, fostered the view that Israel's victory was achieved in the face of 'insurmountable military odds':

> Israel is pictured in these accounts as a little Jewish David confronting a giant Goliath. The war is portrayed as a desperate, costly and heroic struggle for survival with plucky little Israel fighting marauding armies from seven Arab states. Israel's ultimate victory in this war is treated as nothing short of a miracle.[7]

These stories had the effect of concealing traumatic events in the years before 1948 and during the Nakba – the expulsion of most of the Arab people of Palestine. A purposeful, sustained and violent campaign of 'transfer' undertaken by the Zionist movement was depicted as a heroic struggle against the odds so extraordinary that it seemed 'wondrous', even supernatural. These accounts removed from the scene a mass of people who abruptly became refugees, losing their homes and possessions, their communities and social assets, and their histories as people who for decades had resisted British colonial forces and the settler presence. Myths about 1948 established a falsehood at the heart of the Zionist project which has since been embedded in the political culture of Israel and disseminated widely, especially in North America and Europe.

'History is the fruit of power', says Haitian historian Michel-Rolph Trouillot.[8] Stories of the past involve unequal contributions of competing groups and individuals, he suggests, 'who have unequal access to the means for such production'.[9] In 1948 the Zionist movement undertook a campaign of ethnic cleansing that removed most of the Arab population: it also removed the main means by which communities and national groups record their circumstances, experiences and aspirations. Nur Masalha writes:

> In 1948 the Israeli state appropriated for itself immovable Palestinian material assets and personal possessions including schools, rich private libraries, books, pictures, private papers, historical documents and manuscripts, furniture, churches, mosques, shrines, historic public buildings, archaeological sites and artefacts, urban residential quarters, transport infrastructure, seaports and airports, police stations, prisons and railways.[10]

By seizing papers, records, registers and cultural heritage, the Israeli state made it possible for some historians to claim that there was no documented evidence of Palestinian experiences before or during the events of 1948. Rashid Khalidi says 'a meticulously crafted and superficially convincing Zionist narrative was ubiquitous', systematically erasing the Palestinians.[11] This, he adds, 'took up all the oxygen in almost any public space'.[12] By the 1960s, when Israel had been integrated into strategies for control of the Middle East by Western states and for the benefit of corporate capital, the Palestinians had been discarded from stories about what Amy Kaplan has called 'Our American Israel'.[13] In the US, now Israel's key ally, Americans projected their own origin myths onto the Jewish state: 'the biblical promised land, the open frontier, the refuge for immigrants, the revolt against colonialism'.[14] Palestinians had apparently disappeared into an undifferentiated mass of people of the Arab world – until in the late 1960s they abruptly reappeared, women and men declaring for a struggle against imperialism and for an independent democratic Palestine. Within a few years a mass movement of Palestinian resistance had mobilised across states of the region. The Zionist 'miracle' of 1948 had failed to remove the displaced and dispossessed: the Palestinians were back, giving testimony to their fate at the hands of Britain, the colonial settler movement, and Israel's powerful allies.

Resistance

The launch of guerrilla struggles by the Palestine Liberation Organisation (PLO) in 1965 initiated organised resistance that has continued for 60 years. Revitalising Palestinian cultural and academic networks, it also prompted efforts to document the past, placing on the historical record Palestinian struggles against Britain during the years of colonialism and against those in the Zionist movement who sought to evict and 'transfer' them. These accounts of resistance subverted falsehoods that underlay Israeli narratives and *hasbara* ('public diplomacy' or propaganda). The 18th-century French writer Voltaire maintained that history was full of falsification and that lying was a virtue 'when it is useful', adding: 'One must lie like a devil, not timidly, not for a time, but boldly and on every occasion.'[15] Israel spent decades boldly disseminating untruths about the foundation of the state and its attitude towards those expelled during the Nakba. The bigger the falsehood, the more insistent the effort to sustain it – and the greater the violence against those who challenged it. Years of savage attacks on the Palestinians culminated in 2023 with a genocidal assault on Gaza.

Painstaking work by oral historians has re-established accounts of the Palestinian experience, 'bringing to light hidden, suppressed or marginalised narratives'.[16] At the same time, historians working conventionally with written records have revealed much that had been concealed by the Israeli state. Accessing archives that for decades remained closed under official restriction, they have documented stratagems and military initiatives of the Zionist movement before, during and after the Nakba of 1948. Together with autobiographies and personal histories, these now play a role in 'decolonising' dominant accounts of events in Palestine. To write more truthfully about the Nakba and its outcomes, says Nur Masalha, is 'a profoundly moral act of liberation and struggle for truth, justice, equality, return'.[17] It is part of Palestinian resistance and of solidarity with the Palestinian struggle for freedom.

Imperialism

Why have Israeli leaders enjoyed impunity when ordering incessant attacks on Palestinian communities? Assaults on Gaza that began in 2023 are among the most violent military initiatives of modern times. By 2 November – 26 days into the bombardment – the Euro-Med Human Rights Monitor (EHRM) estimated that Israel had dropped 25,000 tonnes of bombs on 12,000 targets – the equivalent of two nuclear weapons over an area of 360 square kilometres, far smaller than the area of Hiroshima assaulted with nuclear devices in 1945.[18]

The organisation reported:

> Israel's use of highly explosive bombs in densely populated areas poses the single greatest threat to civilians in modern armed conflicts…and explains the complete levelling of residential neighbourhoods in Gaza and the overall severity of the widespread devastation there.

An official of the Israeli Defence Forces (IDF) declared that residents of Gaza were 'human beasts' and 'are dealt with accordingly'.[19] Israel had imposed a total blockade on Gaza, he said, 'No electricity and no water, just damage. You wanted hell, you will get hell.'[20] People of Gaza were treated as collectively guilty for attacks launched by Hamas on 7 October 2023. This approach was not new. In the 1920s British forces routinely punished entire villages and neighbourhoods in Palestine for resistance to colonial rule. In the 1930s Britain mobilised tens of thousands of troops to assault communities in which they suspected that 'bandits' (resistance fighters) were present. And Britain armed and trained many members of Zionist militias that in 1948 drove over 700,000 people out of Palestine: people seen collectively as 'guilty' for being in occupation of land that the settler movement wished to seize.

Assaults on the Palestinians and on people of neighbouring states including Lebanon, Syria and Egypt have been a feature of Israeli history. They have included invasions, occupations and massacres. In 1982 Israel supervised mass killings in Beirut at the Sabra–Shatila refugee camp. Under the authority of General Ariel Sharon, later to be prime minister, Israel's allies among ultra-right-wing Lebanese militias murdered thousands of defenceless people. Their collective crime was their status as Palestinian refugees. This pitiless use of violence has been pursued by Israeli leaders from David Ben-Gurion, first prime minister of the Zionist state, through Ariel Sharon to Benjamin Netanyahu, architect of the Gaza genocide. All have acted with confidence that their allies among the most powerful Western states would endorse their actions. Governments in North America and Europe have effectively granted Israel's leaders immunity from criticism, together with assured supplies of weaponry with which to assault people of the region. Israel's 'right to self-defence' has been invoked continuously to secure its overwhelming military advantage in relation to Palestinian resistance and among all states of the Middle East. In 2008 the US Congress placed formally into law a commitment of the American state to guarantee Israel a 'Qualitative Military Edge' (QME) over any state or coalition of states with which it might be in conflict.[21] The QME law confirmed arrangements that had been under way for decades: the US has provided weaponry in quantities that dwarf supplies to any other state worldwide. By 2023, it had delivered a total of almost $350 billion worth of aid to Israel, overwhelmingly in the form of military equipment.[22] This huge sum was not a sentimental gift to 'Our American Israel' but a hard-headed investment in a state long part of imperialist networks in the Middle East.

Since President Franklin D Roosevelt declared in the 1940s that Gulf oilfields were vital to the US, strategists in Washington have focused on the region, seeking sites for military bases and local allies judged capable of backing American interests. Following the 1967 war in which Israel defeated a coalition of Arab states – most important, the radical nationalist regime in Egypt – the value of American arms exports to Israel increased by 450 percent.[23] When the Shah of Iran, a longstanding American ally, was deposed by a revolutionary upheaval in 1979, arms supplies to Israel surged to an annual record of over $15 billion.[24] Israel had become America's chosen 'partner against the spread of anti-Western radicalism' throughout the Middle East.[25] The US has since continuously backed Israel: a preliminary account for 2024 shows that arms exports were at a record level, including missile defence systems, aircraft, fighting vehicles, heavy weaponry, small arms, cluster bombs, 'bunker bombs' and light ammunition.[26] Between October 2023 and August 2024 the US sent Israel more than 10,000 highly destructive 2,000-pound bombs and thousands of missiles.[27] Aerial onslaughts on Gaza and Lebanon were a 'hell' manufactured in the US and among lesser arms suppliers in Germany, Italy, France and the UK, as well as in Israel.

'Exist, resist, return'

Israeli historian Ilan Pappé writes that during the early years of Zionist migration to Palestine, the Arab population appeared to settlers 'as aliens who should not have been there'.[28] When settler organisations appropriated land, 'good' Palestinians were those who allowed themselves to be evicted. 'Those who refused were branded robbers and murderers':

> Later on, wherever Israel would control the lives of Palestinians, such a refusal to collaborate would be the ultimate proof for Palestinian choice of the terrorist option as a way of life.[29]

Their presence in Palestine was sufficient cause for early Zionist leaders to brand the Arab population 'a malignant evil'.[30] Even among socialist–Zionists, Palestinian Arabs were under suspicion, an 'apparently docile mass' capable at any point 'of exploding into irrational and bloody action'.[31] As Jewish immigrants arrived from Europe, most innocent of hostility to the Arab population, they encountered institutions implacably opposed to the Palestinian presence. Like other migrants who settled in European colonies worldwide, they became part of exclusionary projects that sought dominion over territory they occupied. Lorenzo Veracini sees a pattern worldwide in which 'fantasies of ultimately "emptying" in one way or another the indigenous section of the population system inevitably recur'.[32] In Palestine, those who resisted settlement were seen within the Zionist movement as perverse, guilty of 'motiveless and unwarranted violence', of 'rage',[33] of 'hatred and fanaticism', or of succumbing to the influence of 'outside agitators' who pursued antisemitic agendas.[34] Members of the immigrant community who aspired to engagement and co-operation with Palestinian society became a diminishing minority as resistance confirmed their leaders' belief that the land should be emptied in order to achieve comprehensive settlement.

The 'miracle' of 1948 accomplished the key aims of the Zionist project. But the Nakba did not eliminate the Palestinians – it displaced and dispersed them, and when resistance was renewed among people of the diaspora, they came under assault from the Israeli state. Now the PLO was alleged to bear irrational hatreds: its activists were terrorists; its leader was a Palestinian 'Hitler' driven by antisemitism. The Palestinians dared to exist, to resist, and even more shockingly, aspired to return.

Israeli attitudes towards the Palestinians have been marked by increasingly open racism. This is not an aspect of the Jewish character of the state – religious/cultural traditions have not shaped Israel's agendas regarding Palestinians. Rather, racism and exclusion have been an outcome of decades of settlement – first under British colonialism, later as part of imperialist networks in which Israel's leaders pursued visions of the state as what the founding father of Zionism, Theodor Herzl, called 'a rampart of Europe against Asia…the outpost of civilization against barbarism'.[35] Herzl's approach to people of the Middle East drew on centuries of racist ideology towards peoples subordinated by European colonial powers. Embedded in the Zionist state, it has proved extraordinarily persistent. A century after Herzl, Israeli Prime Minister Ehud Barak could assert that Israel enjoyed the status of 'a villa in the jungle': here, says Neve Gordon, Barak sees 'a civilised Western island surrounded by semi-barbaric Arabs and Muslims'.[36]

In this view, Israel is an oasis of harmony and democracy. Ramzy Baroud writes: 'For the Israeli "villa" to remain prosperous and peaceful, according to Barak, Israel needed to do more than merely maintain its military edge; it had to ensure the "chaos" does not breach the perimeters of Israel's perfect existence'.[37] Israeli leaders have constructed a security regime in which residents within Herzl's 'rampart'/ Barak's 'villa' impose their presence on the Arab population:

> Israelis want to be able to kill, without being killed in return; subdue and militarily occupy Palestinians without the least degree of resistance, armed or otherwise; they want to imprison thousands of Palestinians without the slightest protest or even the mere questioning of Israel's military judicial system.[38]

This vision has guided the thinking of successive Israeli leaders. In 2023, Benjamin Netanyahu justified war on Gaza by insisting: 'we [Israel] are in a battle of civilisation against barbarism'.[39]

Here 'barbarism' denotes not only Palestinian resistance but the Palestinian people's existence. Marwan Bishara observes:

> Israel fears all that is Palestinian steadfastness, Palestinian unity, Palestinian democracy, Palestinian poetry, and all Palestinian national symbols [and] Israel hates the Palestinians for being so integral to the history, geography and nature of the landscape it claims as its own... Israel hates them for impeding the realisation of the Zionist dream over all historical Palestine. And it especially hates those living in Gaza, for turning the dream into a nightmare.[40]

'Global' Palestine

The long history of resistance among Palestinians is remarkable but not unique. Many struggles against colonial rule have been undertaken continuously for generations. Ireland's movement for liberation from Britain lasted over two centuries; organised resistance to France in Algeria continued for over 100 years; liberation struggles in Vietnam confronted first France, then the US and its allies. Across Africa, Asia, Australasia and Latin America the lives of billions of people have been shaped by struggles for freedom from colonial rule.

Since the Nakba Palestinians have explored all manner of options to resist. These have included appeals to Arab leaders for action on their behalf, diplomatic lobbying, and legal challenges undertaken through international bodies: all have failed. More effective has been everyday resistance; refusal to collaborate; mobilisation through rallies, demonstrations and strikes; and, intermittently, guerrilla struggles. They have often revealed contradictions and profound difficulties. As in other movements for national liberation, the leadership of the PLO pursued strategies that could not serve the mass of people. Following agendas shaped by the interests of an embryonic Palestinian bourgeoisie, Yasser Arafat and his colleagues isolated most Palestinians from struggles for change across the Middle East, ignoring or even rejecting movements of solidarity. When the Palestinians' remarkable intifadas stimulated mass support and efforts at emulation in states such as Egypt and Algeria, PLO leaders invoked a principle of 'non-interference' in the wider politics of the Arab states. Determined to maintain their links with the kings, emirs and presidents of the region, they inhibited movements for change that challenged rulers seeking their own place in imperialist networks and accommodations with Israel.

Despite these retreats, relentless struggle by the mass of Palestinians eventually won support worldwide. Some 20 years ago the issue of Palestine became 'Global Palestine' as networks of solidarity grew rapidly – first in the form of action for Boycott, Divestment and Sanctions (BDS), later in repeated mass movements of protest when Israel assaulted the West Bank and Gaza. 'Peace' talks organised by the US during the 1990s had delivered for the PLO a 'ministate' that proved no more than a set of tiny enclaves of Palestinian land under Israeli military control. The Palestinian Authority (PA) created to administer these areas lost all credibility as its subordination to Israel demonstrated that PLO strategy had reached a dead end. The Palestinian national leadership, said BDS activist Omar Barghouti, was 'unelected, unrepresentative, unprincipled, and visionless'; it had for years been 'in total disarray'.[41] Young Palestinians resolved to break the isolation imposed on the national movement by the PLO. Inspired by the example of the BDS movement in support of anti-apartheid struggles in South Africa, they launched an international campaign seeking solidarity and an independent Palestinian future. In 2005 a Boycott National Committee supported by 170 Palestinian organisations called for co-ordinated action: for Israel to end its occupation and colonisation of all Arab lands; to dismantle the Apartheid Wall; to recognise the rights of Arab–Palestinian citizens of Israel to full equality; and to promote the rights of Palestinian refugees to return to their homes seized during years of conflict.[42] Dismissed as an irrelevance by Israeli leaders, the campaign grew with striking speed, especially among trade unions, community groups and faith groups. Willie Madisha, president of Cosatu, the South African trade union federation, declared:

> It is time for the global workers' movement to stand firm and principled against hypocrisy and double standards. We cannot remain silent any longer. It is time to stand in word and in deed with the peoples of the Middle East and heed their call to support the struggle against occupation. There will be no peace in this region and in the world, without justice.[43]

Building on opposition to the invasion of Afghanistan launched by the US and its allies in 2001, and in 2003 on widespread opposition to the invasion of Iraq, the BDS movement created opportunities for people worldwide to undertake solidarity with Palestine. Israel was forced to confront a new reality. The influential Reut Institute, a thinktank close to the Israeli government, declared in 2010 that BDS 'tarnishes Israel's reputation, constrains its military capabilities, and advances the one-state solution'.[44] BDS, it said, was an important part of networks with potential to pose an 'existential threat' to Israel – 'a systemic, systematic, and increasingly effective assault on its political and economic model'.[45]

Solidarity with the Palestinians was reflected in protests against repeated Israeli offensives in Gaza. In 2023, when Israel launched a genocidal war, millions of people worldwide joined demonstrations of unprecedented scale.[46] In November 2023, 800,000 people marched in London: the largest-ever solidarity demonstration with Palestine in Britain, the state that had supervised European settlement under its former colonial regime.[47]

Of all expressions of solidarity, however, the most significant appeared during the Arab revolutions that began in 2011. Since the Nakba, Palestinian struggles had been disadvantaged by the fragmentation of the Palestinian working class. Palestine's workers had been dispersed, their organisations – already inhibited by the colonial regime and by Zionist hostility – had been dismembered. In the absence of workplace solidarities and the potential of workers' struggles, mobilisations in Palestine were all the more impressive. But Palestinians lacked the collective power of a working class like that which brought the Egyptian dictatorship of Husni Mubarak to an end. During and after the 'Arab Spring' of 2011, the Middle East witnessed repeated uprisings and revolutionary upheavals. Decades of neoliberalism had brought crises in which organised labour played a key role. Struggles in Egypt, with workers at their heart, removed a regime that had long partnered with Israel's rulers and provided the US with its key Arab ally. As millions declared for Palestine, Israel's rulers shuddered. Such upheavals will reoccur, destabilising imperialist networks on which Israel relies. A key question that confronts young Palestinian activists is that of establishing relations with those preparing for further mass movements, above all in Egypt, where the Sisi regime confronts a population still seeking 'Bread, freedom and social justice', the aims of the 2011 revolution.

Youth

Veteran Palestinian activist Jamil Hilal observes that young people in Palestine have been 'strongly present' each time clashes against the colonising occupation intensified.[48] They do not possess 'magical powers', he says, but give evidence of the vitality of political culture in Palestine and across the diaspora.[49] Ilan Pappé also sees the vigour of young people as 'a silver lining and a ray of hope'.[50] Despite immense difficulties, people of the West Bank and Gaza, he says, have launched 'incredible initiatives that combine the existential daily struggles of young Palestinians with a more strategic outlook: envisioning a better and different future'.[51] He adds:

> Despite being marginalised (and at times even suppressed) by their leaders, they continue to demand a foothold in politics from above, as well as from below. They are adamant about their right to take part in the process of political decision-making that would determine the future of their homeland.[52]

Young Palestinians challenge the two organisations that dominate political life in the West Bank and Gaza: Fatah (in the form of the PA) and Hamas. Each is characterised by elitism and by authoritarian leaders who are intolerant of organisation from below. While Israel continues to assault Gaza and commit to the elimination of Hamas, support for the organisation has increased rapidly. But Islamist organisations, hampered by mistrust of struggles from below, do not provide a perspective for radical change. The youth of Palestine are more ambitious and, like the youth of Egypt, seek social justice that engages the mass of people. Mohamed is one of the leading activists of Egypt's Tahrir Revolution. He says: 'Without the Palestinians the revolutionary movement in Egypt would never have emerged. Their struggles inspired us. Their intifadas confronted Israel and its powerful allies':

> Twenty years ago the Palestinians gave us courage to march in our streets in their support – and to build a movement that became a revolution. Now we think not only about future struggles in Egypt but how our movement can bring change for Palestine. In 2011 the Arab working class shook Israel and will do so again, despite the many problems we face.[53]

For decades the PLO both inspired Palestinian struggles and isolated them. In a new era, imperialism is much weakened in the Middle East and local regimes face continuing challenges from below, including mass protests, democracy movements and revolutionary upheavals: as Mouin Rabbani suggests, the region is 'all shook up'.[54] Despite repression, counter-revolution and intense efforts to suppress these struggles, they continue relentlessly. 'Imperial and neoliberal fetters have consciously, systematically and structurally inhibited human development across the Arab region', writes BDS activist Omar Barghouti;[55] at the same time, the mass of people has demonstrated how such structures of exploitation and oppression can be challenged and overturned.

In *Foreign Affairs*, an American publication often viewed as the house journal of the US foreign policy establishment, Marc Lynch declares that: 'The Arab Uprisings Never Ended'.[56] In 2021, on the tenth anniversary of upheavals in Tunisia and Egypt, he counselled against the view that counter-revolution and military coups meant 'business as usual' in the Middle East: '[T]he revolutionary wave of 2011 was not a passing mirage…the region's autocratic façade is cracking again… More eruptions of mass protest now seem inevitable.'[57] In 2024, as the Assad regime in Syria collapsed, *Foreign Affairs* re-circulated the article, warning its readers that 'the fate of the region…seems more uncertain than at any point since the 2010–11 Arab Spring'.[58] For decades the US and Israel relied upon regimes based on 'corruption, autocracy, failed governance and abuse of human rights': now their rulers shuddered at the prospect of renewed struggles.[59]

Israel's war on Gaza marks a turning-point in the history of Palestine. It has galvanised tens of millions of people worldwide, appalled by the crime scene created by the IDF and by the genocidal declarations of some of its most prominent leaders. The struggle for liberation in Palestine is integral to movements for change across the Global South and in the heartlands of imperialism. Palestinians are our sisters and brothers: their future is in a world we share. Freedom for Palestine is part of our struggle for global justice.

....

The chapters that follow address key developments in Palestine chronologically, from the early years of the 20th century to the recent assaults on Gaza:

Chapters 1, 2 and 3 assess British colonial rule and its association with the Zionist movement. They address the process of European settlement in Palestine, the practices of Britain's Mandate regime and Palestinian resistance culminating in the intifada of 1936 to 1939.

Chapters 4, 5 and 6 consider Zionist strategies for 'transfer' of the Palestinian Arab people, the events of the Nakba and its impacts on Palestinian society. They address the class nature of mass displacement and its influence on Palestinian nationalism and consider the relationship between Israel and its Western allies.

Chapters 7, 8 and 9 follow the re-emergence of guerrilla struggle, the establishment of the PLO and its achievements and failures. They record the impact of a new intifada and the importance of solidarity movements in the Arab states, the appearance of Hamas as a new element in the resistance movement, and the end of the 'two-state solution'.

Chapters 10 and 11 address the impact in Palestine of the 'War on Terror' declared in the US. They assess the character of the Islamist movement, Israel's expanding settlements, and the advance of genocidal agendas regarding Palestinians. They examine the impact of neoliberal policies in Palestine, the revolutionary upsurge in the Arab world and its implications for the Palestinian future.

Chapter 12 examines solidarity with Palestine in the Arab region, its role in stimulating resistance and, in Egypt, its place in the revolutionary movement of 2011–2013. It considers Palestine as part of anti-imperialist struggles across the Middle East.

Chapter 1
Imperialism, racism, Zionism

British colonialism in Palestine. Origins of the settler movement. Arabs and Jews under the Mandate

Meir Baruchin is an Israeli teacher who in November 2023 posted online his opposition to the IDF assault on Gaza: he was promptly charged with treason, imprisoned and placed in solitary confinement. Baruchin had written: 'Horrific images are pouring in from Gaza. Entire families were wiped out… I ask everyone else to do everything possible to stop this madness. Stop it now. Not later, Now!!!'[1] He later reflected on Israeli perceptions of those under attack: 'Most Israelis don't know much about Palestinians. They think they are terrorists, all of them, or vague images with no names, no faces, no family, no homes, no hopes.'[2] Here, Palestinians are faceless/hopeless and, apparently paradoxically, also an active threat – 'terrorists, all of them'. This is the view from within an Israeli 'bubble' – what Israeli geographer Oren Yiftachel calls an 'ethnocratic bubble' in which, after decades of military occupation and subordination of the Palestinians, 'the "Palestinian question" has been internalized in such a manner as to require scant attention or mention, except in the guise of references to "terrorism" or the "Islamic threat"'.[3]

Israel's apartheid wall has for years contained and controlled people of the West Bank; at the same time, it has rendered them invisible to those outside, so that towns and villages of the West Bank have become 'a grim ghetto…wholly out of sight'.[4] Laleh Khalili comments:

> The interaction between Palestinians and their far more powerful adversaries, foremost among them Israel, is as much a struggle against being 'hidden' from potentially sympathetic publics, as it is against marginalisation, dispossession, the constant gaze and monitoring of the state and its violent apparatuses.[5]

Resistance to military occupation makes Palestinians visible in ways that challenge the 'bubble' and intensifies efforts in Israeli media to depict them as enemies – people who are invisible and unknowable and who, at the same time, are malign and threatening.[6] Mary-Jo Nadeau and Alan Sears identify a 'silencing campaign' that originated with the Nakba of 1948 and has continued with the aim of 'dehumanization and silencing techniques aimed at the Palestinian population'.[7] The strategy of silencing, they say, 'has deep roots in the specific history of Palestinian unfreedom, which has centred around sustained efforts to erase Palestinian existence'.[8]

Empire, race and racism

Colonial powers have long viewed subject peoples as both faceless/invisible and as malevolent and threatening. This is especially clear in the Middle East, where, from the 19th century, Britain and France mobilised ideologies of racism that originated with slavery and were reinforced by Islamophobia. The British approach was well-established when in 1920 its officials and military men took charge of 'Mandate' Palestine and were soon confronted by vigorous resistance. They responded with policies that would persist throughout the colonial period, influencing the Zionist movement and the agendas of the Israeli state.

Britain and France occupied Egypt – Palestine's neighbour to the south and west – in 1882, intervening to crush a nationalist revolution led by army officer Ahmed 'Urabi. They aimed to seize control of the Suez Canal, a key strategic asset for imperialist networks. Britain took charge in Cairo and went on to run Egypt as a colony in all but name. After centuries of occupation and exploitation of territories in Asia, Africa and the Americas, its ideologues of empire asserted that Europeans' superiority endowed them with the right to rule people of the Middle East. Palestinian writer Edward Said observes their attachment to 'a type of racial distinction that divided human kind into lesser and greater breeds of men'.[9] During the 19th century, long-standing prejudice towards people of the region, notably Muslims, had been bolstered by biological theories that fused ideas about 'race' and nation, so that Britain – seen as 'advanced and civilized' –

undertook responsibility for 'turning [the natives] into useful human beings under European rule'.[10]

British officials had contempt for the Egyptians. Evelyn Baring, later Lord Cromer, was chief architect of the colonial regime in Cairo. Egyptians, he said, were 'poor, ignorant, credulous' and must be raised from their piteous state by 'the civilized Englishman'.[11] The entire Egyptian population, he said, was *in statu pupillari* – under British guardianship – its future to be shaped by the colonial power and, he added, 'by what we consciously think is best for the subject race'.[12] Alfred (later Viscount) Milner directed financial affairs for the British authorities. He asserted that Britain had rescued Egypt from 'the flame of anarchy' and 'inveterate evil',[13] saving the country from 'forces of poverty and fanaticism'.[14] On the one hand, he said, Egyptians were 'docile and good tempered…a nation of submissive slaves, not only bereft of any vestige of liberal institutions but devoid of any spark of the spirit of liberty'.[15] On the other hand, Egypt was 'eternally abnormal': its people were 'in the grip of a religion the most intolerant and fanatical', leading them to excesses of behaviour including uprisings and 'rebellions' such as that of 1882.[16] Egyptians were damned if they protested at subjugation by the British (intolerant, fanatical) and damned if they did not (passive, submissive).

The British were equally contemptuous towards the people of Palestine. Claude Reignier Conder was an army officer who had participated in the assault on Egypt in 1882 and was later appointed to the Palestine Exploration Fund, charged with surveying the Levant, then part of the Ottoman Empire. He subsequently reported on the land and the people: 'The native peasantry,' he wrote, 'are well worth a few words of description…They are brutally ignorant, fanatical, and, above all, inveterate liars.'[17] They were nonetheless 'good-natured and very docile under recognised authority' and could be developed into 'a useful population', preferably under 'the English scheme of reforms'.[18] These views were shared widely among academics and writers. Robert Alexander Stewart Macalister was an archaeologist who in 1912 reported on history and contemporary affairs in Palestine. He compared the people to 'a community of white ants'.[19] Young children, he wrote, 'are particularly evil-looking morsels of humanity',[20] while Bedouin nomads were 'primitive' and 'wild'.[21] Macalister observed that after the last of the Crusades of the medieval period, 'the country had collapsed into an almost recordless semi-barbarism' only modified by recent colonisation from Europe.[22]

Palestine fell under British domination during the First World War. Its military men and officials shared these views, which, says Zein Ghandour, rested on 'racial and cultural theories and presumptions'.[23] Ghandour summarises the approach set out in many official documents:

> Palestinians rioted regularly. Their farming methods were primitive and inefficient and were in dire need of improvement and modernization. Their land law, a scenic Ottoman relic, was a mess – nothing an overhaul could not fix... Peasants lacked a coherent political consciousness and were incapable of political action beyond a kneejerk defence of their own little patch of land. They were only worth discussion when they posed a threat to law and order.[24]

In this view, says Ghandour, Palestinians were no more than 'a primordial people'.[25] As with Egyptians dismissed by Cromer and Milner, they were 'incapable of political action'.[26] At the same time, they were volatile and likely to disturb good order: like others across regions then described as 'the colonial world', Palestinians were characterised by the British according to 'casual racial stereotypes'.[27] Gardner Thompson comments that 'Europeans of high office had little if any regard for the competence of Arabs...and tended to treat them collectively with a degree of contempt'.[28]

These views were shared by leaders of the Zionist movement, which aspired to establish a Jewish state in Palestine. Their attitude to the Palestinian population was not associated with their ethno-religious identity as Jews; rather, it reflected how Europe's rulers and imperial administrators saw people of the Middle East and more widely of the 'colonial world'. Among early Zionists there was little recognition that a 'native' people populated the land they wished to settle. The historian Derek Penslar observes: 'most Zionists denied the Arab presence or refused to consider it seriously'.[29] The movement was not wholly unaware of the Palestinians, however: Penslar adds, 'a small minority [of Zionist leaders] nervously kept track of Jewish–Arab clashes and predicted future, and more serious, confrontations'.[30] Theodor Herzl was a dominant figure during early phases of the movement, attempting to win support for the settlement project from Ottoman rulers who, until the First World War, controlled the entire Arab East. Herzl visited Palestine in 1898 and travelled widely but 'barely noticed' the inhabitants.[31] He had already set out a plan to facilitate the settlement process: the Zionist movement, he wrote, would acquire land from private owners and then move to expel the resident population:

> We must expropriate gently the private property on the estates assigned to us. We shall try to spirit the penniless population across the border by procuring employment for it in the transit countries, while denying it employment in our own country. The property owners will come over to our side. Both the process of expropriation and the removal of the poor must be carried out discreetly and circumspectly. The property owners may believe that they are cheating us, selling to us at more than [the land is] worth. But nothing will be sold back to them.[32]

Palestinian historian Rashid Khalidi comments on this 'chilling' proposition: 'Herzl clearly grasped the importance of "disappearing" the native population of Palestine in order for Zionism to succeed'.[33] Evidently Palestine was populated but not by people worthy of consideration by those who were to settle on their land: the 'natives' could be treated instrumentally, like those in other regions under European control. In Palestine Herzl met senior Ottoman officials, including Youssuf Zia al-Khalidi, a former mayor of Jerusalem, who later wrote to him warning that mass settlement would have a profound impact upon all the people of the country. Jews were 'our cousins', he said, deploring the treatment of Jews in Europe and expressing understanding for the motivations for Zionism; at the same time, he warned of dangers in establishing a Jewish state in Palestine, a land 'inhabited by others'.[34] Mass settlement would affect all the existing communities of Palestine, including Jews, he said, concluding with an appeal to Herzl: 'In the name of God, let Palestine be left alone.'[35] Herzl replied, says Khalidi, 'dismissing as insignificant the interests, and sometimes the very existence, of the indigenous population'.[36] Jewish settlement in Palestine, he declared, would bring prosperity for all.[37] Khalidi comments:

> With all the smug assurance so common to nineteenth-century Europeans, Herzl offered the preposterous inducement that the colonisation, and ultimately usurpation of their land by strangers would benefit the people of that country... This condescending attitude towards the intelligence, not to speak of the rights, of the Arab population of Palestine was to be serially repeated by Zionist, British, European and American leaders in the decades that followed, down to the present day.[38]

Carving up the Arab East

Herzl went on to establish the Jewish–Ottoman Land Company – a public project for colonisation by Zionist settlers. He died in 1904 before these plans could be advanced and at a time when the Ottoman Empire was increasingly unstable in the face of interventions in the Middle East by European colonial powers. He had nonetheless set out visions of a project that was to be pursued by successive generations of Zionist leaders.

As the Ottoman Empire went into rapid decline Britain became the focus of Zionists' attention. Now the movement's leading figure was Chaim Weizmann, who was convinced that it must win support from within the British ruling class on the basis that a Jewish state could serve the best interests of Britain's empire. Weizmann was able to deal directly with members of the British government. During the First World War, as Britain advanced on German–Ottoman forces in Palestine, he lobbied decision-makers in London, allying with the most aggressive imperial strategists – ministers who sought to extend British control across the Middle East. Danny Gutwein describes these arch-imperialists, including Winston Churchill and the former 'liberal imperialist' Lloyd George, as 'radicals [who] perceived realization of the Zionists' aspirations as a means of advancing dissolution of the Ottoman Empire and extending British imperialism to Palestine'.[39] Herzl had earlier proposed that a state for the Jews would constitute 'the portion of the rampart of Europe against Asia, an outpost of civilization as opposed to barbarism'.[40] Now Weizmann worked to persuade Churchill and others that a Zionist state could serve 'as a colonial border guard in the service of British imperialism'.[41] When British strategists agreed, concluding that the settler movement would reinforce imperial interests, they produced the Balfour Declaration, with its commitment to a 'national home' for the Jewish people.

In 1916 Britain struck a deal with France to carve up Ottoman territories in the Arab East (the Levant and Mesopotamia). Under the Sykes–Picot agreement, agreed secretly between the two states, France would receive Syria and Lebanon; Britain would receive Mesopotamia (today's Iraq) and Transjordan; Palestine would be under shared authority. Britain had a special interest in Mesopotamia. Here, its officials anticipated discovery of major oilfields like those in neighbouring Iran, then controlled by the Anglo–Persian Oil Company (APOC, later British Petroleum (BP)). Oil had been integral to military initiatives during the First World War: Lord Curzon, who was to become British foreign minister, later asserted that 'the allied cause floated to victory upon a wave of oil'.[42] Control over oil-bearing territories in Mesopotamia, together with access to the Arab/Persian Gulf, would bring a further invaluable energy resource. Britain's war cabinet recorded a key strategic aim: to ensure 'continuity of territory or of control both in East Africa and between Egypt and India'.[43] Iraq would come under direct control: the British had also concluded that their presence in Palestine was necessary 'in order to keep France and Russia from the approaches to Egypt and the Suez Canal'.[44] In 1917 they invaded Palestine, sidelining France and preparing to establish a colonial regime.

It was in this context that later in 1917 the British Government issued the Balfour Declaration, an undertaking to the Zionist movement that it would work to establish a 'national home for the Jewish people':

> His Majesty's Government view with favour the establishment in Palestine of a national home for the Jewish people, and will use their best endeavours to facilitate the achievement of this object, it being clearly understood that nothing shall be done which may prejudice the civil and religious rights of existing non-Jewish communities in Palestine, or the rights and political status enjoyed by Jews in any other country.[45]

The population of Palestine was some 670,000, of whom 60,000 were Jews; the rest were Arab Muslims and Christians, and members of small minority groups including Druze and refugees from Algeria and Muslim regions of the Caucasus who had arrived during the 19th century.[46] The 'national home' to be established for the Jewish people had no status in international law or in treaties and agreements but was understood to imply a *state*: the Zionist movement had long since advocated use of the term as 'a synonym for state'.[47] Meanwhile the reference to 'civil and religious rights' for the majority population *excluded* political rights: the settler community was to enjoy the prospect of a state; others, over 90 percent of people in historic Palestine, would have no such option. Avi Shlaim comments: 'The majority of British ministers did not recognize the Palestinians as a people with legitimate national aspirations, but viewed them as a backward, Oriental, inert mass'.[48] Balfour himself, signatory to the Declaration, later wrote: 'Zionism, be it right or wrong, for good or bad, is of far profounder import than the desires and prejudices of the 700,000 Arabs who now inhabit that ancient land'.[49]

Weizmann had aligned the Zionist movement with Britain's most aggressive imperialists. Some had long records of antisemitism. Many believed that a shadowy Jewish presence, especially the role of Jews in international trade and finance, gave them global influence that could assist Britain in the Middle East. Israeli historian Tom Segev comments: 'The men who sired [the Balfour Declaration] were Christian and Zionist and, in many cases, anti-Semitic. They believed the Jews controlled the world.'[50] Mark Sykes, the British official who had concluded the Sykes–Picot agreement, 'harboured an abiding and almost obsessive fear of Jews, whose web of dangerous international intrigue he discerned in many an obscure corner'.[51] His imaginings of Jewish power, fed by antisemitism that was growing in influence in Europe, prompted him to advocate for a Jewish state. He told King Faisal of Saudi Arabia: 'this race [the Jews] is all-powerful and cannot be put down'.[52] Arthur Balfour, signatory to the Declaration, had been an architect of the Aliens Act of 1905, which targeted poor Jewish migrants from Russia and

Eastern Europe for exclusion from Britain. One of his associates wrote that Balfour 'is inclined to believe that nearly all Bolshevism and disorder of that sort is directly traceable to Jews'.[53] Brian Klug comments on the 'irony of antisemitic support for Zionism'[54] – backing from politicians who intended that (imagined) Jewish influence would assist them to make more colonies in the Middle East.

Weizmann continued to deal directly with these racists. In 1918 Britain authorised establishment of a Zionist Commission, tasked with taking 'any steps required' to realise the project for a Jewish national home in Palestine.[55] It soon established departments for settlement and farming and, crucially, began creating an armed force. But the pace of change was too slow for Weizmann, who argued for accelerated immigration of Jewish settlers. This, he argued, would bring 'civilisation' to Palestine, complementing and strengthening British authority and imperial control. In a lengthy letter to Balfour, he expressed fears that 'the present state of affairs would necessarily trend towards creation of an Arab Palestine': this should be avoided at all costs, as the 'treacherous nature of the Arab' threatened to destabilise British authority and good order.[56] His appeal was infused with racist hostility towards the Palestinians. Arabs, he said, were 'corrupt, inefficient', 'arrogant' and 'roué' (wily/cunning); the *fellah* (peasant), he wrote, 'is at least four centuries behind the times', adding that the *effendi* (official/professional) is 'dishonest, uneducated, greedy, and as unpatriotic as he is inefficient'.[57] He offered to counter Palestinian deficiencies by assisting 'enlightened and honest English officials'. A Jewish presence, he suggested, would aid 'the fair and clean-minded English official' – the 'fair and just' Englishman at the head of the colonial administration.[58]

For Weizmann, observes Edward Said, the Arabs were Orientals, 'therefore less human than Europeans and Zionists; they are treacherous, unregenerate etc. Most of all they do not deserve to own a country'.[59] Here, suggests Said, is 'the total identification of Zionism with the most reprehensible aspects of European white and cultural hegemony':

> Both Zionist and European share in common the ideals of fair play, civilisation and progress, none of which the Oriental could understand...ethnocentric ideals, appropriated by Zionism valoriz[ed] the white man's superiority and his right over territory believed to be consonant with those ideals.[60]

The Zionist leadership seized this agenda, notwithstanding that Jews had also been viewed in Europe as 'Orientals', people from the East who, like Muslims and Roma/Gypsy people, were viewed as Other and inferior. In the 19th century ideas about biological difference had been integrated into European racism, intensifying both antisemitism and anti-Muslim racism/Islamophobia, so that 'exclusionary ideas about Jews and Muslims were overlapping currents within the same stream of nationalist or broader Western ideas'.[61] Weizmann recast Jews as privileged Europeans. 'The Arab is primitive and believes what he is told,' he said.[62] The Arab population of Palestine was 'a demoralised race' and there was 'a fundamental difference in quality between Jew and [Palestinian] native'.[63] Palestinian writer Joseph Massad comments that much of what antisemitism had projected onto European Jews was now displaced onto Palestinian Arabs, 'seen to embody the attributes that both Zionism and anti-Semitism insisted had been previously embodied by diaspora Jewry'.[64]

The founders of Zionism had predicted that European antisemites would assist them in settling Palestine. Herzl wrote: '[T]he Governments of all countries scourged by Anti-Semitism will be keenly interested in assisting us to obtain [the] sovereignty we want.'[65] Not only 'poor Jews' would contribute to an immigration fund for European Jews, he wrote, 'but also Christians who wanted to get rid of them'.[66] He predicted that 'honest Anti-Semites, whilst preserving their independence, will combine with our officials in controlling the transfer of our estates'.[67] A generation later Zionist leaders again found some of their most important allies among Britain's racist politicians and imperial officials.

Learning from the British

In 1920 Britain's high commissioner in Palestine, Herbert Samuel, issued a 'land transfer ordinance' that enabled acquisition of farms and property by the settlers; Zionist officials were also granted special authority to oversee immigration. The victorious allied powers of the First World War shortly issued three mandates in territories of the defeated Ottoman Empire: for Syria, in which France would hold authority, and for Mesopotamia and Palestine, ceded to Britain. In the latter a Jewish agency was to be created: 'In effect,' comments Cronin, 'the mandate allowed a Zionist quasi-government to be formed'.[68] The deal with Britain had been sealed, Winston Churchill repeating commitments to a 'national centre and a national home' for the Jewish people: 'We think it will be good for the world,' he said, 'good for the Jews and good for the British Empire.'[69]

Britain's ideologues of empire and those who administered its colonial territories were not only racial supremacists but also designed and implemented policies that involved savage repression. As Zionist settlement in Palestine accelerated, Britain was crushing resistance in neighbouring Egypt and Iraq. On the outbreak of world war in 1914 Britain had imposed martial law in Egypt and militarised the economy, ordering conscription of labour and requisitioning crops and animals. At least 500,000 men were mobilised and vast numbers of draft animals seized, with a huge impact on rural society.[70] The mass of people experienced a significant drop in living standards while a minority, especially landowners favoured by British policies, were enriched. By 1917 there were strikes in Cairo and Alexandria, and protest marches that defied Britain's restrictions on all forms of public politics. In 1919 the British arrested nationalist leaders who had called for Egyptian independence and a mass movement erupted across the country. Demonstrators were confronted by British and Australian troops and several were killed – the start of a nationalist revolution that was to last for almost four years. The British prepared to crush the movement. Their police commander in Cairo set the tone, confronting participants on a protest march in Cairo he described as 'a howling mob of the most horrible roughs I have ever seen':

> The whole mob was shrieking and yelling and waving their weapons in the air. If you can imagine a drawing by Hogarth of a scene made up by Dante's Inferno and the French Revolution, add to that mad Oriental fanaticism – and you have something like this mob.[71]

The 'docile' Egyptians were now 'mad' and possessed by 'fanaticism'. Britain mobilised air power, the Royal Air Force (RAF) attacking demonstrators and bombing villages that had risen against the occupation – an assault that may have been the first use of aircraft against civilians outside Europe. The RAF's commanding officer reported:

> During the last two days aeroplanes have machine-gunned with excellent effect crowds engaged in damaging railways and are now ordered to use bombs when targets offer. Have formed five squadrons from training squadrons and over 100 machines are now occupied.[72]

Demonstrations and strikes continued to spread across the country, involving members of all the country's ethno-religious communities: significantly, Jews joined Muslims and Christians in the uprising.[73] The colonial regime used all means against the movement: British opponents of the war describe 'a campaign of reprisals [by British forces] carried out with terrible severity', resulting in the deaths of 1,000 Egyptians and the destruction of entire villages.[74] (The Egyptian historian 'Abd al-Rahman al-Rifi' suggests that the British offensive may have cost 3,000 lives.)[75] Still the uprising continued, with mass strikes and – for the first time – establishment of a host of trade unions. After three years Britain was compelled to concede notional 'independence', although it maintained control of Egypt and the Suez Canal, retaining a large military garrison.

In the case of Iraq, a British force had been in place for much of the war. Most troops came from the Indian Army and the British imposed legal codes earlier developed in India to facilitate their rule as part of the 'Raj'. British politicians anticipated that they would acquire the region as a colony and debated means of securing control, including by means of 'planting' settlers. As early as the 17th century Britain's nascent nation-state had undertaken 'plantation', notably in Ireland and the Americas, and later in Australasia and southern Africa. In the case of the new Iraq some imperial strategists proposed to mobilise people from India, implanting them in the mode of transportees destined for indentured labour – a practice that for a century had seen people taken from South Asia to British colonies worldwide. According to one proposal presented to the British parliament, Mesopotamia would have 'irrigation works and canals all in working order under the British government…the banks along its rivers populated and cultivated by flourishing Indian colonies transported from the banks of the Indus [in the western provinces of "British" India]'.[76]

The British disposed of people and resources of the Middle East as they saw fit, although 'plantation', a disquieting parallel with the settlement process in Palestine, was never implemented – in part because of mass resistance in both Kurdish and Arab areas. Britain mobilised over 100,000 troops: as the 'Iraqi Revolt' continued, Winston Churchill as Secretary of War ordered the RAF to bomb civilian targets. A senior British flying officer declared:

> The Arab and Kurd…now know what real bombing means, in casualties and damage; they know that within 45 minutes a full-sized village… can be wiped out and a third of its inhabitants killed or injured by four or five machines which offer them no real target, no opportunity for glory as warriors, no effective means of escape.[77]

These brutal assaults were judged highly satisfactory by the British command. A historian of aerial bombardment comments: '"Air policing" of Iraq provided the blueprint for future bombing as the technological and financial advantages to British rule made it the backbone of the whole organisation'.[78] This was terror on the cheap and the British went on to use it in southern Africa, Burma, India – and Palestine – against defenceless populations.

This was the imperial order in which Weizmann was eager to serve 'the fair and clean-minded English official' and within which he saw the prospect of a Jewish state. In 1920 and 1921 there were clashes between Jewish settlers and Palestinians, resulting in deaths and many injuries. The confrontation in 1921, known to Palestinians as the Jaffa

Intifada, led Samuel, the senior British official, to order that Palestinian protestors should be bombed from the air in what was now a well-rehearsed practice in neighbouring states.[79] Churchill decided to establish what he called 'a picked force of white gendarmerie', importing hundreds of police earlier stationed in Ireland, as well as members of the notorious Black and Tans (originally recruits to the Royal Irish Constabulary during the Irish war of independence), who bore a reputation for extreme violence. Richard Cahill comments that they had used 'a wide variety of techniques and strategies in their attempts to squelch the Irish Rebellion', including: 'demolition of homes of suspected rebels or in some cases, entire villages; arrests and imprisonments without warrants, charges or trials; beatings; torture; and rape'.[80] In 1926 the gendarmerie was dissolved and hundreds of its members recruited into the Palestine Police. Among senior officers was Douglas Duff, a sadist whose methods of torture included water-boarding and 'suspension': the colloquial English term 'duffing up' is attributed to rank-and-file troops' description of his methods.[81] The force was riddled with racism: Duff admitted, 'Most of us were so infected by the sense of our own superiority over "lesser breeds" that we scarcely regarded these people as human'.[82] He was particularly hostile to the people of Nablus: they were marked by 'innate fanaticism', he said, adding 'there are few Muslims in Palestine so treacherous, cruel and bigoted as the Nabulsis'.[83]

Land and the people

During the 1920s Britain governed the Mandate territory in much the same way that it controlled colonies across the globe. Acts of public resistance met with brute force; at the same time, British officials worked systematically to weaken the social and political structures of Palestinian society. Rashid Khalidi describes 'a sophisticated policy of divide and rule [that] may have reached its peak of perfection in Palestine after years of maturation in Ireland, India and Egypt'.[84] The British encouraged rivalry between leaders of Palestinian communities whom they recognised only on the basis of religious identity. Whereas Jewish settlers were viewed as part of a 'national' project, Palestinians had no 'national' character, only ethno-religious affiliations. The League of Nations mandate allowed for the creation of a Jewish administration with authority to direct education, health, public works and – crucially – acquisition of land. The British supported Jewish agencies in establishing these functions of a quasi-state; at the same time they treated Palestinian Arabs 'with the same contemptuous condescension they lavished on other subject peoples from Hong Kong to Jamaica'.[85]

In one respect Palestine differed from other British colonial territories. The League of Nations mandate provided (Article 6) that Britain should facilitate 'close settlement by Jews on the land'.[86] It also provided (Article 4) for a Jewish Agency as a public body with authority to undertake development across the territory.[87] The Agency was focused on accelerating immigration from Europe. Initially progress was slow: states worldwide had entered an era of 'autarky' during which borders were closely controlled and migration in general was restricted. The Zionist Executive lobbied Britain intensively and eventually won a commitment to minimal migration controls, so that a Jewish population that in 1918 had accounted for 8 percent of the people of Palestine, by 1926 reached 18 percent.[88] Acquisition of land by Jewish agencies also advanced rapidly, despite many conflicts over land law and claims to ownership. In 1924, in an important ruling, British officials endorsed a huge sale by the absentee Sursuq family of Beirut to Jewish owners. This was a historic development, affecting 22 villages on 70,000 dunams of the most fertile land in Palestine. The British Governor of Haifa noted: 'the inhabitants had to quit… Government consent was granted in pursuance of the [Jewish] national home policy, regardless of the fate of the cultivators.'[89] Similar purchases evicted thousands of families: between 1920 and 1930 some 533,000 dunams (215,000 acres) were acquired by settler agencies.[90]

Peasants were confronted not only by Jewish agencies and British officials but also by Palestinian leaders among whom were landowners with interests radically different from their own. Stein describes how collusion between sellers and buyers of the land avoided both traditional (Ottoman) legal practice and British regulations: 'Legislative protection only applied to a very small percentage of the agricultural population [and] buyer-seller collusion was a common method of circumventing tenants' rights.'[91] The Sursuq case demonstrated starkly how the political economy of Palestine was being affected by these developments. The Sursuqs were a dynasty of landowners, traders and bankers who had been among the wealthiest families in the Ottoman Empire – so successful, says Kristen Alff, that their presence was significant at the global level.[92] Their sale in 1924 of a vast estate strategically located in the centre of Palestine worried even the senior British official in the area, who warned that the deal was 'causing some uneasiness'. The Sursuqs were backed by vast wealth and influence; the buyer, the Palestine Land Development Company (PLDC), had ample funds raised abroad within the Zionist movement; the tenants and landless labourers who worked the estate were poor, largely uneducated and vulnerable in the face of institutional authority. In this unequal confrontation the outcome was 'mass eviction'.[93]

Palestinian landowners who were not absentees also sold their estates and were thoroughly compromised in relation to anti-colonial resistance. Jewish agencies settled the land on the basis that it was 'vacant' – Palestinian cultivators having been evicted, usually by the former owners, so that those who sold land also drove out peasant families and sometimes whole communities. During the 1920s the pace of eviction increased rapidly and when in 1930 a British committee reported on the rural economy, it found that among 104 villages surveyed 28 percent of households were landless: among the rest, few had access to land sufficient to feed their families.[94] Indebtedness was also increasing, stimulated by a huge increase in taxes imposed by the British authorities. The colonial regime and the Zionist agencies, together with landowners, were accelerating destitution and landlessness and prompting protests across the country:

> Peasants resisted both the 'downward social mobility' they experienced and their political marginalisation. Although it has been little acknowledged, their myriad efforts to stay on the land and to reject political effacement and economic displacement were pivotal to forging the restive course charted by the Palestinian national movement in the 1930s and also to stoking the Mandate's increasing recourse to repression, and especially collective punishments, in response.[95]

Protests against dispossession and displacement were largely ignored by Mandate authorities – those involved being barely visible ('faceless'/'hopeless') except when their conduct required punishment. After conflict between settlers and Palestinian protestors in 1921 the British introduced a Collective Responsibility for Crime Ordinance, resulting in massive fines on Arab towns and villages. Further laws on collective punishment created 'an illiberal and repressive template for dealing with Palestinian resistance'.[96] Britain had long used collective punishment to address resistance in the empire, notoriously in its American colonies, where the Intolerable Acts (also known as the Coercive Acts) were imposed on the people of Massachusetts in retribution for the Boston 'Tea Party' protest of 1773. In India the British delegated to local police the authority to detain people without trial, to impose collective fines, and to use force to compel a crowd to disperse – part of a regime of 'punishments and indiscriminate state violence'.[97] The *Manual of Military Law* provided Britain's legal framework in Palestine: it had provision for shooting 'rioters' and allowed for 'collective punishments' and 'retribution'.[98] Troops were told that when coercion was required or 'terrorism' needed to be checked, collective punishments and reprisals which would 'inflict suffering upon innocent individuals' were 'indispensable as a last resource'.[99]

Collective punishment of Palestinians was encouraged by leaders of the Zionist movement: Weizmann personally lobbied Balfour to punish Arab villages in conflict with the settlers.[100] The Gendarmerie, largely raised from the Black and Tans, was responsible for countless violent assaults. When it was disbanded in 1926 many members were recruited to the Palestine Police, which included Jews, Palestinian Arabs and members of minority groups. Recruitment in Britain was restricted to former soldiers and the force operated in paramilitary style alongside the army, continuing to use 'systematic informal, grass-roots based coercion' that reproduced methods used by the Gendarmerie.[101]

The British gave tacit support to armed Zionist militias. In 1921 Weizmann asked Churchill for agreement that his movement could smuggle rifles into Palestine: Churchill assented.[102] Several Jewish regiments had fought alongside the British during the world war: these were disbanded in 1918, but in 1920 the Zionist movement established the Haganah ('The Defence'), with a core of veterans from the Jewish Brigades. Segev notes: 'the [British] authorities made no objections'.[103] The Haganah at first supported settlers in the context of increasingly frequent Palestinian protests. These were seen predominantly within the settler movement as 'pogroms' – antisemitic assaults that linked Arab 'terrorism' to the predicaments of European Jewry. Some Jewish activists of the left in Europe who had confronted intense antisemitism were fiercely critical of this view: one Yiddish writer argued, 'the true pogrom had been perpetrated by the British forces and Zionists on the local Arab communities'.[104]

By the late 1920s Palestinians not only confronted British forces and settlers on the land but also increasing urban poverty. Tens of thousands of dispossessed villagers were moving to the cities, living in shanty towns on the outskirts of urban centres such as Haifa, Jaffa and Gaza. Between 1922 and 1931 the urban Arab population increased by 40 percent to some 475,000, with mass displacement a key driver of urban growth.[105] By the mid-1930s in Haifa alone there were 11,000 Palestinian Arabs living in informal housing, 'in hovels made out of old petrol tin-cans, without any water supply or the most rudimentary sanitary conditions'.[106] British policy allocated a larger share of government jobs to Jews, who were also favoured by higher wage rates.[107] Many government contracts in construction and maintenance were awarded to Jewish-owned firms that excluded Arab labour – a strategy pursued by the Histadrut, the General Federation of Jewish Labour, established in 1920. Its founding congress resolved:

> [To] unite all the workers and laborers in the country who live by their own labour without exploiting the labour of others, in order to arrange for all settlement, economic and also cultural affairs of all the workers in the country, so as to build a society of Jewish labour in Eretz Yisra'el.[108]

Zachary Lockman comments: 'it was obvious that "all the workers in the country" actually meant the Jewish workers alone'.[109]

Ostensibly a trade union, the Histadrut soon controlled a network of institutions dealing with housing, insurance, credit, health, education and planning. It pursued the policy of *kibbush ha'avodah*, 'conquest of labour' – the creation of an exclusive economic sector in which the *yishuv*, the settler community, would engage only Jewish labour and consume only Jewish products. Israeli radicals Haim Hanegbi, Moshe Machover and Akiva Orr comment that it maintained Jews 'in national isolation while they lived in an essentially Arab milieu'.[110]

The policy of *avoda ivrit* ('Hebrew labour') continuously set Jews against Arabs, embedding in everyday life ethno-religious differences that destroyed prospects of united action in circumstances in which there were clear common interests. In 1921 Zionist leaders lobbied the British to replace railway workers who had originally been conscripted by the British as part of the Egyptian Labour Corps, aiming to remove 1,000–1,500 Egyptians and to replace them with jobs for 8,000 Jews.[111] At a conference called to discuss the proposal the British Army's director of labour addressed the issue of hiring 'white [Jewish] labour'; the director of immigration and travel accepted that such 'immigrant' labour was preferable to 'coloured' [Arab] labour.[112] Hiring Jewish labour, he said, was 'the national policy of the country'.[113] Here the overt racism of the colonial power met the aims of Zionist leaders intent on creating an ethnocentric Palestine.

Among Jewish immigrants in Palestine were socialists and Labour Zionists who had a different perspective. In *Comrades and Enemies*, a detailed history of Arab and Jewish workers in Palestine, Zachary Lockman comments that many Jews of the left took their internationalist and socialist principles seriously and felt a moral obligation to pursue common interests with Arab co-workers. But Jewish workers, organised through the ethnically exclusive Histadrut, were soon at 'the very centre of the Zionist project'.[114] Some activists continued to work for solidarity with Arab workers but were systematically marginalised by the organisation's leadership. Left-wing factions were broken up and expelled: Gabriel Piterberg describes purges aimed to shape the Histadrut as part of a 'pure settlement colony'. The leader of the right in the organisation was David Ben-Gurion, later to be first prime minister of Israel, who was implacably opposed to meaningful collaboration with Palestinian Arabs and played a key role in marginalising the left. Leading labour Zionists, says Piterberg, 'had acquired a white settler consciousness': in the 1920s one of the key figures in the movement, Haim Arlosoroff, even compared the Jewish settler community to the white minority in South Africa.[115] In the long run, comment Hanegbi *et al*, 'It is not for nothing that the Histadrut was considered as the central pillar of the Zionist enterprise...or as the Zionists say, "the State in embryo"'.[116]

Chapter 2
Land, crisis, conflict

Ethnic separation, 'economic apartheid', nationalist resistance. Britain arms Zionist militias

Three years after Britain issued the Balfour Declaration, the key components of an embryonic settler state were in place. With the establishment of the Haganah militia, 'close and fairly effective cooperation [between Britain and the Zionist leadership] was achieved in the three most important areas of Zionist activity: immigration, settlement and security'.[1] During the 1920s, some 100 settler communities were established as the Jewish population grew to 156,481.[2] Many immigrants brought capital and were soon engaged in economic activity, especially in the cities. Although the land was a focus for Zionist leaders, 80 percent of immigrants who arrived in the mid-1920s settled in urban areas and by 1925 80 percent of all Jews in Palestine lived in towns and cities, most in exclusively Jewish neighbourhoods.[3]

The key driver for ethnic separation was the principle of Hebrew labour. David Ben-Gurion was general secretary of the Histadrut. He insisted: 'Without Hebrew labour there is no way to absorb the Jewish masses [into Palestine]. Without Hebrew labour there will be no Jewish economy; without Hebrew labour there will be no homeland'.[4] The Zionist Executive pressured Jewish employers to exclude non-Jewish labour and as industrialisation progressed, largely in areas of Jewish settlement, fewer and fewer Arab workers were engaged in Jewish-owned enterprises. Norman Bentwich, a senior British official committed to the Zionist cause, later described these developments as 'economic apartheid'.[5] British policy encouraged segregation. Separate urban settlement on the basis of 'race' was part of the geography of European rule: the British had long established ethnic enclaves for the European elite in the Americas, Africa and South Asia, and in Egypt they built exclusive European quarters in Cairo and in Ismailiya, headquarters of the Suez Canal Company. In Palestine, Haifa – the country's main port – was viewed initially as a 'mixed' city. Anat Kidron describes changes during the Mandate period that 'tell us the story of Zionism's growing influence and dominance', the city moving steadily towards a 'dual society with growing demographic, economy and organizational dominance of the Hebrew community'.[6] In cities across Palestine 'Hebrew spaces' were expanding as what Nur Masalha calls 'de-Arabisation' progressed.[7]

British officials aligned their plans more and more consistently with the priorities of the settler movement, facilitating industrial development in predominantly Jewish cities such as Haifa, where they developed the port, built an oil refinery and railway workshops, and licensed electrification. A modern capitalist industrial sector dominated by entrepreneurs of the settler community was encouraged by 'an increasingly sympathetic British Administration'.[8] Part of the vision of Herzl and the early Zionist leaders was being realised – and as the process of settlement advanced, 'segregation carried the day'.[9] Jewish immigrants now joined communities in which, says Ronen Shamir, separatism was becoming integral to everyday practice, consolidating '[a] conviction that the two societies could not and should not share one national umbrella and that a spatial segregation between Jews and Arabs was not only desirable but also viable and sustainable'.[10]

These developments were also expressed in education. Settler families benefited from investment in schooling supported by Jewish foundations and by the continuous arrival from Europe of qualified teachers and professionals. Proposals for co-education were opposed vigorously by the Zionist leadership, for which 'the Jewish national home needed Jewish education'.[11] By 1931, although Jews constituted less than 20 percent of the population, there were more literate Jews than among all Palestinian Arabs.[12] Ilan Pappé comments that from the earliest period of sustained Jewish immigration to Palestine, segregation in education was 'an essential tool' in advancing the Zionist project.[13]

The 'Iron Wall'

The most aggressive current within Zionism now set out a strategy to accelerate colonisation and achieve an exclusively Jewish state by military means. In 1923 Ze'ev Jabotinsky wrote *The Iron Wall*, a manifesto for military might to confront the Palestinian Arabs. Jabotinsky was the key figure among Revisionist Zionists. He had been an officer in the Jewish Legion attached to the British Army during the First World War and later organised 'self-defence' groups active in the Arab–Jewish conflicts of 1920. In 1922 he split from the mainstream of the movement over the extent of the Jewish state he wished to see established. The British had determined that territory east of the Jordan River was to be part of Transjordan: Weizmann reluctantly accepted the proposition, but Jabotinsky rejected it on the basis that 'Palestine' included all lands on either side of the river. Jabotinsky argued that 'colonisation' of Palestine – his word – had always been pursued against the wishes of its Arab inhabitants. Jewish settlement must either be terminated, he said, 'or carried out in defiance of the will of the native population'.[14] *The Iron Wall* opposed gradual expansion of the Jewish presence, committing to the growth of the *yishuv* (Hebrew: 'settlement') by use of decisive military means. Jabotinsky declared: 'There can be no voluntary agreement between ourselves and the Palestine Arabs. Not now, nor in the prospective future.'[15] Zionism was a colonising movement, he asserted, and there was not 'one solitary instance of any colonisation being carried on with the consent of the native population':

> The native populations, civilised or uncivilised, have always stubbornly resisted the colonists, irrespective of whether they were civilised or savage... Every native population in the world resists colonists as long as it has the slightest hope of being able to rid itself of the danger of being colonised.
>
> That is what the Arabs in Palestine are doing, and what they will persist in doing as long as there remains a solitary spark of hope that they will be able to prevent the transformation of 'Palestine' into the 'Land of Israel'... Zionist colonisation must either stop, or else proceed regardless of the population. Which means that it can proceed and develop only under the protection of a power that is independent of the native population – behind an iron wall, which the native population cannot breach.[16]

On no account should the Zionist movement pursue a negotiated agreement with the Palestinians, Jabotinsky argued. Rather, it should construct an armed Jewish garrison as the basis to establish a sovereign Jewish state.

Masalha quotes Jabotinsky's 'racist contempt' towards the Palestinians: 'We Jews, thank God, have nothing to do with the East... The Islamic soul must be [swept] out of Eretz-Israel [the Land of Israel]'.[17] Arabs and Muslims, he said, were 'a yelling rabble dressed up in gaudy, savage rags'.[18] Jabotinsky founded Betar, an organisation of uniformed youth that held paramilitary displays and marches and trained for military action. If the founding ideas of Zionism had been influenced by nationalism and the imperial obsessions of late-19th-century Europe, the Revisionists, suggests Masalha, absorbed 'authoritarian and militarist tendencies and the cult of personality... of the far right in Europe during the interwar period'.[19] They were hostile to the Histadrut and to labour Zionists, whom they saw as radicals subverting the ideals of the *yishuv*. They actively opposed strikes and organised strike-breaking, attempting to establish an anti-working-class Federation of Jewish Labour.[20] Jabotinsky called the Histadrut 'a gross cancer in the body of the Yishuv'.[21] This was too much for the key figures in the colonising movement. Ben-Gurion, leader of the Histadrut, compared Jabotinsky to Hitler: 'Same words, same style, same spirit,' he said, publicly calling Jabotinsky 'Vladimir Hitler'.[22] For Maurice Edelman, one of Ben-Gurion's biographers, Jabotinsky displayed 'a grim similarity to those of the anti-Semitic nationalism which was the real enemy'.[23]

'Economic apartheid'

As settlement intensified the Revisionists played an important role in exacerbating tensions and prompting conflict with Arab communities. In 1920 settlers held 456,003 dunams of land; by 1930 the figure had reached 987,600 dunams, of which the bulk was concentrated in the most fertile cultivable areas.[24] Mass evictions were driving peasants from the countryside or onto land that could not support the increased population. A British survey showed that by the mid-1940s land under Arab ownership was supporting twice the number of people it was able to sustain.[25] More and more of the rural population, much living precariously on the urban fringes, was drawn into wage labour. There were alternative booms and slumps, especially in construction, which employed Palestinian labourers from an increasingly large pool of former peasants. Many were seasonal workers moving between jobs, making effective collective organisation difficult, especially during workplace disputes when employers readily sourced strike-breakers.[26]

The organisation of Palestinian Arab workers was patchy. In 1925 activists formed the Palestine Arab Workers Society (PAWS), which was initially successful in recruiting among rail workers but struggled to maintain momentum. The Histadrut was now dominated by labour Zionists committed to the principle of Hebrew labour who, paradoxically, also argued formally for working-class unity. The organisation eventually established a trade union section for Arab workers, the Palestine Labour League (PLL). This was largely ineffectual: Lockman observes that the PLL's resources were 'miniscule' and the Histadrut's interest in Arab workers soon declined, becoming a policy of 'benign neglect' accompanied by renewed efforts to compel Jewish employers to dismiss Arab workers and to hire Jews instead.[27] The policy was sometimes enforced by pickets who barred entry to Palestinian Arabs seeking work in Jewish-owned workplaces, meeting them with abuse and physical threats. Steven Glazer records the activities of 'flying pickets' in Jerusalem, Haifa and Tel Aviv: in some cases there were attacks on Palestinian workers[28] and entire Jewish communities were involved, 'voluntarily mobilised for the purpose of picketing'.[29] Deborah Bernstein gives the example of picketing at the Borowski Building site in Haifa that had implications for communities across the city. Scores of Histadrut members took part in a campaign to exclude Arabs: pickets included male and female workers from the organisation's affiliated unions; youngsters from the Histadrut youth movement; members of kibbutzim (agricultural settlements) temporarily stationed in the city; and members of Hapoel Hamizrahi, the religious party allied with the Histadrut.[30] Thousands attended a rally in Haifa to support the pickets, and activists distributed a warning notice across Jewish neighbourhoods:

> The organised Jewish community in Haifa warns all those who employ foreign [Palestinian Arab] workers that by doing so they are causing severe damage to the life of the community and endangering its normal economic development. These transgressions might cause dangerous

> political complications. We extend a serious warning to [Jewish neighbourhoods] and call upon them to prevent the spread of Arab labour... and bring such labour to an immediate halt wherever it is happening. The residents of these neighbourhoods are called upon to use all means at their disposal to prevent foreign labour.[31]

Nathan Weinstock, one of the first writers from the left to produce a comprehensive assessment of Zionist colonisation, comments that the 'definitive foundations of this economic partitioning were laid during this period'.[32]

In Haifa and elsewhere principles of segregation in the workplace were projected into Jewish neighbourhoods and Jewish homes – an example of how 'economic apartheid' had wider social implications. For generations Palestinian society had been characterised by cultural diversity and co-existence between ethno-religious communities. The Ottoman state viewed working relationships between ethno-religious groups as helpful to commerce and to social stability: 'The ideal of a multi-ethnic and multi-national state ruled supreme in Istanbul [the Ottoman capital]'.[33] Like other areas of the Middle East that shared forms of 'cosmopolitanism', Palestinian towns embraced complex social relations between families and communities. Typically, Muslims, Christians, Jews and members of the Druze community celebrated aspects of each group's religious festivals with gift-giving, and figures of authority including rabbis, priests and imams were in general treated with respect across the community. As Jewish settlement progressed during the 1920s many of these relationships were ruptured. In the case of Haifa, creation of new Jewish neighbourhoods separated from Arab neighbourhoods, 'signalled the beginning of the end of informal social relationships'.[34] The policy of Hebrew labour created 'a deep chasm', especially as separatist institutions such as the Histadrut and the Haifa Labour Council set the agenda.[35]

These developments took place in the context of a colonial regime in which Britain treated the Palestinian Arab population primarily on the basis of religious affiliation, which its officials saw as primordial and unchanging. European powers had a long record of treating 'race' and religion as key means of understanding and controlling colonised people, often on the basis of divide-and-rule. In nearby Iraq, Britain had already created an ethnically based militia, the Levies, that it aimed to use against mass movements of opposition among the Kurdish and Arab populations. The core of the Levies was recruited among the minority Assyrian Christians, whom the British believed to be implacably opposed to other religious groups. In Lebanon the French were constructing a confessional state in which they privileged Christians in relation to the Muslim majority. In Palestine, says the historian Noah Haiduc-Dale, British officials were also 'obsessed' with religion, assuming that Muslims and Christians (then some 10 percent of the Arab population) 'existed as separate groups, rather than as parts of a single community'.[36] Officials developed organisational and political structures on the principle 'that religion was the primary element of Arab identification'.[37] Confessional labels in fact concealed important differences, especially differences of class and of regional and neighbourhood loyalties.

Notwithstanding the antisemitism of leading British politicians and officials, the colonial regime in Palestine saw Jewish immigrants as 'modernisers' whose communities should be privileged in relation to 'backward' Muslims and to Christians affiliated to religious currents very different from the dominant Protestantism of the colonial cadre with its 'civilising mission' across the empire and especially in Palestine.[38] While the British gave European settlers representation in administration of the Mandate through the Jewish Agency, Arabs had no such status and were recognised formally only through relations with certain religious leaders. The British complemented and endorsed ethnic separatism, intensifying communal divisions and hostilities.

Conflict and repression

Individuals and groups among the settlers, especially among workers, continued to promote solidarity and the prospect of unity with the Arab population.[39] Underlying changes, however, made unified action increasingly difficult. Peasants confronted by land seizures and evictions had for years been involved in sporadic attacks on Jewish settlements, often described by the British and the Zionists as 'banditry'. In 1929 mass conflict erupted, initially in Jerusalem over access to holy places following a march by Zionists including members of the Haganah and Jabotinsky's Betar movement.[40] Counter-demonstrations followed and within days hundreds had been killed and injured in what became known as the Western Wall or al-Buraq riots. Conflict spread across the country, with many attacks on Jewish rural settlements and the mass killing of Jews in Hebron (al-Khalil), where hundreds were also saved by Arab neighbours.[41] Now a group of settlers attacked a mosque in Jaffa and in a further revenge assault the Jewish quarter of Safed was assaulted. Clashes spread nationwide, claiming almost equal numbers of fatalities among Jews and Arabs.[42] The British rushed in three army battalions from Egypt and the RAF attacked Arab 'looters' from the air.[43] The Mandate authorities issued numerous death sentences on Arabs and two on Jews: most were commuted but in an indication of repression to come, three Arabs were executed and massive fines imposed on the Arabs of major towns and several villages, using Britain's Collective Punishments Ordinance.

For Jews in Palestine and for the Zionist movement worldwide, killings in Hebron and Safed were pogroms – and the perpetrators were antisemites against whom new measures should be taken. Pogroms had a long history in Europe as offensives organised purposefully by antisemitic movements and/or by state authorities that targeted Jews, often resulting in mass killing. In Palestine, however, there were both Jewish and Arab victims of conflicts associated directly with the process of colonisation and the policies of the Mandate authority. Arab involvement showed a distinct national dimension: over half of Jewish rural settlements were attacked and there were clashes in Nablus, Haifa, Jaffa, Beisan, Jerusalem, Safad and Hebron in which Arab protestors fought with settlers and with the British colonial police.[44] Saposnik comments that the events proved 'a critical turning point in the emerging national conflict – a "zero hour" and a formative moment in the crystallization of the Palestinian Arab national movement'.[45] They reflected countrywide crisis: loss of peasant landholdings; accelerating rural-urban migration; urban poverty; and political marginalisation of Arab society by the colonial regime.

The British Government ordered a report, the Shaw Commission: it concluded that the fundamental cause of the events was 'the Arab feeling of animosity and hostility towards the Jews consequent upon the disappointment of their political and national aspirations and fear for their economic future'.[46] The report recommended controls on Jewish immigration and land purchases, and proposed that Arab peasants should be protected from eviction – a reflection of new anxieties among some colonial officials. Britain already faced problems in neighbouring states: in Iraq a renewed Kurdish rebellion had begun, with demands for an independent Kurdistan; in Egypt, the energies of the revolution of 1919 had not been suppressed and a new political current, the Muslim Brotherhood, had just come into being: already it was growing with startling speed. A national uprising in Palestine would stretch British resources in the region beyond breaking point at a time when world economic crisis was prompting fears about the security of imperial networks. A further commission of enquiry was established and a White Paper published (the Passfield Report) that offered concessions to the Palestinian Arabs, criticised Zionists' separatist forms of organisation, and proposed to limit Jewish immigration and provide protections for the peasantry. For the first time since the Balfour Declaration British officials contemplated serious restrictions on the settler movement.

Zionist leaders were furious and organised to reverse the policy. The settler movement had institutional strengths: the Jewish Agency; the Histadrut; the Haganah militia; a host of educational and welfare networks; mass media; and a range of political currents from labour Zionism to the Revisionist parties. Chaim Weizmann met British Prime Minister Ramsay MacDonald on their behalf, winning a complete retreat in what Segev calls 'a stunning turn of events'.[47] Weizmann received a public message, the MacDonald Letter, in which the British government abandoned the White Paper proposals. Paul Kelemen writes that the Letter, 'in all but name declared the Yishuv's paramountcy in British policy'.[48] In a detailed account of the events Tom Segev comments that 'there is no rational explanation' for Britain's policy reversal.[49] Fear of deepening world economic crisis and of instability in a region in which anti-colonial resistance was growing rapidly, together with reluctance to confront the well-organised settler community in Palestine, seem to have been decisive in shaping MacDonald's decision. Faced with a choice between the settler state-in-construction and the weak and disorganised Arab leadership, British strategists opted for the Zionists as 'the empire bowed its head'.[50] A few years later Ronald Storrs, who had been military governor of Palestine, reflected on the choices offered by rival Jewish and Arab communities in a region of growing instability. He concluded:

> [T]he enterprise [Zionism] was one that blessed him that gave [Britain] as well as him that took [the Zionist movement] by forming for England a little loyal Jewish Ulster in a sea of potentially hostile Arabism.[51]

Crisis of leadership

Zionists' success in obtaining renewed British support exposed the vacillating and incoherent leadership of Palestinian Arab society. The events of 1929 witnessed the emergence of an incipient national movement already moving beyond the influence of traditional leaders. When clashes began, the old elite of landowners, commercial families and religious figureheads issued a call to end disorder:

> We call upon you, O Arabs, in the interests of the country, which you place above all other considerations, to strive sincerely to quell the riot, avoid bloodshed, and save life. We request you all to return to quiet and peace, to endeavour to assist in the restoration of order and to turn a deaf ear to...unfounded reports and rumours. Be confident that we are making every possible effort to realise your demands and national aspirations by peaceful methods.[52]

The appeal was ignored – most importantly by peasants, Bedouin, workers and youth. Conflict continued, not only with settlers but increasingly with the British police. In a significant development an armed group appeared in the countryside near Safed in Galilee (al-Jalil). *Al-kaf al-khadra* (the Green Hand), mounted attacks on Jewish settlements and on the police for six months until suppressed by the British Army. In a unique, detailed assessment of Palestinian resistance in this period, Charles Anderson comments on the Green Hand's 'precocious effort at armed insurrection' – a marker of the gulf between elite nationalist leaders and the rest of Palestinian society and of developments to come.[53]

For a decade the Arab Executive had claimed leadership of Arab Palestine. Founded in 1920 by a small group from landed families it was later expanded to include members of the urban elite. The Executive operated as if Palestine was still under Ottoman rule and its members' authority as traditional 'notables' who mediated with the imperial centre was intact. Compromised by Arab landowners' sales of their estates and by disinterest in the peasant crisis among the urban elite, the Executive was sidelined by the events of 1929. It sent several delegations to London to lobby the British government – all failed to win serious attention and were in effect humiliated by the MacDonald Letter, dubbed the 'Black Letter' by Palestinian activists. The Executive subsequently opposed calls to boycott the colonial administration and to organise a tax strike.

The Zionist movement mobilised robust communal institutions under leaders with long experience of dealing successfully with the British: in contrast, the Arab Executive was a staid, defensive body isolated from the mass of people and passive in the face of the colonial power. It proved unable to voice demands for national independence like those that challenged Britain across the empire. In Egypt, the British had been compelled to deal with a mass movement under leadership of the Wafd Party; in Ireland, they had faced demands for independence advanced by the nationalist Sinn Fein; in India an anti-colonial movement under leadership of the National Congress was undermining British rule. In Palestine, the colonial power successfully exploited divisions and rivalries among the elite, restricting formal representation of Arab society to individual religious leaders. In political terms, writes Smith, Arab society was 'reduced to virtual oblivion'.[54]

The example of neighbouring Egypt was particularly important. Here the Wafd, like Palestine's Arab Executive, represented landowners and the commercial elite. Under pressure from below, however, its members challenged the British by participating in mass protests, the home of Wafd leader Sa'ad Zahglul becoming *bayt al-umma* ('House of the Nation') during the nationalist uprising of 1919.[55] The Wafd was also compromised by the politics of its leaders but placed itself within the movement, gaining credibility that eventually produced partial concessions from the British.[56] In Palestine the Arab Executive was paralysed, its interest in the status quo outweighing urgent calls for change coming from the mass of people. Throughout the Mandate period class interests of Palestinian landowners had diverged from those of the peasantry, workers and urban poor. As the Zionist project enriched both absentee landowners and resident holders of the great estates, it also led to the formation of a network of brokers, lawyers, surveyors, accountants and estate agents affiliated to the landowning families. Porath quotes the editor of the Arabic daily paper *al-Karmil* on the impact of these changes:

> The British Government should not be blamed for their refusal to heed our demands. We are to be blamed since we charged with the running of our affairs, the untrustworthy, the sellers, the brokers and the office-seekers, whom the British despise and the people...belittle.[57]

In effect the Arab leadership was a party to processes of change that, under British supervision, alienated the land and embedded a settler population. Independent organisations had already started to emerge, especially among youth – scout groups, sports clubs, cultural associations, and most important the Young Men's Muslim Association (YMMA), founded in 1928 and soon established across Palestine. The YMMA co-ordinated with railway workers and with the unemployed, committing to 'organise unions of Muslim workers to help advance the Muslim worker to preserve his existence and rights and to advance his standard of living'; at the same time it worked for unity of interests between Christians and Muslims.[58] In an echo of developments in Egypt, where the Muslim Brotherhood was expanding rapidly, the YMMA also established schools and clinics and offered legal advice.[59]

In 1929 a congress of Arab students in Jaffa called for full independence for Palestine: many of the participants were soon involved in conflict with the British.[60] The gap between traditional leaders and youthful activists was widening fast. After clashes with settlers in Jerusalem in August 1929, key figures of the Arab Executive called for an end to the conflict. They included heads of the most powerful families, the Husseinis and the Nashashibis, bitter rivals within factional struggles. Their mutual hostility had long been exploited by the colonial regime, but they feared the movement from below and the challenge to their status. Anderson comments that Britain's response to the 1929 events led to popular perceptions among the Arabs that it was the colonial regime above all that enabled and protected the Zionist project – an idea that further threatened the position of the elites, who sought to 'walk a tightrope between roiling public sentiment and their own unshaken belief in the necessity of a national strategy based firmly in diplomacy'.[61]

Under pressure from below the Executive called a national strike – then reversed the call and, under challenge from the YMMA, reinstated it. Youth took the initiative, organising a nationwide boycott of Jewish goods that included pickets of Jewish-owned businesses. The Executive was compelled to participate; meanwhile Zionist organisations intensified a counter-boycott consistent with their long campaign to support Hebrew labour and Hebrew products. The British eventually suppressed the Arab boycott, using collective punishment and a policy of internal exile under which activists were imprisoned far from their homes. The Arabic newspaper *al-Sirat al-Mustaqim* challenged the Executive:

> The Palestinian leadership is not worthy of its position. This leadership does not act in support of the national interest and does not let others act…our situation is gradually declining precisely due to this leadership.[62]

In 1930 Indian nationalist leader Mohandas ('Mahatma') Gandhi organised a 'salt march' across north-western India, protesting against British taxes and colonial rule, that grew to involve tens of thousands of protestors. Inspired by India's mass movement, young Palestinians prepared a similar initiative. The British intervened, arresting a key organiser who was sentenced to internal exile. Grassroots activism was taking on a stronger anti-colonial character, with the British viewed not only as facilitators of Jewish settlement but also as an imposition on the whole of Palestinian Arab society. A Youth Congress, initially formed with support of the Executive, soon moved beyond control of the notables. After a large protest in Jerusalem the British High Commissioner in Palestine wrote:

> It is noteworthy...and symptomatic of a new orientation of Palestinian nationalism that the cries of the demonstrators were 'Down with the English' and 'Down with the colonisers'. Arab feeling in Palestine is definitely becoming anti-British and anti-government.[63]

In 1932 activists in Nablus founded the Istiqlal (Independence) Party. This proposed to organise independently of the old elite, of family and regional alliances, and of religious differences. Inspired by the Istiqlal founded earlier in Syria, it argued for reintegration of Arab countries separated by the colonial powers: Palestine had an Arab character, it said, and was a natural part of Syria. But the Istiqlal was also elitist, confining its membership to dissident members of the leading families and to intellectuals and members of the urban middle class. It invoked the Palestinian people to more active political engagement against Britain and the Zionists, but its appeals were often moralistic, lacking the conviction of grassroots activism. When in 1933 events took a new turn, the Istiqlal was marooned and soon faded from the scene. The Youth Congress proved more resilient. Originally intended to subordinate young activists to the Arab Executive, it opposed the conservatism and factionalism of the traditional elite and grew quickly to become the largest nationalist association of the early 1930s, counting several thousand members in branches across Palestine and soon playing a key role in mass protests.

'Guardian at the gates of Palestine'

In Europe fascism marked an historic advance when, in January 1933, Adolf Hitler was installed as Chancellor of Germany. His regime immediately began attacking Jews, communists, socialists, trade unionists, and others deemed by the Nazi Party to be enemies of the state. Jews were banned from many jobs and Nazi stormtroopers attacked Jewish homes and businesses. Using emergency powers, the Nazis seized thousands of people and placed many in concentration camps.

The assaults came at a time of hyper-nationalism in Europe and North America. Since the early 1920s states had been pursuing policies of self-sufficiency in economic affairs that included tight control on the movement of goods, the strengthening of borders, and restrictions on the movement of people. International migration, which until the First World War had been proceeding at a hectic pace, all but ceased. Now states focused upon exclusion of 'aliens', especially those – notably Jews – who had been targeted by legislation such as Britain's Aliens Act and the Johnson–Reed Act introduced in the US in 1924. Within days of Hitler's accession to power, Jews from Germany began to arrive at British ports seeking entry as refugees. The British government viewed Jewish immigration as problematic, ostensibly because 'destitute' migrants would be a charge on the state – the same disingenuous reasoning that justified the antisemitic Aliens Act of 1905. Anthony Grenville sums up the government's policy – to restrict admission of refugees 'while trying to maintain an appearance of humanity'.[64] In reality, German Jews were accepted on the basis of their instrumental value to the British state. The Cabinet agreed formally that it should seek to secure 'prominent Jews' – those who had 'achieved distinction whether in pure science, applied science, such as medicine or technical industry, music or art':[65]

> This would not only obtain for this country the advantage of their knowledge and experience but would also create a very favourable impression in the world, particularly if our hospitality were to be offered with some warmth.[66]

British policy, observe Lisa Schuster and John Solomos, amounted to 'cynical manipulation of the Jewish exodus for practical and propaganda purposes'.[67] The US also treated victims of fascism as a cultural commodity, accepting leading academics, musicians and literary figures in order 'to symbolise both the barbarism of Nazi Germany and the best aspects of American democracy'.[68] Barnet Litvinoff comments that 'competition waxed furious among the world's universities for celebrated writers and scientists. Everyone wanted the Nobel laureates'.[69] He adds: 'money too could speak all languages', so that those who could escape with their capital, or with means of securing it, were also accommodated.[70]

Mass displacement is always influenced by relations of class.[71] Celebrity status assisted some Jewish refugees to gain entry to Britain but more important was capital. Grenville comments: 'Those who had sufficient financial resources to provide for themselves were at an advantage throughout...otherwise refugees risked being turned back at the port of entry'.[72] Wealthy applicants were also more likely to have passports, to acquire visas or other forms of documentation required to enter Britain, and were more likely to have access to international networks that could facilitate their journeys and arrivals.[73] In 1934, in the face of compelling evidence of Nazi persecution, Britain accepted just 1,882 German Jews as refugees – the mass of victims of fascism were left to their fate.[74] Government policy not only reflected continuing hostility to 'aliens' but also the antisemitism of leading figures of the British establishment. Many members of parliament expressed antisemitic views publicly: William Joynson-Hicks, home secretary for much of the 1920s, had a long record of antisemitism,[75] and Neville Chamberlain, later prime minister and who in 1933 was chancellor of the exchequer, 'acknowledged finding prejudice against Jews understandable and he himself felt it'.[76] More important for the British government than the fate of German Jews was maintenance of good relations with the state in which they faced persecution. Louise London writes: 'Britain's determination to limit public criticism of Germany's internal affairs was matched by concern to prevent the refugee issue from damaging relations with Germany.'[77]

The government made sure that territories of the British Empire were also closed to most victims of Nazism. The British 'dominions' – Australia, Canada, New Zealand and South Africa – all maintained exclusionary policies, reinforced by official communications from London informing their governments of steps taken to prevent, 'Communists and other undesirable aliens from Germany' entering Britain 'in the guise of refugees'.[78] Palestine, however, was an acceptable destination. During the early 1930s the Mandate authorities accepted most refugees from Germany. They were supported by leaders of Britain's Jewish community. Louise London notes: 'Zionists and non-Zionists [among leaders of Anglo-Jewry] agreed that their priority was to encourage immigration into Palestine and that it should occupy the pre-eminent position as a refuge for Jews from Germany'.[79] For Jewish leaders the British government was seen less as holder of the keys to the United Kingdom, 'than as the guardian at the gates of Palestine'.[80] The British intermittently imposed controls on certain applicants, especially those without capital or professional skills, but most travelling to Palestine found means to enter. Louise London quotes a senior foreign official who declared in 1935 that Palestine was 'our contribution to the refugee problem'.[81]

Resistance and repression

Jewish organisations in Palestine also initially expressed concern about the immigrants. Israeli historian Benny Morris records discussions among their leaders about the preferred ages and backgrounds of those to be accepted: leading figures in Mapai (the early Labour Party, affiliated to the Histadrut) were concerned about the arrival in Palestine of 'undesirable [Jewish] immigrants'.[82] Events in Europe soon changed the terms of debate: as the 1930s progressed millions of people faced savage Nazi persecution and urgently required a place of sanctuary. In 1934 Ben-Gurion suggested that there was room in Palestine for four million Jews; two years later he spoke of eight million 'at the least'.[83] At the same time, Ben-Gurion and other Zionist leaders began to view the catastrophe engulfing Europe's Jews as a means to strengthen the *yishuv*. Segev records Ben-Gurion's observation that, 'We want Hitler to be destroyed but as long as he exists, we are interested in exploiting that for the good of Palestine'.[84] Consequently, Segev comments, 'the Zionists took action to ensure that Europe's Jewish refugees would come to Palestine rather than go elsewhere'.[85]

Between 1929 and 1935, the Jewish population of Palestine more than doubled to 355,157.[86] Most came from Germany and Eastern Europe, driven by the reality of life under fascism and the prospect of Nazi expansion across the continent. The Mandate regime maintained a leaky system of border controls with neighbouring states. Officially, 'illegal' immigrants (those without formal documentation) were to be deported: in fact, thousands arrived by irregular means and few were expelled.[87] At the same time, the impact of world recession was felt in rising unemployment among both Jews and Arabs. Construction, which had for years been a key driver of economic growth in Palestine, contracted abruptly, leaving tens of thousands of Arabs without jobs – a much larger proportion of the workforce than in the Jewish sector.[88] The issue of land acquisition continued to be a source of anger and distress. Land sales now involved smaller plots and more often it was Jewish settlers rather than Arab landholders who organised evictions, so that direct confrontations became more frequent. The rapid rise in numbers of immigrants was widely seen by Palestinian Arabs as likely to lead to their future 'expulsion' and even 'extermination'.[89] Under intense pressure from below even members of the Arab Executive issued a statement targeting the Mandate regime and endorsing 'any acts' undertaken to protect Arab Palestine:

> The Arab people believe that the [British] Government of Palestine aims, through its policy and by various means, at their destruction and replacement by Jews... The Arabs are of the opinion that Government has deprived them of all their political rights and has taken every measure to undermine their existence and entity. Thus Government is considered by the Arabs as a destructive body...
>
> The Arabs, who observe the continual undermining of their national existence through the admission of tens of thousands of Jews into Palestine, without giving any consideration to Arab opinion, consider themselves to be acting in self-defence should they themselves adopt any means in order to prevent the flow of immigration and any act which may be taken in opposition to their so doing will be unjust.[90]

In defiance of the British ban on demonstrations, the Executive eventually backed public protests. Jamal al-Husseini, one of its leading members, told British officials that it was under unrelenting pressure:

> We as leaders confess that we have not done our duty in the past to the people because we have never adopted other than peaceful means. We have never in the past resorted even to peaceful demonstrations;

> now we have been pushed to it by the people themselves. Being so pushed, we hope that government would help us and not force us to lead people to more serious trouble.[91]

Musa Kazim Pasha, another of the traditional leaders, told the British: 'You tell us to do nothing, to wait as we have waited in the past, to wait to be slaughtered. I assure you that if it were in my power I would try to stop this demonstration but…the people prefer to die'.[92] In October 1933 a demonstration of some 10,000 Palestinian Arabs assembled in Jaffa, including many peasants and urban workers joined by supporters from Syria and Transjordan. Dockers and members of the Youth Congress organised and stewarded the protest. British police killed 19 participants, wounding 70 others. On the basis of official records, Kolinsky identifies perpetrators as members of a police 'firing squad' that shot directly into the march.[93] Protests erupted across Palestine: in Haifa thousands surrounded the police station on successive days: barricades were set up in the city and four demonstrators were killed. In Nablus, police attacked protestors, killing one.[94] The British mobilised police across the country and there were further killings.

The Arab Executive announced a general strike that was widely supported but called it off after a week. British officials continuously pressured the Executive to bring the movement under control: at the same time, they recognised privately that it had passed beyond the influence of traditional leaders. The High Commissioner, Arthur Wauchope, who was strongly supportive of the Zionist movement, told the Colonial Secretary in London that 'genuine national feeling' among the Palestinian Arabs was 'growing constantly more powerful…and more bitter against [the] British Government'.[95] He added: 'Arabs of all parties [are] united in abusing Government…for preventing Arabs for 15 years from carrying out their national aims and for encouraging establishment of a Jewish National Home.'[96]

The British understood well the challenge of 'national feeling' across the empire and had long responded with extreme violence to protests and to liberation movements. As recently as 1919 British soldiers had massacred hundreds of demonstrators at the Jallianwala Bagh in

Amritsar, India. In Iraq from the early 1920s the British maintained a garrison of over 100,000 troops to suppress nationalist opposition, as well as raising the Assyrian Levies. As in Egypt, they mobilised air power, attacking towns and villages in both Arab and Kurdish areas.[97] The assault on Palestinian demonstrations in 1933 was consistent with imperial practice. After killings by police in Jaffa, an official report exonerated those involved. Recycling long-held prejudices, it declared: 'It is clear that an Arab crowd in Palestine is mercurial and excitable and when excited [is] dangerous'; police who had shot at and charged demonstrators were said to have acted with 'forbearance and restraint'.[98] The High Commissioner heaped praise on British forces, including those who had baton-charged the crowds, telling officials in London, 'The charge was magnificently executed and was completely successful.'[99] In one respect, however, the engagement of British forces in Palestine differed from their conduct elsewhere. The police were working more and more consistently with settler communities and organisations. They protected what they called 'Jewish colonies', placing sealed armouries containing weapons to be used, they said, for 'defensive' purposes in or near 74 Jewish settlements.[100] The British also supplied weapons directly to the Haganah,[101] supporting the growth of the militia and in effect facilitating the establishment of a more aggressive settler current committed to organised violence. In 1931 the Revisionists, led by Jabotinsky, set up Haganah Bet (Haganah B). This recruited to a large paramilitary unit: within a few years it had some 3,000 men under arms. Now it was the issue of arms and armed conflict that would precipitate societal crisis.

Chapter 3
Intifada

Palestinians contest the colonial regime. The 'Great Revolt' – from petition to armed struggle

In October 1935 Arab dockers at Jaffa discovered that a ship they were unloading contained hidden arms, including hundreds of rifles, half a million rounds of ammunition, and parts for a large number of machine-guns, all destined for the Haganah.[1] The scale of the weapons haul suggested that Zionist militias were preparing for major conflict – and Arab organisations and newspapers reacted with anger. Now divisions between the traditional leadership and Arab youth deepened. Activist groups, co-ordinated through the Youth Congress, demanded that the British search for and seize arms held by settlers. The Congress called a general strike, widely observed with rallies and marches that targeted the British as facilitators of Zionist settlement and protectors of Jewish colonies. Young Palestinians called for armed self-defence; at a meeting in Haifa a representative of the YMMA from Nablus argued that Palestinian Arabs needed their own Haganah.[2] Guerrilla activity, like that undertaken by the Green Hand in and around Safed, had already surfaced fitfully in other areas, with clandestine networks committed to armed resistance extending their influence across the country. Initially local groups undertook military drills and weapons training: in 1935, after discovery of the arms shipment at Jaffa, they began co-ordination, with calls for insurrection.

Former members of the Istiqlal, local scout groups and activists of the YMMA took the initiative. Leadership came from the urban middle class, but soon local groups embraced a wide cross-section of Palestinian Arab society including workers, the urban poor, and – in significant numbers – the peasantry. 'The weakness of the national leadership's representation of rural interests,' writes Anderson, 'including the bulk of the country's population of agricultural producers, led many peasants, like youth, to take their own initiatives'.[3]

Pre-eminent among groups that began guerrilla resistance were fighters affiliated to 'Izz al-din al-Qassam. A Syrian strongly influenced by the *salafi* movement that from the late 19th century sought revival of Islam by means of restoration of its founding principles, he pursued *jihad* ('striving'/'exertion') as a struggle against European colonialism. Qassam had attempted unsuccessfully to travel to Libya to confront Italian forces and later fought the French in Syria. He eventually settled in Haifa, where he encouraged establishment of trade union organisation among rail workers and formation of branches of the YMMA. After the conflicts of 1929 he organised for armed struggle against the colonial power, enlisting and training fighters with the aim of igniting a mass uprising. In 1935 his group took to the hills of the north, where Qassam was soon killed in a confrontation with British forces. His funeral in Haifa was said to be the largest public gathering in Palestinian history, with some 25,000 attending.[4] Qassam took on legendary status, popularly seen as an intransigent Muslim activist committed to a model of mass mobilisation that focused upon the poor and dispossessed.

Michel Mitri, leader of the Arab Workers Society (AWS) – a trade union network established in 1934 – convened a national union conference in Jaffa to contest Arab unemployment, the settlers' campaign for Hebrew labour, and the Zionist project. When the British refused to address his demand to employ Arab workers on government contracts, the AWS adopted the Histadrut's tactics, Arab workers picketing building sites where Hebrew labour prevailed.[5] When pickets were arrested the AWS called for a mass presence at construction sites, quarries and other locations that excluded Arabs. Now trade unionists, youth activists, members of Palestine's small communist party (the PCP), and Qassamists linked up at a further meeting in Haifa. Zachary Lockman comments:

> The tide of worker unrest had itself been fuelled by al-Qassam's resort to arms…and the popular sentiments it unleashed, and more generally by the poverty and despair in the shantytowns and working-class neighbourhoods of Haifa and Jaffa, which in turn nourished al-Qassam's movement.[6]

Activists produced the first co-ordinated demands of the mass movement, telling the colonial regime that they required self-determination and the granting of independence; a block on land transfers of any kind from Arabs to Jews; and a halt to Jewish migration to Palestine. The British offered a tame 'legislative council' in which a minority of seats would be elected and the British would retain control of key policies, including that on immigration. Now Arab Palestine was at boiling point, with meetings, protests and rallies taking place across the country. In April 1936 followers of al-Qassam who had re-formed as a guerrilla group were involved in clashes with settler paramilitaries, resulting in deaths on both sides. Conflict spread, focused on Jaffa where, according to British records, seven Jews and two Arabs were killed – the Arabs having been shot by British police.[7]

General strike

Activists called a further, indefinite general strike and 'national committees' sprung up across the country. The strike was to last for six months – one of the longest such mobilisations in world history. It marked the first phase of an intifada dubbed by the British – in imperial fashion – the Palestinian 'Revolt', and which continued for three years. Smith comments that it was 'as significant for the future of the Middle East as the [contemporaneous] Spanish Civil War for Europe'.[8]

Traditional leaders attempted to assert control, belatedly endorsing the mobilisation and forming an Arab Higher Committee (AHC) that included all factions of the old elite. It was radical activists, however, who set the agenda. Energised by action from below, the strike was led initially from the towns, where workers paralysed Arab motor transport and Jaffa dockers shut down the port. The PLL, which had been feebly supported by the Histadrut, collapsed in all but a few workplaces as Arab-led PAWS played the key role. Within days the strike had spread across the countryside. Over a third of peasants were now landless and the majority of the rural population cultivated plots insufficient to meet household needs.[9] Half the male rural workforce engaged in seasonal work, largely in construction, entering wage labour in an economy that was in rapid change and placing rural and urban workers in closer relationships, facilitating collective action.

The strike gave evidence of change affecting much of the Middle East. Since the mid-19th century capitalist development had accelerated across the region, destabilising class relations based upon landholding and on the dominance of rural dynasties and the urban commercial elite. Industrial development reflected the priorities of European powers, their demand for raw materials and for certain locally manufactured goods, notably fine textiles. Extraction of oil – initially from Iran, then from Iraq and the Gulf – saw construction of refineries and pipelines that crossed the Arab East. Infrastructural development brought modern docks, railways, roads and dams, and upgrades to the Suez Canal. Market relations penetrated the countryside: land was progressively commodified, with huge implications for those dependent upon subsistence methods; indebtedness of rural households increased rapidly. The influence of urban centres over the countryside became more pronounced as many peasants were drawn from the land into new workplaces in and around the cities, becoming full-time workers or part-time cultivators.

Palestine represented a special case of these developments. Here change accelerated during the 1920s as Britain established the Mandate regime and Jewish settlement intensified. More and more peasants were forced from the land but – as Britain favoured industrial and infrastructural development for the Jewish sector and Jewish organisations implemented the policy of Hebrew labour – many were rapidly impoverished. At the same time, wages in key industries collapsed: during the 1920s average wages for Arab workers in the wool and soap industries fell by 70 percent, and by 1936 the majority of workers in Jaffa, a key industrial centre, were living below subsistence level.[10] Industrial workers, semi-proletarians of the countryside, the peasants, and the urban poor not only faced a European power and an emerging colonial-settler regime but also the reality of immiseration. It was in these circumstances that the uprising 'spread like wildfire, gripping the cities and country alike and giving rise to an unprecedented armed insurrection'.[11]

Radicalisation and solidarity

In May 1936 rural committees (significantly called 'national committees') agreed a programme for the villages, including non-payment of taxes and opposition to the British policy of establishing police stations in the countryside – for which the colonial authorities demanded payment from the local population. Armed groups went onto the offensive, attacking British communication links and Zionist settlements, and even sabotaging the pipeline which carried oil from Iraq to Haifa for the Iraq Petroleum Company, in which Britain had a major stake.

Young activists in Palestine were increasingly influenced by political developments in neighbouring states. In January 1936 the national movement in Syria declared a general strike to demand freedom from France. After the French army killed dozens of protestors there was a wave of solidarity in Lebanon, Iraq, Jordan – and in Palestine. Under public pressure in France the Popular Front government opened talks with Syrian activists, agreeing to negotiate a treaty of independence. This outcome inspired Palestinians, among whom extensive social networks stretched across territorial borders with Syria and Lebanon that had come into existence barely a generation earlier. Thomas Hodgkin, an official in the British administration, reported from Haifa that Palestinian activists hoped to 'follow the lines of the recent [strike] in Damascus, which lasted seven weeks and succeeded in getting all the Syrian demands granted'.[12] In Egypt, also connected closely with Palestine through economic and social links, the British were retreating in the face of demands for genuine national independence. In May 1936, only weeks after the start of the Palestinian intifada, the Wafd – which had been sidelined by the British – returned to government in Cairo, extracting from the colonial regime a commitment to full formal independence.[13] Here there was also a surge in working-class activity, inspired in part by strike waves in Europe – in France, Spain, Belgium and Greece – which were widely covered in the Arabic-language press.[14] Joel Beinin and Zachary Lockman describe 'an explosion of labour militancy' in Egypt, with strikes in the chemical industry, at textile mills, on the transport network, and at the country's main sugar refinery. Activists created a Committee to Organise the Workers' Movement as the basis for a national network of Egyptian trade unions. Palestinians were encouraged by these developments, in particular by the energies mobilised from below, contrasting them with the passivity of their own national leadership. Convinced that further attempts to negotiate with the British would be fruitless, they were 'ready to emulate their Arab brethren' by intensifying mass struggle.[15]

In a marker of many similar episodes to come, the Palestinian intifada also stimulated solidarity across the Arab region. In Egypt there were demonstrations of support, and the Muslim Brotherhood declared backing for the uprising, pledging to raise arms for the Palestinian struggle and to send a detachment of fighters to join the guerrillas. Gudrun Kramer points out that this stance on the Palestinian issue played a key role in advancing the Brotherhood as the largest and most energetic organisation in Egypt opposing the British regime and in projecting the organisation and the Islamist agenda onto the international stage.[16] Volunteers arrived in Palestine from Syria, Transjordan and, notably, from Iraq under the army officer Fawzi al-Qawuqji, who declared that the Palestinians' general strike was 'a great means to begin the revolution' – the struggle to liberate the Arab region from colonial control.[17]

For many months the general strike paralysed the Arab sector of the economy and seriously affected the British administration and the settler enclave. Thomas Hodgkin wrote: 'The strike seems to be going on with much determination… As far as one can see the movement is out of the hands of the [traditional] leaders and in the hands of the people.'[18] Local committees were the focal point for grass-roots democracy. In a radical atmosphere, old social conventions were challenged, notably by the active engagement of women, whose militancy, says Ellen Fleischmann, 'reached new heights'.[19] An Arab Women's Association of Palestine (AWA), founded in 1929, organised mainly women of the elite and the middle class; significantly its leading members came from both Christian and Muslim families. The AWA had supported strikes and demonstrations in the early 1930s: now, in developments that echoed the activity of women in the Egyptian Revolution of 1919, Palestinian Muslim women gave speeches in churches and Christian women spoke in mosques.[20] When demonstrations took place in Jerusalem, the British High Commissioner noted 'a new and disquieting feature' of the events – 'the prominent part taken by women of good family as well as others'.[21] When the uprising began in 1936, women's participation 'underwent a transformation and radicalisation commensurate with that of the rest of the country'.[22] Women of the elite took part in demonstrations; collected money to fund the uprising; helped to form rural women's committees; held secret meetings to support the militants; and deluged the Mandate regime with written protests.[23] Women of the villages were even more intensively involved:

> Myriad village women joined rural *faz'a* ['alert'] alarm calls for inter-village mutual help... Women protected their villages and resisted security force searches, and were beaten up and, occasionally, shot for their troubles... [W]omen played their part in revolt and pacification, both as subjects of attritional imperial control and as active agents of rebellion...rebels' use of women to avoid security force searches helped the national struggle; women supporting their menfolk or as warriors themselves added to rebel fighting power...[24]

At least one woman is recorded as killed in battle with British forces[25] and Matthew Hughes comments that 'nameless women died elsewhere'.[26] Most schools participated in the general strike and female students were active in making what the British police called 'political and inciting' speeches.[27] Fleischmann writes:

> Throughout the country, most of the government schools went on strike and closed down, and the students formed their own Strike Committee, joining forces among different schools. These committees harassed students who did not observe the strike, particularly those attending missionary schools.[28]

British reports noted 'bellicose' female agitators in many villages who instigated young men to become combatants, warning that, 'women are taking an active part in village affairs and are constantly urging the men to take definite action for the safety of their homeland'.[29] Women's role as activists and as leaders expressed the embracing character of the intifada – a national uprising that, like similar movements to emerge decades later, engaged Arab society as a whole. The Labour Zionist leader Moshe Shertok, later prime minister of Israel, commented that women's militancy 'bore eloquent witness to the depth of Arab national feeling'.[30]

Class and 'rebel state'

The general strike saw not only establishment of 'national' committees at the local level but also specific committees for workplaces, for provisioning, for medical relief, for financial support, for legal services, and for boycott of Jewish and British goods. Young activists dominated: everywhere, traditional leaders struggled to assert their authority. As the strike progressed into the summer of 1936 it became clear that arrangements imposed by the British and which accommodated the old Palestinian elite were no longer effective. Everywhere the movement was marked by differences of class. Radical activists demanded contributions from the wealthy to support the struggle: those who would not comply faced threats and coercion. The movement created local groups to deal with recalcitrant merchants and others with wealth, and with strike-breakers and ill-disciplined activists. In Haifa the local committee called for suspension of rent payment and encouraged landlords and lenders not to take legal action or foreclose on debtors.[31] The national network, argues Anderson, was so effective that it constituted 'the first step in the process of rebel state formation'.[32] In effect, he suggests, the uprising was approaching a situation of dual power in which neither the British and the settler movement on the one hand nor the Palestinian uprising on the other was able to assert full authority over the wider society and its institutions:

> The network aimed to delegitimize the colonial state while proffering an alternative vision of an incipient popular sovereignty, materialised through everyday practices and struggle. The organs of the strike accorded themselves powers of communal mobilisation and resource management that are usually reserved for the state and even displayed a degree of functional specialisation (as in a bureaucracy). While the state-making capacities of the rebels remained constrained and limited,

> the dynamic of popular state formation – that is, the drive for institutionally embodied self-organisation, combined with the active rejection of external sovereignty and governance – cannot be gainsaid.[33]

But the uprising did not have the economic weight or the co-ordinated political organisation to make a decisive challenge to traditional leaders, the British and settler institutions. In October 1936 the AHC asked the kings of neighbouring Arab states to appeal to Palestinian activists to call off the strike on the basis that Britain would directly address their grievances; at the same time Britain threatened martial law and the introduction of overwhelming military force. Each of the monarchs of Egypt, Transjordan, Iraq and Saudi Arabia had been endorsed – in effect, anointed – by the British and readily complied with the AHC's wishes. Now traditional leaders took advantage of frustration and exhaustion, the threat of starvation among the most vulnerable Palestinian communities, and tensions between committees in the rural and urban areas. The AHC announced an end to the general strike and most collective action petered out. Anderson comments: 'Without a clear victory and in the wake of the elite assertion of will that terminated the strike, popular forces were left in relative disarray and the moment of their revolutionary authority lapsed.'[34]

Partition

The intifada was far from over: within a year the national movement resumed activity in the form of armed struggle that made much of Palestine ungovernable by the colonial regime. But the British had already exacted a heavy price for the general strike. When it began in April 1936 High Commissioner Arthur Wauchope authorised the use of brutal methods against those involved. He introduced 'protective custody' – detention without trial – an approach that had been pursued for generations across the British Empire. Activists were seized and imprisoned in what the Colonial Office in London called 'concentration camps', a term first used for incarceration of those interned by Britain during the Anglo-Boer War in South Africa at the end of the 19th century. Palestinian detainees, referred to officially as 'convicts', were held far from their homes; initially they were confined close to an army camp at Sarafand in central Palestine that was the largest British military base in the Middle East. Over the course of the intifada, Britain established 13 camps, continuing to describe them as 'concentration camps', notwithstanding evidence from Europe of how such prisons – *Konzentrationslager* in Nazi Germany – were being used to isolate and murder victims of fascism. In Palestine the internees were compelled to undertake labour, notably in quarries and on the railway.

The British freely used mass arrest and collective punishment, and the death penalty was imposed for shooting at British forces, throwing bombs and attempted sabotage. In one episode, hundreds of homes were destroyed during an assault on the Old City of Jaffa based on what the Colonial Office called 'punitive demolition'.[35] Residents were given a few hours' notice to leave, with evacuation notices dropped from the air – a precedent for later aerial offensives including the repeated assaults undertaken in Gaza by Israeli forces that began in 2023. Cronin quotes a directive from the Air Ministry in London to the RAF to 'bomb the houses of criminals or of their sympathisers'.[36] By September 1936 British troops had killed or wounded more than 1,000 Palestinian Arabs. When resistance could not be suppressed, Wauchope declared: 'His Majesty's Government will continue with military action till all resistance is ended.'[37]

A team arrived from London charged to investigate 'the underlying causes of the disturbances...and to ascertain whether...either the Arabs or the Jews have any legitimate grievances.[38] The Palestine Royal Commission, known as the Peel Commission, addressed a crisis that expressed problems of empire worldwide. Britain was in retreat: a declining power unable to police its colonies and struggling to find means of maintaining its strategic interests. In 1935 the British parliament had passed the Government of India Act, an attempt to defuse the movement for Indian independence. This introduced direct elections and made major concessions to demands for local government. In Egypt, Britain faced massive demonstrations and strikes in the biggest protests since the nationalist revolution of 1919. In Iraq, it had already conceded a form of independence and now manoeuvred to keep control of the oilfields and its military bases. Facing an insurgent movement in Palestine, Britain despatched a team of aristocrats and officials embedded in the imperial past – Segev comments that they arrived in Palestine from London wearing top hats and tails.[39] The leading figures had long records of service in India, where the Raj was unravelling: others had served in Kenya, Ireland, and Burma. Now they received a 'royal warrant' to resolve conflict in Palestine.[40]

In 1937 the Commission produced its report – the first formal document to propose partition of Palestine. Its recommendation to the British government was to divide Palestine into three parts: a Jewish state, an Arab state, and a permanent mandate in the area around Jerusalem together with a corridor to the Mediterranean coast. Transfers of population would create two new ethnocentric entities, overwhelmingly involving displacement of Palestinian Arabs, among whom hundreds of thousands were to be moved compulsorily. Arab organisations were unanimous in rejecting the plan; after debate, Zionist organisations accepted it with reservations. Britain hesitated and sent a further group, the Palestine Partition Commission, known as the Woodhead Commission, to produce detailed plans for borders and transfers. By 1938 the project had been abandoned but the idea of partition, of new borders and mass population movements, had been established as an agenda for addressing the continuing crisis. It was to have profound consequences.

Falsehoods and deceptions

The Peel Commission's report attempted to vindicate Britain's record in Palestine, to identify an exit strategy from territory the Mandate regime could no longer control, and to secure Britain's remaining strategic interests in the Middle East. The Mandate had been undertaken in good faith, the Commission declared, with the aim of meeting Jewish aspirations and of progressing Arab Palestine to self-government. This was 'in harmony with British principles – the same principles as have been put into practice since the [First World] War in different circumstances in India, Iraq and Egypt'.[41] There was a problem, however: the Mandate was unworkable, the report declared, because Palestine was in the grip of a 'disease' in the form of irreconcilable differences between two 'races':

> The Arab community is predominantly Asiatic in character, the Jewish community predominantly European. They differ in religion and in language. Their cultural and social life, their ways of thought and conduct, are as incompatible as their national aspirations.[42]

Arabs and Jews would not behave in accordance with the principles of the Mandate and with the values of the mandatory power, the report declared. Britain had done its best and was now saddled with finding a solution: 'We [the British] are responsible for the welfare of the country. Its government is in our hands. We are bound to strive to the utmost to do justice and make peace.'[43]

The report and its conclusions were based on blatant falsehoods. The Mandate had been conducted on the basis of commitment to 'well-being and development' of the whole population of Palestine, it asserted, and the Arabs had been the main beneficiary. This myth had already been exploded by one of Britain's senior staff. Thomas Hodgkin was secretary to the High Commissioner, with access to inner circles of the colonial regime. Appalled by British repression and hypocrisy, in 1936 he resigned and was expelled from Palestine, writing a personal testimony of the harms done to Arab society. 'The Palestine Arabs have for the last eighteen years endured an undiluted British autocracy,' he said.[44] Palestine was in reality a Crown Colony and resistance was the 'natural response to the Government's continued frustration of all peaceful efforts of the Arabs towards independence'.[45] Far from serving the whole of Palestinian society, the British had 'annexed Palestine by force...and was holding the Arabs down by force'.[46] Far from providing justice and peace, Britain had created enduring conflict.

The Commission's report also carried gross misrepresentations of British policy regarding Jewish people. Britain had demonstrated an historic commitment to the Jews of Europe, it proposed. 'Nowhere have Jews found it easier to live and prosper than in Britain', the report declared: 'Nowhere is there a more genuine desire to do what can be done to help them in their present difficulties.'[47] Britain had for years excluded the most vulnerable victims of fascism, particularly Jews who sought asylum in the face of intensifying antisemitism and the murderous policies of the Nazi regime. By the late

1930s, there had been some 600,000 applications for asylum in the United Kingdom from German and Austrian refugees: one in ten had been successful.[48] Jews had discovered that Britain was closed to most applicants and Palestine became a key destination. Here, Britain accommodated mass settlement of Jewish immigrants and suppressed Arabs who contested landlessness and poverty. Thompson comments on 'a profound, continuing, nimbyist and arguably anti-Semitic reluctance' to open British doors to the refugees of Europe.[49] It was not Britain's responsibility to address Europe's Jewish crisis: the Arabs must solve the problem.

Partition – secrets and 'imaginings'

The Peel Commission 'investigated' a crisis made in the Colonial Office and in Government House, Jerusalem. It blamed the victims and sought an outcome that would leave Britain free to pursue its remaining interests in the Middle East, most importantly in Egypt and Iraq. As Penny Sinanoglu points out in a detailed analysis of the Commission's procedures and conclusions, Britain's strategic interests – including control of the Suez Canal and of air routes and land communications – were a key consideration for imperial planners and military chiefs. These were reflected in the report but went 'unnoticed and unexposed'.[50]

During the Commission's visit to Palestine evidence was gathered in open sessions at which Zionist leaders presented their case, the AHC at first boycotting the procedures, then, after pressure from the king of Transjordan, agreeing to participate. The Commission also held numerous sessions in camera, 'private sessions', also referred to as 'secret sessions', that involved many discussions with the Zionist leadership in which plans for partition were advanced vigorously by the settlers' leadership. Transcripts of the secret meetings were classified and, under British governmental procedures, were not revealed until 2017. Laila Parsons's analysis of the transcripts reveals that many Zionist leaders and British officials gave secret testimony: no Palestinian leaders participated in these sessions.[51] As the hearings proceeded, Parsons observes, 'Zionist leaders and British officials sound[ed] more and more like partners in a joint project':

> The way the secret testimony unfolded without the Palestinians reflected what was happening on the ground, as Jewish immigration to Palestine increased and a Jewish state in-the-waiting was being built.[52]

The secret testimony makes it clear that the British were not merely working closely with Jewish institutions but relied on them for much routine administration and in crucial policy areas such as immigration. The Zionist movement in effect already operated alongside the colonial regime. As one British official observed during the secret sessions, his government was not 'the colonising power here; the Jewish people are the colonising power and in order to facilitate immigration you must use such organs as they have created for the purposes of colonising'.[53]

Britain and the Zionist leadership were not always in agreement, especially over levels of immigration, land acquisition, and what the British called the 'absorptive capacity' of the country. Britain attempted to exclude Jewish refugees from Europe who had not received entry permits, intercepting ships bearing 'illegal' immigrants, fining their captains, and interning some passengers in the British colonies of Cyprus and Mauritius. Tensions were later to erupt into open conflict, with assaults on British forces and institutions by the Revisionist militias. But Britain was primarily a facilitator of settlement in Palestine: between 1931 and 1938 almost 200,000 Jewish immigrants were admitted to Palestine by the colonial authorities, twice the total that had arrived during the earlier years of the Mandate.[54] By 1939 the settler community numbered 450,000, or a third of the population of Palestine.[55] It is in this context that Thomas Hodgkin, who had left the Palestine administration in 1936, commented that although Palestinian Arabs viewed Zionism as a Jewish 'act of aggression', Zionism was 'in reality a British colonising movement': Zionism and British policy, he observed, were 'a single enemy'.[56]

'Transfer'

Key figures of the Zionist movement greeted the Peel Commission's report with surprise and in some cases with delight. Segev quotes Ben-Gurion's diary: the report, wrote Ben-Gurion, was 'our declaration of independence'.[57] Israeli historian Benny Morris also quotes Ben-Gurion:

> The compulsory transfer of the Arabs from the valleys of the proposed Jewish state could give us something which we never had… We are being given an opportunity which we never dared to dream of in our wildest imaginings.[58]

In fact, Zionist leaders had not only dreamed of a state in Palestine that would be free of Arabs but had pursued the idea with British politicians over many years. In 1930 Weizmann proposed the idea of 'transfer' – forcible movement of Palestinian Arabs – with British officials and ministers. The notion of expulsion had been on the Zionist agenda since the time of Herzl but was not advanced seriously by the settler movement until discussions that followed the conflicts of 1929. Then Weizmann, head of the Jewish Agency, suggested that Transjordan – which the movement had long considered part of Palestine – provided the space into which Palestinian Arabs should be directed. During his talks with British officials, colonial minister Sir Thomas Drummond Shiels agreed that 'a transfer of the Arab population was desirable'.[59] Weizmann then formalised the idea, presenting to the Colonial Office proposals for a loan of one million Palestinian pounds to be raised from Jewish financial sources for the resettlement of Palestinian peasant communities into Transjordan.[60] On this occasion British ministers rejected the proposal, known as the Weizmann-Rutenberg Plan, but it entered wider discussions as a 'solution' to the Palestine crisis. Weizmann pursued it in an article published in London:

> No statesmanlike view…could ignore the fact that Transjordan is legally part of Palestine…that in race, language and culture its people are indistinguishable from the Arabs of Western Palestine: that it is separated from Western Palestine only by a narrow stream [the River Jordan]: that it has been established as an Arab reserve, and that it would be just as easy for landless Arabs or cultivators from the congested areas to migrate to Transjordan as to migrate from one part of Western Palestine to another.[61]

The project of 'transfer' now appeared repeatedly in discussions between Britain and the Zionist leadership and in international forums. In 1931 the Jewish Agency submitted a proposal to a British-appointed committee to study the situation of dispossessed Arab farmers, including those evicted from lands sold to Jewish owners, the Agency proposing to remove the peasants directly to Transjordan. In 1932 the Zionist Organisation at the League of Nations suggested in a secret memorandum that Palestine should be partitioned, with 120,000 Arabs removed from the area designated for Jews.[62] At the same time transfer was discussed more and more openly within the Zionist movement. Menachem Ussishkin, a veteran Zionist and President of the Jewish National Fund, told a meeting in Jerusalem that transfer was a matter of principle:

> We must continually raise the demand that our land be returned to our possession. If there are other inhabitants there, they must be transferred to some other place. We must take over the land. We have a greater and nobler ideal than preserving several hundred thousands of Arab fellahin.[63]

Ussishkin declared: 'I am prepared to stand and defend the moral aspect [of transfer] before God and the League of Nations.'[64] Few Zionist leaders disputed the desirability of expulsion – the key issue was how to achieve their aim by persuading the British to carry it out. The Jewish Agency established a Committee on Population Transfer to assess who should be moved, to what destinations, in what order, and at what cost. The Weitz Plan proposed to move the Arab peasantry first, using financial inducements, with the 'aim of reducing the [Arab] population by a third in two to three years'.[65] Other proposals envisaged transfer of the whole population by force. The Committee agreed to undertake a detailed study of the rural sector of Arab society – collecting evidence on Arab villages and landholdings in preparation for their 'evacuation' following sale to Jewish owners and/or by direct compulsion. Ben-Gurion favoured negotiated deals with neighbouring states which were to receive displaced peasants. He was not, however, satisfied with only part of the country, arguing at the Committee: 'After we build up a strong force following the establishment of the state we will abolish the partition of the country and we will expand to the whole Land of Israel'.[66] Acquisition of a portion of Palestine was 'only a stage in the realisation of Zionism', he explained:

> It should prepare the ground for our expansion throughout the whole country through Jewish-Arab agreement...the state, however, must enforce order and security and it will do this not by moralising and preaching 'sermons on the mount' but by machine-guns, which we will need.[67]

The Committee continued to debate the desirability of inducing Palestinian Arabs to move or compelling them to do so. Meanwhile, the weapons so important to Ben-Gurion were being put to a more immediate use, as Zionist militias joined the British in suppressing a new and more intense phase of Arab resistance.

Armed struggle

In 1931 Haganah B had re-organised as the National Military Organisation, the Irgun Tzvai Leumi (IZL, or the Irgun), known in Hebrew as Etzel. This armed group prepared for confrontation with the Palestinian Arabs on the basis that they should be expelled en masse. At the start of the general strike in 1936 the organisation was involved in attacks on Arab neighbourhoods, targeting markets and public places.[68] In 1937 most of its members joined the Haganah, now numbering over 20,000 well-organised militiamen, taking with them the Revisionists' intense hostility towards Arabs and their commitment to expulsion of the entire Arab population. In 1939, Revisionist leader Jabotinsky wrote: 'There is no choice: the Arabs must make room for the Jews in Eretz Israel. If it was possible to transfer the Baltic peoples, it is also possible to move the Palestinian Arabs.'[69] In 1940 a split from the Irgun led by Avraham Stern founded Lehi (Lohamei Herut Yisra'el), known widely as the Stern Gang. Stern described the Arabs as 'beasts of the desert, not a legitimate people'.[70] The Arabs were not a nation, he said, 'but a mole that grew in the wilderness of the eternal desert. They are nothing but murderers'.[71] Lehi advocated ruthless confrontation with those it saw as enemies of the Jews in Palestine and was later to call on the United Nations for compulsory evacuation of the entire Arab population.

The Haganah had been boosted by tacit support from the colonial regime and both open and clandestine supplies of arms. It now had a new role: the British were no longer in control of events in Palestine and it was the settler movement they had incubated that became a partner in suppressing Arab resistance. The general strike declared in April 1936 precipitated a profound crisis for the British: Matthews comments that it brought collapse of the 'system of colonial control' in Palestine.[72] Arab youth activism, worker solidarity, women's initiatives and a national network of committees and local groups had upended the relationship between the colonial regime and the traditional leadership upon which British control had depended. When the strike came to an end the British hoped to reinforce the old order, but in November 1937, just two months after publication of the Peel Commission report, guerrilla fighters assassinated a senior British official known to be a supporter of the Zionist cause. When the regime reacted with punitive measures the intifada resumed, this time in the form of armed struggle, and now Jewish militias came to the fore.

Beginning in the north, veterans of Qassamist groups organised in many villages and extended their influence into the mountainous areas of the West Bank. They avoided pitched battles, ambushing British troops and even destroying RAF aircraft on the ground. Anderson describes their tactics: 'The rebels answered the colonial regime's superior firepower and manpower with flexible formations whose ability to rapidly dissolve and disappear into their surroundings was, as in 1936, critical to their survival and longevity.'[73] Villages and entire rural areas became 'no-go' for the British. The cities were also mobilised, with Jerusalem (al-Quds) and Hebron (al-Khalil) strongholds of the armed movement. Some local networks remained under the influence of traditional leaders, but much activity was autonomous, with young radicals to the fore. They attacked police stations, government offices and Jewish settlements, targeting Arab collaborators and those who advocated coming to terms with the British. The Arab component of the British police disintegrated as a loyalist force, many joining the intifada and fighting with guerrilla groups. Shepherd describes a movement that paralysed the colonial regime:

> The rebels commandeered supplies and reinforcements from the villagers; they raided banks in the towns; they set up rival courts, with clerks writing on typewriters stolen from British offices; and handed down penalties and sometimes death sentences against those who resisted them.[74]

The British were in serious trouble. In Egypt they were also struggling to maintain control, challenged by the workers' movement and continuing growth of the Muslim Brotherhood. They opted for maximum repression, invoking their *Manual of Military Law* to justify unlimited use of force against those involved in insurrection. Reprisals, collective punishments and destruction of Arab property became routine. Two full infantry divisions of the British Army – some 25,000 men – were mobilised, many taking on policing roles in villages and Arab neighbourhoods in the cities.[75] The Royal Navy was also deployed, its ships shelling villages said to have 'pro-bandit' sympathies.[76] Arab activists were viewed as 'brigands': among those captured, torture at the hands of British troops was routine; extrajudicial executions (shooting 'out-of-hand') became common.[77] Gratuitous violence was encouraged by the senior command. Hughes describes the 'banality of brutality' as 'destruction and vandalism became a systematic, systemic part of British counter-insurgency operations'.[78] He writes:

> During army searches, soldiers would surround a village – usually before dawn so that they could catch any suspects before they fled – the men and women then divided off, held apart from the houses, often in wired 'cages', while soldiers searched and often destroyed everything, burnt grain and poured olive oil over household food and effects. The men meanwhile were 'screened' by passing hooded or hidden Arab informers who would nod when a 'suspect' was found, or by British officials checking their papers against lists of suspects.[79]

There were reprimands for rank-and-file troops who hesitated to perpetrate these crimes by not 'doing their stuff' in wrecking houses and destroying their contents; at the same time looting was common and largely went unpunished.[80] Unable to strike an elusive and effective enemy, the British increasingly operated on the basis of revenge attacks, collective punishments and reprisals including mass demolitions. Meanwhile they censored Arabic-language newspapers: commanders such as Major-General Bernard Montgomery, later to be celebrated for leading British forces during the Second World War, banished newspaper reporters so that his men could carry on their work untroubled by the media – an approach later favoured by Israeli governments.[81]

Partnership - Britain and the Zionists

Jewish organisations operated as if they were part of the regime. British intelligence-gathering, run by the RAF, worked closely with the Jewish Agency and its network of informers. In an account favourable to the Zionist cause, Naomi Shepherd writes that information about rebel bands, their composition, location and arms, and their connections with Arab politicians was gathered by Arabic-speaking settlers and passed on to the British.[82] The colonial administration recruited and armed 6,000 Jewish police and continued to channel weapons to the Haganah, which by 1938 numbered 50,000 men in its front-line and reserve detachments: according to Colonial Office reports, it had 'thousands of guns concealed in all towns and colonies [Jewish settlements]'.[83] The settler militias also supplied recruits for a new force established by Colonel Orde Wingate, a veteran of British army service in Egypt and Sudan. His Special Night Squads (SNS) of British troops and Jewish 'supernumeraries' were charged to protect the oil pipeline from Iraq and to attack Arab villages seen as supportive of the intifada. Wingate was a fervent Christian Zionist who identified strongly with the settler movement. He worked closely with the Haganah: according to Yigael Allon, then a key commander in the settler forces, Wingate 'co-operated illegally' with Haganah units, training them in novel methods of counter-insurgency.[84] Wingate became notorious for extreme cruelty: he engaged in provocations in Arab neighbourhoods and markets, tortured villagers and shot dead 'suspects' in cold blood.[85] Segev describes the Special Night Squads as 'virtually a private army' so vicious that even some Zionists distanced themselves from its methods.[86]

The intifada was so widespread and guerrilla bands so successful in attacking British forces, that in December 1937 the government in London directed Sir Charles Tegart, then a senior official in India, to join the regime in Palestine. Tegart had a long record of suppressing Indian nationalists and set about containing and then eliminating Palestinian guerrillas. He ordered the construction of 70 large concrete forts, positioned strategically at key crossroads and vantage points across Palestine. Contracts to build these strongpoints, together with a 50-mile fence in the north-east known as 'Tegart's Wall', were given to Solel Boneh, the construction company affiliated to the Histadrut, which employed Jewish labour protected by the 'supernumerary' Jewish police. The Jewish Telegraphic Agency wrote:

> The barbed-wire 'fence' under construction today along the northern frontier of Palestine will be a barricade such as exists on no other border in the world, not even the most troubled. The 'fence' is actually an entanglement of the most substantial and permanent wartime type, over six feet high and six feet deep, strung on stakes set in concrete. There are 200 yards of wire coiled in an impenetrable tangle in every yard of length of the barricade.[87]

It was widely reported that the vast lengths of barbed wire required were imported from Mussolini's Italy.[88] The forts, placed across Palestine on elevated terrain, were 'monuments of power and machines of control and territorial expansion':

> The architectural language was brutalist and repellent, expressing military iconography par excellence. The architectural design imposed power and control over the observer, as well as a real ability to control and survey through their panoptical design. These stony white structures that dotted the landscape were brutal both in image and in use, serving as centres of torture, interrogation, and investigation.[89]

The forts were to play a key role in successive conflicts, before, during and after the Nakba of 1948, eventually becoming part of the military resources of the Israeli state.

The MacDonald Paper

Still the British and their settler allies failed to suppress the intifada. In March 1938 the government in London replaced Wauchope with another imperial veteran, Sir Harold MacMichael, formerly Governor of Tanganyika. He told the Colonial Office: 'The position is deteriorating rapidly and has reached a stage at which rebel leaders are more feared and respected than we are'.[90] The 'revolt', he said, was 'an attempt to achieve the complete reversal of government policy regarding partition and Jewish immigration'.[91] Now Britain determined to use all means to impose control. Following the Munich Pact with Nazi Germany, Britain felt free to mobilise a further division of troops in Palestine – over 12,000 men together with armour, artillery, engineers and signals units. The regime launched a campaign of 'rolling mass incarceration', based on what Anderson calls a 'colonial model of concentration camps'.[92] Arab sources suggest that 40,000-50,000 men were held for various periods in detention centres.[93] Together with intelligence provided by settler organisations, increasing factionalism, and ineffective co-ordination among insurgent groups, this assault gradually weakened the intifada. By the end of 1938 the movement was in decline. The High Commissioner crowed at the turn of events, declaring: 'the leaders are now hunted rather than hunting'.[94] Lacking ammunition, fighters were increasingly isolated. When an international conference on Palestine was organised in Cairo, traditional leaders were able to reassert some of their former influence, boosted by British assurances that proposals for partition of Palestine had been abandoned.

The impact of events in Europe was felt directly in Palestine. War was coming and British strategists turned to the Middle East, just as they had done during the conflict of 1914-18. Then the Allies 'had floated to victory on a wave of oil': now they urgently sought to secure the Suez Canal; the oilfields of Iran, Iraq and of Bahrain (where oil had been discovered in 1932); and the vast oil resources of Kuwait and Saudi Arabia, which had just been located. Palestine had renewed importance: having used the greatest brutality against the national movement, the British sought to stabilise control and in May 1939 the government produced a new White Paper that repudiated partition and advanced proposals for a unitary state – superficially an accommodation to Arab interests. The MacDonald Paper proposed to limit Jewish immigration to Palestine and to introduce 'self-government':

> The objective of HMG [His Majesty's Government] is the establishment within 10 years of an independent Palestinian state...in which the two peoples in Palestine, the Arabs and Jews, share authority in government in such a way that the essential interests of each are shared.[95]

Leaders of the Zionist movement were enraged. Ben-Gurion inveighed against an 'evil, foolish and short-sighted policy'.[96] He alleged that the British had revoked the Balfour Declaration: 'Satan himself could not have created a more distressing and terrible nightmare.'[97] In protest demonstrations in Palestine, Jews carried banners comparing the White Paper to the antisemitic Nuremburg Laws of Nazi Germany and MacDonald to Hitler.[98] Now the Irgun attacked British targets and stepped up its assaults on Palestinian Arabs. Over the course of a few months it murdered over 130 people.[99] Arab leaders, mistrustful of the British, were disinclined to accept the proposals. It was too late: as Rashid Khalidi observes, Britain was soon at war in Europe; importantly, Winston Churchill, 'perhaps the most ardent Zionist in British political life', was prime minister.[100] But now the British and their empire were no longer to play the key role in shaping events: '[A] new world was about to be born in which Britain would at best be a second-class power. The fate of Palestine would no longer be in its hands.'[101]

Chapter 4
Displacement and dispossession

Zionist plans for 'transfer'. The Nakba and Palestinian resistance

World war rapidly accelerated the decline of European colonialism in the Arab East. Movements for national independence were growing rapidly and political radicals were making headway. France was soon to leave Lebanon and Syria; in Egypt and Iraq, Britain was on borrowed time. In Palestine, Britain was also on the retreat, but here the post-colonial order would not reflect aspirations for an Arab region free of European control; rather, an independent Jewish state was to emerge focused on integration into a world dominated by new imperialisms.

Britain's hold over large areas of South Asia had lasted for two centuries: the Palestine Mandate had been sustained for only three decades, largely because persistent Arab resistance made effective control impossible. As German military offensives in North Africa came to an end in 1943, British politicians and officials concluded that Palestine was no longer a strategic asset. The colonial secretary had already concluded that 'Palestine is a millstone around our necks'.[1] Britain prepared to retreat, aiming to retain a presence in Egypt and Transjordan and to focus on key assets in oilfields of the Gulf. They would be leaving a country in which European settlers now enjoyed economic, political and military advantages over an Arab population that Zionist leaders were increasingly determined to remove by means of 'transfer'. Josef Weitz was director of the land department of the Jewish National Fund (JNF) and a key member of the Transfer Committee established in 1937. In 1941 he wrote: 'We have clashing interests with the Arabs everywhere...only [Arab] population transfer and evacuating this country so it would become exclusively for us is the solution'.[2] Weitz was increasingly focused on this project. His diary notes:

> Amongst ourselves it must be clear that there is no room for both peoples in this country. No 'development' will bring us closer to our aim to be an independent people in this small country. After the Arabs are transferred, the country will be wide open for us; with the Arabs staying the country will remain narrow and restricted, when the war is over, and the English have emerged victorious and when the judging nations sit on the throne of law, our people should bring their petitions and claims before them; and the only solution is the Land of Israel, or at least the Western Land of Israel [Palestine], without Arabs. There is no room for compromise on this point.[3]

Weitz was emphatic: 'The only way is to transfer the Arabs from here to neighbouring countries, all of them, except perhaps Bethlehem, Nazareth, and Old Jerusalem. Not a single village or a single tribe must be left. And the transfer must be done through their absorption in Iraq and Syria and even in Transjordan.'[4]

Weitz wrestled with the problem of clearing the Arab population. After discussion with colleagues he determined: 'From now on we must work out a secret plan based on the removal of the Arabs from here'; he continued: 'today we have no other alternative...we will not live here with the Arabs'.[5] He travelled to Syria to inspect areas into which Palestinian Arabs could be 'evacuated', favouring the al-Jazira region in the far north of the country, which he described as 'a huge absorption home for people – workers, peasants, townspeople, and others'.[6] Iraq, he suggested, could also absorb Palestinian Arabs. The problem of accomplishing 'transfer' became a preoccupation of the Zionist leadership. Could the British be pressured by diplomatic means to undertake the project? Should the movement confront the colonial regime, as some Revisionists advocated? Should the settler community and its institutions prepare to expel the Palestinians en masse?

Ben-Gurion initially favoured working with and through the British. The settler community had continued to expand – during the Second World War some 60 new settlements were established in Palestine and Ben-Gurion anticipated that pro-Zionist ministers in London such as Churchill could be won to the prospect of an independent Jewish state. Some among Revisionist leaders favoured outright conflict with Britain. Menachem Begin had become leader of Etzel (Irgun), advocating Jewish claims to the whole territory of historic Palestinian and beyond – 'from the Nile to the Euphrates', he said.[7] In 1944 Begin issued a 'declaration of war' against Britain and attacked the mainstream of the settler leadership as feeble and treacherous. Lehi (the Stern group) meanwhile attempted assassination of leading British officials, succeeding in 1944 in killing Walter Guinness, Lord Moyne, Britain's senior official in the Middle East. Lehi declared: 'We accuse Lord Moyne and the government he represents, with murdering hundreds and thousands of our brethren; we accuse him of seizing our country and looting our possessions. We were forced to do justice and to fight.'[8] Two years later Irgun bombed the headquarters of the Mandate Authority and the British armed forces in the King David Hotel in Jerusalem, killing almost 100 civilian and military personnel.

Despite strategic differences Zionist leaders held in common the aim to achieve 'transfer'. They anticipated further significant conflict with the Palestinian population and, in an important development, key settler institutions began to prepare by surveying villages and towns in which confrontations were likely to occur. The Jewish National Fund (JNF) had for years undertaken surveys of the land, initiating purchases from Arab landowners and supervising evictions. It had started to compile 'Village Files', providing information about local topography, village demographics and religious affiliations, and assessments of community organisation and 'hostility' towards the British and the settlers.[9] In 1940 Shai, the Haganah's intelligence section, began to collect more detailed information, including by use of 'scouting missions' to produce perspective sketches, maps, drawings and photographs of each village and its surroundings. It also undertook aerial photography conducted by means of clandestine activities designed to evade British restrictions. Rona Sela quotes one of those involved: 'I told myself that if we find ourselves in a war, we will have to conquer these villages.'[10] Haganah member Moshe Pasternak recalls that the project was unreservedly militaristic; the Village Files were designed to serve as a database of intelligence information that could be used to coordinate paramilitary operations against Palestinian targets:

> We had to study the basic structure of the Arab village. This means the structure and how best to attack it…the Arab village, unlike the European ones, was built topographically on hills. That meant we had to find out how best to approach the village from above or enter it from below.[11]

The Village Files became a key resource for Zionist forces employed in offensives that eventually facilitated 'transfer' in the form of mass displacement and dispossession – the Nakba of 1948.

Overwhelming force

The Zionist movement, says Segev, 'had hitched itself to the British Empire, advancing under its sponsorship to the verge of independence'.[12] Acquiring land and autonomous institutions, it had also built a large and effective military apparatus. An Anglo-American Committee of Enquiry into events in Palestine which reported in 1946 gives evidence of these armed forces. The Haganah could call on an army of 16,000 trained fighters and a reserve force of 40,000; the Palmach units, founded in 1941, numbered 2,000 with 4,000 in reserve. The report estimated the Irgun guerrilla group as 3,000-5,000-strong, and the Stern group as 200-300-strong.[13] When sustained conflict with the Palestinian Arabs began in 1948, says Shlaim, the Haganah (renamed the Israel Defence Forces, IDF) fielded 35,000 troops, not counting second-line troops in the settlements. By mid-July 1948 the IDF fully mobilised 65,000 men under arms; by September the number rose to 90,000; and by December 1948 it reached a peak of 96,441.[14]

For years the Zionists' military cadre had, in effect, been tutored in strategy and tactics by the British. It had observed practices developed in the face of resistance to British colonialism worldwide and now directed against the Palestinian Arabs: collective punishment; curfews; exile and banishment; demolitions; destruction of trees, crops and livestock; occupation of villages; arbitrary arrest; detention without trial; assassination; torture; concentration camps; covert operations; hit squads; the use of collaborators, informers and 'human shields'; controls on movement; attacks from the air and the sea; construction of walls and fortified emplacements; the use of military law against civilians...the full panoply of techniques employed in imperial rule. The British systematically mistreated Palestinians whom they seized and detained: the prison system was 'militarised and brutalised' and '[British] security personnel went about their work as they wished'.[15] During 1938 the British detained at least 96,000 Palestinians – 11 percent of the Arab population, or 22 percent of male Palestinians.[16] Hughes calculates that during the intifada of April 1936 to September 1939, British forces (army, police and auxiliaries) detained 528,000 people – 37 percent of the entire population of Palestine.[17] They undertook mass assaults: 'The Army pulled in whole villages for periods of incarceration and labour, hundreds of people at time.'[18] These startlingly high rates of incarceration, says Hughes, 'emphasise continuities in British colonial security state imprisonment regimes during revolt crises, from Egypt, Iraq, and Ireland after 1916 to Kenya and Malaya in the 1950s'.[19]

Zionist leaders and rank-and-file activists were close observers and sometimes participants in the repression. In a unique, detailed account of the military aspects of colonial rule, *Britain's Pacification of Palestine*, Matthew Hughes concludes that sharing of intelligence between Britain and the Zionists, plus military training of Jewish recruits to the Special Night Squads and the police, 'toughened the [Jewish] community for the next war with the Palestinians and the Arabs in 1948'.[20] Britain's role in arming and training Jewish 'supernumary' police and kibbutzniks (residents of agricultural communities) had its impact upon settlers who, says Hughes, had 'a visceral stake in the unfolding counter-insurgency and who unlike the [British] soldiers were not going "home" after the fighting was over'.[21]

At the end of the Second World War, Britain had 100,000 troops stationed in Palestine at a cost of £30 million a year.[22] With a weakened empire and chronic domestic problems, it was preparing for rapid retreat. Withdrawal from India was imminent and in February 1947 the government declared that the following year it would hand over the Palestine Mandate to the newly formed United Nations. The UN set up a commission which presented another report recommending partition, and in November 1947 the General Assembly voted to establish two states in Palestine, one for Jews and one for Arabs. The

Jewish state was to receive twice as much territory as under the previous British partition proposal – 52 percent of historic Palestine – with 42 percent for the Arab state and the area in and around Jerusalem to be placed under international control.[23] The mainstream of the Zionist movement accepted the plan – what Edelman describes as 'the miraculous prospect of the Jewish state' – which was received with delight by most of Palestine's settler population:

> In Tel Aviv, Jerusalem and Haifa great crowds streamed into the streets as the news was passed from mouth to mouth. Men, women and children danced in the streets. The State! The State!... At last the world had acknowledged the Zionist claim to a State, and Herzl's dream had been fulfilled.[24]

Arab leaders rejected the UN plan, not least because the proposed Jewish state would contain more than half a million Palestinian Arabs while 10,000 Jews would be placed within the boundaries of the Arab state. Like Britain's partition plan for India, which had already produced intense conflict, mass displacement and enormous suffering, the UN proposal was a formula for disaster.

Ethnic cleansing

Clashes between Palestinians and Zionist militias began almost immediately, resulting in scores of victims, and for months intermittent conflict continued. The British attempted to close off neighbourhoods in which confrontations were particularly intense; meanwhile Revisionist groups attacked Arab villages and volunteers from some Arab states entered Palestinian territory to join the resistance. In January 1948 the Zionists took decisive steps as militias under the movement's mainstream leadership moved to the strategy of 'takeover, occupation and expulsion'.[25] In February 1948 Zionist forces began what Ilan Pappé calls 'major cleansing operations': it was only then, he says, 'that the meaning of the imminent catastrophe began to dawn on the [Palestinian] people'.[26]

Britain had announced that its forces would leave Palestine on 15 May 1948. In March the Zionist leadership authorised Plan Dalet

('Plan D'). Palestinian historian Walid Khalidi records the entire document, which should be read in full to grasp its key aims – to 'wipe out' resistance and to expel the population from territory that Zionist leaders intended should form the basis of a new Jewish state.[27] Extracts from the Plan set out numerous offensive measures against the Palestinian population:

- The objective of this plan [Dalet] is to gain control of the areas of the Hebrew state and defend its borders. It also aims at gaining control of the areas of Jewish settlement and concentration which are located outside the borders [of the proposed Hebrew state] against regulars, semi-regulars, small forces operating from bases outside or inside the state...

- Launching pre-planned counter-attack on enemy bases and supply lines in the heart of his territory and within the borders of the country [Palestine] and in neighbouring countries...

- Applying economic pressure on the enemy by besieging some of his cities in order to force him to abandon some of his activities...

- The lands of the state, such as roads, bridges, main passes, important crossroads, paths, etc. must be blocked by means of: acts of sabotage explosions, series of barricades, minefields, as well as by controlling the elevations near roads and taking up positions there...

- Destruction of villages (setting fire to, blowing up, and planting mines in the debris), especially those population centres which are difficult to control continuously...

- Mounting combing and control operations according to the following guidelines: encirclement of the village and conducting a search inside it. In the event of resistance, the armed force must be wiped out and the population must be expelled outside the borders of the state.[28]

Striking features of the Plan include continuous references to the Palestinian Arab population as 'the enemy' and the mobilisation of tactics used repeatedly over preceding decades by the British –

reflecting the fact that half the men available to the Haganah at this point had been trained by the colonial power.[29]

Plan Dalet set out 13 operational offensives, beginning with Operation Nachshon, undertaken in central Palestine and which was to prove a model for successive initiatives in which sudden mass expulsions were achieved through surprise attacks. Pappé records the directive to Zionist commanders who began Nachshon: 'You will move to State Dalet…the villages which you will capture, cleanse or destroy will be decided according to consultation with your advisors on Arab affairs and the intelligence officers.'[30] Palmach units were told: 'The principal objective of the operation is the destruction of Arab villages [and] the eviction of the villagers'.[31] Pappé comments that villagers were trying to continue life as normal – 'within a few days most of them would be expelled forever from the homes and fields where they and their ancestors had lived and worked for centuries'.[32] He records efforts at resistance and attempts to retake villages overwhelmed by Zionist militias, but sustained attacks meant that 'one by one [villages] were surrounded, attacked and occupied, their people expelled and their homes and buildings demolished'.[33] Information gleaned over the years and placed in the Village Files proved crucial in guiding local offensives. 'We [had been] through every village in Palestine,' recalled an Israeli officer, 'and estimated its character, whether it meant trouble or not; and we had a map in which the strategic characters of every Arab village and the quality of its inhabitants were indicated. We had a file with the details.'[34] The 'details' were, in effect, part of the militias' battle plans.

In April 1948 Zionist forces led by Revisionist militias occupied Deir Yassin near Jerusalem and massacred almost 100 of its people.[35] The episode was used as a propaganda initiative – broadcast as a warning to other villages and neighbourhoods of what awaited those who would not flee in the face of the militias. One after another nearby villages were also attacked, buildings destroyed and the population expelled. Zionist forces moved on to major urban centres, assaulting Tiberias, Haifa, Safad and Jerusalem. British troops were present throughout the events but, with the exception of one incident, remained onlookers.[36] A further series of towns soon fell: Jaffa was the last to be taken, on 13 May, 48 hours before Britain's termination of the Mandate. Its population of 50,000 was expelled en masse: by mid-May 'the occupying Jewish forces had emptied and depopulated all the major towns and cities of Palestine'.[37]

Benny Morris, initially one of Israel's 'New Historians' who used Zionist archives to investigate events during 1948, attests to the importance of violent, exemplary attacks on Palestinian villages, including Deir Yassin.[38] Notwithstanding efforts by Israeli ideologues to deny outright the perpetration of massacres by Zionist forces, he observes:

> Everyone, at every level of military and political decision-making, understood that a Jewish state without a large Arab minority would be stronger and more viable both militarily and politically. The tendency of local military commanders to 'nudge' Palestinians into flight increased as the war went on. Jewish atrocities...(massacres of Arabs at Ad Dawayima, Eilaboun, Jish, Safsaf, Majdal Kurum, Hule (in Lebanon) Saliha and Sasa, besides Dayr Yasin and Lydd and other places – also contributed significantly to the exodus.[39]

Here, massacres 'nudge' Palestinians in fear of their lives to leave villages and neighbourhoods, meeting the aims of Plan Dalet and the project of 'transfer'. Focused use of terror to achieve mass displacement had been used routinely by the British and was now integrated into Zionist military strategies.

On 14 May Ben-Gurion declared establishment of the State of Israel, but the assaults were not over: over the next six months 'cleansing' operations continued, targeting areas in which villages had successfully resisted and those displaced Palestinians who attempted to return to their homes. Zionist forces also tackled units of troops from Egypt, Transjordan, Syria, Lebanon, Iraq, Saudi Arabia and Yemen – ostensibly part of an Arab Liberation Army (ALA) – that had entered Palestine with the formal aim of freeing it from occupation. Conflict between these regular army forces and Zionist militias has entered mainstream Israeli history as a battle with hostile forces bent upon genocide and a joint effort 'to throw the Jews into the sea'.[40] Israeli historian Avi Shlaim addresses these claims, including biblical images of David confronting Goliath in tumultuous struggles for a Jewish state – accounts since continuously invoked in Israeli state narratives. Typically, he says, these identify struggles of the few against the many in the form of a 'desperate, tenacious, and heroic struggle for survival against horrifyingly heavy odds'.[41] But, writes Shlaim, forces despatched by Arab states 'were nowhere as powerful or united as they appeared to be in Arab and Jewish propaganda'.[42] Arab armies, most in the form of expeditionary units, were deeply divided and affected by 'backstage manoeuvres, labyrinthine intrigues, and [Arab leaders'] sordid attempts to stab each other in the back'.[43] They were largely ineffectual or worse – failing in leadership, co-ordination and in elementary military strategy: 'The Arab coalition was one of the most divided, disorganised and ramshackle coalitions in the entire history of warfare', suggests Shlaim.[44] Zionist militias (combined as the IDF) outnumbered and outgunned Arab forces, so that: 'In this war, as in most wars, the stronger side prevailed'.[45]

Resistance

If the forces of Arab states deployed in 1948 have since been viewed in Israel as an existential threat to the new Jewish state, Palestinians in contrast have been depicted as passive and at best reactive, apparently abandoning their homes in response to directions from the AHC and from Arab kings and presidents. On this view, Palestinians walked away from their towns and villages – part of the 'miraculous' events that presented the Zionist movement with a land free of people.

There were in fact many episodes of resistance. Anne Irfan observes that Palestinians' own accounts 'clearly undermine any suggestion that they were purely passive in the Nakba'.[46] Zionist forces in northern Galilee (al-Jalil), part of the UN-designated Arab state, adopted Britain's policy of dropping leaflets from the air, calling on villagers to surrender and following up with massive aerial bombardment. Across the area, however, Palestinian villages 'turned themselves into strongholds…holding out with what meagre arms they had before being overpowered by the assailants'.[47] Most villagers refused to flee, remaining in their homes until forcibly evicted: 100,000 Palestinians from the area were eventually compelled to move north across the border to Lebanon. Others in Central Galilee were able to maintain resistance and to remain in their villages, despite intensive efforts by the IDF to evict them. Adel Manna observes that many resisted the policy of expulsion: 'Survivors in this part of Palestine decided to cling to their homeland and face their conquerors barehanded'.[48] Palestinian oral history gives testimony of countless similar efforts. Muhammad Hallaj describes how Qalqilya and nearby villages co-ordinated resistance. People of the town organised a collection to buy guns and ammunition, and erected fortifications:

> Soon Qalqilya was completely surrounded by a defensive trench. The men also built a number of round concrete structures with little openings to serve as watchtowers. Every able-bodied man between the ages of 18 and 45, if I remember correctly, was to stand guard one night a week...
>
> Qalqilya not only defended itself in 1948, but it also helped to defend a number of smaller neighbouring villages, such as Taybeh, al-Tira, and Jaljulya. The town installed a siren on the top of the mosque's minaret, and when reinforcements were needed to help another village the siren was sounded to alert men to go to their aid. When they heard the siren, they assembled in the little square in front of the municipality, and trucks carried them to wherever the battle was taking place.[49]

Walid from Safad recalls confrontations between Zionist militias and the town's irregular forces until, inhibited by lack of arms and ammunition, inhabitants were compelled to leave. 'We had many battles,' he relates:

> But we were mainly irregular forces, with different kinds of arms, British, Belgian, German, Italian and Greek. The Jordanians [part of the ALA] said they would send us ammunition according to the types of arms we had. But they distributed ammunition to the wrong fighters.[50]

In nearby Mi'ilya, Elias Shoufani records effective co-operation with a small unit of regular troops from Yemen, as people of the village resisted a siege:

> The battle welded the village, the militia and the ALA into an integrated body. Every soldier was at the front fighting. Every man in the village was busy lending a hand in the common effort… Women carried food and water to the embattled men.[51]

Collecting accounts from scores of those engaged in the events of 1948, Rosemary Sayigh observes that large numbers of Palestinians tried to avoid leaving the country, notwithstanding immense pressure exerted by Zionist forces. 'It seems that the majority moved about within Palestine for as long as possible,' she says, remaining as close as possible to their homes, and in at least one case, al-Birwa, the community succeeded in recapturing its village from the settler militia.[52] She concludes: 'Although Zionists continue to protest that Palestinians left Palestine of their own accord, without pressure, the testimony of 800,000 refugees refutes them.'[53]

Eventually most people from Galilee were forced north to Lebanon and Syria, those from central Palestine were compelled to move to the West Bank, under Jordanian control, and people of southern Palestine and the Negev (al-Naqab) were expelled to Gaza or into Egypt. Further massacres took place, notably at the village of Dawaymeh near Hebron (al-Khalil): Pappé describes 'increasing levels of [Zionist] ruthlessness and cruelty'.[54] By 1949 Palestinian Arab villages across the length and breadth of the country had been depopulated and most of their people 'transferred'. Dawn Chatty comments: 'For the Zionists, it was the culmination of a dream… For Palestinians it was the time of expulsion, exodus, and destruction of their land and society.'[55] Palestine ceased to exist, says Edward Said, 'except as a memory or, more importantly, as an idea, a political and human experience, and an act of sustained popular will'.[56]

'Wall of silence'

In the years following the Nakba a number of Arab writers recorded the events of 1948.[57] Widespread dislocation caused by mass displacement, however, meant that it was several decades before researchers began systematically to address their meaning. In 1979 Rosemary Sayigh published *Palestinians: From Peasants to Revolutionaries*, a pioneering work on the experiences of people displaced into Lebanon.[58] Their stories, said Sayigh, had been 'suppressed, ignored or distorted': it was time 'to penetrate the wall of silence'.[59] The reasons for flight from their homes, says Sayigh, were so obvious that only deliberate mystification could have obscured them. 'The primary causes,' she concludes, 'were direct military attack on the villages; terrorism; lack of leadership; lack of arms; in short, chaos and fear'.[60]

During the 1980s, Walid Khalidi and over 30 other researchers collected data on Palestinian villages destroyed or depopulated in 1948, compiling records supported by maps, statistics and photographic evidence. *All That Remains: The Palestinian Villages Occupied and Depopulated by Israel in 1948*, published in 1992, is a monumental work of forensic archaeology and contemporary history that presents evidence of the fate of more than 400 villages and of post-1948 Israeli settlements established on confiscated village lands.[61] Palestinian testimony and material evidence provide a compelling picture of the Nakba as an intensive, sustained and violent assault on all aspects of Arab society – the people, their villages and towns, their social networks and cultural resources.

A further development exposed hitherto hidden histories of 1948. During the 1980s Israel's 'new historians' addressed Palestinian testimony and examined Israeli, American, British, and United Nations documents previously ignored or which, as 'classified' material, had not been available for historical study. Their work broke what Michal Ben-Josef Hirsch calls Israel's 'taboo' on questioning mainstream Zionist accounts of 1948 – an 'avoidance practice' that evaded not only responsibility for mass displacement of Palestinian Arabs but also its implications for contemporary politics.[62] For the first time, one of these critical historians, Ilan Pappé, addressed the Nakba as a sustained episode of ethnic cleansing based upon a 'master plan of expulsion and destruction'.[63]

An important part of Israel's foundational myths and of the narrative of 'miracles' is the idea that in 1948 Palestinians evacuated villages and towns under the direction of their traditional leaders and of Arab governments. Israeli historian Simha Flapan comments:

> The claim that the exodus was an 'order from above', from the Arab leadership, proved to be particularly good propaganda for many years, despite its improbability. Indeed, from the point of view of military logistics, the contention that the Palestinian Arab leadership appealed to the Arab masses to leave their homes in order to open the way for the invading armies, after which they would return to share in the victory, makes no sense at all.[64]

Quoting state archives and records of the Zionist militias, together with Ben-Gurion's war diaries, Flapan concludes that the AHC 'vigorously opposed' the departure of Palestinians.[65] References to directions by the Committee were 'largely fabricated' by Zionist historians and others, Flapan asserts. He continues:

> When, after April 1948, the flight acquired massive dimensions, Azzam Pasha, secretary of the Arab League, and King 'Abdallah [of Jordan] both issued public calls to the Arabs not to leave their homes, Fawzi al-Qawuqji, commander of the Arab Liberation Army, was given instructions to stop the flight by force and to requisition transport for this purpose. The Arab governments decided to allow entry [to their territories] only to women and children and to send back all men of military age…
>
> Why did such pleas have so little impact? They were outweighed by the cumulative effect of Zionist pressure tactics that ranged from economic and psychological warfare to the systematic ousting of the Palestinian population by the [Zionist] army.[66]

Walid Khalidi combed Zionist records for 1948 to identify evidence that Palestinians had been directed by their leaders to evacuate. After examining records of the Arab League and of Arab media, he observed: 'There is no trace in them of an order.'[67] On the contrary, like Flapan, he found that broadcasts and statements in the press ordered Palestinians to remain in their homes. Irish journalist Erskine Childers also sought evidence of evacuations directed by Palestinian leaders and Arab states. In 1961 he wrote:

> Examining every official Israeli statement about the Arab exodus, I was struck by the fact that no primary evidence of evacuation orders was ever produced. The charge, Israel claimed, was 'documented'; but where were the documents? There had allegedly been Arab radio broadcasts ordering the evacuation; but no dates, names of stations, or texts of messages were ever cited. In Israel in 1958, as a guest of the [Israeli] Foreign Office and therefore doubly hopeful of serious assistance, I asked to be shown the proofs. I was assured they existed, and was promised them. None had been offered when I left, but I was again assured. I asked to have the material sent on to me. I am still waiting.[68]

Like Walid Khalidi, Childers checked detailed records of radio broadcasts during 1948. He notes: 'There was not a single order, or appeal, or suggestion about evacuation from Palestine from any Arab radio station, inside or outside Palestine, in 1948.'[69] Rather, he says: 'There is repeated monitored record of Arab appeals, even flat orders, to the civilians of Palestine to stay put.'[70] Khalidi concludes that it was after the main events of the Nakba, in 1949, that Zionists decided to counter the damaging influence that mass displacement of Palestinians was having on their cause, producing novel accounts favourable to the Zionist militias and to the new state.[71] 'The story of the Arab evacuation order would hit two birds with one stone,' Khalidi writes: 'It would absolve the Zionists from the responsibility for the refugees, and it would pin this responsibility on the Arabs themselves.'[72] This account was to play an important role for Israeli ideologues – politicians, professional historians, archivists, educators and media people – who shaped and disseminated understandings of the birth of the nation. The evacuation myth proposed that Palestinians were active only to the extent that they walked away, leaving their land free for the settlers. It also had the function of legitimising seizure of Palestinian property by the settlers and later by immigrants from Europe and the Middle East who joined them. Maurice Edelman, an enthusiastic Zionist, comments that after 1948: 'The State cried out for immigrants, and they swarmed in, filling the towns and villages from which the Arabs had fled.'[73] Here, Palestinian homes were in effect gifted to the new owners.

These falsehoods were integral to stories about Israel, its history and contemporary reality that Israeli leaders told themselves and the wider world. They concealed the purposeful violence enacted upon the Palestinians by Israeli forces and, at the same time, made Palestinians responsible for their own fateful exit from territory of the new state. This was not a novel practice: modern nation-states have for generations told stories that 'forget' key events and processes associated with their establishment, installing other accounts that legitimise a new order. Ernest Renan, a 19th-century French republican writer, observed:

> Forgetting, I would even say historical error, is an essential factor in the creation of a nation and it is for this reason that the progress of historical studies often poses a threat to nationality. Historical inquiry, in effect, throws light on the violent acts that have taken place at the origin of every political formation, even those that have been the most benevolent in their consequences. Unity is always brutally established.[74]

Israel is not unique in 'forgetting' key events in its early history, but these have special significance because of later developments and its current policies. The work of the new historians, based upon archival materials earlier concealed from researchers, is compelling and consistent with Palestinians' accounts of their experiences at the hands of Zionist forces. In particular, exposing the falsehood that Palestinians left their homes in 1948 as a wilful act of compliance with directions from Arab leaders has focused attention on Palestinians' continuous calls for justice and above all the right of return.

The Zionist movement, says Shlaim, accomplished 'one of the most successful public relations exercises of the 20th century'.[75] Its version of the emergence of Israel and of subsequent conflicts was 'selective, simplistic and self-serving'.[76] Israel's new historians targeted these accounts, 'the sacred cows that all Israeli school children had been educated to respect and revere'.[77] They met with a furious reaction. Israeli writer Aharon Megged alleged a 'suicidal impulse', charging that the new historians provided ammunition to enemies of Israel and delegitimised the Zionist project in ways that could endanger the very existence of the state.[78] Efraim Karsh devoted a book to the issue, written, he said, to empty the 'balloon called New Historians before their academic manipulations will spread into public knowledge and from there into the education system…it is a gang that aim to systematically falsify the past of the state'.[79] In 2001 Prime Minister Ariel Sharon declared that Israeli children 'must be taught Jewish-Zionist values, and the 'new historians' must not be taught'.[80] His education minister, Limor Livnat, said that she would dedicate her life to 'root out the influence of the revisionist historians'.[81] In 2010 Avi Beker, former secretary-general of the World Jewish Congress, described their impact on Israeli and Zionist historiography as 'disastrous'.[82]

Britain arms the militias

If the Palestinians did not walk away in 1948 in compliance with directions from their leaders, what accounts for their 'disappearance' from hundreds of towns and villages? Palestinian oral history and critical analyses of the new historians point to overwhelming force exercised by Zionist militias. The capacity to fight and overwhelm 'enemy' forces, however, was not merely the result of Zionist energies and organisation: it was also closely associated with British support in the form of arms, training and intelligence.

Britain had finally suppressed the intifada of 1936 to 1939. In 1938 the Munich Pact with Germany allowed its military command to direct tens of thousands of troops to Palestine, delivering a final blow to the resistance movement, 'to smash the most serious challenge to the Zionist project in its history and to bring the Palestinian uprising to a conclusion'.[83] When the Second World War began in September 1939, most leading activists of the national movement had been killed or were in prison or in exile. The AHC had been dissolved and key members deported. With a huge garrison in place the British hoped to target further systematic resistance. Here they could rely upon the settler community and its militias.

British policy towards the Zionists reflected the uncertainties of a dying colonial power. Since the 1920s, controls on migration to Palestine had been relaxed and tightened according to the changing agendas of successive governments. On the outbreak of world war in 1939, Britain imposed new controls, often evaded by 'illegal' migration routes established by Zionist networks: some 120,000 Jewish immigrants reached Palestine during the war, so that by 1947 the Jewish population of the country numbered some 608,000.[84] Policy on military co-operation was different. Concerned to maintain control over the Palestinians and to reinforce its garrison in the face of German advances in North Africa, Britain worked increasingly closely with the settler movement.

Zionist militias, police and 'supernumeries' had for years played a significant role for the colonial regime. The Haganah had been established early during the Mandate period and had grown rapidly – initially with tacit British approval, later with British encouragement and weaponry. By 1938 there were also 6,000 Jewish recruits, both 'regulars' and 'supernumeraries', in the British-led police force. High Commissioner MacMichael noted that all were provided with rifles by the colonial regime and that almost all were drawn from the Haganah.[85] Working closely with Orde Wingate and the Special Night Squads (SNS), the Haganah had developed new tactics and techniques. Hughes describes the violence and effectiveness of the SNS, based on longstanding British practice across the empire: 'British SNS brutality prompted Jewish soldiers, taught them how to deal with insurgency and insurgents and set this within a colonial legal framework of collective punishment and punitive action that normalised draconian action.'[86] In a sympathetic account of relations between Britain and the settler forces, Shepherd comments that working as part of the SNS, 'For the first time, Jews acquired the skills – night fighting, and surprise attacks – to carry the conflict into the Arab villages.'[87] Wingate also provided training for the militia's newly established intelligence service, Shai, later to become Israel's General Security Service, Shabak. Hughes comments:

> [T]he mutually beneficial relationship during the Arab revolt between the Jewish and British intelligence communities underpinned British military operations... The Jews helped to direct British operations, as counterinsurgency demanded good intelligence and the Yishuv (the Jewish community in Palestine) had the upper hand here, as its intelligence on the Palestinians was so good.[88]

Among Wingate's senior Jewish officers in the SNS were Yigal Allon, Moshe Dayan and Yitzak Sadeh – each to become key figures in Israeli national life. According to Sadeh, 'in him [Wingate] we found our leader'.[89] Hughes observes that Wingate and the SNS 'taught the Jews to use cold steel' against the Arabs, providing a case study 'of how imperial powers will use an indigenous loyalist colonial community to help pacify rebels'.[90] The SNS were disbanded in 1938 but Britain continued to work closely with Zionist militias: in 1940, writes Shepherd, the British army provided money, arms and training for the Palmach, soon 'to become the nucleus of the future Israeli army'.[91] This 'extraordinary episode' was organised by Britain's Special Operations Executive (SOE), created by Winston Churchill, and which operated largely independently of the military bureaucracy.[92] The Palmach was established ostensibly to resist potential German military advances in the Arab East but soon, writes Pappé, 'its zeal and activities were directed against the Palestinian rural areas'.[93] The Jewish Agency embraced the project, in addition offering support with intelligence-gathering and offering to place Haganah agents at the disposal of the British. A senior British officer saw settler recruits as 'extraordinarily useful...as their connections are widespread and their organisation and intelligence service very efficient':

> No better human material could exist for our [British] purposes; these are honourable fanatics who will stop at nothing, physically and mentally tough, highly disciplined and used to guerrilla warfare.[94]

Here, 'guerrilla warfare' was action against Palestinian resistance to both the colonial regime and the settler militias. In further plans British officers committed to training a select 'attacking force' described as 'a small irregular band of toughs based in Palestine'.[95] For over a year, members of the Haganah trained with the British at a secret camp: one of those later involved in operations was Moshe Dayan, who had already served with Wingate's SNS and was to hold ministerial posts in Israeli governments of the 1950s, 1960s and 1970s. In 1942 the British set up the Palestine Scheme, involving hundreds of Jewish volunteers recruited for training in the use of explosives and in sabotage, initiated officially in case of German activity in the Eastern Mediterranean. Involvement of Jewish recruits was said within British special operations to have developed to 'enormous proportions and we are evidently committing ourselves very deeply'.[96] Using expertise gained within the Scheme, settler militias set up their own training camps: the British officer in charge cautioned that 'Palestine Jews...were unable to identify solely with the war effort but continued to try to promote their own parochial nationalist aspirations'.[97] This assessment did not inhibit Britain from recruiting over 27,000 settlers into a Jewish Brigade (some 7,000 Palestinian Arabs also joined up).[98] The overall impact of these initiatives, writes Shepherd, was to introduce the Haganah to regular warfare: 'the experience of belonging to a highly organised, modern army, fighting in an all-out war, was an education'.[99]

These developments explain the scale and readiness of settler militias in 1948. At this point, says Morris, the Haganah had developed the capabilities of a regular army:

> During the course of that year it emerged and efficiently functioned as a large conventional force, beating first the Palestinian Arab militias and then the combined irregular and regular armies of the Arab states. By April–May 1948, it was conducting brigade-size offensives, by July multi-brigade operations; and by October, divisional, multi-front offensives.[100]

Palestinian and Arab forces in contrast were 'unorganised and leaderless'.[101] Deeply affected by defeat of the intifada of 1936 to 1939, they had fewer combatants than the Zionist militias and were poorly equipped. Military historian Richard Hughes describes the Palestinian leadership as 'weak, maladroit'.[102] Rifles distributed by Palestinian leaders in Jerusalem were described by a senior Palestinian official as 'junk' and attempts to collect for new weapons and ammunition as 'pathetic': Arab leaders were accused of 'incompetence, corruption and treason'.[103] In an unequal contest, Zionist forces – now the IDF – achieved the key aims set out in their project of 'transfer'.

Britain had long prepared the ground for Zionist offensives: Cronin comments, 'By the time they had decided to quit, the British had already created the conditions necessary for the ethnic cleansing of Palestine.'[104] Its relationship with the settler movement and repeated diplomatic manoeuvres and evasions, he suggests, made Britain midwife to the Jewish state.[105] Less a miracle, Israel had been born as part of the long and tortuous retreat of European powers from the Arab East.

Chapter 5
Palestine in a new era

Displacement and class formation. Palestinian capitalists and the Gulf economies

The Nakba abruptly changed Palestinian Arab society. More than 80 percent of the population had been displaced and dispossessed: most had been compelled to move to over 60 refugee camps established initially by the Red Cross and local charities in Lebanon, Syria, Jordan, the West Bank and Gaza.[1] Some 160,000 people remained within borders of the new state of Israel.[2] The United Nations made a first assessment of numbers and distribution:

> Where did the refugees go when they left their homes? About 70,000 crossed the Jordan River to the east and are now in the Hashemite Kingdom of Jordan. About 97,000 fled into Lebanon, just north of Galilee. Some 75,000 are clustered near the south and western boundaries of Syria, and in and around Damascus and other towns. About 200,000 are crowded into the tiny coastal desert area called the Gaza strip, at present held by Egypt. About 280,000 are in that part of Palestine not occupied by Israel – west of the Jordan – from Jenin in the north to Jericho and the Arab portion of Jerusalem and on beyond to Bethlehem in the south. About 4,000 crossed the desert to Baghdad in Iraq, far to the east. In addition, some 31,000 Arabs and 17,000 Jews, classed as refugees by the international relief agencies, are in Israel.[3]

Palestinians occupying the camps came overwhelmingly from the most vulnerable sections of a society that had remained largely rural and poor. The impact on their communities was shattering: some villages and neighbourhoods had been widely dispersed, some were atomised after repeated journeys back and forth across Palestine and the new borders of Israel. Most institutional structures were destroyed, as Palestinians were redistributed across neighbouring states. Rosemary Sayigh describes typical experiences:

> Settled peasants, many of whom had never been outside their sub-district...were suddenly expelled into an alien world in which others would look on them as different, threatening or even contemptible: 'refugees', 'displaced persons', 'strangers'.[4]

The refugees were initially regarded worldwide as victims of war – a view encouraged by Israeli leaders, for whom the conflict of 1948 was seen as a 'war of independence' of the Jewish people. There was an assumption, shared even by Israel's friends in European and North American governments, that people displaced in such a conflict would be repatriated – returned to their places of origin, – a reflection of urgent efforts in Europe to return millions of refugees compelled to migrate during the Second World War.[5] Israeli leaders told the UN that they would not admit the Palestinians, as 'they would constitute [a] fifth column [and] their space was needed for Jewish immigrants'.[6] Israel maintained that refugees were not their responsibility:

> The Government of Israel must disclaim any responsibility for the creation of this [refugee] problem. The charge that these Arabs were forcibly driven out by Israel authorities is wholly false; on the contrary, everything possible was done to prevent an exodus which was a direct result of the folly of the Arab states in organising and launching a war of aggression against Israel.[7]

In October 1948 the UN General Assembly declared for 'The right of the Arab refugees to return to their homes in Jewish-controlled territory at the earliest possible date'.[8] Israel rejected the idea outright. The Israeli Foreign Ministry had made a secret study of the refugees. It asserted:

> The most adaptable and best [Palestinian Arab] survivors would manage by a process of natural selection, and the others will waste away. Some will die but most will turn into human debris and social outcasts and probably join the poorest classes in the Arab countries.[9]

This chilling assessment captured the mood among Zionist leaders – both triumphalist and aggressively racist. Ben-Gurion decreed, also in a then-secret statement, 'They may not return'.[10] The meaning was clear: for Israel, displaced Palestinians were not refugees as defined by the UN; rather they were 'human debris', people removed by ethnic cleansing and who had no future within their historic homeland. The logic of 'transfer' as pursued by leaders of the Zionist movement had reached a grisly conclusion.

Displacement continued as Israeli forces drove out Palestinians attempting to return to their villages and neighbourhoods. In May 1949 US President Harry S. Truman sent a secret message to Ben-Gurion. He said:

> The Govt of the US is seriously disturbed by the attitude of Israel with respect to a territorial settlement in Palestine and to the question of Palestinian refugees [and urges] the acceptance of the principle of substantial repatriation and the immediate beginnings of repatriation on a reasonable scale…
>
> The US Govt and people have given generous support to the creation of Israel because they have been convinced of the justice of this aspiration… The US Govt is gravely concerned lest Israel now endanger the possibility of arriving at a solution of the Palestine problem in such a way as to contribute to the establishment of sound and friendly relations between Israel and its neighbors.[11]

Washington had anticipated that Jerusalem, a city of immense importance in the Islamic world, would be 'internationalised' as a *corpus separatum* ('separate entity') as envisaged in the UN partition plan – but now half the city was under Israeli control. The Americans were worried about continued attempts of Israel to seize land and the presence of large numbers of refugees in a region in which it now had vital strategic interests. Eliahu Elath, Israeli ambassador to the UN, dismissed Truman's appeal, declaring that the US should 'not underestimate Israeli determination to preserve the security of Israel at all costs'.[12] Angered by the response, the US threatened to withhold development aid unless Israel accepted the return of

200,000 refugees. The Israelis refused and Truman caved in. Donald Neff comments:

> It was a fateful capitulation by Truman for it signalled to Israel that it could literally do what it wanted without undue worry about American protestations. After this debacle, the Truman administration apparently made no further effort to exert overt pressure to bring Israel in line with U.S. policy...
>
> Israel completely ignored America's advice and went about ruthlessly imposing its rule in its expanded frontiers, tightening its grip on Jerusalem, and relentlessly propagandizing its claim that the suffering refugees were not its responsibility.[13]

New world order

Across the region Palestinian refugees were received with solidarity – but also sometimes with suspicion. There was a surge of sympathy among the mass of people, mixed with a sense of humiliation that an Arab movement had been so comprehensively defeated. Public ignorance of events in Palestine was widespread and Israeli versions of the Palestinians' flight, largely unchallenged in the West, were circulated in some Arab media.

Palestinians had been ejected into states in which local rulers were particularly insecure. France had left Syria and Lebanon less than two years earlier; Egypt was in turmoil as the pro-British monarchy struggled to hold onto power; in Jordan a fragile ruling group was dependent on British support. Sayigh comments that Arab governments saw Palestinians as a threat to stability and order, prioritising control over the refugees by placing them in camps where their movements could be restricted through special regulations.[14] The UN took a similar approach, again reflecting developments in Europe, where states and military leaders had sought to corral and contain refugees displaced by war, fearing their involvement in radical movements and even revolutionary upheavals, although here the emphasis was on return to countries of origin. In 1943 Allied states in Europe had created the United Nations Relief and Rehabilitation Administration (UNRRA).[15] At the end of the war it was provided with a huge staff and an enormous budget of $3.6 billion and charged with repatriating the 40 million people displaced across Europe.[16] Driven by a compulsion to return refugees to their 'national' locations, UNRRA used the military to force refugees onto trains and held those unwilling to travel in special camps with the aim of isolating them from other displaced persons. Within five months of the end of the war it had succeeded in repatriating 75 percent of all refugees.[17]

In Palestine the UN took a very different approach. It first established the Disaster Relief Project (UNDRP) and shortly afterwards the UN Relief for Palestinian Refugees (UNRPR). In 1950 it created the United Nations Relief and Works Agency (Unrwa), with responsibility for displaced Palestinians. It did not attempt repatriation: since the US had been rebuffed by Israel, Western governments focused on establishing and maintaining camps in which Palestinians could be contained and supported with basic services. This new regime, comments Anne Irfan, 'was predominantly driven by the Global North': the refugees were not consulted by the agency or by governments disinterested in the refugees' own aspirations.[18] Unrwa's 'works' programme was directed to jobs creation – in effect it was a resettlement project in which Palestinians were to remain in Arab states. The key decision-makers in relation to Unrwa, the US and Britain, saw the organisation as 'a tool for implementing the refugees' permanent resettlement outside Palestine'.[19] In the refugees' eyes, comments Irfan, 'the UN and Unrwa were part of the same power bases that had created Israel and turned them into refugees'.[20] Fawaz Turki was one of the first Palestinians to write a full account of his family's displacement and subsequent journeys to a refugee camp. From the small town of Balad al-Sheikh near Haifa the family had been compelled to move to Lebanon. Here, says Turki, 'I was an outsider, an alien, a refugee, and a burden.' Unrwa soon created a culture of control and dependency: for Turki, it was 'our contemptuous stepmother'.[21]

The US provided most of Unrwa's funding and was the key influence on its policies. With the retreat of the European powers, the US had become the key player in the region, its strategy shaped by twin concerns: access to the Gulf oilfields and Cold War rivalries with the Soviet Union. During the Second World War Truman's predecessor

Franklin D. Roosevelt had declared Saudi Arabia to be of vital interest to the American state. In 1938 oil had been discovered in Saudi provinces close to the Gulf, with indications that the reserves were the largest in the world. In 1943, after talks with the Saudi king, Roosevelt declared that 'defense of Saudi Arabia is vital to the defense of the United States'.[22] Two American corporate oil giants, Standard Oil Company of New Jersey (later Exxon) and Standard Oil Company of New York (Socony, later Mobil), soon became shareholders in the Arabian–American Oil Company (Aramco), which controlled production across Saudi Arabia. Washington's deal with the Saudi monarchy created a new strategic base for the US in the Arabian Peninsula, particularly important because of the advance of political radicalism in neighbouring states. In Iran, British influence over the oilfields was threatened by an insurgent nationalist movement and by Soviet involvement in autonomous republics declared in the Azeri and Kurdish regions. In Iraq the communist movement was growing in influence, threatening the pro-British monarchy, and in Egypt the anti-colonial movement was surging as communists and Muslim Brothers led strikes and mass protests.

In 1947 President Truman announced an aggressive strategy designed, he said, to confront Moscow and its allies. The 'Truman Doctrine' proposed that the US should intervene forcefully where it identified the growth of communist influence – in effect, the US aimed to suppress movements from below perceived as a threat to Western capitalism. 'The free peoples of the world look to us for support in maintaining their freedoms', Truman declared, winning massive funding from the US Congress to aid with offensives on mass movements in Greece and Turkey.[23] If communism should succeed in these states, others would be likely to fall, Truman argued. With the European colonial powers in retreat, he said, 'We are the only country able to provide...help.'[24] In the same year, US diplomat George Kennan published a document that soon became a key text for American Cold War strategists. 'The Sources of Soviet Conduct' argued that 'counterforce' was necessary to contest the Soviet Union's global ambitions.[25] The US must be alert to all challenges, aiming continuously to pressure Moscow to achieve 'either the breakup or the gradual mellowing of Soviet power'.[26] Kennan set an agenda for US imperialism in the post-war era, widely seen as a blueprint for a 'new world order'.[27]

Now Palestine, located at the heart of a region of increased strategic importance for Western capital, took on global significance. Toby Craig Jones comments that Middle Eastern oil had 'enchanted global powers and global capital since the early twentieth century'.[28] After the Second World War its allure became particularly powerful for the US and links with the Saudi monarchy became one of the Americans' most important international relationships, 'preserving the security not just of Saudi Arabia but of the entire Persian Gulf region and the flow of Middle Eastern oil'.[29] Maintaining relations that served corporate interests in the region became a priority for US strategists.

In 1951 the Iranian government of Mohamed Mossadeq nationalised the Anglo–Iranian Oil Company (formerly the Anglo–Persian Oil Company), claiming sovereign rights over the oilfields, and in 1952 the pro-British monarchy in Egypt was deposed by army officers expressing commitment to the Palestinian cause. Radical nationalism was intensifying across the region: one response of the US and its allies was to impose tight controls on Palestinian refugees – people with potential to participate in mass movements in half a dozen states. Provision of basic services for the refugees aimed to minimise the attraction of 'political extremism'.[30] Those in charge at the agency repeatedly emphasised its 'positive impact on stability in the Middle East': its director spoke proudly of how the agency's work 'kept the situation [in the refugee camps] under control'.[31] Irfan comments:

> In the context of the Cold War, the biggest Western fear...was communism, and there was particular anxiety that without aid many Palestinian refugees might be susceptible to its charms. In providing basic services to forestall absolute poverty, Unrwa's work thus became a crucial part of the strategy for combating communism and preventing revolution across the Middle East.[32]

Unrwa was dedicated ostensibly to humanitarian assistance. In practice, writes Smith, it managed a system in which refugees 'were to become the wards of international charity and a pool of cheap labour for the Arab countries'.[33] When in 1951 states worldwide agreed an international treaty on refugees and their rights, the Palestinians were excluded. The Convention Relating to the Status of Refugees, often called the Geneva Convention, specified that displaced people already under the supervision of UN bodies, including Unrwa, would not be included in its provisions, with the result that Palestinians, uniquely, were left in a 'nebulous realm'.[34] In Jordan they received citizenship and some with secondary education were recruited to governmental and professional posts; at the same time, popular protests were ruthlessly suppressed and the camps kept under continuous surveillance. In Syria, Palestinians formally received equal rights with the local population but remained non-citizens. They were forbidden to buy land or property without authorisation and camp residents were forbidden to change residence without permission. In Egypt, the state accepted Palestinians but soon dismantled two camps originally constructed to accommodate them and the refugees were excluded from services offered by Unrwa. In Gaza the population increased threefold as a result of the Nakba, 200,000 refugees entering the 'Strip' – a sliver of territory within historic Palestine that, following Israeli offensives, was just 45 kilometres from north to south and six to 12 kilometres wide. Here much of the population, the Gazan 'locals', were affected by arrival of the refugees and the establishment of eight camps, taking a large proportion of available land. Most Gazans were ineligible for assistance from Unrwa and poverty was widespread. In Lebanon, Palestinians experienced economic marginalisation and intense political repression. They were excluded from all public employment and required permits for work with private employers. They were also under close surveillance – viewed by the Lebanese ruling establishment 'as a threat to internal political and social stability' – and only a fraction of the refugees, mostly prosperous Christians, received Lebanese citizenship.[35] A special section of the military-security service, the Deuxième Bureau, was established to monitor Palestinian communities, soon developing a reputation for intrusion and violence. The overall effect, writes Turki, was that Palestinians in Lebanon were 'considered aliens' and forbidden to engage in political activity.[36]

The works programme initiated by Unrwa was short-lived. After large sums of money had been invested, it became clear that the main beneficiaries were the 'host' governments and the programme was abandoned. For refugees in the camps economic prospects varied widely. Everywhere they were disadvantaged, although in Jordan and Syria they were formally of equal status and could seek employment. In Lebanon, official discrimination meant that many refugee families experienced absolute poverty as household incomes collapsed to a fraction of earnings before the Nakba.[37] Later, Palestinians' vulnerability made them attractive as cheap labour: when the Lebanese economy boomed in the 1950s and 1960s, many were employed at poverty wages in construction, agriculture and services:[38] by the early 1970s almost 70 percent of all employed Palestinians from camps in Lebanon were still paid on a daily rate.[39] Poverty was embedded in the refugee regime.

New bourgeoisie

Not all Palestinians faced such predicaments, however. Mass displacement greatly exaggerated differences of class: peasants, workers and the urban poor were most likely to have been displaced abruptly by Zionist militias and to have had the most limited choice of where to seek safety. Those with capital, professional status and/or connections to international networks were usually the first to move from Palestine and to exercise choice in means of travel and destination. They were more likely to possess documentation that facilitated border crossings and entry to other states, to acquire visas and successfully navigate immigration controls and police checks. Not least, they were most likely to have family and personal connections that enabled journeys to destinations of choice. Many moved early to Arab capitals – Beirut, Damascus, Amman, Cairo – and to Palestinian communities in Europe and the Americas. Pamela-Ann Smith comments:

> The simple act of possession, of having some capital, tangible or intangible, amidst the general poverty and confusion, set these Palestinians apart from their fellow refugees and they formed the basis for the Palestinian bourgeoise which was to emerge, in an expanded form, throughout the mid-50s and the early 1960s.[40]

A small Palestinian capitalist class had prospered in the 19th century in towns including Jaffa, Haifa and Akka – centres for local and regional trade in olive oil, soap and textiles. Industries included flour milling, soap-making, weaving, glass-making and quarrying. Palestinian merchants were active in Ottoman commercial networks and more widely in Mediterranean trade that reached as far as France and Britain.[41] Contrary to Zionist accounts in which capitalist enterprise appeared in Palestine only with arrival of the settler population, a nascent bourgeoisie was embedded in Palestinian society and initially grew during the Mandate period: between 1918 and 1927, as Jewish settlement advanced rapidly, 60 percent of new enterprises were established by Palestinian Arabs.[42] British policy, favouring industrialisation of the Jewish sector, was increasingly a factor stimulating its growth as Palestinian entrepreneurs were marginalised. They nonetheless remained a significant presence: Sherine Seikaly identifies them as 'Men of Capital' engaged in finance, construction and commercial agriculture, and as middlemen, commission agents, and franchise-holders for international businesses.[43] Their resources meant that many were able to leave Palestine before the full impact of ethnic cleansing in 1948. Others who were able to recover some of their capital, usually through banks, legal or diplomatic action, or to retrieve cash and valuables, became part of this neo-capitalist network. They were able to set up households outside the refugee camps and to integrate more readily into neighbouring Arab economies and the emerging states of the Gulf. They too were refugees: the Nakba did not distinguish between Palestinian Arabs – all were targeted for expulsion. But their experiences in the years after 1948 were markedly different from the mass of those displaced.

This was particularly clear in Lebanon, where despite discriminatory policies, Palestinian capitalists and members of the professional middle class made rapid progress. Yusuf Beidas, a Jerusalem banker compelled to leave Palestine in 1948, established a series of companies including Intra Bank, Middle East Airlines and Arabia Insurance Company, becoming part of the boom of the 1960s that channelled 'petrodollars' through Beirut, amassing a huge fortune. Palestinian professionals – doctors, lawyers, accountants, engineers – especially those educated in

English during the Mandate, took up leading positions in Lebanon's corporate bodies. Others, including commission agents, import-export merchants, wholesalers and those who had held franchises in Palestine from North American and European companies reopened in Beirut. Soon small communities of prosperous Palestinians were established in central Beirut and the city of Saida, 'where their style of life stood in marked contrast to the tens of thousands of others housed in the camps or in the sprawling shanty towns outside the major cities'.[44]

Yusuf Beidas became a major player in the economy of the Arab East. So too Abdul-Majid Shoman from the village of Beit Hanina, who had migrated to the US, returning to Palestine in 1929 with the ambition of establishing a pan-Arab bank. He collaborated with Talat Harb, the leading Egyptian capitalist of the period, before establishing the Arab Bank in Jerusalem. It soon became a key institution under the Mandate, enjoying close relations with the traditional leadership of the AHC. After the Nakba, the bank transferred to Amman, Shoman eventually opening branches across the region and investing widely in infrastructure and industrial projects.[45] His son, Abdul-Hamid Shoman, continued to expand operations across the Middle East, with hundreds of branches, notably in states of the Gulf. In the 1960s the Arab Bank became the first Arab financial enterprise to establish a presence in Switzerland, alongside Europe's leading financial institutions. Lesser financiers, merchants and entrepreneurs followed a similar trajectory.

During and after the events of 1948 many members of the Palestinian middle class migrated to states of the Gulf. Saudi Arabia, Kuwait, Bahrain and later the United Arab Emirates and Qatar were in the process of construction as oil economies in which commercial networks and governmental institutions sought professional staff. Saudi Arabia in particular soon depended upon Palestinians – doctors, engineers, lawyers, teachers, media people, managers and consultants, and as diplomats who staffed Saudi embassies and consulates worldwide. In Kuwait by 1965, Palestinians comprised 41 percent of employees in the private sector and 48 percent of employees in the public sector.[46] Across the Gulf, some Palestinian families were integrated into traditional merchant networks that were expanding rapidly as the petro-boom advanced.[47] Twenty years after mass displacement, some 200,000 Palestinians were living in states of the Gulf and in Libya, which also had an expanding oil economy. By 1980, 554,000 Palestinians were living in such states: most in Kuwait (278,000) and Saudi Arabia (127,000).[48] The total amounted to 12.6 percent of the Palestinian population.[49]

Resistance

Like refugee populations worldwide, Palestinians in the Gulf were energetic in attempting to overcome the loss of resources that resulted from mass displacement. So too with many people in the camps. Despite controls imposed by the UN and the Arab states there were continuous efforts to retrieve resources from areas occupied by Israel. On countless occasions during and after 1948, Palestinians crossed the borders of Israel to secure possessions from their homes, to collect livestock and crops, and to reunite with family members who had become part of Israel's minority Arab population. They faced extreme danger; defined by Israel as 'infiltrators', they were likely to be shot on sight or instantly deported. Israeli criminologist Alina Korn writes:

> From the beginning of the 1950s, infiltration was linked with terrorist attacks and the word 'infiltrators' (*mistanenim*) became synonymous to a gang of murderous terrorists. The term 'infiltrators' was inscribed in the collective Israeli consciousness and received a terrifying and threatening meaning.[50]

During and shortly after the process of mass expulsion the Israeli parliament passed a series of 'emergency ordinances' that confiscated the land, settlements and other resources of Palestinians. Their rights of residence and property were deemed to have been transferred to Israeli 'custodians' such as the ministry of agriculture, which claimed ownership of 'absentee' lands. Palestinians who attempted to return were aliens and, by definition, criminals whose presence required executive action by the police and armed forces. Great numbers of Palestinians made these journeys, however: between 1949 and 1956, Israeli officials recorded up to 15,000 'infiltrations' each year.

Many more went unrecorded: Israeli police estimated at least 1,000 unrecorded events each month.[51] According to historian Benny Morris, up to 5,000 Palestinians who crossed borders were killed by army, police and civilians between 1949 and 1956.[52] The majority were unarmed, people categorised even by the Israeli authorities as 'motivated by economic and social factors' and who met with extreme violence[53] – part of the process of ethnic cleansing and racist exclusion. Palestinian feminist Nadera Shalhoub-Kevorkian writes: 'The simple fact of being-at-home [in Palestine] constituted, according to the Israeli state, an act of terrorism and an incitement to violence'.[54]

Sometimes Palestinians crossed borders that were unmarked but were nonetheless intercepted and shot or instantly 'deported' across an invisible line – the outcome of what Morris calls 'accidental infiltration'.[55] British soldier and diplomat John Bagot Glubb was in charge of military operations in the West Bank, under Jordanian authority. He reported to officials in London:

> A great many of these wretched people [Palestinian refugees] are killed now, picking their own oranges and olives just beyond the [border] line... If the Jewish patrols see him he is shot on the spot, without any questions. But, they will persist in returning to their farms and gardens.[56]

While Israeli laws banned Palestinians from the territory of the new state, all people worldwide claiming Jewish ancestry could assert their right to Israeli citizenship. In 1950 the Israeli parliament passed a Law of Return providing that 'Every Jew has the right to come to this country as an oleh' (Article 1).[57] The Israeli state was encouraging mass immigration, especially of Jews from countries of the Middle East, who were sought energetically to maintain the process of settlement in Palestine. Ben-Gurion posed the issue as a crisis, insisting:

> The main thing is the absorption of immigrants. This embodies all the historical needs of the state... We might have captured the West Bank, the Golan, the entire Galilee but these conquests would not have reinforced our security as much as immigration. Doubling and

> tripling the number of such immigrants gives us more and more strength... That is the most important thing, above all else... Settlement, that is the real conquest.[58]

Ben-Gurion feared that the Zionist movement would not be able to populate its new territories fast enough. 'For thousands of years we were a nation without a state,' he said, 'Now there is a danger that Israel will be a state without a nation.'[59] Settlement proceeded rapidly: in the first two years after Israel's declaration of independence, 400,000 immigrants arrived, some from Europe, most from Jewish communities of the Middle East and North Africa, many of whom were directed to the function of what Oren Yiftachel calls 'socio-spatial' control – the strategy of populating areas along Israel's borders.[60] In these 'frontier regions', development towns and *moshavim* (agricultural co-operatives) were peopled largely by new immigrants. By 1954, 350 new settlements had been established. Orit Rozen writes:

> Initially, the establishment of new Jewish settlements was aimed at preventing Palestinian refugees from returning to their homes and lands. Later, security and settlement policy-makers argued that new settlements could help to seal Israel's borders and reduce infiltration of all types.[61]

The effect of this policy was that Palestinians attempting to reach their homes and lands were often intercepted by Israelis who had not even been present during the events of 1948. Many new immigrants were Arabic speakers who had much in common with Palestinian culture but whose role, writes Ran Greenstein, was to prevent the return of the refugees 'by serving as a physical barrier along the border [and] as cannon fodder'.[62] Some were recruited to Israel's Frontier Guard, established in 1948, together with members of the state's minority communities such as Bedouin, Druze and Circassians (descendants of 19th-century immigrants from the Caucasus). Martin Van Creveld comments that a good command of Arabic was an important qualification for membership of the

Guard, adding: 'squeamishness was definitely not included in the job description'.[63] Forming paramilitary units, later to become the Border Police, they were soon notorious for violence towards Palestinians, notwithstanding that most of those who crossed the new borders were unarmed. Oren Bracha quotes an Israeli police report of 1952 which specified that all 'infiltrators' were to be viewed as '[intending to] carry out hostile actions, such as theft, robbery, murder, sabotage, and even espionage'.[64] The Guard was officially limited to operations within Israel's borders but in reality operated alongside units of the IDF that carried out cross-border punishment missions against Arab villages targeted for 'failing to stop the infiltrators'.[65] Moshe Dayan, now a senior IDF officer, declared that this type of retaliation, however 'unjustified and immoral', was the only 'effective' way to put an end to infiltration.[66] While the army assaulted such villages and demolished houses, Israeli planes attacked them from the air. Van Creveld comments:

> The proceedings were rather unappetizing, the IDF responding to civilian killings [of Israelis] by indiscriminately killing infiltrators – including, on some occasions, some who were unarmed or had surrendered – torturing captives, and mutilating bodies.[67]

Shalhoub-Kevorkian observes: 'The very state of being Palestinian within or near the borders of Israel became cause for surveillance, legal intervention, and military control.'[68] It is in this context that attempts by Palestinians to visit family, friends and their lands demonstrated strong attachment to homes and communities, and active resistance to the Israeli state. Far from accepting passively the prospect of exile, hundreds of thousands of Palestinians undertook long, risky journeys in knowledge of the dangers involved and the likelihood of retribution. Writing a history of Palestinian resistance, Mazin Qumsiyeh notes that against the odds many Palestinians did succeed in reaching their homes and lands: this, he says, 'in itself was a major act of resistance during and after the *nakba*'.

The petro-economy

Palestinian nationalism had its origins among the landowning elite, the commercial bourgeoisie and urban intellectuals of the mid-19th century.[69] Contrary to Zionist assertions that a Palestinian identity emerged only in relation to Jewish settlement, proto-nationalism emerged in response to overbearing Ottoman control, developing much more fully during the years of British colonialism. Like national movements across the European empires, it mobilised mass support for independence and self-government. After the Nakba, however, a new imperialism shaped circumstances in which the movement would be re-established and that eventually mass struggles would resume.

For almost 30 years after the Second World War, Western capitalism experienced continuous growth. The 'long boom' marked a dramatic change from earlier decades of recession. Between 1913 and 1950 the average annual increase in Gross Domestic Product per capita in the US had been 1.61 percent; between 1950 and 1973 this increased to 2.45 percent.[70] In Western Europe the figures were more striking, with a rise across 16 countries from 0.78 percent to 4.86 percent.[71] Post-war reconstruction, a surge in industrialisation and greatly increased levels of arms production associated with the Cold War demanded expanded supplies of energy. Initially this came from coal but within 20 years oil was the dominant source – not only because of increased reserves and new technologies but also because of persistent lobbying by the powerful oil corporations.[72]

In Washington strategists had a vision of the post-war era as 'the American century'. The US was to be guardian of a world order based upon American economic and military influence – an agenda for Western imperialism that depended upon relations with ruling classes in regions of special importance. Timothy Mitchell coined the term 'petroknowledge' to describe how economists and political strategists viewed prospects for world oil production and how the drive to locate cheap sources of energy shaped foreign policy.[73] During the 1950s access to oilfields with significant reserves became a key issue, as 'a symbiotic relationship formed between postwar U.S. global strategy and oil'.[74] David Painter writes:

> Controlling oil helped the United States contain the Soviet Union, end destructive political, economic, and military competition among the core capitalist states, mitigate class conflict within the capitalist core by promoting economic growth, and retain access to the raw materials, markets, and labor of periphery nations in an era of decolonization and national liberation.
>
> As part of this strategy, the U.S. military established a vast archipelago of overseas bases that allowed the United States to project its power into almost every region of the world. The forces necessary for this strategy, mainly sea and air power, could and were used to maintain access to overseas oil reserves. These forces were also dependent on oil.[75]

By the early 1950s US corporations held oil concessions in Saudi Arabia, Bahrain and Kuwait, and 'petroknowledge' suggested that other areas of the Gulf would soon disclose oilfields with large reserves, emphasising the importance of the region. Kingdoms and emirates of the Arab Gulf had embryonic state structures – systems of civil administration that provided basic services – but all lacked institutions required to underpin capitalist control. Crucially, core repressive functions of the state associated with what Frederick Engels described as 'instruments of coercion' – including the police and the army – were undeveloped, and the autocratic rule of kings and princes made the regimes especially vulnerable.[76] In 1951 the nationalisation of oil in Iran prompted extreme anxiety among Western governments which feared the Iranian example would be contagious, affecting states across the Gulf. Iran had become the world's fourth largest exporter of oil and was supplying 90 percent of Europe's petroleum.[77] Cold War paranoia was at its height, with US strategists identifying the hand of the Soviet Union in every anti-colonial movement: in the case of Iran, said President Truman, the Soviets were 'sitting like a vulture on the fence waiting to pounce'.[78] American security officials declared:

> It is of critical importance to the US that Iran remain an independent and sovereign nation firmly aligned with the free world... It is important that there be a government in power in Iran on the side of the free world, capable of maintaining internal order and determined to resist Soviet aggression.[79]

US Secretary of State John Foster Dulles declared: 'If Iran succumbed to the Communists there was little doubt that in short order the other areas of the Middle East with some 60 percent of the world's oil reserves, would fall into Communist control'.[80]

In 1953 the US and Britain organised a coup against the Iranian government, removing Prime Minister Mossadeq, bolstering the monarchy, and striking new deals for the oil corporations including significant holdings for American companies. Another monarch had meanwhile fallen on the other side of the Arabian Peninsula: in 1952 nationalists in the army seized power in Egypt and soon removed the pro-British King Faruq. Both Britain and the US attempted to negotiate with the new Egyptian leader, Gamal Nasser, anxious to minimise Soviet influence and to maintain control of the Suez Canal, now of added importance as a key means of transporting Gulf oil to Europe.[81] It was in these circumstances that Israel presented itself as a strategic resource for the US and its allies – a state possessed of apparently robust institutions and armed forces recently successful against a Palestinian nationalist movement similar to others that were threatening imperialist interests across the region.

The Americans had constructed an airfield in Saudi Arabia at Dhahran on the Gulf, built during the Second World War to safeguard nearby Aramco facilities. In 1951 this was incorporated into the Strategic Air Command network, making it 'the largest US installation between Germany and Korea'.[82] Now an Israeli initiative proposed additional means of supporting American interests by establishing a permanent base for Western imperialism in the form of an allied state in an unstable region. An editorial in the leading newspaper *Ha'aretz* set out a strategic vision in which Israel would serve as a 'watchdog' for the West:

> The West is none too happy about its relations with states in the Middle East. The feudal regimes there have to make such concessions to the nationalist movements, which sometimes have a pronounced socialist-leftist colouring, that they become more and more reluctant to supply Britain and the United States with their natural resources and military bases… Therefore, strengthening Israel helps the Western powers maintain equilibrium and stability in the Middle East. Israel is

> to become the watchdog. There is no fear that Israel will undertake any aggressive policy towards the Arab states when this would explicitly contradict the wishes of the US and Britain. But if for any reason the Western powers should sometimes prefer to close their eyes, Israel could be relied upon to punish one or several neighbouring states whose discourtesy to the West went beyond the bounds of permissible.[83]

Israeli Marxist Moshe Machover later commented that this was 'a very shrewd and accurate assessment'.[84] It was not for several years, however, that the US aligned with Israel and provided means to 'punish' those who threatened Western interests. Neither President Truman nor, initially, President Eisenhower, elected in 1953, provided arms directly to Israel. Both maintained that a close alliance would stimulate hostility to the US in the region, opening opportunities for the Soviet Union. At the same time, Eisenhower encouraged France, Canada and Nicaragua to supply weaponry, including French tanks and advanced fighter jets. The Americans also provided Israel with aid: from 1953 to 1956 it dispensed $250 million in 'technical assistance', commodities and forms of tax relief on transactions – a sum that greatly exceeded the combined totals directed to Arab states.[85] The US was moving closer to Israel, as Eisenhower 'gradually came to regard the Israelis as potential allies against the Soviet Union and Soviet-backed revolutionary Arab nationalism'.[86] In 1956 Israel invaded Egypt, ostensibly to tackle Palestinian 'infiltrators' and to gain access to sea routes in the face of an Egyptian blockade, its forces seizing Gaza and the Sinai Peninsula. Israeli Foreign Minister Golda Meir declared that: 'the Gaza Strip is an integral part of Israel', as the IDF killed some 400 Palestinians in the Khan Yunis and Rafah refugee camps.[87] France and Britain joined the offensive, each motivated by opposition to Nasser's nationalisation of the Suez Canal in which they had held stakes since the late 19th century. The Israelis intended to bring change across the region, even contemplating, together with France, a 'far-reaching secret plan for creating a "new order" in the Middle East', including Israel's annexation of Gaza and Sinai; the overthrow of Nasser; the dismantling of Lebanon and the annexation of southern Lebanon to Israel; and the partitioning of Jordan between Israel and Iraq.[88]

The US was infuriated – Israel and its allies had taken an initiative without its approval, Washington believing that the invasion would win wide support for Nasser and for radical nationalism across the region. Faced with forceful American action the invasion forces were withdrawn but not before Israel had impressed the Americans with a quick victory over the Egyptian army. Now Congress agreed to use its own military force in the region and to provide up to $200 million in economic aid to any Middle Eastern state threatened by direct or indirect aggression 'from any country controlled by international communism'.[89] In 1957 the US intervened to protect the Jordanian monarchy when Nasserist officers attempted a coup, moving an American fleet to the eastern Mediterranean. At the same time, Eisenhower declared that American policy 'embraced the preservation of the state of Israel'.[90] In 1958, Syria and Egypt unified to form the United Arab Republic and nationalist officers in Iraq overthrew the pro-British monarchy, initiating revolutionary struggles that were to continue for several years as radical currents grew in influence.[91] CIA Director Allen Dulles declared that the Gulf region was 'the most dangerous place in the world today'.[92] Meanwhile in Lebanon nationalists battled with supporters of right-wing Christian president Camille Chamoun: the US invaded with 14,000 marines, declared a nuclear alert and mobilised for further strikes across the region, while Britain airlifted troops to Jordan using Israeli airspace. Israel offered to 'erect effective sandbags' against the rising tide of radical Arab nationalism and the Americans sent small arms, then military helicopters.[93] In 1962 the US agreed to Israel's key demand – for Hawk anti-aircraft missiles.

When Nasser sent troops to assist the nationalist movement in Yemen, where guerrillas were battling British troops, the liaison with Israel was sealed, the Americans supplying tanks and fighter jets. Lyndon Johnson was now president, offering 'renewed assurances of our willingness and capability to safeguard Israel'.[94] Increasingly confident of its military superiority over neighbouring states, in June 1967 Israel launched strikes against Egypt and Syria, confronting what a leading Israeli politician called 'the Hitlerite-Nasserist barbarianism'.[95] In less than a week Israeli forces occupied Gaza, Sinai, the West Bank and the Golan Heights, increasing by more than three times the territory under Israel's control. The IDF seized East Jerusalem as Moshe Dayan, now minister of defence, declared: 'We have returned to our most holy places, returned in order never to be separated from them again.'[96] The West Bank, he asserted, was 'part of the flesh and bones – indeed the very spirit – of the Land of Israel'.[97] The impact on Arab governments was profound: their forces had been comprehensively defeated and Israeli expansion had seized over a million Palestinians – people of the West Bank and Gaza. In Egypt, Nasser resigned as president, accepting responsibility for the failure of his army, which had occupied a key place in nationalist strategies.

Following the conflict, Western states and media expressed admiration and appreciation for Israel. In London the *Economist* declared: 'It is not only Israel's chestnuts which have been drawn out of the fire; it is those of Britain and America as well'.[98] Israel's victory, the *Economist* argued, had global ramifications. By denying Nasser a victory and means to unite the Arab world, Israel had denied the Soviet Union increased influence in the Middle East.[99] In the US, the *Los Angeles Times* produced a book to mark the occasion, declaring:

> It was a short, decisive and brilliantly fought war. Unlike Vietnam it did not rend this country [the US] in two and sorely trouble the conscience of so many Americans. It was a war with bigger-than-life heroes; it was a religious spectacle; it was the underdog triumphant, David versus Goliath.[100]

The Vietnam conflict had been a key factor shaping American foreign policy. Bogged down in South East Asia and confronted by a growing movement of domestic opposition to the war, Israel's alliance with the US appeared as a relatively cost-free means of addressing problems in the Middle East. For Washington, Nasser represented 'an intolerable challenge to US hegemony' in the region and by 1967 Israel's ability to defeat Egypt was viewed as an important asset.[101] Key American strategists had already begun to conceive of Israel as a "Sparta" that could dominate the Middle East in the interests of American power'.[102] Washington had already ensured that Israel enjoyed a military advantage over the Arab states and shortly before the June conflict the director of Israel's intelligence agency, Mossad, had visited Washington and received 'an unspoken green light to attack'.[103] The outcome of the war appeared to confirm the expectations of American strategists: now, writes Cheryl Rubenberg, 'Israel could serve as an instrument of American power, a strategic asset to US regional interests'.[104]

Contradictions

Israel's expansion during the 1967 war brought another million people under control of the Zionist state. Palestinians of the West Bank and Gaza came under military occupation, together with Syrians of the Golan Heights and Egyptians of Sinai. Israel was not only a partner of the US in bolstering American interests but now also a sub-imperial power, exercising expanded influence in its own right and pursuing further territorial gains. Nur Masalha writes:

> The overwhelming Israeli victory, the seizure of the remainder of Palestine with its sizeable Arab population, the resultant outburst, and later upsurge, of messianic Zionism and growing Israeli confidence all contributed to the prompt and inevitable revival of the project of territorial expansion.[105]

Within weeks Israeli settlements were under construction in the Golan Heights; within months the first settlements were established on the West Bank. Boosted by European and American arms and integrated into imperialist agendas for control of the Middle East, Israel was already engaged in new projects of expansion and of subordination of people of the region.

These events intensified a contradiction facing both Palestinians who remained in their homeland and those of the diaspora. As another 300,000 became refugees and some 700,000 fell under direct Israeli control, the same processes of capitalist advance and imperial control that facilitated Zionist expansion were enriching a minority of their compatriots. Across the Arab world and most notably in the states of the Gulf, 'diaspora millionaires' had emerged. By the mid-1960s Palestinian entrepreneurs controlled a network of corporations and trading companies active across the Middle East.[106] Together with a growing middle class – the professionals who administered much of the new oil economy – they represented an aspiring capitalist class, one prospering *within* the imperialist networks. Class differences among Palestinians had been widening fast: hundreds of thousands were still contained and controlled in refugee camps, many living in absolute poverty. At the same time, as the petro-economy expanded under the supervision of the US and its allies, Palestinians were active agents of capital accumulation and hundreds of thousands of middle-class functionaries had become integral to construction of the new states. As Palestinian struggles continued, these contradictions were to have a profound impact on a rejuvenated national movement.

Chapter 6
'Our American Israel'
Oil, imperialism and the 'watchdog' state. Israel, Palestine and world media. Rise of the PLO

During the mid-1960s Middle East oil production surged ahead of output in the US, the historic source of world supply. For decades American oilfields had provided capacity to meet rising demand; now states of the Gulf played the key role, strengthened by the establishment in 1960 of the Organisation of Petroleum Exporting Countries (Opec), soon a powerful producer cartel. In the light of nationalisations in Iran and Iraq, the CIA warned of growing dependence on the region, coupled with the danger of 'confiscation of important U.S. properties in the area'.[1] Israel's comprehensive victory in the 1967 war provided a new strategic option for the US – a local ally capable of suppressing challenges to American interests. There was soon a huge surge in American arms supplies: between 1967 and 1968 the value of weapons provided to Israel increased by 450 percent and Washington agreed to provide 50 Phantom fighter-bombers, giving the Israelis a huge advantage over all other states in the region.[2] During the 1960s, US aid to Israel had totalled $834.8 million, of which 30 percent was in military support; during the 1970s aid increased to $16.3 billion, of which 71 percent was in military support.[3] These sums dwarfed US aid and weapons supplies to all other states: a new alliance had been cemented, as Israel became America's 'partner against the spread of anti-Western radicalism throughout the Arab world'.[4] The vision of Israel as 'watchdog' had apparently become a reality.

Under President Richard Nixon, Washington declared that it was 'firmly committed to Israel's security and to her military superiority in the Middle East, for only Israel's strength can deter attack and prevent a call for direct American intervention': here, Israel was recognised formally as a proxy for US military power.[5] For President Jimmy Carter, the two states enjoyed 'a special relationship':

> It's absolutely crucial that no one in our country or round the world ever doubt that our number one commitment in the Middle East is to protect the right of Israel to exist, to exist permanently, and to exist in peace. It's a special relationship... And obviously part of that is to make sure that Israel has adequate means to protect themselves [sic] without military involvement of the United States.[6]

American military support continued accordingly, with ever-more sophisticated weaponry. In 1979 Carter quadrupled military aid to $4 billion and over the next decade Washington delivered over $28 billion of aid, more than half in the form of arms;[7] in addition, in 1981 all US economic assistance was converted from loans to grants.[8] Israel was highly favoured but not to the exclusion of selected states to which Washington was also sub-contracting policing roles in the region. Since the 1950s, Israel had been encouraging the US to strengthen relations with its allies. Ben-Gurion told President Eisenhower that Israel was drawing closer to Iran and Turkey, with the aim of 'erecting a high dam against [the] Nasserist-Soviet tidal wave'.[9] He proposed an unofficial alliance, which the US – already allied with the Shah of Iran – backed with increasing volumes of arms. By the early 1970s, the Americans were supplying 80 percent of Iran's military hardware, including advanced fighter jets and heavy artillery.[10] For several decades Washington maintained a 'Twin Pillar' policy, based on what American strategists called the 'regional influentials', Israel and Iran.[11] Then, in 1979, a revolutionary movement in Iran deposed the Shah – a shocking setback to the US that soon benefited Israel, now seen as the Americans' sole reliable ally in the region. In the year after the revolution, US arms supplies to Israel reached an unprecedented $13.2 billion.[12]

Israel had meanwhile developed a wider role in the Global South, working closely with African, Asian and Latin American states linked to the US and its allies. After creating an international aid programme in 1958, Israel soon had working relations with 60 countries: by the early 1970s, 4,000 Israelis had served abroad and 15,000 trainees had been sent to study in Israel.[13] In its relations with the Global South Israel presented as a newly independent and apparently non-aligned state willing to provide valuable technical assistance. Radical critics in

Israel saw the strategy differently: as an initiative encouraged by the US to develop 'a channel through which money and ideology can be routed to neo-colonial countries', furthering 'a collusion of interests between Israel and imperialism'.[14] Relations with South Africa were of special importance. One of the architects of apartheid, Hendrik Verwoerd – prime minister of South Africa – had praised Israel fulsomely. Notwithstanding his aggressive antisemitism and enthusiastic support of Nazi principles, Verwoerd highlighted Israel's ethnic exclusivism, drawing parallels with the experience of European settlers in Africa: 'The Jews [sic] took Israel from the Arabs after the Arabs had lived there for a thousand years', he said, 'Israel like South Africa is an Apartheid state'.[15] During the 1950s and 1960s, Israel and South Africa grew close.[16] As anti-colonial movements challenged racist regimes in southern and central Africa, South Africa's rulers sought advanced weaponry: by the late 1970s they were Israel's largest international customer for arms.[17] Other destinations for Israeli hardware included right-wing dictatorships such as Chile, Argentina, Brazil, Nicaragua and Guatemala, and in Africa, Zaire, Uganda, the Central African Republic, and the racist regime of Southern Rhodesia. In 1986 General Matityahu Peled, member of the Israeli parliament, told the Knesset that after decades of supplying pariah states in which rulers, paramilitaries and others lacked 'legitimate' sources of weaponry, Israel had been acting as the United States' 'dirty work contractor'.[18]

'Our American Israel'

The 1950s and 1960s were years of rapid growth of mass media and unprecedented coverage of world events on radio and television. Conflicts in the Middle East and – in the context of the Cold War, their potential for superpower involvement – brought huge interest and overwhelmingly favoured Israel. Jérôme Bourdon argues that 'Israel became central to the image of the entire region'.[19] A dense network of relations between the settler movement in Palestine and societies of Europe and North America had earlier helped to present favourable accounts of Zionism to Western audiences. From the 1940s, revelations of the reality of the Holocaust played their role in winning support for Israel, although Holocaust denial proved resilient, especially in some European states.[20] Israel's leaders saw their country's international profile as a key issue: foreign journalists were encouraged to visit and provided with written materials, special communications and information officers as part of the project of *hasbara*, literally 'explaining', or creative propaganda. Cummings writes that open access and attention lavished on reporters 'reinforced Israel's advantage in international public opinion, ensuring further interest and sympathetic coverage'.[21]

In its early years Israel's national narrative was the subject of intense domestic debate, but key themes emerged – Israel was projected at home and abroad as modern, European, secular, technologically advanced and, at the same time, as energetic and heroic in struggles against external threat. Bourdon writes, 'In an age of rising global media, first radio, then television, Israel had all the elements of a good journalistic story':

> It provided colorful leaders and characters, many of whom were part of a new, personalized political landscape, one rendered more visual by television... The development of Israel fitted another major 'grand narrative' of the period: that of faith in technological progress as the ultimate solution to the world's pervasive problems. In this vein, throughout the period, Israel continued forging its image, via new agricultural programs and technological advances, as a modern nation – an image that also impacted its relations with (and its image in) the Third World.[22]

People who until 1948 had been the majority in Palestine were not present in these stories disseminated widely by Israeli institutions. Ilan Pappé notes the importance of this central aspect of memoricide in Israeli society and in Israel's projection of its past: 'the absence of the Palestinian tragedy from the Israeli historical account'.[23] From 1948 to 1967, he observes, 'the Palestinians were mostly ignored'.[24] A series of books published in Israel during this period became key texts for the Israeli public. They included *The History of the Resurrection*, produced by the History Branch of the IDF, and *The History of the War of*

Independence, by Netenel Lorch, which explained historic conflicts as the outcome of 'incomprehensible and unintelligible hate' on the part of Arab society, 'against which the Jewish forces defend themselves with valour and determination'.[25] This self-image encouraged a view internationally that both celebrated the state and its achievements, and promoted 'indifference, even hostility, towards the Arabs as people who were almost universally depicted as backward' – a view that became general in Western media but was also exported 'far beyond the West'.[26]

Powerful images were disseminated worldwide: of importance were photographs taken by Robert Capa, a celebrated photojournalist and founder of the influential Magnum agency. Jørgen Jensehaugen comments that, 'Visually speaking, Robert Capa made Israel'.[27] Providing hundreds of photographs to the world's media, he 'served the origin myth that Israel was established in a defensive war and that the first Israelis made the desert bloom, completely overlooking the destruction of the territory's native Palestinian society'.[28] Palestinian Arabs were almost entirely absent from his images. By endorsing Israeli accounts, says Jensehaugen, Capa – 'perhaps the most famous photographer of his age' – also 'erased Palestine'.[29] The practice continued, with American media in particular offering overwhelming support for Israel. In 1967 Israel's instant victory against the Arab armies was contrasted to America's grinding war in Vietnam. Amy Kaplan traces the rise of popular support for Israel during this period as 'a successful replica of America – an even shinier, more robust model' and 'our American Israel'.[30] An enduring narrative was established, says Kaplan, 'the familiar plot of plucky David trouncing a lumbering Goliath'; soon, she says, 'Americans en masse fell in love with Israel'.[31]

British journalist Tim Llewellyn observes that during the 1950s and 1960s the Palestinian cause was ignored in Western media. The main story, he says, was of 'Plucky little Israel fighting off the great hordes of the Arab masses, who were, we were led to believe, about to descend on plucky little Israel and eliminate it at any moment, if they were given half a chance'.[32] Complaints to the BBC in 1968 about its partisan coverage produced a formal response from the corporation:

> Journalists doing an honest job in this country have to take account of the fact that Israeli or Zionist public relations are conducted with a degree of sophistication, which those on the other side have rarely matched. An accurate reflection of publicly expressed attitudes on the issue may well inevitably reveal at times a preponderance of sympathy for the Israeli side.[33]

Here, sustained efforts by Israel to project its favoured narratives were largely successful. Palestinians, Llewellyn concludes, 'weren't getting a look in'.[34]

'Memoricide'

Palestinians had been 'invisibilised'. As Israel removed their physical presence from the landscape and attempted to erase their lives and histories from the consciousness of Israeli citizens, world media lost sight of the Palestinian people. Following the ethnic cleansing of 1948, political leaders in Israel had debated the fate of the refugees. Some were prepared to negotiate deals for return of a fraction of the displaced; others including Yosef Weitz, one of the architects of 'transfer', were adamant that none should reappear on conquered territory. Ben-Gurion concluded that time was on Israel's side, as 'the refugees would become absorbed wherever they happened to be, and thus the source of conflict would completely disappear'.[35]

The state did all it could to erase evidence of the Palestinian presence on the land. Ilan Pappé writes of 'memoricide' as 'a systematic, scholarly, political and military attempt to de-Arabise the terrain'.[36] Some Palestinian villages had been occupied by immigrants when estates were bought in the 1920s and 1930s by Zionist agencies and the inhabitants evicted. Arabic names had been abandoned, replaced by novel Hebrew names chosen by the naming committee of the Jewish National Fund (JNF). This had originally been active in the 1920s: in 1949 it was reconvened by Ben-Gurion, providing new names for a host of Palestinian villages while in some cases the Fund eradicated evidence of their earlier existence, including by creating national parks and forests where villages had stood. 'The true mission of the JNF', writes Pappé, 'has been to conceal these visible remnants of Palestine not only by the trees it has planted over them, but also by the narratives it has created to deny their existence'.[37]

The JNF's 'green mission', since part of its official agenda, has been based upon a sustained programme of demolition of Palestinian settlements.[38]

For many years Israeli authorities denied that they were flattening and concealing hundreds of villages. In 1973 Israeli human rights activist Israel Shahak took a stand against 'this falsification', what he called 'one of the most guarded secrets of Israeli life'.[39] Citing the work of Palestinian researcher Arif al-Arif, confirmed by local activists, he listed 385 villages that had been eliminated: 'destroyed – in almost all cases – destroyed *completely*, with their houses, garden-walls, and even cemeteries and tombstones, so that literally a stone does not remain standing, and visitors are passing and being told that "it was all desert" [emphasis in original]'.[40] Shahak continued:

> No publication, book or pamphlet gives either their number or their location. This of course is done on purpose, so that the accepted official myth of 'an empty country' can be taught and accepted in the Israeli schools and told to the visitors.[41]

Enormous efforts were directed to erase the Palestinians, their society and culture from the landscape and from publicly accessible records and educational curricula – part of projects to assert legitimacy of the settler presence in Palestine and to celebrate achievements of the Zionist movement.[42] These were deemed key issues for young Israelis and promoted in school texts and classroom instruction. Israeli historian Elie Podeh observes that for several decades after 1948 Israeli academics and educators pursued predominantly a 'national' approach to accounts of modern and contemporary history. He quotes Mihael Ziv, head of Israel's department for secondary education, to the effect that 'the values underlying the official historical narrative, as introduced in the classroom, must accord with society's principal values'.[43] Material chosen for this purpose, Ziv insisted, had a specific aim:

> [to] instill love and respect for our most important and cherished values, and encourage the young to identify utterly with [Israeli] society's goals, fight for its continued existence and play an active role in its development and progress.[44]

The project was not unique: construction of stories about nations and belonging were as old as the nation-state. In the case of Israel, however, it had special significance as an ongoing process of physical exclusion of Palestinian Arabs conducted aggressively by the armed forces while foundational myths of the state were made central to its ideological agendas. Israeli sociologist Uri Ram writes that during its early decades the realities of the Nakba became 'a strict "taboo"' in Israeli culture – 'something not spoken about in the open and made unknown to most new-born or new-coming Israelis for at least one or two generations'.[45] The realities, however, were difficult to conceal. In 1969, in an unusual, revealing assessment at odds with the dominant narrative, Moshe Dayan – full of confidence as Israel's defence minister – gave his own account of changes in the landscape of Palestine:

> We came to this country, which was already populated by Arabs, and we are establishing a Hebrew, that is a Jewish state here. In considerable areas of the country we bought the land from the Arabs. Jewish villages were built in the place of Arab villages. You do not even know the names of these villages, and I do not blame you, because these geography books no longer exist. The Arab villages are not there either... There is not one place in this country that did not have a former Arab population.[46]

Meanwhile, Israeli prime minister Golda Meir told the official story, asserting in 1969 that: 'There was no such thing as Palestinians', and adding: 'It was not as though there was a Palestinian people in Palestine considering itself as a Palestinian people and we [Israelis] came and threw them out and took their country from them. They did not exist.'[47]

The 'Revolution'

The fact of the matter, Edward Said wrote in 1980, 'is that today Palestine does not exist' – except, he added, as an idea, a human experience, and an act of sustained popular will.[48] When Palestinians renewed mass resistance in the mid-1960s, they defied Israeli expectations and a view held worldwide that Palestinians were no longer active participants in events in the Middle East.

Ten years after the Nakba there was intense frustration among Palestinians that Arab leaders had no meaningful strategy to address their needs: Nasser's biographer Robert Stephens writes: 'They felt that the Arab governments were complacently shelving their claims or treating them simply as a refugee problem.'[49] As before, Arab kings and presidents had continuously made promises: in Lebanon refugees were told, '"All you have to do is eat and sleep. The Arab armies will get your country back for you." ...Unfortunately the battle never seemed to come.'[50] By the late 1950s presidents Nasser of Egypt and Qasim of Iraq were vying for the status of most high-profile nationalist in the region. Qasim began to promote the idea of a 'Palestinian entity' – an independent republic with its own institution on the lines of the provisional government established by the Algerian liberation movement in its struggles with colonial France. But in 1964 Nasser admitted that he had 'no plan' for the liberation of Palestine.[51] Instead he set up Voice of Palestine, a radio station that broadcast from Cairo, and encouraged appointment to the Arab League's Political Committee of its first Palestinian representative, the conservative lawyer Ahmed Shuqeiri.[52] A Palestine National Council met under the chairmanship of Shuqeiri, notionally representing people across Palestine and the diaspora. It declared a National Charter, asserting: 'the Palestine people have a right to self-determination following the liberation of their country'; that the Arab people were lawful owners of Palestine; and that 'Jews of Palestine origin' were to be regarded as Palestinians 'proving they are willing to abide peacefully and loyally in Palestine'.[53]

At a further meeting the Council established a Palestine Liberation Organisation (PLO) and a Palestine Liberation Army (PLA) to be composed of members of the armed forces of Arab states. There was a furious response from remnants of the traditional Palestinian leadership, the AHC – now headquartered in Lebanon – which described the PLO as 'a colonialist Zionist conspiracy aimed at the liquidation of the Palestinian cause'.[54] The organisation soon had momentum, however. Small groups of young activists had begun to organise in the refugee camps, especially in Lebanon, and some Palestinians had secretly received military training in Syria and Algeria. Nasser still hoped to contain their increasing frustration and growing determination to take 'direct action' in the form of armed struggle.[55] Within a year, however, Palestinians had set a new agenda with the launch of guerrilla raids against Israel, initiating what was soon widely seen across the diaspora as 'The Revolution'.[56]

Israel's victory in the 1967 war was *al-Naksa* – 'the setback'. Remaining confidence in the Arab states collapsed, as Palestinians declared for self-emancipation. Shuqeiri resigned as chair of the PLO, which soon fell under the control of armed Palestinian groups. But within years of the PLO advance it was compelled to retreat. Affirming Palestinian agency, at the same time PLO leaders sought to minimise its impact on the presidents, kings and princes who had failed them for so long.

Karama

Nasser had hoped to contain Palestinian energies, establishing the PLO 'as a means of canalizing Palestinian national emotions and containing any rash adventures into guerrilla warfare'.[57] His initiative came too late: Palestinian politics was already being reshaped by two distinct developments. One was the growing determination of young activists in the camps; the other was the aspiration of the Palestinian bourgeoisie.

When in 1967 Shuqeiri resigned and armed groups entered the PLO, the group that soon dominated the organisation was al-Fatah ('the opening'/'the victory').[58] It had not been founded in the camps but in communities of the Gulf by a group of young Palestinians among whom some had become wealthy during the oil boom of the 1960s. The key figure was Yasser Arafat, born in Cairo to a family from Gaza and who had trained in Egypt as a civil engineer. After living in Jerusalem, he returned to Cairo to study, forming with others a Union of Palestinian Students in Egypt that aimed to pressure the Nasser regime to take action on Palestine. Unsuccessful in lobbying Egypt's leaders, they moved to the Gulf, taking jobs in Kuwait and Saudi Arabia. Arafat at first worked for the Kuwaiti state, then on his own account. Alan Hart, one of Arafat's biographers, comments that Kuwait was undergoing 'a sensational development explosion. There were fortunes to be made'.[59] For several years, says Hart, 'he [Arafat] did make a great deal of money'.[60] In 1959, with other young activists, Arafat established Fatah, producing the magazine *Our Palestine, The Call of Life*, published in Beirut.[61] This stressed Palestinian self-reliance: according to Arafat's colleague Salah Khalaf:

> We were convinced, for example, that the Palestinians could expect nothing from the Arab regimes, for the most part corrupt or tied to imperialism, and that they were wrong to bank on any of the political parties in the region. We believed that the Palestinians could rely only on themselves.[62]

The group was inspired by the Algerian liberation struggle and in 1962 Arafat attended celebrations in Algiers to mark independence from French rule. Fatah members assumed that they could emulate Algerians of the National Liberation Front by pursuing guerrilla warfare against Israel. They were also influenced by models of guerrilla struggle like that promoted by China: Arafat later said that the People's Republic of China was 'the biggest influence in supporting our revolution and strengthening its perseverance'.[63] According to Khalaf, the group 'worked feverishly' to collect arms and in January 1965 launched its first attack on Israel in the name of *Al Asifa* ('The Storm').[64] Asifa's Communique Number 1 declared its aim of 'showing to the colonialists and their henchmen, and to world Zionism and its financiers, that the Palestinian people remains in the field; that it has not died and will not die'.[65]

During 1965, Fatah mounted almost 40 attacks, gradually developing confidence to conduct operations in its own name and winning huge support across Palestine and the diaspora. For the next two years it recruited steadily with the aim of launching sustained guerrilla warfare in territories under Israeli occupation. In 1967 it attempted wider armed action in the West Bank, hoping to win backing from the local population. Israel reacted quickly and violently, using techniques learned from the British – imposition of curfews, house demolitions, round-ups of 'suspects', and collective punishments – and seizing a thousand of Fatah's *fedayeen* ('sacrificers'/'fighters'). Arafat had joined the operation and was almost captured, escaping through Jordan. Regrouping, the organisation continued attacks, achieving its greatest success in 1968 at Karama in the Jordan Valley. When thousands of Israeli troops, tanks and aircraft assaulted a Fatah base a few hundred fedayeen stood their ground, avoiding defeat. In Arabic, *karama* means dignity, and the episode brought huge excitement and enthusiasm for the Palestinian cause across the region: according to Salah Khalaf, over the next 48 hours over 5,000 potential recruits applied to join Fatah.[66] Armed raids continued, causing continuous problems for Israeli forces and projecting the Palestinian resistance to an audience worldwide.

Nineteen sixty-eight was the year of the Tet Offensive in Vietnam, of mass protest against the Vietnam War in the US and across Europe, of the May Uprising in France, and the rise of the Civil Rights Movement in Ireland. Palestinian activists produced a stream of statements and pamphlets, arguing that they too were part of struggles against imperialism and capitalist crisis. They presented the Palestinian cause in a new form, 'as that of a stateless nation of liberation fighters rather than a group of Arab refugees and a propaganda tool of the regimes in Cairo and Damascus'.[67] Fatah, together with the Palestinian left – notably the Popular Front for the Liberation of Palestine (PFLP) and the Popular Democratic Front for the Liberation of Palestine (DFLP) – placed Palestine within a movement for Third World liberation that contested imperialism and neo-colonial regimes. Now Palestinians were 'a heroic resistance movement striking against the forces of global imperialism'.[68]

There was an immediate impact in Egypt, where the Palestinians played their part in stimulating mass protest against the Nasser regime involving students and workers, including at the key industrial centres of Helwan, Shubra al-Khaima and Alexandria. In Helwan workers surrounded the offices of Nasser's Arab Socialist Union, Egypt's sole legal political party, chanting 'No pity for the traitors',[69] and 'There is no socialism without freedom'.[70] Strikes continued and demonstrations filled city centres, including Cairo's Tahrir Square, expressing 'sympathy and admiration for the Palestinian guerrilla action' and anger at the oppression of their own regime.[71] Even the pessimistic (and later pro-imperialist) academic Fouad Ajami wrote:

> When Palestinians struck out on their own in early 1968 and proclaimed the beginning of a guerrilla war of national liberation, they posed a deep psychological challenge to Egypt's sense of pre-eminence and confronted the Egyptian leader [Nasser] with a set of thorny problems. For more than a decade it had been an article of faith that the hope of doing something for the Palestinians rested on Nasser and his army: that was Egypt's burden and role. Now, in a dramatic reversal of fortunes, Egypt stood paralyzed and ineffective and Palestinians were raising bright banners... Palestinian defiance and guerrilla incursions provided reassurance that not all was lost.[72]

Ajami continued: 'They [Palestinians] were new and he [Nasser] was old; they were the revolution and he was a missed opportunity.'[73] Many Egyptians identified with the young guerrilla activists, gaining confidence to challenge military rulers who had failed to meet expectations of the earlier mass movement against Britain's colonial occupation that had facilitated the army's rise to power. In the 1940s and early 1950s Egypt had been alive with discussions of radical change. Nasser had suppressed the movement and failed the people of Palestine; now talk of revolution re-entered political debate and, as the protests of 1968 continued, Egyptians again had 'a sense of their own power'.[74]

There had long been a relationship between struggles in Palestine and those in the wider Arab world. For decades, millions of people across the region had confronted European colonialism, participating in mass strikes, intifadas and uprisings. In the Arab East there had been continuous interactions between movements in Syria, Lebanon, Iraq, Egypt and Palestine – often a surge in struggles in one area of the region stimulated others. By the 1960s Palestine alone remained under colonial occupation but events there continued to influence movements for change in Arab states – now with the effect of challenging post-colonial regimes. Palestinians had a radical agenda: in defying Israel they encouraged mass protests like those in Egypt that demanded freedom of expression, a free press and 'a new society'.[75] The more that Israel aligned with Western interests the more clearly Palestinian struggles were identified with anti-imperialism and with the repression of the Arab regimes.

In Lebanon, renewal of Palestinian struggles challenged a sectarian state established by France before its belated departure in 1943. The French had created a confessional system under which Christians would always dominate Muslims in the state apparatus in a ratio of six to five. The aim had been to privilege the Maronite (Catholic) Christian minority with which France claimed special affinity – an expression of Islamophobia common to the colonising powers. By the 1960s, Maronite dynasties together with an elite of Sunni Muslim merchants controlled the state and a highly repressive security force. The rejuvenated Palestinian movement ruptured this system. During a few months in 1969, the people of all 17 refugee camps in Lebanon ejected the police, the army and the hated Deuxième Bureau. Declaring *Al Thawra*, 'The Revolution', they successfully challenged the agencies of repression.

During the 1960s the aggressive approach of the Lebanon state had produced a change of mood in the camps, 'from one of patience and suppressed anger to one of revolutionary readiness'.[76] Anne Irfan writes:

> The impact was immediate and transformative. As the camps were released from state authority, internal activities became demonstrably 'Palestinised'. The camps turned into hotbeds of nationalist expression, guarded by *fidaiyyin* rather than by Lebanese police, and dominated by displays of the Palestinian flag.[77]

Palestinian activists were joined by people of cities and villages in Lebanon's south, expelling the police and security agencies. Rosemary Sayigh comments:

> The activism liberated by the restoration of camp Palestinians' self-respect set in motion changes in their relations with the Lebanese population around them, as well as their own international social relations.[78]

Activists set up popular committees, organising defence, political discussion, sports and cultural activities, and military training. Now the camps were no longer means of containment and control but sites for political radicalisation and militarisation – a change soon formalised by the Cairo Agreement of 1969 between the Lebanese government and the PLO, which gave Palestinians control over the camps and over swathes of southern Lebanon, where much of the population held their own grievances against the state and its repression. Basing its headquarters in West Beirut, the PLO established a 'quasi-state' administration and military command, confident in its support in nearby camps such as Sabra and Shatila, Tal al-Zaater and Bourg al-Barajneh, and in extensive working-class areas in the south of the city. Now Palestinians began to travel from across the diaspora to join the movement in Lebanon, receive training and engage in political debate.

For the first time since the 1930s women were leading activists, participating in military training and appearing as key figures in Palestinian communiques and broadcasts. Rosemary Sayigh recorded experiences from the camps of Lebanon: typical was a testimony from Nahd al-Bared camp near the city of Tarablus:

> The circle of fear was over, and now there was active movement in the camp. For the first time in our history women took their right role, and there was military training for girls as well as boys. We felt we had regained our identity, not just as Palestinians, but as human beings.[79]

Julie Peteet describes changes to the typical wartime sexual division of labour in which 'men carry the gun and fight; women provide the sustenance'.[80] In Shatila camp, West Beirut, she notes, 'Women are affiliated to the Resistance in a number of ways: as fulltime members or "cadres", as members, friends, students and employees':

> New social realities – women's presence in the public political sector, usually associated with men – have disturbed and unsettled gender relations and ideologies. New ideas took hold and new forms of social relations emerged with a measure of legitimacy... The construction of gender and gender relations was a conscious process among women who were vividly aware of the historical moment.[81]

At the grassroots a rejuvenated Palestinian movement was initially participatory, democratic and radical. The traditional leadership had been marginalised and the PLO had become a focal point for those seeking change across the Arab world. Fatah declared that it provided 'a model of resistance to neo-imperialist domination'.[82] But its successes were short-lived as the new leadership pursued a strategy that was fatally flawed. Rather than challenging imperialist domination, paradoxically Arafat and his colleagues were also working to secure the status of ruling classes across the region. In Black September 1970 they experienced a reverse from which the armed movement never recovered.

'Non-interference'

For 20 years after the Nakba, Palestinians in the Gulf had enjoyed remarkable material success. In 1982 Eric Rouleau asked, 'Are there 100 or 300 Palestinian millionaires in the Gulf?' Estimates vary, he said, 'but they include merchants, entrepreneurs, bankers and world-class wheeler-dealers'.[83] Hundreds of thousands of Palestinians also occupied key roles in public service and were well-paid by regional standards, enjoying privileged status in relation to the mass of people across the Middle East. A nascent Palestinian bourgeoisie had emerged, together with an elite of senior state employees and professionals whose conditions of life were dramatically different from those of people in the camps. In 1948 mass displacement at the hands of the Zionist militias had emphasised existing relations of inequality: in the years that followed class differences were strongly exaggerated, so that the circumstances and experiences of Palestinians across the diaspora were more and more distinct.

The politics of Arafat and his colleagues were shaped within the Gulf diaspora. According to Salaf Khalaf, all the founding members of Fatah were businessmen, senior state officials or teachers. 'Most of us had good positions', he said. 'Compared to Palestinians living in other Arab countries we were privileged.'[84] Fatah made a direct appeal to this proto-bourgeoisie – people of privilege but who lacked political rights in the Gulf states. Few were citizens of countries such as Saudi Arabia and Kuwait: most were stateless, prosperous but also insecure. Although they espoused free enterprise and the development of 'Western-style capitalism', they lacked a territorial base in which to secure property rights and legal hegemony, and the ability to move freely across borders and to operate as part of the global economy.[85] The nascent bourgeoisie of the 1920s and 1930s had already been denied a state like that pursued by others who contested colonial rule. Its project to advance free trade, profit and private property had been obstructed by the Mandate authorities and by settler colonisation.[86] Now a new generation of capitalists sought a state in which to pursue its ambitions – what Pamela-Ann Smith called a 'rightful place in the government and administration of an independent Palestinian state'.[87] Raja Khalidi writes:

> It might have been expected that the class interests of Palestinian diaspora capitalists and middle-class professionals would dictate that they keep their distance from such dangerous radicals [as Fatah and leftist groups] and continue to serve the Arab regimes within which they had become increasingly integrated. But they too were disillusioned with the defeat of official and popular ideologies of the preceding decades. They were attracted by the pull of national unity and inspired by this younger generation of fearless soldiers of national liberation who were willing to sacrifice themselves for the cause.[88]

They were also reassured by undertakings provided by the Fatah leadership, which developed close relations with rulers of states that included the most active Palestinian business communities. According to Bassam Abu Sharif, a Palestinian activist and once a left-wing critic of Fatah, Arafat was particularly active in liaising between Fatah and the Gulf states, reassuring their rulers that his organisation was focused exclusively on challenging Israel and that on no account would the movement engage in the domestic affairs of other countries.[89] The founding charter of the PLO, agreed in 1964 under the leadership of Shuqeiri, had included the provision (Article 26) that, 'The Liberation Organisation co-operates with all Arab governments each according to its ability, and does not interfere in the internal affairs of any state.'[90] Arafat made the idea of 'non-interference' a rigid principle of Fatah strategy and practice, providing a formal guarantee of economic and political security to both the Arab ruling classes and the Palestinian bourgeoisie. Fatah received a stream of contributions from communities in the Gulf –

a stream that became a flood when, in the mid-1960s, Palestinian capital faced a new challenge within the Arab states.

Having earlier welcomed Palestinians to participate in construction of the Gulf economies, in the mid-1960s governments in Saudi Arabia and Kuwait moved to advantage their own citizens at the Palestinians' expense. Non-citizens already faced severe restrictions on ownership of property and rights to engage in commerce, especially import-export activity. New regulations specified that contracts for construction and infrastructural development were to be awarded to companies owned by 'nationals', who also received tax breaks and special credits. In Kuwait, the government compelled Palestinians to turn over shares held in local companies or lose rights to operate in the country.[91] In a further blow, in 1966 the Palestinian-owned Intra Bank collapsed. Based in Lebanon, the bank had played a key role in the region's financial networks, notably by investing Palestinian capital in Europe and the US. Hostility to its Palestinian owners seemed to have played a key role, as stakeholders in Saudi Arabia, Kuwait, Qatar and Lebanon withdrew their support. *Time* magazine reported that 'the smell of blood is in the air', as tens of millions of dollars was withdrawn and Lebanon's Central Bank refused support,[92] apparently in response to demands from the country's Maronite dynasties that Palestinians' financial influence should be reduced. Intra's affiliated companies, including airlines, shipbuilders, port operators, and media interests, were all abruptly lost to Palestinian ownership. Smith comments:

> Palestinians of all walks of life drew the conclusion that the bank had failed, or been allowed to fail, because it was Palestinian. Henceforth, they argued, Palestinians would either have to share their profits with the Arab rivals...or invest their funds in an area where Palestinians had a say in the government and in the way affairs of the economy were handled... [T]he only answer to many Palestinian businessmen in the diaspora after the collapse of Intra seemed to be creation of a place where economic influence could be secured and maintained by political power, namely through establishment of a state of their own.[93]

Saudi connection

Fatah's activist recruits came largely from the camps. Its leadership had emerged from the diaspora of the Gulf but frontline troops came overwhelmingly from the refugee communities of Jordan, Lebanon and Syria – not only impoverished former peasants and workers but also teachers, journalists and writers, doctors and engineers – people without capital but with an urgent desire for change. Together they formed a new movement that demanded solutions to the national question – and the more effective they became the more they posed a problem for regional and global powers. The kingdoms and principalities of the Gulf, said Rouleau, were as 'sensitive as a seismograph to tremors in any country of the region'.[94] Still lacking a stable state apparatus, each was vulnerable to political upheavals, doubly challenged by rejuvenation of the Palestinian movement – its impacts in the Arab East and among diasporic communities of Saudi Arabia and Kuwait, and which had now been established in the UAE and Qatar. 'The Palestine problem', suggested Rouleau, 'generates agitation, revolutions, and wars which threaten to shake these fragile and vulnerable regimes to the very foundations.'[95] The Gulf rulers hoped for resolution of the Palestine issue with minimum disruption: while supporting the PLO as the only viable Palestinian national body, 'they hesitate to do anything that would put in question their property and their stability'.[96] It was to the Gulf rulers that Fatah now turned, however, seeking the means to continue its guerrilla offensives and to build the institutions of the liberation movement.

In 1969 Khalid al-Hassan of the Fatah leadership met King Faisal of Saudi Arabia, apparently convincing him that Fatah was composed of trustworthy Muslims engaged in a religious cause.[97] Saudi rulers calculated that the organisation could be influenced by mobilising a fraction of the kingdom's vast financial resources. They had faced an earlier form of Palestinian radicalism, when in 1953 and 1954 skilled workers employed by Aramco led strikes for wage increases, union recognition, and improvements in housing: over 150 were arrested and deported. In 1955 another 100 Palestinians were arrested for engaging in political activity and in 1956 Palestinians in the Gulf participated in protests over the Suez War and Israel's assault on Gaza.[98] Within two years Palestinian participation in the workforce in the Gulf had been limited to those with professional qualifications. Ten years later some restrictions had been eased but now the national movement had revived and workers were under pressure to restrict political activity. Offered undertakings by Hassan that Palestinians would honour the principle of 'non-interference', Faisal agreed to supply Fatah with money and arms, and to levy a 5 percent 'liberation tax' on the income of all Palestinians working in Saudi Arabia, to be directed to the PLO. Huge sums of money now flowed to Fatah: Palestinian economist Yusuf Sayigh notes that by the 1980s, official Saudi government contributions to the PLO amounted to $30 million 'every few months'.[99] Hart comments:

> The significance of Saudi Arabia's support for Fatah cannot be exaggerated. As time proved, with Saudi Arabia on its side, Fatah was indestructible – as long as it was pursuing policies the Saudis could endorse.[100]

Chapter 7
Guerrilla strategy

Fatah – the crisis of strategy. 'Black September' – the movement retreats

Revitalisation of the Palestinian movement was achieved against enormous odds: it also presented a series of testing new challenges. Leaders of the Zionist movement had succeeded in placing Israel within imperialist networks in the Middle East: they had in effect made good on the strategy of Theodor Herzl to engage with dominant powers in the region. The PLO intended to disrupt this project but resolved not to challenge local regimes committed to the status quo. It embraced a contradiction: its leaders sought to stimulate Palestinian struggles that also energised people across the region, including those with good reason to confront their own rulers. The principle of 'non-interference' was implausible: the more that Palestinians succeeded in mobilising against Israel, they more they challenged the Arab regimes. Confrontation was inevitable – and came less than three years after the heady events at Karama, as Palestinian forces were assaulted by the army of Jordan's King Hussein.

Arafat and his colleagues were focused, they said, solely on Palestinian national concerns. Their main influences came from conservative political currents. In Cairo, Yasser Arafat, Salah Khalaf and Khalil al-Wazir had all worked with the Muslim Brotherhood during a period when it was in rapid retreat.[1] They had no known connections with the left. In Kuwait they were part of the most privileged section of the diaspora, including wealthy businessmen and senior state officials closely connected to the regime. Helga Baumgarten writes: 'It is difficult to overestimate the extent to which the diaspora experience shaped the formation and ultimate success of Fatah.'[2] Its leaders were bourgeois nationalists, seeking an independent state like others in the Middle East that had already struggled free of colonial rule. Across the Global South, leaders of such movements often allied local capitalists with middle-class professionals with the aim of securing control of states without disturbing existing economic and social relationships. Distinct from these movements were radical nationalists who challenged some aspects of imperialist rule and who implemented at least partial economic and social reforms – such as the Free Officers in Egypt and the National Liberation Front in Algeria. Fatah's leaders wished for an independent Palestine in the mould of most other Arab states: they held a cautious bourgeois nationalist agenda. At the same time, their call for armed struggle and mobilisation in the camps had the effect of radical nationalism, raising expectations that went far beyond their leaders' vision of change.

The call for armed resistance harked back to the intifada of the 1930s and guerrilla leaders such as Izz al-Din al-Qassam. It was also associated with contemporary struggles conceived as 'people's wars' for liberation. In an early document Fatah wrote:

> Revolutions all over the world are inspiring us. The revolution in Algeria lights our way like a bright torch of hope. When the Algerians took up their revolution in 1954, they were only some hundred Arabs facing 20,000 French troops and well-armed settlers... The revolution in Algeria proved to us that a people can organize itself and build its military strength in the very process of fighting.[3]

The examples of China, Vietnam and Cuba also inspired Fatah leaders. Having visited Algeria in 1962, two years later Arafat travelled to China, hoping to obtain arms. He described Fatah's strategy to his hosts as an attempt to launch guerrilla warfare and win over the mass of people across historic Palestine. They responded sceptically:

> They told us: 'What you are proposing is unbelievable. You can't do it. You have no bases in the territory to be liberated and no prospect of creating them. From where will you start? There are no conditions for guerrilla warfare.'[4]

When a Fatah delegation visited North Vietnam in 1970, says Salah Khalaf, they received a similar response.[5] In fact the strategy had already been tested in 1967, with disastrous results. The initiative seems to have been planned at Fatah's first congress, held earlier that year, when as an outcome of the June war a million Palestinians had fallen under Israel's control. Now, participants concluded, 'conditions were right for a popular war of liberation':

> Those who entertained this idea believed they could now apply Mao Tse-Tung's thoughts about revolutionary armed struggle. The one million Palestinians under Israeli occupation would be the revolutionary sea in which Mao's fish – in this case the Palestinian guerrillas – would swim. On the West Bank and Gaza the oppressed Palestinian masses would give aid and shelter to their fighters in the short term and in the long term they would rise up against the Israelis.[6]

There were huge differences between China and the West Bank, and in 1967 – under Israeli assault – Fatah was soon forced to retreat to bases in Jordan from which it conducted sporadic cross-border attacks. The strategy was not attempted again. Did Fatah revise its approach – or had its leaders never held a realistic expectation that the West Bank would rise defiantly in their support? According to Khalid al-Hassan, also one of the founders of Fatah in Kuwait, the organisation had aimed to pressure Arab regimes into military action against Israel:

> We intended to provoke and capture the imagination of the Palestinian and Arab masses. We thought we could create a new atmosphere in which no Arab leader would dare to ignore the subject of liberating Palestine...when the Arab leaders were coming under pressure for action from their own masses, we would engage them in dialogue. We would ask them to join us in planning a co-ordinated strategy for the actual liberation of our homeland.[7]

But putting Arab leaders under pressure from their own populations violated Fatah's principle of 'non-interference'. Khalid al-Hassan added:

> If they [the Arab leaders] turned us down we would lead a confrontation between the Palestinian refugees and the regimes. And the aim of this confrontation would be to provoke a real Arab revolution that would end with the bringing to power of regimes that would have the power to fight Israel.[8]

Fatah had never seriously contemplated such a strategy and when genuine mass movements demanding action on Palestine erupted in Arab states, they were ignored by the organisation's leaders. In February and September 1968 mass strikes and protests in Egypt challenged President Nasser for his failures, highlighting the successes of the fedayeen, whose performance at Karama brought thousands of applications from Egypt to join the guerrillas. In February, pro-Palestinian student societies were established across Egyptian universities.[9] Mahmoud Hussein wrote: 'Popular aspirations crystallized around the Palestinian resistance. The profound admiration this struggle inspired in the masses gave them renewed confidence in the validity of mass struggle against the occupiers'.[10] A further surge of activity in November brought student occupations, strike committees and wide involvement of the Egyptian public in confrontations with the army and the police. Fatah remained entirely passive in relation to this powerful movement: it was not clear whether events in Egypt registered with its leaders or if their silence marked unwillingness to address the impact of Palestinian struggle in the most populous state in the region.

Edward Said comments that following events in Karama the movement surged in popularity; at the same time, a 'besetting' issue began to affect the PLO – vacillation 'between a revolutionary direction (liberation) and one that seemed to transform the structures of Palestinian power into those of an Arab state (national independence)'.[11] Mobilising arms and finance provided by rulers of the region, Fatah could not pursue 'revolution'. Its leaders wanted parity with other ruling classes: political status that accorded with the economic standing of that part of the diaspora from which they had emerged. The French communist leader and PLO sympathiser Alain Gresh later wrote:

> The Palestinian Resistance was locked into a contradiction that has marked its entire history right down to the present day. On the one hand it cannot hope to win without the support of the Arab states… on the other hand, its very development leads to contradictions with these countries.[12]

Radical critics

Fatah dominated the PLO. The state-like structures it created were controlled by Fatah cadres, who maintained a tight grip on finances, arms and internal bodies. But in the radical atmosphere of the late 1960s, the Palestinian left drew significant support. It had its origins in the Arab Nationalist Movement (ANM), founded in the early 1950s by Palestinians and others at the American University in Beirut, Lebanon. 'They thought of themselves', writes Walid Kazziha, as forming 'a kind of widely inclusive political tendency, whose purpose was to mobilise the whole Arab nation in its struggle for Palestine'.[13] Hostile to Arab rulers they held responsible for the defeat of 1948, they were also opposed to the communist left, which they saw as divisive and – due to Soviet support for Israel – as complicit in the Nakba. The ANM supported the Nasser regime in Egypt and was enthused by the declaration in 1958 of a United Arab Republic (UAR) combining Egypt and Syria. When the UAR collapsed in 1961 ANM leaders began moving steadily to the left but maintained the idea that the Arab world should unite under the leadership of Egypt. In 1964 they established a National Front for the Liberation of Palestine (NFLP), which aimed to undertake military action with the aim of detonating a war in which Arab states led by Nasser would confront Israel. At this point the ANM was larger than Fatah but focused principally on internal ideological debates. After the June war of 1967 it moved more sharply to the left, declaring that the Arab regimes were 'petit bourgeois', that the 'Arab revolution' depended upon leadership of the 'toiling social classes', and that a successful confrontation with Zionism and imperialism required 'popular armed struggle'.[14] In December 1967, George Habash and a group of Palestinian members of the ANM established the Popular Front for the Liberation of Palestine (PFLP). In 1969 a group led by Nayef

Hawatmeh left the PFLP to form the Popular Democratic Front for the Liberation of Palestine (DFLP), declaring for 'socialism' (see Chapter 12).[15] The ANM was now overshadowed by Fatah, however, and soon challenged by a crisis that brought to a head the decisive issue of relations between the armed movement and the Arab regimes.

Fatah's achievement in winning mass support for the resistance was continuously undermined by its contradictory approach to the regimes. In a further statement of strategy, Khalid al-Hassan had declared:

> We will make actions, the Israelis will make reactions. Now the Arab governments either will support us against the Israelis or will fight us. If they fight us, the people will support us. When the people will support us the governments either will support us or they will confront us with their own people.[16]

In the event, it was an attack by the Jordanian regime that clarified Arab rulers' approach to the PLO. By 1970, under Fatah's leadership, Palestinians had succeeded in building a quasi-state apparatus in Jordan. Palestinian historian Yezid Sayigh describes the host of institutions run independently by the Resistance: military police, security apparatus, revolutionary courts, information offices, media, trade unions, full-time armed forces, and liberated zones in the refugee camps.[17] The movement enjoyed wide support: 70 percent of the Jordanian population was of Palestinian heritage and the regime's base was narrow, resting ultimately on armed forces emplaced by the British. Following the Battle of Karama, King Hussein had been forced to declare: 'I think we have reached the point now where we are all fedayeen.'[18] Fatah believed that even Hussein's army could be won to the Palestinian cause, claiming that some units were ready to back the resistance[19] – a view confirmed by Yezid Sayigh, who observed that Fatah enjoyed much support at all levels of government and 'had extensively penetrated the army and security services'.[20] Several Jordanian army officers advised Fatah to go onto the offensive, challenging the Hussein regime. The DFLP argued that the regime was hostile to the PLO and that the movement should prepare to confront it; the PFLP called for establishment of 'an Arab Hanoi' in the Jordanian capital, Amman.[21] Fatah attempted to restrain them, arguing that Palestinians 'must understand the imperatives of Arab security in all Arab countries, and understand the need for internal Arab stability'.[22]

King Hussein was preparing a showdown, bolstering his support among Bedouin communities from which he drew loyalist officers. Arafat and the Fatah leadership continued passively to observe events, despite calls from the DFLP for more energetic engagement with the mass of Jordanians, the creation of 'popular councils', and preparations to bring down the monarchy.[23] The PFLP argued that it was time for an assault on the state, calling for 'revolution, revolution and continued revolution until victory'.[24] There was widespread talk of 'dual power' – a situation in which neither the Jordanian state nor the PLO had decisive influence, and one that implied major conflicts to come.

The events of 1970 have often been viewed exclusively as a conflict between the monarchy and the PLO – as an intra-Arab dispute focused upon local control of Jordanian territory. In fact, they had global significance. The success of the PLO in re-energising the Palestinian movement and raising support across the region had implications worldwide, suggests Paul Thomas Chamberlin. The Resistance, he suggests, was 'the world's first globalized insurgency', influencing radical movements across the continents.[25] US government documents classified for 30 years eventually revealed that President Nixon, his adviser Henry Kissinger, and American foreign policy strategists viewed the Jordanian crisis as an issue of pressing importance.[26] In 1970 the Cold War was in full flood, the US taking a close interest in a 'precarious balance between radicals and moderates in the Arab world'.[27] American strategists were intent on limiting the influence of both the Soviet Union and China. Facing intractable problems in South-East Asia, they feared new guerrilla movements that drew inspiration from the National Liberation Front in Vietnam. As events in Jordan unfolded President Nixon asserted: 'You cannot separate what happens to America in Vietnam from the Mideast or from Europe or from any place else.'[28]

Black September

For Nixon, Kissinger and Washington's imperial strategists, the PLO was attempting to occupy 'a new front that had to be fortified'.[29] As Arafat and Fatah continued to prevaricate, the US developed closer relations with Hussein, who was struggling to deal with the evident strength and popularity of the fedayeen. In June 1970 Hussein offered Arafat a role as prime minister and freedom to form a cabinet of his choice: Arafat declined and the crisis deepened.[30] Hawatmeh of the DFLP later insisted, 'the cities, villages and camps of Jordan were in our hands…the balance of forces was titled in the direction of the revolution and people'.[31] He referenced the Bolshevik experience in the Russian Revolution of 1917, arguing that a decisive move against the regime would swing the population behind Palestinian forces. The DFLP raised the slogan 'All power to the Resistance';[32] the PFLP called for a joint effort to split the Jordanian army. Even leading members of Fatah believed that the PLO had the resources – and an urgent need – to move against the king. Abu Daoud Oudeh (Abu Daoud) was commander of overall guerrilla operations. He later asserted:

> I was of the opinion that we not only could but should knock off Hussein…this was the feeling not only of the leftists and so-called radicals in the other guerrilla organisations, it was also the feeling and the wish of the majority of us in Fatah – the fighters and the young officers… We discussed the question of overthrowing Hussein very seriously and very frequently. We also discussed our views with Arafat, and I told him on more than one occasion that I thought we were making a terrible mistake by not moving against Hussein… Arafat always said 'No'. He told us that making war against Hussein or any Arab regime was not the way to liberation.[33]

In the summer of 1970 Washington put forward a 'peace plan' to address conflict between Israel and Egypt (the Rogers Plan), also aiming to divide the Palestinian movement by engaging with the Arab regimes and with traditional leaders on the occupied West Bank. To the horror of the Resistance, Nasser gave provisional support. News of the plan was greeted by huge demonstrations of protest in Amman, where turnout was said to be the largest ever seen in the city, with tens of thousands filling more than three miles of city streets.[34] In Lebanon there were also mass protests and calls for the government formally to join the fedayeen in struggle against Israel. Arafat declared against the plan and called for wider support for the armed movement: still, however, he refused to intervene against the monarchy. Weeks passed with intermittent clashes between the fedayeen and Jordanian forces amid demands from the Resistance that the PLO should seize power before Hussein struck decisively: even the PLO Central Committee (which included representatives of all the armed groups) warned of the dangers of 'encirclement and annihilation [and] a terrible and bloody massacre'.[35] In early September the PFLP hijacked a series of aircraft, forcing three to land at a remote air base in Jordan. Intended to focus world attention on the Palestinian cause and the Front's call for action, it brought the standoff in Amman to a head. Now Arafat called a general strike, demanding a people's assembly for Jordan that would include Palestinian representatives.

The US saw a threat to states across the region. For Kissinger, victory for the fedayeen would mean, 'one more radical state in the Middle East where the U.S. is barred. A radical fedayeen base there [Jordan] would strengthen the movement against Saudi Arabia, Kuwait and the Persian Gulf states'.[36] Kissinger's strategic task group on Jordan considered sending an American invasion force 'to clean out the city [Amman]' and to move jointly with Israel 'to sustain Hussein against the Palestinians, Iraqis, and Syrians'.[37] The President's instincts, said Kissinger, 'are to crush the Fedayeen now'.[38] It was agreed that if the crisis deepened the US would support intervention by Israel, backing the IDF with arms and ammunition and bolstering the Lebanese Army in case of an uprising in Beirut.[39] Such was the regime's anxiety that Hussein told US officials if fighting resumed, 'he [Hussein] had had it'.[40] Washington assured him of American commitment to the Jordanian state, moving the US Sixth Fleet into the Eastern Mediterranean and co-ordinating with Israel. In the event of direct involvement of the Israelis, Kissinger's task group agreed to provide the IDF with 'expendables' – arms and ammunition – at a rate of up to $100 million a month.[41]

With Hussein's confidence boosted by assurances from the US and Israel, his forces launched an all-out assault on the PLO. Units of the Syrian army crossed the border, quickly achieving control of Jordan's northern cities and heading for Amman, ostensibly to protect the fedayeen. Iraq had maintained a large force in Jordan since the 1967 war and now warned that it would not allow the PLO to be defeated. With Hussein's onslaught in full swing, however, the Syrians retreated while Iraqi forces remained passive. Now Nasser, compromised by his support for the Rogers Plan, raised the alarm over 'a terrible massacre'.[42] After a ceasefire and an agreement with Arafat to control PLO activities, the Jordanian army attacked again, forcing Palestinian fighters out of their bases and isolating them in the north, where most eventually retreated into Syrian territory. At least 3,000 Palestinians (and as many as 20,000)[43] were killed and much of the PLO infrastructure was dismantled. Hussein claimed total victory.

Understanding defeat

The events marked both a high tide of Palestinian armed resistance and a defeat from which the fedayeen never recovered. The movement had been a negligible military force until the June war of 1967, after which it had mobilised mass support within and beyond Palestinian communities. Drawing upon the resolve of tens of thousands of activists from the camps it had, in effect, made Jordan a sanctuary in which Palestinians were able to realise a form of self-expression denied since the time of the Nakba. This notable achievement demonstrated that, notwithstanding the assertions of Israeli leaders such as Meir – 'No such thing as the Palestinians' – resistance remained strong, determined and extraordinarily energetic.

The events highlighted emergence of the radical left. Organisations such as the PFLP and DFLP had no historic precedent in the Palestinian movement, having crystallised within the ANM as a response to the 1967 conflict. Led largely by middle-class professionals they nonetheless reflected the aspirations of many Palestinians who were not part of the Gulf elite but faced continued marginalisation at the hands of regimes in Lebanon, Syria and Jordan. This was expressed in a rapid move to the left during the late 1960s, in insistent calls for radical change, and by 1970 for 'revolution'. After the 1967 war the ANM concluded that the disaster of 1948 had been the responsibility of the Palestinian 'feudal and bourgeois classes', and that Israel's victory in the June War was an outcome of the inability of the petit bourgeoisie (the Nasser regime) to confront imperialism and Zionism. The 'road to national salvation', it said, lay in adoption of 'the ideology of the proletariat' and closer relations with the Arab revolutionary movement (see Chapter 12).[44]

Some assessments of Black September see the left as responsible for the PLO defeat. Rashid Khalidi views the events as a 'debacle' during which the Palestinian movement was unable to discipline its own ranks.[45] The PFLP, he concludes, 'provoked the Hashemite regime beyond tolerance', leading the movement into a devastating crisis.[46] This is consistent with the views of key figures in the Fatah leadership, among whom some concluded that the left should have been confronted militarily by the mainstream of the Resistance. Khalid al-Hassan (Abu Said), one of the historic Fatah leaders, maintained:

> I think we made a very big mistake by not using our superior military force to deal with the leftists and the so-called radicals...we could have done it at any time in 1969 and before August 1970... The first and biggest [mistake] was allowing the leftists to be part of the PLO in the first place.[47]

His brother Hani al-Hassan (Abu Tariq) agreed:

> I think we lost Jordan because Arafat refused to discipline the leftists. I think we were right to debate with the leftists and the radicals without putting any pressure on them, but when we had decided our line, which was to co-operate with Hussein, we should have disciplined and punished those who did not follow it.[48]

Here responsibility was displaced away from the Fatah mainstream, deemed to be in error only by failing to confront the radicals. Other key figures from the Fatah leadership disagreed, however. Abu Daoud testified that the majority of Fatah's cadre wished to confront Hussein before he assaulted the movement – and that in August 1970, after months of hesitation and delay, even Fatah had talked of creating a 'secret apparatus' that would challenge the monarchy.[49] For Bassam Abu Sharif – once of the PFLP, later of Fatah – the key issue was intervention by Hussein's forces: 'Our own Arab brothers had taken up arms against us: a catastrophe for the Palestinian cause.'[50]

The senior leadership of Fatah had been paralysed for months before the September assaults. Michael Hudson observes that since 1967 the PLO had become 'more radical ideologically, a development which reinforced its overall cohesion':[51]

> It developed a degree of leadership, organization, and mass support quite superior to earlier efforts during the British Palestine Mandate and to those of other political movements in the Arab world. It developed a modest violence capability against Israel which the Israelis found politically intolerable. More significant, however, was the challenge it posed to the authority of all the Arab regimes.[52]

'What went wrong?' Hudson asks, suggesting: 'The resistance leadership was consistently unable to make the necessary decisions that would protect its independence and integrity, and it misjudged the dynamics of Arab interstate politics in the Middle East crisis.'[53] The Resistance was in the process of becoming a highly mobilised anti-imperialist movement, emphasising self-activity and increasingly sceptical about the promises and intentions of the Arab regimes. It had evicted the army and security services from the camps of Lebanon and had created extensive areas of self-government in Jordan. These were real and substantial gains for a movement that earlier had been clandestine and marginal to Arab politics. At the same time, the Fatah leadership remained focused on hopes of working with and through the regimes. A confrontation with the latter was inescapable – and a collision with Palestinian activists more and more certain of their own role in the struggle was inevitable.

Left-wing groups were a minority among the PLO guerrilla forces but exerted growing influence ideologically. To Fatah's strategy of armed resistance they added another element, says historian John Chalcraft: 'revolution in the Arab states, especially the reactionary ones, which would have to come about before such states would join a revolutionary confrontation with Israel'.[54] The PFLP argued that Fatah lacked understanding of the Jordanian regime, which it said was 'totally and organically linked to American imperialism...a force for oppressing the masses'.[55] Despite emotional support for the Palestinian cause, it said, the mass of people in Jordan were not directly engaged in struggle by the PLO leadership: 'Emotional support is one thing, conscious revolutionary mobilisation is another'.[56] The PFLP observed that during the crisis in Jordan neither the monarchy nor the Resistance was able to exert full authority. In the event this 'dual power', which lasted from mid-1969 to September 1970, 'was resolved decisively in favour of the reactionary regime and the class forces on which it depends':

> History shows that dual power leads to a situation of disintegration in the state system which cannot continue for very long. If, in such a case, the revolution does not act to resolve this situation to its benefit, then no doubt counter-revolution will... The leadership of the revolution faced the situation of dual power without a plan. Thus it abandoned the Jordanian masses.[57]

The PFLP concluded: 'The resistance created a situation of dual power and then stood idly by...[the leadership's] own policies led to its defeat'.[58] For the DFLP's Hawatmeh, it was impossible to avoid a conflict with the monarchy, given its long collaboration with Zionism and Israel, colonial roots, imperial alliances, expansionism, and need to maintain hegemony at any cost.[59] Fatah's Salah Khalaf (Abu Iyad) later agreed, declaring of the Jordanian regime that, 'its supremely ingenious tactic was to bide its time while we made our mistakes; then, in September and later, it struck the fatal blow'.[60]

Evaluating the strategies of competing currents within the Resistance, Hudson concludes: 'The mainstream leadership acted as if it were ignorant of the realities of politics, yet it had been repeatedly warned at the highest levels of the consequence of its behaviour':[61]

> The guerrilla and PLO leadership, while repudiating in general terms the traditional Palestinian leaders, had been unable to commit itself to a total and coherent radical strategy, nor had it severed the ties that bound it to regimes that could only tolerate it as a weak and non-radical movement, useful primarily for propaganda in the West... The temptations of power and prestige dimmed the perceptions of danger that co-optation entailed.[62]

Palestinian radicals were convinced that there could have been a different outcome. Successful efforts to remove the kings of Egypt and Iraq had earlier resulted in the establishment of republics committed initially to radical change. There could be no certainty that a challenge to Hussein would resolve the crisis in Jordan, suggested the PFLP, but it would have strengthened the mass support and continued the battle against the regime, 'eventually putting an end to it'.[63] Like recent movements in Egypt, Iraq and Algeria it would have had a radicalising impact across the region. In the event, defeat in Jordan was not only a blow against the Palestinians but also against the mass of people across the Arab world.

Lebanon – 'too many enemies'

During the 1920s and 1930s traditional Palestinian leaders organised in the Arab Executive and the AHC attempted continuously to strike compromises with the British colonial regime, inhibiting the national movement and facilitating Zionist settlement. Decades later Fatah attempted its own policies of restraint in Jordan: in the words of a key member of the leadership, Hani al-Hassan, it aimed consciously 'to co-operate with Hussein'.[64] This attempt at cohabitation was doomed from the beginning. Rex Brynen comments: 'The mere presence of a revolutionary movement within a dissonant state and society constitutes a structural threat to those who rule it'.[65] Black September of 1970, he continues, 'was the military reaction of a conservative elite faced with a potential revolutionary threat to its power and position'.[66] Fatah had attempted to contain the energies of an insurgent movement and, in doing so, had led it to defeat.

'Co-operation' led to further mass displacement, as 30,000 Palestinians were compelled to move via Syria to Lebanon – a state in which they had already faced years of marginalisation and oppression. Armed resistance had recently brought relief from the attentions of state security agencies, but Palestinians were still marginalised and had much in common with the mass of Lebanese, who also experienced multiple deprivation, especially in the countryside and cities of the south. Beirut's financial institutions had played a key role in the petro-economy, enriching a tiny minority while most Lebanese faced poverty and a significant number were identified as 'destitute'.[67] But widespread social discontent was often displaced into tensions and rivalries encouraged by leaders of the country's confessional groups. The 'logics of sect and patronage' directed fundamental issues of class conflict towards communal hostilities formalised at the level of a state still dominated by the Maronite Christian elite and its allies.[68] Support for the Palestinians was widespread: when three PLO leaders were assassinated in Beirut in 1973, some 250,000 people attended their funeral – testimony not only to sentiments of solidarity but also awareness among many Lebanese that the Palestinians were allies in struggles for social justice.[69]

Right-wing organisations, especially those linked to the Maronite elite, expressed intense hostility to the PLO. Prominent among these was the Phalange and its paramilitary wing, usually jointly referred to as al-Kataeb ('The Battalions'), which worked aggressively to advance Maronite interests: in 1958 it supported US troops that had invaded Lebanon to suppress mass protests against the pro-imperialist Chamoun regime. Like other organisations associated with Maronite communities, such as the Zgharta Liberation Army and the Guardians of the Cedars, the Kataeb combined paramilitary organisation with Islamophobia, embracing the racist hostility of French colonial rule towards Lebanon's Muslim population. As most Palestinians were Sunni Muslims, they were seen by leaders of the Christian Right as representing multiple threats – as foreigners, Muslims and armed activists. In the 1970s both Jordan and Israel saw opportunities for alliances with the Kataeb and other right-wing forces: by 1973 Jordan was training Phalange militiamen and financing sectarian chiefs hostile to the Palestinians. More serious was direct and indirect Israeli intervention: by 1975 the IDF was raiding Lebanese territory on average 17 times a day and the following year it established covert links with the Phalange.[70] These ties with an organisation standing in the tradition of European antisemitism, ethnic exclusivism and street violence marked Israeli intentions. The Kataeb was to become Israel's key ally in Lebanon, with murderous implications for the Palestinians. Rosemary Sayigh, who observed these unfolding challenges, saw emerging crises for the Resistance, confronted by 'too many enemies'.[71]

New colonies

The rise of the Resistance as a movement of armed struggle had taken place as Israel was creating new colonies in Palestine. According to Yigal Allon, then Israel's foreign minister, territories captured in 1967 provided 'strategic depth' and 'defensible borders' – buffer zones that, he argued, would give protection in future conflicts.[72] Of importance in the context of Zionist ideology was acquisition of land seen as central to the historic project of settlement and, within weeks of capture of the West Bank, Allon directed cartographers to include the area in maps of Israel. In official documents it was now to be designated as 'Judea and Samaria', long seen by Zionist leaders as integral to creation of 'Eretz Israel'.[73] Shortly after the 1967 war an opinion poll showed that 91 percent of Israelis favoured permanent control over East Jerusalem; 89 percent were for keeping the Golan Heights; and 71 percent wanted to keep the West Bank.[74] Allon declared: 'The last thing we must do is to return one inch of the West Bank'.[75] The Israeli government promptly annexed East Jerusalem and nearby Palestinian Arab villages; within weeks it had demolished hundreds of Palestinian homes in the city and approved establishment of 'work camps' and 'settlement outposts' in what it called 'the administered territories' of the West Bank and Golan Heights.[76]

Israel's senior lawyer dealing with international issues told the government that civilian settlement in the territories would contravene the Geneva Convention, to which Israel was a signatory. Israel's Cabinet kept his ruling secret as settlement proper got under way.[77] Beginning with villages of the Etzion Bloc, south of Jerusalem – earlier occupied by Zionist settlers displaced during the conflict of 1948 – settlements were at first established slowly, accelerating after 1974 when Gush Emunim (Bloc of the Faithful), a group of messianic activists, received approval for a site near Nablus on the West Bank. By 1977, 4,500 Israelis lived in 36 settlements established either at the government's initiative or with its acquiescence – 31 in the West Bank and five in the Gaza Strip. For the first time the Likud Party was elected to government under Menachem Begin, the Revisionist Zionist who had been leader of Etzel (Irgun). Now the pace of settlement accelerated rapidly: by 1981 there were 16,000 settlers in the Territories; by 1990 there were 78,000; by 1993 there were almost 200,000.[78] Karen Tenenbaum and Ehud Eiran comment: 'Likud's intent was to ensure that no future Israeli government would find it politically possible to withdraw from the West Bank as part of an overall settlement'.[79] When the Labour Party returned to power in 1992, it declared that there would be no new settlements but promptly increased construction of housing units on existing sites: by 2005 there were 231,000 settlers living in more than 175 settlements in addition to almost 200,000 who were living in the annexed portion of Jerusalem.[80]

Likud minister Ariel Sharon, later to be prime minister of Israel, planned for two million settlers across the Occupied Territories, where Israel now ruled by dictat, enabling all manner of controls over people and resources.[81] In June 1967, the Commander of the IDF in West Bank had declared that 'any power of government, legislation, appointment, or administration with respect to the region or its inhabitants shall henceforth be vested in me alone'.[82] Settlement sites were viewed in effect as part of Israel: millions of dollars were invested in road networks that connected them to territory seized in 1948, and in electricity lines, water pipelines, deep-bored wells, underground irrigation systems, and in private and public housing. Settler families received unprecedented state support: Sadot for example, constructed in the Egyptian territory of North Sinai, required an initial government/Jewish Agency investment of some $275,000 for each settler family.[83] Meanwhile over 1.5 million Palestinian Arabs were under military occupation: tens of thousands had fled the offensives of 1967 but the great majority remained in their homes and in camps in which they had lived since 1948.

Towards intifada

Years after the 1967 war, Shlomo Gazit – who had been head of research for Israel's military intelligence – wrote: 'At the end of the sixties the world was already watching the end of the era of colonialism, and precisely then Israel found itself marching in the opposite direction.'[84] The Zionist movement had in fact been 'marching' alongside European colonialism for many decades. Some of its leaders had been explicit about their aim to secure land and to expel the inhabitants: others were evasive, disingenuous or denied outright the colonial character of their venture. In 1967 senior figures in Israel's foreign ministry and intelligence services sent urgent messages to the government warning of the 'stain' of colonialism. Occupation of the West Bank, they warned, required careful thought, because 'internationally, the impression could be created…that Israel is maintaining a colonial regime'.[85] Decision-makers were less coy, opting for military control and programmes of settlement that established hundreds of new colonies.

According to Gavit, Israeli leaders had long since determined to seize the Territories.[86] Drawing on the experience of a brief occupation of Gaza during the 1956 war with Egypt, they had devised an elaborate scheme for control of the West Bank. The Shacham Plan (officially 'The Organisation of Military Rule in the Occupied Territories') divided the area into administrative units and gave Israeli officers powers as 'absolute monarchs' in zones under their authority.[87] As in 1948, Israeli leaders planned to impose laws and regulations from the British Mandate period, including use of military courts with powers to impose the death sentence. Elaborate arrangements were in place four years before the war of 1967 – what Pappé calls a 'successful blitzkrieg' that ended in military occupation.[88]

In 1967 there were 820,000 Palestinian Arabs in the West Bank; 80,000 in East Jerusalem; and 450,000 in Gaza.[89] Israel variously attempted to remove them, exploit them and imprison them. During the earliest phases of the occupation there were sustained attempts to prompt 'emigration'. This hidden history of ethnic cleansing gave evidence of Zionist leaders' continuing commitment to 'transfer' – the key aim of the settler movement since the time of Herzl. Citing classified documents, concealed from public view for decades, Omri Shafer Raviv shows how in 1967 Israeli strategists aimed to remove Palestinians, particularly those in Gaza, by 'pushing individuals to leave of their own accord'.[90] The government 'hoped to create a demographic shift in the Gaza Strip so that [its] vision of annexation would slowly, but safely, become a reality'.[91] Within weeks of the June war, Moshe Dayan – in charge of the conquered territories – ordered provision of a 'daily shuttle' to move people from Gaza to the border with Jordan. Later, claiming success in moving Gazan labourers over the Jordan River to the East Bank, Dayan declared: 'This is their transfer.'[92] A Transfer Subcommittee undertook more elaborate planning based on a 'push and pull' strategy. Gazans were offered grants to move to the West Bank in the expectation that they would subsequently move east across the border into Jordan. When in October 1967 the government finalised a secret policy for all newly occupied areas it set as a priority (Clause 2) the reduction of the number of Arabs in the territories and (Clause 3) the 'evacuation' of inhabitants of the Gaza Strip. In a further strategic document, the government resolved to move Gazans systematically to the West Bank and then to the East Bank (Jordan 'proper'). It noted: 'movement to the East Bank is one-way'.[93]

In 1968 Prime Minister Levi Eshkol directed a senior official to undertake, covertly, a programme to eject Palestinians by prompting movements across the continents. 'Find ways and paths that will help the Arabs to emigrate,' he said, encouraging efforts to focus on South America. 'It's possible to move people there [so] that no one would even know about their existence in the world.'[94] Israeli officials approached states including Brazil and Australia: in the case of Brazil, said Eshkol, the country was large enough that once Palestinians arrived there 'no one will even know they exist'.[95] In 1969 Israel signed a clandestine agreement with Paraguay to provide 60,000 Palestinians with work visas which would be valid in four South American countries. On leaving, Palestinians were required to sign a form declaring, in Hebrew and Arabic, that they departed willingly and understood that they would not be able to return without a special permit.[96] 'Few Israelis knew of the transfer project,' writes Tom Segev: 'Everything was done secretly, as if it were something to be ashamed of.'[97] The two governments operated furtively, confirms Raviv: 'After all, it was a conspiracy.'[98] The project collapsed after only a handful of Palestinians had been induced to participate.

Bantustan Palestine

Movements out of Gaza soon diminished: in the period after the 1967 war just 31,000 Palestinians 'emigrated', mostly women, children and dependent older relatives travelling to Jordan and Syria with the aim of maintaining the integrity of family networks.[99] Over the next two decades, permanent 'transfer' of Palestinians became less important for the Israeli state than availability of cheap and vulnerable Arab labour. By 1988, 100,000 Palestinians from the West Bank and Gaza were at work in Israel, most in low-paying jobs. Forty percent of all construction workers and one in six farm workers in Israel were Palestinians, most as day-labourers who commuted from their homes.[100] Shir Hever writes that certain areas, especially in the big cities, became gathering places that Israelis nicknamed 'slave markets':

> Palestinian workers would wait in these areas for hours, hoping to be picked up for work. Those who were picked up (those judged by the contractors to be young, fit and hard-working), would be paid for a single day of work, with no guarantees for another day of employment and no social benefits whatsoever. Those who weren't picked up had to return home empty-handed, after wasting half a day.[101]

The West Bank and Gaza were now closed zones in which economic activity was shaped by Israel's political agenda and economic priorities. Sara Roy identifies a process of 'de-development' in which Palestinian labour was readily exploited by Israeli employers while Palestinian communities provided markets for all manner of Israeli goods, anchoring the Territories in the Israeli economy and in Israel's wider trade relations.[102] Change was rapid: by 1974, Palestinians' earnings in Israel amounted to a quarter of GNP in Gaza and the West Bank;[103] by 1988, the Territories had become Israel's second-largest 'export' market.[104] Drawing on histories of southern Africa, the Territories were said to be undergoing 'bantustanisation' – transformation into de facto labour reserves.[105] A Palestinian bantustan, suggested Azmi Bishara, was 'a place that lacks sovereignty and at the same time is not part of Israel. It is neither one nor the other'.[106] In the mode of controls exercised under the Pass Laws of South Africa's apartheid regime, African workers were monitored by complex regulations on movement. In South Africa successive governments had shaped the bantustans to serve labour policy: African workers were to be supplied in huge numbers to serve employers in the apartheid state. In the case of Israel, the Territories were abruptly integrated into the economy, the process of bantustanisation an outcome of strategies of control and of racist policies of exclusion. Palestinians lacked protections provided for Israeli workers: excluded from the Histadrut, they were irresistible to Israeli employers seeking cheap and easily disposable labour. In 1977 workers from the Territories received on average 40 percent of wages paid to Israelis in comparable jobs.[107] Ten years later average incomes in Israel were four times higher than in the West Bank and ten times higher than in Gaza.[108] One Israeli organisation described Gaza as 'the labour camp of Tel Aviv...the Soweto of the State of Israel'.[109]

In the 1970s colonial projects constructed worldwide by European powers were 'in remission', writes Hever; in the case of Israel, however, colonisation proceeded apace, as settler enclaves were constructed within zones in which the population was subordinated by a military regime.[110] Israeli forces protected fortified sites in which settlers enjoyed lives of privilege. In Gaza the Jewish population constituted 0.4 percent of the population: each settler had access to 2.6 acres of land while Palestinians of the territory had on average 0.006 of an acre, living in densely populated areas that were among the most overcrowded worldwide.[111] Settlers consumed on average 19 times more water than Palestinian residents of the camps, most of whom had no regular water supply and no mains drainage.[112] Israeli troops patrolled borders of the Territories and the streets of Palestinian camps and towns; Israeli administrators ran legal and educational institutions. The occupation attempted forcefully to suppress Palestinian identity: it was illegal to organise independent trade unions, school or university associations, to fly the Palestinian flag, to distribute or even read 'subversive' (nationalist) literature.

Resistance nonetheless continued: Raviv describes armed attacks on Israeli troops and civilians as 'a routine sight' even during the earliest days of the occupation,[113] so that during 1969 alone there were almost 500 attacks on Israeli targets.[114] At the same time, there were repeated mass protests: as in the 1930s, young women at high school were among the most prominent activists. Using civil disobedience tactics, they attended school in the morning, then exited their classrooms together, marching through the streets with resistance slogans and raising forbidden Palestinian flags. Israeli forces saw a serious challenge, turning high-pressure water hoses on demonstrators, arresting leaders, and beating demonstrators with clubs. 'But', says Raviv, 'the demonstrations, just as the armed resistance, persisted.'[115]

Throughout the 1970s and into the 1980s there were countless episodes of protest. Between 1977 and 1982 protests averaged 3,700 a year.[116] Once more Israeli turned to techniques learned from the British colonial regime, repeatedly imposing collective punishments: between 1985 and 1987 alone more than 100 Palestinian homes were demolished.[117] More and more often the Israelis encountered Palestinian youth – young women and men who were members of an Occupation Generation that knew only the experience of repression. In Gaza, the number of people aged 25-34 doubled in a decade; by 1987 those under the age of 14 made up half of all residents. Schools and university campuses were key battlegrounds: many students were killed by Israeli troops, thousands were arrested and beaten, hundreds imprisoned without trial. Increasingly *al-shabab* – 'the youth'/'the guys' – stood their ground. Steeled by years of confrontation with the police and the army, youth resistance erupted into mass defiance – and in 1987 into a powerful new intifada.[118]

Chapter 8
Intifada renewed

Intifada and struggles from below. Solidarity, Arab regimes and the ministate

The intifada that began on 8 December 1987 was one of the great mass movements of the 20th century. Initiated in Gaza, it quickly spread to the West Bank and soon involved Palestinian citizens of Israel. For six years a movement organised from below engaged youth, women, workers, peasants, Bedouin – every area of Palestinian society became active in ways that profoundly disturbed the Israeli state. As protests began, Haidar Abdel-Shafi, head of the Palestinian Red Crescent, observed that 'the slightest spark ignites a fire': there was a 'chain of confrontation' across the country', he said.[1]

Israeli Defence Minister Yitzak Rabin ordered reinforcements into the Territories, pledging to crush the uprising. But within days Palestinians in Israel had called a general strike in solidarity, confronting police in towns such as Jaffa, Akka and Lidd. Israelis were stunned: for the first time since the 1930s, all Palestinian Arab communities were mobilising to support their national rights. Israeli leaders had thought the PLO, and by extension the national movement as a whole, had been defeated. A few years earlier the IDF and its allies of the Lebanese Right had expelled Palestinian guerrilla forces from Beirut and occupied swathes of territory in Lebanon's south. Undefended, Palestinian camps had been assaulted and massacres had been perpetrated by the right-wing Kataeb. Now Rabin declared:

> Gaza and Hebron, Ramallah and Nablus [all in the Occupied Territories] are not and never will become Beirut, Sidon and Tyre [former PLO guerrilla strongholds in Lebanon]...here we shall fight united and with all our strength, and it is great, against every force that tries by violent means to undermine our full control of Judea, Samaria and the Gaza Strip.[2]

An 'iron fist' policy, similar to that which had been imposed in Lebanon, would be put into operation in the West Bank and Gaza, said Rabin. Israeli troops were to use 'force, power and blows' against demonstrators: 'We will make clear who is running the Territories', he insisted. 'We are adamant that violence will not achieve political ends'.[3] But the IDF could not suppress the movement: its heavy weapons proved ineffective against young activists armed with catapults and stones. Soon the *Jerusalem Post* observed:

> The streets, both in Gaza and the West Bank, and in East Jerusalem, are thus in effective control of the youth. It is a situation of our 20-year-olds battling their 20-year-olds – ours using armour, helicopters and guns; theirs, clubs, rocks and primitive Molotov cocktails.[4]

One account suggests that during the early stages of the uprising Israel placed more troops in the Territories to manage the intifada than it took to capture them from the Arab armies in 1967.[5] Still resistance continued. Israeli leaders resolved to starve the Palestinians into submission. Once more using tactics learned from the British Mandate regime – and which were to be implemented at terrible cost in 2023 – they imposed curfews on camps in Gaza. Food and water became scarce; meanwhile troops attacked residents in their homes and Israeli planes dropped gas canisters from the air. Thousands of Palestinians were seized and imprisoned; by mid-January 1988 at least 50 had been killed.[6] Still the intifada gathered momentum: Palestinian workers took prolonged strike action, refusing to work in Israel. For the first time in decades, industrial workers demonstrated the impact of collective action: in Israel, employers appealed to the government to find labour for construction, to operate hotels and restaurants, and to harvest fruit and vegetables.

Sparked by the killing of Palestinians in Gaza by Israeli troops, the uprising had begun spontaneously. At the same time, it was an expression of long-term developments – not only sustained repression but also the emergence of networks that for years contested the occupation by establishing groups focused on self-reliance and local collaboration. Often led by radical activists, volunteers reclaimed and cultivated land, paved roads, fixed sewage, cleaned streets, and improved conditions in the camps and the poorest areas. Husain Jameel Bargouti describes how these initiatives became the basis for popular committees that led the intifada:

> The VWCs [Voluntary Work Committees] were based on democracy, not bureaucracy: there were no headquarters, no official documents, no 'orders' and no fixed plans which could not be changed at any moment by the volunteers directly involved in implementing them. The simplicity, efficiency, flexibility, democracy and diffused leadership of the VWCs have been sources of inspiration in the formation of the popular committees of the uprising.[7]

Self-reliance was a response to the economic domination of the Territories by Israel. The West Bank and Gaza had become captive markets for Israeli products. By 1986 they imported $780.3 million of Israeli goods – 89.4 percent of all imports into the Territories.[8] At the same time, Israel imposed quotas on the types and quantities of goods from the Territories that could be exported to Israel, banning completely the sale of some products. Over two decades economic activity in the Territories had been shaped to the needs of Israeli capitalism, so that local agriculture and industry stagnated, radically reducing employment opportunities and compelling Palestinians to seek employment elsewhere, primarily in Israel. By 1987, says Israeli researcher Zeev Rosenhek, 108,900 Palestinians were commuting from the Territories to work in Israel; at least a third were 'irregular' workers without work permits, their vulnerability to the authorities encouraging employers to pay the lowest wages and to evade regulations on employment rights:

> [T]he incorporation of Palestinian non-citizens [from the West Bank and Gaza] conformed with the interests of most Israeli political actors. It provided employers and the Israeli economy in general with cheap and unprotected workers who helped to restrain wage levels and to increase private sector profits... [I]ncorporation of Palestinian workers was in line with important political interests of the Israeli state concerning management of the occupation and the conflict with the Palestinians.[9]

At the same time, Israel effectively banned trade union organisation – harassing and intimidating Palestinian activists and closing union offices. Workers' organisation went underground, strengthening clandestine networks and nationalist loyalties. The combined effect of Israeli policies was to stimulate rapid growth of grassroots organisations. Samih Farsoun and Jean Landis comment that efforts to atomise, degrade, control, and dispossess a native population triggered 'a dialectical oppositional response'.[10] As the struggle intensified, Palestinian unity strengthened, developing a determined movement of the oppressed against a colonial oppressor.[11] As in earlier mass movements, says Nadia Nasar-Najjab, women played a prominent role, 'far removed from the symbolic appointment of women to political positions or the ongoing fixation of international organisations on 'empowering' Palestinian women'.[12] Participants in the uprising describe how, due to Israeli misconceptions about Palestinian women's role and the targeting of men, 'women were present in the public sphere leading, organising and mobilising protests and activities'.[13]

When the intifada began, resistance committees were established across the West Bank and Gaza. These soon combined as the Unified National Leadership of the Uprising (UNLU), committing to the PLO and the exile leadership but maintaining freedom of decision-making that marked the movement as different from the centralised structures of the armed Resistance. UNLU co-ordinated across the Territories, with strikes and boycotts of Israeli goods, extending the campaign for Palestinian self-sufficiency. 'The campaign has a role for every Palestinian', said one report from the West Bank:

> The multiplicity of modes of struggle politicises the most mundane aspects of life and expands enormously the number of active participants in the intifada beyond those directly engaged in stone-throwing or formal political organising.[14]

Such was the effectiveness of the boycott movement that within six months Israeli 'exports' to the Occupied Territories had halved.[15] The movement was resilient: when the Israeli authorities declared all popular committees to be illegal and intensified repression, the uprising maintained its momentum. After 12 months, Israel's Deputy Chief of Staff Ehud Barak reported that the army had used an average of 10,000 troops each day, investing 3.5 million days in attempts to suppress the uprising.[16] They had failed, although at heavy cost to people of the Territories: by December 1988 at least 30,000 Palestinians had been seized by Israeli troops; by February 1989 the IDF had killed one in every 3,300 people of the West Bank and Gaza.[17]

Co-optation – the Village Leagues

Continuing resistance defied direct repression by Israel and its efforts to create a layer of local collaborators through the Movement of Palestinian Leagues, widely known as the Village Leagues. Drawing on colonial practices worldwide, notably British strategies of 'indirect rule', the Likud government of the 1970s attempted to co-opt community leaders, bypassing elected local councils and refusing development aid and infrastructural support unless these came through bodies that rewarded Palestinians prepared to distance themselves from the PLO leadership. The strategy also recalled efforts by the Jewish Agency in the 1920s to establish a 'Farmers Party' in the Nazareth, Nablus, and Hebron regions as an alternative to the traditional Palestinian leadership which, deeply conservative, was nonetheless seen as an obstacle to growth of the early settler movement. In both cases, writes Salim Tamari, the Agency and then the Israeli state attempted to use 'all internal political factions' within Palestinian society, especially religious differences and clan rivalries.[18] The Leagues were said by their leaders to be the 'vanguard of the peace forces in the West Bank and Gaza – whose historic task is to mobilise the Palestinian people in a peace movement...against bigotry and [Palestinian] terrorism'.[19] Israel provided them with their own budgets, uniformed militias, prison cells and interrogation centres, and a bi-weekly newspaper: in effect the Leagues were a sustained attempt to develop an armed rural alternative to the nationalist movement. The main objective, said a leading collaborator, was to fight against PLO influence and to negotiate on behalf of the Palestinians with the state of Israel.[20] The policy failed, Israel recruiting largely marginal figures from a small number of villages. Efforts to manipulate religious differences by focusing on predominantly Christian communities, comments Tamari, marked the futility of relying on confessional-based politics in a society that had achieved a relatively high degree of secularisation and nationalist identification.[21]

The initiative also struggled against the background of a different Israeli policy – the intensification of settlement in the West Bank and Gaza under Israeli Prime Minister Menachem Begin, a zealous coloniser eager to extend the Jewish presence across the Territories. From the mid-1970s settlements proliferated, constructed in the West Bank on high ground above Palestinian villages and – as a precise strategy – separating Palestinian lands. At the same time the government approved construction of large urban settlements that attracted residents of Tel Aviv and Jerusalem seeking subsidised homes and easy commuting. Gorenberg comments that 'the settlement effort spurred Palestinian nationalism – and was also spurred by it'.[22] For the most energetic proponents of colonisation such as Gush Emunim, continuing Palestinian resistance increased the urgency of securing what they called 'The Whole Land'. By 1986 Israel had confiscated or brought under military control over 52 percent of land in the West Bank and between 30 and 40 percent of land in Gaza.[23] By 1987, there were 18 settlements in Gaza and 118 across the West Bank – a 'creeping' de facto annexation of the Territories.[24]

'Butcher of Beirut'

During the 1980s new networks of resistance had emerged in which young Palestinians were particularly active. Fouad Mougrabi observed, 'The new generation of Palestinian youth has iron in its soul. It has shown moral courage in defying the occupation and has fashioned from existing cultural materials new ways of resistance and political behaviour.'[25] Joost Hiltermann comments that local organisations generated their own leadership, 'elected routinely in the democratic process, who would promptly pledge their allegiance to the PLO'.[26] Relationships between the armed Resistance, based since 1970 in Lebanon, and people of the Occupied Territories had for years been viewed as a major problem for Israel. In 1982 Israeli strategists proposed that by attacking and decapitating the armed movement in Lebanon they would strike at the heart of Palestinian nationalism. Emboldened by the quick victory of the 1967 war they anticipated a deadly strike against guerrilla bases in Beirut and south Lebanon, and tighter control in the West Bank and Gaza, facilitating the process of colonisation. Sending a massive invasion force into Lebanon in June 1982 they assaulted bases of the Resistance and eventually expelled guerrilla forces from Beirut.

The offensive was facilitated by increasingly close relations between Israel and the US. American President Ronald Reagan had declared that revolution in Iran in 1979 re-emphasised the importance of Israel as America's key ally in the Middle East:

> Our own position would be weaker without the political and military assets Israel provides… [T]he fall of Iran [sic] has increased Israel's value as perhaps the only true remaining strategic asset in the region on which the United States can truly rely.[27]

American military supplies to Israel rose in proportion to the Pentagon's fears for its interests in the Gulf, where Iranian revolution had inspired an uprising in Saudi Arabia in 1979 and an Iraqi invasion of Iran's southern provinces in 1981. Washington increased supplies of advanced weaponry to Israel, much in the form of direct grants. When Israel revealed to the US in 1982 that it intended to invade Lebanon, its leaders received supportive messages – Secretary of State Alexander Haig telling Prime Minister Begin that 'no one has the right to tell Israel what decision she must make in order to defend her people'.[28] Similar messages from American leaders to their Israeli counterparts were to become routine – up to and including the offensive on Gaza launched in October 2023. In June 1982 an invasion force of 40,000 troops entered Lebanon from the south, supported by hundreds of tanks, aircraft and naval vessels.[29] The PLO and its Lebanese allies faced an immense challenge, although their continuous resistance slowed the attack. One Israeli military correspondent wrote that the steadfastness and motivation of the guerrillas 'must stir within us uneasy feelings':

> The PLO fighters whom we had treated as rejects showed in this war a tenacity and intelligence which should not be underestimated. Israeli soldiers, who have shown contempt for the fedayeen for years, have tasted this truth in the most bitter way.[30]

The Israelis eventually encircled Beirut, together with the Kataeb and other right-wing militias. For 70 days the west of the city was bombarded from land, sea and air in a siege that provided precedents for many later assaults on Gaza: some 2,500 people were killed by this barrage.[31] In August 1982 PLO militias were expelled – some 14,000 Palestinian fighters were evacuated by sea to countries including Tunisia, where the PLO set up a new headquarters. Palestinian communities in Lebanon were now undefended. In September the Kataeb and an Israeli proxy force, the South Lebanon Army, murdered between 1,500 and 3,500 people in the Sabra neighbourhood and nearby Shatila refugee camp in West Beirut. They were supported by the IDF, which closed exits from the area and provided illumination with flares during night-time killings which, said Israeli human rights activist Amnon Kapeliouk, were 'planned in advance and executed in cold blood'.[32] An international commission later concluded that Israel bore responsibility, declaring the events a form of genocide.[33] Under international pressure, an Israeli investigation – the Kahane Commission – identified the IDF as 'indirectly' responsible, forcing Defence Minister Ariel Sharon to resign. Sharon – the 'Butcher of Beirut' – was later to become prime minister, to ignite the Palestinian intifada of 2000, to direct savage attacks on the people of the West Bank and Gaza, and to initiate construction of Israel's apartheid wall.

Solidarity and emulation

Menachem Begin had declared that removing the PLO from Lebanon would bring secure treaties with Israel's neighbours and would provide '40 years of peace'.[34] But resistance in the West Bank and Gaza intensified: activist networks proliferated, with women and young people particularly prominent, and in December 1987 mass defiance became an intifada. The *Guardian* commented: 'The uprising has succeeded brilliantly in many ways – most of all in putting the Palestinian cause back on top of the international agenda and creating unprecedented unity in Palestinian ranks'.[35] It had a profound impact across the Arab world. Within days there were demonstrations of support in Algeria, Tunisia, Morocco, Bahrain, Kuwait, Lebanon, Jordan and – most important – in Egypt. Soon the solidarity movement spread to Sudan and to Turkey.

The uprising confirmed a process at work for decades: Palestinian resistance to British colonialism and later to Israel inspired solidarity and highlighted the character of imperialism, with implications for regimes across the Middle East. In 1968 Palestinian resilience at the Battle of Karama stood in contrast to the failure of Arab armies and the humiliation of defeat in the 1967 war. Then Palestinians had appeared as a model of anti-imperialist struggle against the odds. In 1987 an even more potent image rallied millions of people: youth of the Occupied Territories armed only with stones confronted Israeli forces backed by the US and its allies. Now the Palestinian headscarf – the *kufiyya* – became a symbol of resistance to Israel, to imperialism and to the oppression of rulers across the region. The uprising made plain that struggles for liberation were possible against all odds. Despite assaults on the guerrilla movement, Palestinians remained intensely active, their intifada a catalyst for resistance to ruling classes across the region.

Arab regimes identified the danger. After three weeks of the uprising, President Assad of Syria organised a solidarity rally in Damascus. The Syrian regime had a long record of duplicity and hostility towards the Palestinians. Its Saiqa militia was a dangerous, unreliable element within the PLO; in 1970 its forces stood aside during Jordan's Black September assault; and in 1976 the Syrian army attacked Palestinians in Lebanon. 'Support for Arafat in Syria is tantamount to high treason,' wrote Khalid Qassem.[36] Millions of Syrians nonetheless expressed their support for the imagination and persistence of 'the "revolt of the stone-throwers"'.[37] Recognising the implications of popular support, President Hafez al-Assad hurried to organise solidarity rallies. Qassem observed:

> The government here, as throughout the Arab world, has been left to play catchup or clampdown to stem the tide of anti-government sentiment spurred by its [the intifada's] success... [A]s self-styled leader of Arab forces of 'progress and confrontation' [with Israel] Syria is playing catch-up and co-opt as hard as anyone.[38]

As the intifada intensified Assad brought prominent PLO leaders onto public platforms and television screens alongside government spokesmen and declared 12 February 1988 a 'voluntary workday' to benefit the uprising.[39] In Algeria a similar government-sponsored rally was attended by Yasser Arafat of Fatah, George Habash of the PFLP, and Nayef Hawatmeh of the DFLP.[40] But the regimes' formal support for the Palestinians was not enough for millions of people stimulated by the Palestinian movement. In Tunisia, which now hosted the headquarters of the PLO, an unofficial demonstration of support was attacked by police. When leaflets calling for solidarity action were distributed in Baghdad, Iraqi police arrested Palestinians in the city. When students in Fez, Morocco, organised a demonstration, troops attacked, killing several participants. In Amman, Jordan, an unofficial march was assaulted by police, and students at Yarmouk University, Irbid, were arrested alongside hundreds of Palestinian activists elsewhere in the country. In February 1988 Kuwaiti ruler Shaikh Jaber al-Ahmad al-Sabah praised 'the blessed resistance [in Palestine]' and donated $5 million to the nationalist cause. Police then broke up a demonstration in Kuwait City. The Kuwaiti newspaper *Al-Ra'i al-'Am*, giving the official view, observed: 'Such demonstrations could be exploited by those who fish in troubled water to create disturbances.'[41]

The intifada prompted international solidarity and the potential for emulation. It was subversive of Arab regimes, among which many also owed their continued existence to imperialism, to weaponry supplied by the US and its allies, and to intelligence services, troops and training programmes provided with the aim of securing corporate assets and strategic interests. Across the region these states, and others that had earlier implemented radical nationalist reforms, were now strongly influenced by the neoliberal agenda and drawn relentlessly towards the priorities of western capitalism. Collating reports from across the region, London-based *Mideast Mirror* commented:

> Official expressions of support throughout the Arab world for the Palestinians and the current Uprising are legion but private enterprise demonstrations bring a chill to ruling bones and are actively discouraged.[42]

'Demonstrations are impermissible'

Protests continued to spread. In mid-February police broke up a demonstration in Istanbul, Turkey; in March thousands marched in protest to the American embassy in Khartoum, Sudan, during a general strike called in support of the uprising.[43] In Egypt demonstrations had begun in December 1987 and continued for months – a special case of solidarity with profound implications for the Palestinian movement. Here the regime of President Husni Mubarak had banned all forms of protest. The issue of Palestine was particularly sensitive, highlighting contentious relations with Israel – officially 'at peace' with Egypt since 1978 – and Mubarak's close relationship with Washington. For more than a decade Egypt had been a key site in the Global South for imposition of neoliberal economic policies. Since the introduction in 1974 of the 'open door' policy (*al-infitah*) encouraged by the International Monetary Fund (IMF), Egypt had been a pioneer in efforts to dismantle the state sector in favour of private capital. Economic and social reforms introduced under the Nasser regime had been abandoned in favour of local business and of global corporations and financial institutions. Government-supported food subsidies were reduced year-by-year, wages fell and public services decayed while state repression intensified.[44] President Anwar al-Sadat, architect of the 'open door', had been fortunate to survive a national uprising in 1977 – an 'intifada of bread' involving millions of people infuriated by the greed of a voracious bourgeoisie often described as Egypt's 'fat cats'.[45] Mubarak had since received unprecedented American military support – supplies of weaponry were exceeded only by those provided to Israel. With public protest banned and tens of thousands of oppositionists – notably Muslim activists – imprisoned, Egypt was in a state of high tension. The intifada, initiated in Gaza on Egypt's border, was greeted with huge public enthusiasm and by regime anxiety that the Palestinians might encourage an Egyptian movement of similar potential.

Under Sadat, Egypt had been the first Arab state to recognise Israel and the regime was widely seen as having abandoned the Palestinians. Official Egyptian media for years disseminated views of 'the bad Palestinian' which aimed, writes Karem Yahia, 'to justify in Egyptian eyes the separate peace with Israel':

> Attitudes of the following sort began to flourish: the Palestinians sold their land to the Jews and are therefore solely responsible for their tragedy; the Palestinians live like millionaires and profit from their national cause; ignorant and backward Arabs are envious of Egypt's stability and superiority and want to fight Israel to the last Egyptian; the wars Egypt waged against Israel 'for Palestine' are responsible for its economic woes, so peace should bring prosperity; and so on… Palestinian organizations were referred to as 'terrorist,' and the Palestinian leadership was judged 'misguided,' 'cut off from the people,' made up of 'agents of Arab and foreign regimes,' even 'nightclub militants,' and other insulting epithets. Meanwhile, the image of the Israeli had undergone parallel changes within the framework of the cultural normalization policy, and the media abandoned the long-utilized words and formulas derogatory to Israel.[46]

Following Israel's invasion of Lebanon in 1982 there was somewhat more favourable coverage, but the Egyptian regime and a compliant media remained deeply suspicious of Palestinian struggles. Despite opposition from Arafat, in April 1987 the Palestine National Council (the Palestinian parliament-in-exile) criticised the 1978 Camp David accords between Egypt, Israel and the US, and Mubarak immediately ordered closure of all PLO offices in Egypt. When the intifada began nine months later Egyptian media began to report from Gaza and the West Bank but as the uprising continued the regime clamped down. Scenes from Palestine disappeared from television screens and

Egyptian newspapers: at the same time, a nationwide movement of solidarity emerged, defying the regime and soon meeting intense repression. Demonstrators supporting the Palestinians were attacked by police in the streets, on university campuses and at mosques. From Cairo, the *Los Angeles Times* reported:

> Bullets fired by Israeli troops to quell the disturbances have echoed loudly here in Egypt, Israel's largest neighbor and peace treaty partner...a popular revolt by fellow Arabs against an unwanted occupation and the disadvantaged economic, social and political conditions that occupation imposes upon them.[47]

Solidarity was becoming emulation as Egyptians targeted 'disadvantaged economic, social and political conditions' imposed by their own rulers. On 30 December 1987 hundreds of demonstrators in Mehalla al-Kubra, an industrial city in the Nile Delta, fought the police and marched to the local headquarters of the ruling National Democratic Party. Mehalla was the site of the largest workplace in Egypt, Misr Spinning and Weaving, a textile mill with a workforce of 40,000 and a history of struggle going back to the 1930s. Here slogans in support of the Palestinians were combined with demands for Egypt to break links with Israel. The government was declared a servant of the West and there were calls to bring down President Mubarak.[48] The *Los Angeles Times* observed:

> Mindful of the riots over food prices here 10 years ago [the 'intifada of bread'] and of the rebellion by thousands of police conscripts only two years ago, the government is particularly allergic now to street demonstrations of any kind.[49]

Egypt's Interior Minister, Zaki Badr, announced that he would not allow protests 'to provoke domestic unrest' and that he would use force against 'any irresponsible attempt by hooligans under the pretext of supporting the Palestinians'.[50] Egypt backed the Palestinian people, he said, 'but the government will not permit this situation to be used in sabotage and incitement'.[51] There were more demonstrations

– the regime was involved in a running battle with activists as Badr declared that 'Leftists and Muslim activists are plotting to subvert the government'.[52] On 6 January 1988 students fought police at Ain Shams University in Cairo and riot police surrounded the headquarters of the Lawyers Syndicate where a meeting nonetheless established a Popular National Committee for Solidarity with the Palestinian People. A week later, meetings at Ain Shams denounced 'the regime's capitulationist policies' regarding Israel and the US, Mubarak's submission to IMF demands 'to starve the Egyptian people', and his repression of the solidarity movement.[53] The next day 200 students were arrested at the University of Alexandria and further conflict at Ain Shams resulted in detention without trial of 250 participants.[54] Badr declared: 'I will sever any foot that attempts to march in demonstrations…demonstrations are impermissible even if peaceful in support of the Palestinian people in the occupied lands and we will meet this with all our firmness.'[55] When hundreds of Egyptian demonstrators assembled at Rafah on the border with Gaza in a show of solidarity they were attacked by troops using live fire. Protests continued until the regime gradually regained control.

The 'ministate'

The solidarity movement in Egypt had engaged large numbers of students, professionals including lawyers and journalists, and industrial workers. It was inhibited, however, by the leadership of the cause that participants wished to support. As demonstrations in Egypt continued, Yasser Arafat visited Kuwait, where he made a personal effort to smooth relations with the regime. He praised Kuwaiti rulers' formal support for the intifada, in effect condemning local solidarity activists and strengthening the position of those in the local Palestinian community who had declared public mobilisation 'a tactical mistake'.[56] He also visited Cairo several times – not to endorse solidarity action but to confer with Egyptian leaders, among them Interior Minister Zaki Badr, resolute enemy of the mass of Egyptians and who was later to call for the expulsion of all Palestinians from Egypt.[57]

Arafat substituted for mass action the prospect of diplomatic manoeuvre. He had emerged from battles in Lebanon still in control of the PLO, although the organisation was weakened and in rapid decline. Tareq Ismael comments that the eventual demise of his leadership and of the PLO itself appeared inevitable. 'It seemed that Palestinian nationalism had run its course', Ismael observes, until in December 1987 the intifada restored legitimacy to the movement and to Arafat's flagging leadership. As the uprising progressed Arafat advanced a plan consistent with Fatah's policy of 'non-interference' – he would use instability associated with the uprising to secure the status of the PLO among the Arab states. His close colleague Khalil al-Wazir (Abu Jihad) observed that some Arab regimes were 'more afraid than Israel of what is happening in the occupied homeland'.[58] Fatah aimed to mobilise these anxieties to strengthen the exiled PLO leadership, and in June 1988, at an emergency summit of the Arab League in Algiers, Arab leaders who had assaulted movements of solidarity with the uprising combined to salute its achievements. They reported to the UN:

> The Conference hailed the uprising of the Palestinian Arab people, which constituted a link in the chain of its struggle that has continued for more than half a century... The Conference also hailed with pride and admiration the acts of heroism performed by the Palestinian people in resisting the Israeli occupation and that people's magnificent resolve to liberate its occupied territory and exercise its right to return, its right to self-determination and its right to establish its independent State on its national soil, under the leadership of the Palestine Liberation Organization, its sole legitimate representative.[59]

The summit pledged to provide huge sums of money to the PLO, 21 states agreeing to deliver more than $350 million for the year, in addition to individual state donations. The quid pro quo was a renewal of commitments by the Fatah leadership to 'non-interference' and to politics by means of cautious diplomacy.

Arafat was compelled to address a new situation in which Palestinians of the West Bank and Gaza 'had claimed for themselves a vanguard role'.[60] Grassroots leaders had activated the uprising: few, however, had emerged at the level of national leadership. This reflected intense Israeli repression, including policies like those earlier imposed by the British in Mandate Palestine. Many leading activists had been deported, an approach intensified by Yitzak Rabin as part of his 'Iron Fist' strategy. Helena Cobban writes:

> The net political effect of these deportations was similar to that of earlier waves of deportations: they drove the resident wing of the nationalist movement [in the West Bank and Gaza] deeper underground and broadened its organizational dispersion while increasing the residents' reliance on the diaspora for overall leadership.[61]

Cobban observes that among leading figures remaining in the Territories who were able to conduct public politics neither traditional leaders (the 'old notables'), nor those she calls 'the nationalist intellectuals', attempted to supplant the PLO leadership.[62] The intifada nonetheless posed serious problems for Arafat and the Fatah leaders. Mass struggle had weakened their status within the national movement, which was now also challenged by the growing influence of Islamist currents in the form of Hamas and Islamic Jihad (see Chapter 9). They also faced intense pressure from Arab regimes which sought urgently to bring under control a movement that was destabilising the whole region. Cobban observes that PLO leaders sought 'to harness the tremendous power of the intifada' with a key aim: 'To seek entry to a negotiation through which the occupation would end and to establish a Palestinian state in the West Bank and Gaza'.[63]

As the intifada progressed, Fatah leaders pursued manoeuvres that would soon lead to historic developments – to PLO recognition of Israel, its legitimacy and rights to Palestinian land, and to plans for a 'ministate' in the form of a Palestinian entity on a fraction of the historic homeland. Randa Farah comments that, 'Most analysts today look back at the intifada and observe that it was hijacked by Arafat'.[64] In fact the Fatah leaders had been working for years to revise the movement's original project of national liberation. In the early 1970s PLO leaders had issued a 'working paper' proposed by Fatah that called for recognition of the right of Palestinians 'to establish a national authority on any lands that can be wrested from Zionist occupation'.[65] This set out Palestinian political goals as: (1) the strategic goal of total liberation and independence; and (2) 'the present and direct goals' of forcing Israel to withdraw from the West Bank and Gaza where an 'independent authority' could be established.[66] A Palestinian 'authority', says Arafat's biographer Alan Hart, was 'agreed PLO code' for a 'ministate' – a Palestinian entity in the West Bank and Gaza in return for which the national movement would recognise Israel in its 1967 borders.[67] This excluded from the Palestinian future millions of people of the diaspora, including those living in camps outside historic Palestine; it made implausible the prospect of return of refugees; and it reconciled the national movement to the presence of a colonial state with claims of sovereign rights to Palestine. Hart points out that the ministate policy 'would require the Palestinians to accept the loss, perhaps for all time, of 70 percent of their original homeland':

> If in 1974 Arafat and his senior colleagues had openly admitted the true extent of the compromise they were prepared to make, it and they would have been repudiated by an easy majority of the Palestinians who were actually engaged in the liberation struggle.[68]

There were strong reactions against the plan among the most deprived members of the diaspora, especially in the refugee camps of Lebanon where the armed resistance recruited extensively. Salah Khalaf (Abu Iyad) later recalled that in Tal al-Zaater camp in Beirut he found 'to my amazement the walls of this desperately poor shanty town plastered with slogans denouncing the Palestinian ministate'.[69] Fatah leaders were focused on a different audience. As early as 1974 they had won support at a conference of Arab leaders in Morocco which resolved:

> To affirm the right of the Palestinian people to establish an independent national authority under the command of the Palestine Liberation Organisation, the sole legitimate representative of the Palestinian people, in any territory that is liberated. This authority, once it is established, shall enjoy the support of the Arab states in all fields and at all levels.[70]

Here, for the first time, the PLO had in effect been recognised by Arab rulers as a Palestinian state-in-exile and the ministate placed on the regional agenda. Arafat was jubilant, describing the Arab summit as 'a Palestinian wedding feast'.[71] A month later he spoke at the United Nations in New York appearing, he said, with 'the olive branch and the freedom fighter's gun'. The PLO was admitted to the UN with observer status and a host of states granted the organisation full diplomatic status. It was another five years before Fatah could win the Palestine National Council (PNC) fully to the ministate project but in the global arena it considered that key goals had been secured. For Salah Khalaf: 'All our objectives on the international stage had thus been reached.'[72]

'Unthinkable concession'

In 1968 the PNC had affirmed that the aim of the national movement was, 'To liberate the Palestine homeland in its entirety'.[73] The following year it asserted that proposals to establish a Palestinian state on the West Bank were unacceptable because, 'This pseudo-entity will become, in effect, a colony exploited by Israel'.[74] When PLO leaders advanced the idea of just such an 'entity' a few years later, they were offering an 'unthinkable concession', observes Hart.[75] Arafat spent most of the 1970s attempting to sell the idea to the PNC.[76] Using the full weight of Fatah he eventually won a majority at the Council, which in 1979 agreed to provide Arafat with authority to negotiate a ministate in international forums and peace talks. Muhammed Muslih comments that since its founding Fatah had been focused upon 'liberation' and establishment of 'a democratic, non-sectarian, secular Palestine in which Jews, Muslims and Christians would live together as Palestinian citizens with equal rights and duties'.[77] This was now replaced by the aim to establish an 'entity' on a fraction of Palestine, conceding de facto recognition of Israel. The change reflected increased pressure on the PLO from Arab states, suggested Muslih, as leading PLO members argued that it was in the interest of the movement to endorse "solutions' submitted by "our friends" [sic]'.[78] The Soviet Union, now ostensibly allied with the national movement, was also pressuring Arafat and in 1975 the PLO and the Soviet Union declared in a joint statement the right of the Palestinians to 'establish their national state upon the Palestinian land according to U.N. Resolutions'.[79]

Writing in 1980, Edward Said observed that Arafat and his colleagues wielded unmatched authority in the PLO. At the same time, their approach to politics was pragmatic, 'giving much time, attention and skill…to manoeuvring and tactics, much less to ideology and disciplined strategy'.[80] Their energies went into short-term, expedient initiatives while perspectives on the Palestinian future were vague and understanding of relations with world powers was undeveloped. He noted criticisms levelled by radicals within the PLO:

> What is the Fatah vision of the future Palestinian society? Why is there no clear Fatah determination on the problems of imperialism, a determination that eliminates once and for all every kind of flirtation with the United States and its allies? Above all, how long can Palestinian politics led by Fatah get away with a little bit here, a little bit there?[81]

PLO policy was often incoherent, said Said, too often influenced by changing relations with states of the region, each eager 'to assure itself of some sort of influence, proxy voice or an actual party at work in Palestinian politics'.[82] What were Arafat's intentions? Where was the PLO going?

Arafat had never been viewed as corrupt or focused on personal material advance. Although he had been wealthy during his years in Kuwait, he was known for an austere lifestyle and continuous, intensive activity on behalf of the national movement. He was also ambitious, however, for a Palestinian state, 'entity', or 'authority' that mirrored modern Arab states, even if established on a fraction of historic Palestine. His expectation was of a Palestine that would be part of the established order in the Middle East. Here, Palestinians would conduct relations with other states as equals and Arafat, as president, would enjoy status similar to that of the kings, emirs and presidents of the region. His appearance at the UN in 1974 appeared to confirm Arafat's standing on the international stage: now he jetted from capital to capital across the Middle East, collecting large cheques and handsome promises. But the regimes' support for the Palestinian cause was self-interested and cynical. Said observed that 'the cachet of legitimacy and authority given Arab politicians by a connection with the

Palestinian struggle' was a powerful incentive to provide material and rhetorical backing.[83] There was a contradiction: 'The Palestinian cause is highest on every Arab government's agenda, but the number of Palestinian dead at every Arab government's hands is appallingly high.'[84]

Contagion

In 1988 the 'pseudo-entity' took on even greater significance. Solidarity action across the Middle East had prompted a group of Arab states to press the US for concessions on the Palestine issue. Washington prevaricated, hoping to maintain business as usual in the region by backing Israel and its repression in the Occupied Territories. But on October 4 another regime was shaken by mass protests – Algeria erupted, as strikes and demonstrations opposed the regime of President Chadli. Hundreds were killed by police and troops and Chadli declared a state of siege. Still the protests continued, led by young people armed with stones in the manner of the Palestinian uprising. *Mideast Mirror* reported: 'Arab leaders don't want an Algerian intifada', adding:

> With the likely spread of Palestinian-type intifadas into their own territories a major concern, Arab kings and presidents have been prompt in sending messages of sympathy and support to beleaguered President Chadli Benjedid.[85]

Events in Algeria were of importance to the US and its allies. The Chadli regime was a key target for the IMF, the World Bank and American foreign policy strategists. For 20 years after the war of liberation from France, Algeria had followed the state capitalist path. As with post-colonial regimes in Egypt and Iraq, key resources were nationalised and power concentrated in the hands of a ruling bureaucracy that had inherited its authority from the Front de Libération Nationale (FLN), once an armed resistance. Successive Algerian governments had aligned with the Soviet Union and the Eastern Bloc, but in the 1980s, with problems of indebtedness and under growing pressure from world financial institutions, Chadli had adopted neoliberal policies that imposed austerity and abruptly increased unemployment.[86] These pressures combined with anger at the regime's repression to produce 'a rupture between the state and the people' – protest at policies that violated the values of the liberation struggle.[87] On demonstrations, banners proclaimed: 'Rise up, Youth', 'Chadli assassin', 'We demand all our rights' and, 'We are men'.[88] Protesters set fire to police stations and kidnapped officials whom they put 'on trial' in the street. There was particular hostility to commission agents and private businesses seen to be profiting from the economic 'opening' – developments seen ten years earlier during the 'intifada of bread' in Egypt.

For months Algerian television had showed scenes of Palestinian youth defying Israeli troops with no more than stones – conduct it endorsed as a legitimate struggle against oppression. When protests erupted in Algerian cities the methods were similar, some demonstrators wearing Palestinian scarves. Former Algerian president Ahmed Ben Bella, long exiled to France, called on the Algerian people 'to unite and take matters into your [own] hands like the Palestinians did in their intifada'.[89] Since President Chadli could only speak 'the language of tanks', the people should resist, said Ben Bella, 'even with stones like the Palestinians'.[90] The Saudi newspaper *al-Sharq al-Awsat*, a mouthpiece for the regime, denounced instability in the region as 'contagious':

> It has become obvious over the past few days that all the Arab countries realise the importance of continuity in beloved Algeria. Hence the eagerness of the leaderships, without exception, to see demagogy contained and peace and stability restored.[91]

In Egypt, Mubarak declared: 'We are as keen on Algeria's stability and security as we are on Egypt's'.[92] Summarising the reactions of rulers across the region, *Mideast Mirror* observed that 'Arab leaders don't want an Algerian intifada', adding: 'the likely spread of Palestinian-like intifadas into their own territories' had prompted kings and presidents to sound the alarm.[93] They lobbied the US, with which many were allied, for an international initiative on the Palestine issue before 'contagion' spread further. Reluctantly, President Reagan – long a passionate supporter of Israel – authorised contact with the PLO and talks with Israel. Arafat responded immediately: for the first time, the PLO recognised Israel and renounced 'terrorism', accepting 'co-existence with Israel in a two-state division of Palestine'.[94] Despite the energies of the intifada, Palestinians were heading towards a 'division' of their land that would end in further tragedy under Arafat – president-in-waiting of a 'pseudo-entity'.

Chapter 9
Hamas intervenes

'New American Century' – neocons, oil and imperialism. Hamas takes the stage

Events in Algeria in 1988 reflected economic and political changes under way worldwide. In the Global South neoliberal measures based on the 'Washington Consensus' aimed to dismantle reforms of the post-colonial era, eroding or reversing nationalisations of industry, finance and commerce, and removing price controls, subsidies, and import tariffs. They were accompanied by 'deregulation' of labour – measures to negate workers' rights and to intensify exploitation of the working class. In the Middle East the neoliberal programme had been pioneered during the 1970s by Egypt's President Sadat. In exchange for loans from the IMF, his *intifah* ('opening') aimed to transfer public assets to private hands – to local capitalists and international corporations, banks and trading companies. It produced years of turmoil as rocketing inflation and rising unemployment brought successive waves of demonstrations and strikes, and in 1977 the 'intifada of bread', which ended only when Sadat mobilised the army against the people. Pressure from Western states, the IMF and the World Bank to implement 'free-market' reforms continued relentlessly, producing a series of upheavals described by Walton and Seddon as 'IMF riots' in countries including Jordan, Tunisia, Lebanon and Algeria.[1]

The drive to impose neoliberal policies was accompanied by renewed determination in the US to secure access to Gulf oil. In the early 1980s world recession, particularly severe in North America, had resulted in a fall in energy use and a decline in oil imports, especially from the Middle East. By the end of the decade demand had surged: at the same time, in Europe oil production from the North Sea was declining and in East Asia expectations of new offshore oil finds had failed to materialise. Projections suggested that Western Europe, Japan and the US were 'on the verge of becoming increasingly dependent on Middle East oil supplies'.[2] In 1991 the US led a large coalition of states – most from

North America and Europe – to war in the Gulf, occupying Kuwait to expel the invading army of Saddam Hussein, president of Iraq. Oil supplies were at stake, together with flows of petrodollars invested by Gulf states that were vital for 'the entire structure of global finance capital, and banking interests'.[3] Gulf investments in the US alone were estimated in the early 1990s at $1 trillion, making a key contribution to American capitalism.[4] President George Bush Senior declared that in a post-communist world, a 'new world order' was emerging and that the US would play an historic role in bringing security and justice to the Middle East, initially by penalising Saddam Hussain of Iraq.[5]

Israel did not participate in the 1991 conflict: it neither took the initiative against Iraq nor received an invitation from Washington to join the 'Desert Storm' coalition. This absence from the battlefield, says Avi Shlaim, marked the conflict as 'the strangest war in Israel's war-scarred history'.[6] The US had determined that to keep Arab states onside Israel should be excluded from the coalition. Israeli forces were on full alert but the order to strike against Iraq never came. Shlaim comments:

> Behind this policy of non-intervention there was a general assessment that the Iraqi invasion would benefit Israel in the short term by focusing international attention on Iraq as the primary source of tension in the area and by letting the Arab world stew in its own juice. There was also the expectation that the crisis would result in an easing of US pressure on Israel to begin negotiations with the Palestinians and revive Israel's role as a strategic partner of the United States in the Middle East.[7]

In Gaza and the West Bank the intifada continued, maintaining extraordinary momentum and denying Israel its aim of undisputed control over the territories. The IDF pursued a shoot-to-kill policy that, according to human rights organisation B'Tselem (the Israeli Information Centre for Human Rights in the Occupied Territories), had by 1990 resulted in 670 deaths and thousands of severe injuries.[8] When the Gulf War began most Palestinians, including those in the Occupied Territories, backed Iraq – seeing in Saddam Hussein an Arab leader whose rhetoric apparently challenged Israel and its allies. The PLO received large donations from Iraq and Saddam Hussein warned Palestinians not to oppose him. Arafat initially adopted an ambiguous position: eventually he declared for Iraq and immediately became 'persona non grata in the Gulf'.[9] After a swift American-led victory over Iraqi forces, Palestinians across the region were victimised. In Kuwait, which had been home to some 300,000 Palestinians, hundreds were arbitrarily arrested, beaten and tortured, leading to many deaths. The majority of Palestinians fled, most to Jordan; others were expelled: within weeks the Palestinian population had been reduced to some 10 percent of its former size. Palestinian deposits in Kuwait banks were seized, together with other assets. Philip Mattar comments: 'Kuwaitis sought to punish the PLO by destroying the Palestinian community.'[10] Some 100,000 Palestinians living in other Gulf states were also expelled as the national movement was ejected from the region in which it had been incubated.[11]

Between 1991 and 1993 the PLO lost some $10 billion: Graham Usher comments that the abrupt halt to Gulf funding 'triggered a dynamic of disintegration throughout the organisation'.[12] Thousands of its officials were laid off, missions abroad were closed, and educational, welfare and social services for refugees were suspended. In the Occupied Territories remittances from the Gulf that for years had been a lifeline for Palestinian families abruptly disappeared. At least 30,000 people who had fled the Gulf arrived in Gaza and the West Bank to find the economy already seriously affected by closures and curfews, and where per capita income now fell to half the level recorded in 1987.[13]

The national movement faced a paradox: at a time when the intifada had summoned mass resistance at a level not seen since the 1930s, winning solidarity across the Middle East, the PLO was gripped by crisis. Its problems were intensified by historic developments in the Soviet Union and Eastern Europe. When the regime in Moscow collapsed and the Eastern bloc disintegrated, PLO leaders were denied the political space in which they had attempted to manoeuvre between Western powers and the state capitalisms of the Soviet Union and its satellites. The Soviet collapse also brought a windfall for Israel, which between 1990 and 1992 received almost 400,000 emigrants, their reception and integration supported by $10 billion in guarantees from the US.[14] Prime Minister Yitzak Shamir celebrated, proposing that their arrival necessitated a 'Big Israel' in order 'to house all the people' and planning 106,000 housing units in the West Bank to accommodate 400,000 settlers.[15] Shamir aimed in particular to settle immigrants in the area around East Jerusalem, where the government intended that demographic engineering would turn the Palestinian Arab majority into a minority.[16] Many young immigrants went straight into combat units in the Israeli army.[17]

Neoconservative alliance

Swift victory over Iraq in 1991 brought general satisfaction in Western capitals. Joshua Rovner wrote:

> The cumulative result was a clear victory for the United States both in terms of brute force and coercion. It had restored the political status quo in the Persian Gulf region while retaining the political support of local Arab regimes. It had kept oil flowing to market. It had compelled Iraq into accepting a serious loss while making substantial concessions.[18]

But some American strategists and politicians were not satisfied. They wanted 'regime change' – the removal of Saddam Hussain and his regime as an exemplary statement of intent for governments that would not comply in full with the Washington Consensus and their own plans for American hegemony. The key critics were members of a neoconservative current that was growing rapidly in influence, boosted by the collapse of the Soviet Union and, in the words of neocon ideologue Francis Fukuyama, 'the end of history' and the triumph of Western capitalism and liberal democracy.[19] They were shortly to establish the Project for a New American Century, dedicated to the principle that 'American leadership is good both for America and for the world'. Its founding principles declared:

> As the 20th century draws to a close, the United States stands as the world's preeminent power. Having led the West to victory in the Cold War, America faces an opportunity and a challenge… We [need] a military that is strong and ready to meet both present and future challenges; a foreign policy that boldly and purposefully promotes American principles abroad; and national leadership that accepts the United States' global responsibilities.[20]

The Middle East featured centrally in these plans: the US was to use all efforts to prompt economic and political change across the region. At the same time, the neocons argued, it should energetically support Israel – a fraternal state that embodied many of their own values. Setting aside conspiracy theories and misplaced (and often antisemitic) ideas about the 'Jewish lobby' in the US, Ilan Peleg and Paul Scham identify close links between American neocons and neo-Revisionist currents in Israel as represented by a succession of leaders including Menachem Begin, Yitzak Shamir and Benjamin Netanyahu:[21]

> In both cases, these movements combined assertive nationalism, unrestrained unilateralism, and unabashed militarism in response to what they viewed as external challenges to their societies, while reflecting at the same time their own internal missionary, 'exceptionalist', position. While the Neo-Revisionist mission has been to establish Greater Israel in the Middle East and the Neoconservative mission (internationally) has been to sustain and enhance US hegemony, largely via a worldwide 'democratization' project, the regional Pax Israeliana and the global Pax Americana have been based on remarkably similar intellectual and ideational foundations.[22]

Right-wing American academic Adam Fuller concurs: a consistent message among American neocons, he observes, is that it is 'imperative' for the US to support Israel's 'existential defence crisis' (ie its military and strategic needs).[23] Neocons continue to believe, he suggests, that Israel 'is of paramount concern to neoconservatives...and should also be important to America'.[24] During the 1990s the neocons and the Israeli right played key roles in shaping American Middle East policy and later the drive to invasion of Afghanistan and Iraq. It was in this context that in 1991 the US initiated talks for 'settlement' of the Palestine issue, what US President George Bush Senior called a 'comprehensive peace' to be grounded in the principle of 'territory for peace'.[25]

At this point the intifada was beginning to falter. Israel had moved to a strategy of targeting individuals and groups of activists, especially by using house demolitions – an approach inherited from the British Mandate regime.[26] The Defence (Emergency) Regulations passed by the British in 1945 included the sanctions of deportation, demolition of housing, imprisonment without trial, and expropriation of land. When Israel occupied the West Bank and Gaza in 1967 it determined that the regulations remained in force (alongside the decision to ignore the Geneva Convention on civilians under occupation). After years of assaulting participants in the intifada by use of 'force, might and beatings' and with a sustained policy of deportation, from 1990 the Israelis added punishment by demolition. No trials or 'proof of guilt [sic]' were involved, says Efrat Silber; rather, the IDF destroyed buildings at will. 'Search operations' blew up scores of houses on the hunch that 'terrorists' might live in them.[27] Silber comments that the policy 'was considered necessary for the preservation of the nation [Israel]'.[28] By 1993, 847 homes had been demolished: almost 50 houses for every 100,000 residents.[29] Meanwhile Israel intensified recruitment of collaborators, using threats against families and communities to build intelligence networks mobilised to undermine local solidarities. In an atmosphere of anxiety and suspicion there was an increase in retributive killings of Palestinian collaborators and outbreaks of factional violence together with 'a drift to internecine struggle'.[30]

Hamas advances

Unity across the West Bank and Gaza expressed through UNLU, which had solidified support for the PLO leadership from the start of the intifada, had also fractured. For the first time, the national movement in the Occupied Territories saw an 'indigenous, authentic and mass opposition completely outside its sway',[31] as the Islamic Resistance Movement – *Harakat al-Muqawwama al-Islamiyya*, known by its acronym Hamas ('zeal'/'fervour') – recruited rapidly. Hamas expressed intense hostility to 'peace' negotiations initiated by the US in 1991. American strategists had judged that success in engaging Arab states in the invasions of Kuwait and Iraq advanced their plan for hegemony in the Middle East and presented an opportunity for talks on Palestine favouring Israel and the US. At a conference in Madrid, George Bush prepared to give undertakings to the Palestinians about a territorial settlement (a 'ministate') but only on the basis of huge concessions to be made by the PLO. Arafat won agreement in the PLO Executive Committee to join the conference – in effect recognising Israel and its claims to sovereign control of Palestinian land seized in 1948. When Israel insisted that the PLO should not participate, Palestinians were represented by a combined delegation with Jordan that included Israeli-approved figures from the Occupied Territories. The 'Madrid process' that followed amounted to three years of tortuous negotiations while Israel bought time to accelerate expropriation of land and construction of new settlements. During the talks Israeli land grabs increased threefold over 1990 levels: 'This was de facto annexation,' writes Usher, 'and it was no longer creeping: it was raging'.[32] Hamas intervened forcefully, rejecting the Madrid process and the PLO's claim to be sole representative of the Palestinian people.

Hamas had been founded at the start of the intifada as an activist response to occupation. On 14 December 1987 leaders of the Muslim Brotherhood in Gaza, speaking in the name of the new organisation, issued a call for mass resistance.[33] The Brotherhood (officially *al-Ikhwan al-Muslimin*, the Society of the Muslim Brothers) had been established in 1928 in Egypt and had long been active on the issue of Palestine. In the 1930s it had created Palestinian branches in Gaza, Haifa and Jerusalem but remained a marginal current within the anti-colonial movement. By 1945 it was said to have 25 active groups in Palestine, later dispersed – like all other organisations – by the impacts of the Nakba.[34] In the 1950s, when the organisation was banned by the Nasser regime in Egypt, its group in Gaza was also suppressed and went underground. Few members remained in Palestine and when Fatah and the radical nationalists grew fast in the 1960s its own orientation on Islam and religious identity made little impact. When the Brotherhood in Egypt grew in strength in the 1970s, it eventually saw a revival, focusing on welfare activities that had been a feature of the organisation's work for decades.

Unlike Fatah and the left the Brotherhood was not a target for Israeli repression and made steady headway in the West Bank and Gaza, benefiting from Israeli efforts to divide and weaken Palestinian society. Israel had followed the British imperial practice of divide and rule, attempting to exploit differences in Palestinian communities on the basis of local loyalties, clan and religion. Despite the failure of its

Village Leagues, the occupation regime believed that it could undermine the PLO by facilitating activities of the Brotherhood, whose members had already demonstrated their hostility to Fatah and the Palestinian left. Israeli officials permitted activities of *Al-Mujamma' al-Islami* (the Islamic Centre) established by the Brotherhood in 1973. Filiu comments that: 'The occupying power did not go so far as to give official sanction to the Mujamma' but instead opted for a benevolent – but by definition reversible – tolerance.'[35] In 1979 Israel officially recognised the Mujamma', which was granted a licence to operate legally. Are Knudsen writes: 'This was not a tactical blunder by the Israelis but a strategic move to support any organisation that could undermine the secular nationalists and over time mount a political challenge to the PLO.'[36] Acting on the advice of Orientalist 'experts', says historian Baruch Kimmerling, Israelis in charge of the occupation regime supported the Brotherhood in the belief that its leaders were more 'submissive' than PLO nationalists.[37] The strategy was to produce spectacular blowback.

The Brotherhood extended its influence through a network of mosques that grew quickly under the occupation. Israel controlled much of the economy in the Territories and permitted a boom in construction of Islamic institutions: between 1967 and 1987 the number of mosques in the West Bank increased from 400 to 750; in Gaza the number rose from 200 to 600.[38] In Egypt the Brotherhood had for decades organised through mosques to which they often attached clinics; schools and nurseries; youth, sports and cultural clubs; and women's centres. As Israeli strategists knew well, the Islamists' political activities advanced alongside these welfare and cultural initiatives – what Robinson calls 'social Islamisation'.[39] The Islamic Centre also gained control of zakat committees, which administered the obligatory alms tax, providing an important source of revenue used to aid needy families as well as to run the organisation's medical, educational and religious facilities.

At various points Israel harassed, seized and imprisoned key figures in the Brotherhood, notably Shaikh Ahmed Yassin – often viewed as the founder of Hamas – who was jailed in 1983 for storing weapons. At the same time, Israeli strategists' willingness to endorse the construction of mosques provided a unique organisational network. Mosques were generally not subject to interference from the authorities, operating as 'sanctuaries' in which the Brotherhood could undertake political work and recruit followers. Ziad Abu-Amr comments:

> The mosque in particular played a significant role as a rallying point and as a place for launching demonstrations and other intifada activities. Hamas used the mosque as a platform and turned it from a place of worship into a centre of learning, and later on as a place for political organisation. The pro-PLO nationalists did not possess a parallel mechanism of equal function and significance.[40]

For years the Brotherhood extended its networks, benefiting from Israeli policies that facilitated its influence in labour unions, professional associations 'and throughout all sectors of Palestinian society'.[41] It faced continuous criticism from organisations of the PLO for inaction in the face of repression, but the realities of occupation were bringing change. In the early 1980s activists impatient with the Brotherhood's policies formed Islamic Jihad (*al-Jihad al-Islami*), which began attacks against Israeli forces. They found a ready audience among younger members of the Brotherhood, invoking the organisation's history of challenging Britain and the settler movement in the 1930s and 1940s, when its founders in Egypt sent volunteers to join the armed struggle for Palestine. When the intifada began in 1987, Hamas 'rapidly absorbed the mantle and commandeered the institutions of the Muslim Brotherhood'.[42] It established the Izz al-Din al-Qassam Brigades, named after the guerrilla leader of the 1930s who had been strongly influenced by Islamist ideas, and declaring for armed resistance. Hamas did not represent a break with the Muslim Brotherhood; rather, suggests Robinson, 'it was a reorganization with a new name and mission'.[43]

Islamist currents had been growing across the region, stimulated by the economic and political crises of the Arab regimes and by the retreat – and sometimes the collapse – of the organised left (see Chapter 12). During the 1980s the Muslim Brotherhood gained status in Palestinian universities, notably the Islamic University in Gaza, founded in 1978 and which provided preachers for mosques across the West Bank and Gaza. By 1987 the Islamic Bloc at the University was the dominant force in campus politics, winning student elections with comfortable majorities over candidates of Fatah and the left.[44] When the intifada began at the end of that year, Hamas was a force that could challenge the PLO for hegemony in the national movement. Abu-Amr observes that it had rapidly gained ground 'in the context of disillusionment with the Palestinian secular political movements and with the frustrated hope of achieving salvation from the Israeli occupation through them'.[45]

For 20 years Israeli strategists believed that they could co-opt the Islamists: 'The Brotherhood could organize, demonstrate, and speak with little fear of arrest, whereas their nationalist colleagues were punished for similar actions.'[46] Israeli policy makers chose to ignore a history of activism, including armed struggle, that had been supported energetically by the Brotherhood in the 1930s and during the Nakba of 1948. In a report from Gaza, the *Wall Street Journal* later concluded:

> A look at Israel's decades-long dealings with Palestinian radicals – including some little-known attempts to cooperate with the Islamists – reveals a catalog of unintended and often perilous consequences. Time and again, Israel's efforts to find a pliant Palestinian partner that is both credible with Palestinians and willing to eschew violence, have backfired. Would-be partners have turned into foes or lost the support of their people.[47]

As the Madrid talks trundled on Hamas led militant resistance to PLO accommodation with Israel. By 1991 it was mounting attacks against the IDF and was involved in street battles with Fatah, claiming leadership of an independent national movement that refused to recognise Israel and a two-state solution, and insisting that it would maintain armed struggle. Hamas now had an extensive following in Gaza: its call for demonstrations and strike days brought an overwhelming response and the organisation became increasingly confident. When February 1994 right-wing Israeli settler Baruch Goldstein killed 29 worshippers at the Ibrahimi Mosque in Hebron, the Izz al-Din al-Qassam group undertook revenge suicide attacks, killing scores of Israelis. For Knudsen, 'The attacks proved that Israel could neither contain the political violence nor protect its citizens.'[48]

Removing the Brotherhood

The Madrid talks were accompanied by a long series of secret negotiations in Norway involving the PLO and Israeli officials – the 'Oslo Channel'. This proposed to integrate the Occupied Territories into the Israeli economy as a means to facilitate final agreement. When the Madrid Process petered out, the Oslo talks moved towards a deal in which portions of the West Bank and Gaza would be the basis for a ministate attached to Israel: settlements were to remain and Israel would continue de facto military control of the Territories. Hamas, Islamic Jihad and PLO radicals rejected the deal. Arafat accepted and in September 1993 issued a declaration in which for the first time he formally recognised Israel, renouncing 'the use of terrorism and other acts of violence' and undertaking to discipline Palestinian activists.[49] Israel responded by recognising the PLO as representative of the Palestinian people. Arafat was on his way to presidential status while Fatah and Hamas moved into persistent violent confrontation.

Since the renewal of Palestinian national struggles in the 1960s, Israeli politicians, academics and media people had declared Fatah a 'terrorist' organisation. They echoed the approach of the Zionist movement in relation to Palestinian resistance under the British Mandate: traditional Zionist historiography, observes historian Joel Beinin, saw 'nationalist, anticolonial, and anti-landlord aspects of the [Palestinian] movement' as acts of terror.[50] For Ilan Pappé this was part of a continuous effort to depict 'motiveless and unwarranted violence against innocent settlers'.[51] Since 1967 the Muslim Brotherhood had been viewed differently – as an organisation easily managed that would be a counterweight to the PLO. When Hamas emerged at the start of the intifada there was a sharp change: now it was also a 'terrorist' organisation and a target for intense repression. In 1992, 415 leaders and activists of Hamas were deported to Lebanon, where they were deposited in 'no-man's land' in the border zone. The expulsions included most front-line leaders and large numbers of second- and third-tier leaders and other activists: in effect Israel was removing the Brotherhood cadre that it had favoured for almost 20 years. In 1993 Abu-Amr commented that the resulting leadership vacuum would likely 'pave the way for the appearance of a new militant leadership'.[52] It was a prophetic observation: Islamists shaped by the intifada and who had reasserted the Brotherhood's tradition of armed struggle were to lead Hamas throughout further uprisings, up to and including the offensive of 7 October 2023.

Towards the ministate

In 1994 Gaza was placed under a Palestinian National Authority (PA) run by Fatah – the first move towards establishment of a ministate. Arafat flew in as provisional leader together with a chaperone, Egyptian President Husni Mubarak, whose presence aimed to demonstrate Arab regimes' support for the US-brokered deal. Now it was Hamas that faced unrelenting hostility from Israel and the US, including an Israeli campaign of 'targeted killings' (assassinations) of its leaders and attempts to isolate the organisation from its domestic and international networks. Khaled Hroub comments:

> [I]n addition to Israel's policy of assassinating and arresting its [Hamas's] cadres, the PA is under constant pressure to demilitarize [Hamas], its funding channels have been blocked, intelligence services exchange information on its movements and membership, Arab states are pressured not to meet with its officials and to close down Hamas offices within their jurisdictions, its network of charitable institutions is under assault, and efforts are ongoing to outlaw Hamas's political wing as a terrorist organization worldwide.[53]

Opinion in Israel regarding the Islamists had aligned with that of neocons in the US, who had earlier embraced Islamophobia as part of their vision for the New American Century. As the end of the Cold War approached, American strategists had searched for rationales for a new global mission. Hostility to Islam had a long history in Europe, heightened by the colonial encounter with Asia and the Middle East.

In the US, suspicion of Islam and of Muslims became more general in the 1950s and 1960s, stimulated by resistance to imperialist interests in the Middle East and through the work of writers who focused on the 'irrationality' of Islam in the face of modernising Western agendas.[54] Bernard Lewis, a key figure in Middle East Studies in the US, originated the theory of a Clash of Civilisations, in which Muslims whom he said were unable to address the prospect of change would increasingly confront 'the West'.[55] In 1993 Samuel Huntington delivered a lecture at the American Enterprise Institute – a right-wing thinktank – that further developed the idea of a global 'clash' of cultures. Directed to politicians and policy makers, this was soon published in a hugely influential article and later in a book, *The Clash of Civilizations and the Remaking of World Order*. Huntington proposed that with the end of the Cold War global politics would be shaped by conflict between cultural 'blocs', most importantly by an elemental clash between 'Islam' and 'the West'.[56] In this context, Americans would learn their true identity and mission because, he said, 'We know who we are only when we know who we are not and often only when we know whom we are against'.[57] With the demise of communism the global enemy was to be Islam, Muslims in general and Islamists in particular. The neocons, a rising force in US state circles, adopted Huntington's approach as a key element in their vision for the New American Century.

For Edward Said, the 'clash' theory was 'relentlessly aggressive and chauvinistic', its author 'really most interested in continuing and expanding the Cold War by other means'.[58] Israeli leaders, however, responded with enthusiasm: Jonathan Cook notes that within months of publication of Huntington's thesis, Yitzak Rabin, Shimon Peres and Ehud Barak were all speaking in the same terms, 'claiming that the West and Islam were doomed to be in a permanent state of confrontation'.[59] Israeli politicians of the left and the right were in accord, endorsing the American neocons, their vision of a new imperial role for the US in the post-Soviet era, and the importance of a co-ordinated stance in relation to Islam and religious activism. According to Shlomo Gazit, Israel's influence radiated across the Middle East. It would now act 'to prevent or halt the processes of radicalization and to block the expansion of religious zealotry', providing a 'vital service' for local regimes and for the industrially advanced states, all of which, he observed, 'are keenly concerned with guaranteeing the [sic] stability in the Middle East'.[60] Gazit had headed the occupation regime in the West Bank and Gaza and was later Israel's head of military intelligence. Once the protector of Islamists, he now proposed to suppress their activities across the region, placing Israel in the front line of states engaged in an imagined 'civilisational' conflict.

The deal signed by Arafat with Israel and the US in 1993 marked capitulation by the PLO leadership. Edward Said wrote: 'Let us call the agreement by its real name: an instrument of Palestinian surrender, a Palestinian Versailles'.[61] The PLO had apparently ended the intifada, Said said, although the uprising did not embody terrorism or violence – which Arafat had publicly renounced – but the Palestinian right to resist:

> So far from being seen as the victims of Zionism, the Palestinians were characterised [by the agreement] as its now repentant assailants: as if the thousands killed by Israel's bombing of refugee camps, hospitals and schools in Lebanon; Israel's expulsion of 800,000 people in 1948 (whose descendants now number about three million, many of them stateless); the conquest of their land and property; the destruction of over four hundred Palestinian villages; the invasion of Lebanon; the ravages of 26 years of brutal military Occupation – it was as if these sufferings had been reduced to the status of terrorism and violence, to be renounced retrospectively or passed over in silence. Israel has always described Palestinian resistance as terrorism and violence, so even in the matter of wording it received a moral and historical gift.[62]

Arafat had not only conceded issues of principle that for decades underpinned the national movement but had entered a working agreement with Israel on security in Gaza and the city of Jericho – the first fragments of Palestine that were to be the basis of a ministate. Israel set the terms of the deal, exploiting a PLO leadership that was 'bankrupt, divided and on the verge of collapse'.[63] In a turn of events that revealed both the cynicism and ineffectiveness of Israeli strategy on Palestinian resistance, Prime Minister Yitzak Rabin also intended that the PLO was to be 'a useful tool in the struggle against the Islamic groups and their terrorist activities'.[64] Having earlier been allocated their own role in containing PLO 'terror', the Islamists were now to be suppressed by Fatah, operating under Israeli supervision.

Israeli writer Amos Oz called the Declaration of Principles (known as the Oslo Accords) signed by Israel and the PLO 'the second biggest victory in the history of Zionism'.[65] In 1995 a further agreement provided for slow expansion of the PA. Ultimately the treaty would divide the Occupied Territories into three zones: in Zone A, covering about 18 percent of the West Bank, the PA would have administrative and (ostensibly) security control but not sovereignty; in Zone B, covering a further 22 percent of the West Bank, the PA would run affairs jointly with Israel; in Zone C, covering the rest of the Occupied Territories, Israel would maintain full control. Israel would also control access to PA territories and authority to collect customs fees and to tax Palestinian products.

Life in the ministate

Many people of the West Bank and Gaza initially welcomed 'self-rule' under the PA. Their expectations soon changed to disillusion and anger. Israel had begun closures of the Territories in 1991, preventing movement out of the area except for those granted special passes. The number of Palestinian workers in Israel was radically reduced (one response to strike action during the intifada) and travel between the West Bank and Gaza became impossible for most people. In 1993 East Jerusalem was incorporated into the 'no entry' regime, so that centres of Palestinian population were isolated from one another. The fragile economy shrunk dramatically: one study estimated the cost of closures between 1993 and 1996 at $2.8 billion, amounting to 70 percent of a year's GDP in the Territories and double the amount of aid disbursed over that period.[66] The PA was delegated to operate a pass system that was more and more tightly controlled: Israeli journalist Amira Hass describes a 'special bureaucratic-military machinery' developed with heavy input from Israel's intelligence service Shin Bet.[67] Now 'Palestinian officials became the middlemen who either transferred the Israeli-approved permits to their fellow Palestinians or transmitted the rejection'.[68] The pass system, says Amira Hass, took on definite class overtones: the political, economic, social, and intellectual elites always found ways to get permits, 'sparing them the constant pressures of being locked up and feeling suffocated'.[69] From the time the PA was established, PLO and PA officials enjoyed free movement in and out of the West Bank and Gaza Strip to Jordan and Egypt, and later free movement into Israel. The mass of Palestinians was restricted to enclaves which most were forbidden to leave.

Israeli settlements meanwhile grew rapidly, linked by high-quality bypass roads that connected to Israel 'proper'. Roadblocks proliferated, interrupting even short journeys and bringing Palestinians into constant contact with the IDF. When a 'final status' agreement was completed in 1995, writes Hass, the West Bank had become 'a confusing mosaic of pieces of territory' under different regimes of control, while in Gaza 20 percent of land was set aside for the Israeli army and for settlers who comprised 0.5 percent of the local population.[70]

PLO leaders had established their status in the PA by imposing a regime described by Tareq Ismael as 'police control, corruption, and intimidation'.[71] In 1996 Arafat won the PA presidency with an overwhelming vote. His officials excluded from the poll, and from elections for the Legislative Assembly, even Fatah members who had hinted at independence of the leadership.[72] Leftist groups boycotted the process; Arafat imprisoned some Islamists and courted others, attempting to draw them into an electoral pact. When Hamas did not stand, the election became a competition among Fatah loyalists 'seeking to position themselves in the emerging Palestinian political system'.[73] Israel effectively controlled the vote, confirming lists of voters and in some areas refusing entry to polling stations.[74] The process eventually returned 71 Fatah members or affiliates to the 87 seats on the Council.

The Oslo deal provided for 30,000 Palestinian police to operate in PA territory – a huge force in relation to communities under Fatah's authority. Additional security agencies were soon added, Arafat creating a General Intelligence section, Military Intelligence, Preventive Security (PSS), and an elite Presidential Guard known as 'Force 17'. These organisations were assembled in close collaboration with the CIA. Israeli security analyst Shlomo Shpiro observes that from 1994 the Americans operated an intensive programme of 'assistance':

> Between 1994 and 1996, hundreds of PA security officers participated in CIA-run training courses, initially in Palestinian-controlled areas, then later at CIA facilities in the US. Palestinian officers were trained in the recruitment and running of agents, covert communications, interrogation techniques, staff work, IT, information security, database investigations, intelligence analysis and reporting, firearms training, sniping and physical security... The CIA also arranged for Palestinian security officers to participate in FBI and police training courses in the US, where they specialised in forensic sciences, bomb disposal and counter-terrorism operations.[75]

The CIA financed construction of a lavish headquarters for the PSS, which was headed by Arafat appointees Jibril Rajoub (Abu Rami) in the West Bank and Muhammed Dahlan (Abu Fadi) in Gaza. Meanwhile, according to Shpiro, the CIA established an office in Gaza and 'operation rooms' in the West Bank towns of Jericho, Hebron, Ramallah and Nablus.[76] Almost overnight the PA had constructed core repressive institutions of the modern nation-state – albeit that this shrunken 'entity' operated under strict American and Israeli surveillance. It was indeed a 'pseudo-entity' – a ministate without independence – just as Fatah had once anticipated.

The regime was highly repressive: thousands of Palestinians were arrested and imprisoned. Amnesty International concluded that prolonged detention without trial almost invariably involved those suspected of support for Hamas or Islamic Jihad – their detention closely linked to pressure from Israel to arrest individuals involved in 'terrorism'.[77] In 1994 the police banned all 'unauthorised' political meetings in Gaza and Jericho, and suppressed demonstrations that challenged PA leaders.[78] Waves of arrests were accompanied by widespread torture: the PA regime was reproducing practices of the Israeli state and of Arab regimes that for decades had aimed to subdue the Resistance.

Economic and social relations operated largely on the basis of patrimonial ties (patron-client relationships) and increasingly through divisive clan loyalties. Within a few years corruption was rife. Although Arafat was not accused of seeking personal gain, he used access to PA funds, including resources officially directed to national development, to secure the loyalty of Fatah officials and to sustain a bureaucracy that soon grew to over 100,000 personnel – people whose livelihoods were tied to their fidelity to the president.[79] Israel facilitated corruption: according to Israeli peace activist Gershon Baskin, its officials encouraged 'ripping off' the Palestinian people through all manner of shady deals that weakened the hold of the Authority.[80] Israeli strategists wished both to exploit PA leaders and to undermine them. Soon Arafat and the PA regime faced an intense crisis of legitimacy.[81]

Al-Aqsa intifada

In September 2000 a new intifada erupted – a movement that rejected economic collapse, fragmentation of the land, and apartheid-like restrictions on daily life. The 'peace process' associated with the Oslo Accords – and which was supposed to continue towards settlement of the Israel–Palestine conflict – had been revealed as a 'charade', observed Ilan Pappé.[82] The PA operated as Israel's 'sub-contractor', working to control Palestinian activism: the Israeli government nevertheless denounced terrorism and alleged 'misbehaviour' and made a 'final offer' of a Palestinian micro-state to be administered from the village of Abu Dis near Jerusalem. In a further development, American and Israel officials made clear that a conclusive deal would forbid the Right of Return for Palestinian refugees. When in September 2000 the leader of the Israeli opposition, former general Ariel Sharon – the Butcher of Beirut – undertook a calculated and provocative tour of the most sacred Islamic site in Palestine – the Haram al-Sharif, location of the Al-Aqsa Mosque – there were mass protests in Jerusalem, followed by demonstrations across the West Bank and Gaza and a retributive crackdown by the IDF. Israel immediately imposed total closure, banning the movement of labour, goods and materials between the Occupied Territories and Israel, as well as between and within the West Bank and the Gaza Strip.

The Al-Aqsa intifada was to last for almost five years. It differed from the mass movement of 1987 to 1993. Israeli repression was more violent and intense and Palestinian responses less organised than in earlier years. Affected by years of fragmentation and closure, Palestinian communities were less able to sustain collective action. Resistance continued, however: Amira Hass describes 'an amazing resilience' as all manner of individual and collective actions defied the Occupation.[83] She also observed, however, that: 'Organising serious protest is not possible without the participation of a political and intellectual vanguard.'[84] The PA, run by Fatah, was hopelessly compromised: 'The Palestinian leadership, having underestimated the effects of Israeli policies and having been blinded by the personal benefits Oslo offered, failed [the] challenge.'[85] Radical Palestinian groups had been greatly weakened and Islamists at this point pursued a strategy of suicide bombing, declining to engage in mass civil disobedience.[86] Writing in 2002, Hass concluded:

> There is no intifada now in the real sense of the word. There is no mass civilian participation in anti-occupation activities. There is, however, a spirit of intifada, which is now expressed in the individual but massive resilience in the face of a relentless siege… [T]hree million individuals are drawing on immense personal reserves to bear the hardships of siege without surrender [emphasis in original].[87]

The full implications of Israeli policy since the Oslo Accords had become evident. The West Bank and Gaza were wholly economically dependent on Israel. In 1998 Israel took 96 percent of West Bank and Gaza exports, up from 90 percent in the 1980s, and was the source of 76 percent of all imports to the Territories.[88] Before Oslo, over a third of West Bank and Gaza workers were employed in Israel, the majority in construction. With continuous partial closures, the number of workers had dropped from a high of 116,000 in 1992 to less than 36,000 in 1996, then rising to 125,000 early in 2000.[89] Full closure in 2000 excluded all Palestinian labour, with devasting impacts: Leila Farsakh notes that every unemployed person represented a six-person family.[90] Sara Roy, who had earlier traced the 'de-development' of the Territories, concluded that impoverishment and social decline were proceeding at an unparalleled rate.[91]

In 2003 the United Nations reported that during the first two years of the Al-Aqsa intifada unemployment in the West Bank and Gaza increased from 36 percent to 50 percent and that half of all Palestinian households had lost over half their usual income. According to the

UN, by the end of 2002, poverty levels had risen to 60 percent across the Territories, with a higher level in Gaza. The UN also reported that closures had divided the West Bank and Gaza into 50 isolated pockets, giving Israel a new mechanism with which to maintain control over Palestinian resources, most importantly, labour, land, and water.[92] The political implications were profound, says Roy:

> Closure and territorial dismemberment not only prevent Palestinians from moving freely within their own territory and from engaging in normal patterns of commerce, trade, and business, but also preclude a unified territorial base on which to organize a sovereign state, economy, and society.[93]

Two states – or one?

During the Al-Aqsa intifada, Israel's prolonged blanket closures in effect annexed the West Bank and Gaza, isolating them from the wider world and rendering meaningless the much-discussed 'two-state solution'. For decades, Israel's allies in North America and Europe had proposed that conflict would be resolved by agreement to establish two states in historic Palestine. The Palestinian nationalist movement of the 1930s had aspired to one state in which all religions and ethnicities would have equal status. When the PLO came into existence in the 1960s, it too proposed a single democratic state. The Zionist movement, in which the mainstream was committed to ethnic separatism, forbade such an outcome. Supported by its Western allies, it divided the land, even while its most zealous separatists aimed to seize all of Palestine – a policy that continued long after the violent birth of Israel in 1948. In the words of the Likud Party manifesto in 1969: 'There will be only Israeli sovereignty applied between the Mediterranean Sea and the Jordan River'.[94] Here Israeli leaders insisted on sovereign rights *from the river to the sea*.

Battered and isolated by defeats in Jordan and Lebanon, the PLO leadership of the 1980s resolved to pursue an 'entity' in any area of Palestine over which it could obtain authority. Kimmerling comments that PLO leaders had 'made the ultimate concession… In the Oslo agreements, they had recognized Israel's right to exist in 78 percent of historical Palestine'.[95] Israel now shaped the 'entity' as part of efforts to extinguish the prospect of an independent state. In 2001 Sharon was elected prime minister as leader of Likud, standing in a tradition of Revisionist Zionism that went back to Jabotinsky and his 'Iron Wall'. Israel began construction of an Apartheid Wall that would enclose the West Bank, seizing further Palestinian land. At the same time, Sharon evacuated some 9,000 Israeli settlers from Gaza while increasing settler numbers in the West Bank by almost 100,000.[96] In 2003 Kimmerling observed:

> Under Sharon, Israel has become a state oriented towards one major goal: the politicide of the Palestinian people. Politicide is a process whose ultimate aim is to destroy a certain people's prospects – indeed, their very will – for legitimate self-determination and sovereignty over land they consider their homeland.[97]

In 2006 new Likud leader Ehud Olmert declared that the Apartheid Wall (described by the Israeli government as a 'separation barrier') would become a permanent border. The wall integrated the largest settlement blocs on the West Bank and aligned with Israel's networks of connecting roads. The International Court of Justice declared that it was 'tantamount to *de facto* annexation'.[98] A Palestinian state with geographical contiguity had become unthinkable: the proposed 'entity' was a patchwork of pockets of land overlooked by settlements that were armed and protected by Israeli forces. When Yasser Arafat died in 2004, there were almost 450,000 settlers in the West Bank, living in armed communities that divided his ministate into fragments.[99] In addition, over 130 'outposts' had been established by settlers aiming to establish further permanent sites.[100] Israel had in effect already declared for one state – a territory in which its colonies expanded relentlessly while Palestinians were confined under military rule.

In 1996 Arafat established PA headquarters near Ramallah. His *muqata'a* ('district centre') had originally been one of the Tegart Forts built by the British during the Mandate Period and had later been an Israeli military base. In 2002 the IDF placed the muqata'a under siege and demolished its main structures, bulldozing most of the site. Until his transfer for medical treatment in 2004, Arafat was living in the few rooms left intact – a tragic epitaph for the 'entity' and the two-state solution.

Chapter 10
'War on Terror'

'War on Terror'. Gaza under siege, settler vigilantes and the far right

Assessing the life and times of Ariel Sharon, Baruch Kimmerling places the Israeli leader's policy of repression in the West Bank and Gaza in the context of 'politicide'. Sharon led an occupation regime, says Kimmerling, committed to 'murders, localized massacres, the elimination of leadership and elite groups'.[1] In addition, he observes, Sharon ordered physical destruction of public institutions and infrastructure, land colonisation, starvation, social and political isolation, re-education, and ethnic cleansing.[2] These were among practices condemned by US President George W. Bush in 2001 as he declared a 'Global War on Terror'. Following the 9/11 attacks in the US, Bush announced Executive Order 13224, giving American agencies new powers to designate individuals and organisations as 'terrorists' to be targeted for punitive action:

> For the purpose of the Order, 'terrorism' is defined to be an activity that (1) involves a violent act or an act dangerous to human life, property, or infrastructure; and (2) appears to be intended to intimidate or coerce a civilian population; to influence the policy of a government by intimidation or coercion; or to affect the conduct of a government by mass destruction, assassination, kidnapping, or hostage-taking.[3]

In the West Bank and Gaza, where the IDF had for years undertaken 'violent acts' against people and property, coercing the entire population and engaging in mass destruction, assassination and kidnapping, Israel's conduct seemed to fit without difficulty into Bush's category. In October 2001, however, it was organisations of the Palestinian national movement that were placed on the terror list.

In November 1988, then Vice President George HW Bush (George Bush Senior) had declared:

> The difference between terrorists and freedom fighters is sometimes clouded. Some would say one man's freedom fighter is another man's terrorist. I reject this notion... Terrorists kill and maim defenseless men, women and children. They murder judges, newspaper reporters, elected officials, government administrators, labor leaders, policemen, priests, and others who defend the values of civilized society.[4]

Bush produced an index of terror groups by region, listing eight Palestinian organisations including Fatah but not Hamas – perhaps because Washington's ally Israel was struggling to address the activities of the Muslim Brotherhood, which it had indulged for some 20 years. The list was testimony to the cynical and expedient approach to terrorism as defined by American politicians and strategists. It included the African National Congress (ANC), whose 'terrorist' leader Nelson Mandela was to be greeted with acclaim in 1990 by the US Congress and by then-President George HW Bush. By 1994 the ANC was in power in South Africa, with Mandela as president, showered with praise by American politicians and media. The discourse of terror had long been used instrumentally, so that today's 'terrorist' – Nelson Mandela – was indeed tomorrow's 'freedom fighter'. The US had long sustained its own policies based on the use of terror. In 1946 it had created the School of the Americas, located in Panama, where the American military and the CIA trained recruits for 'counterinsurgency'.[5] Most of the officers who led the right-wing military coup in Chile in 1973 were trained at the school, which also produced operatives directed to assault trade unions, peasant organisations, students, human rights defenders, and parties of the liberal establishment and of the left throughout Latin America. They were active in Guatemala, El Salvador, Nicaragua, Colombia, Peru, Argentina and further afield in Africa and South-East Asia. Tens of thousands of people were murdered, tortured and 'disappeared' by shadowy paramilitary death squads and state security forces trained by the US. Lesley Gill describes, 'an imperial project that brutalized and oppressed peoples around the world'.[6] President Richard Nixon had in addition established a Cabinet Committee to Combat Terrorism in 1972, licensing American agencies and task forces to confront terrorism, defined in effect as any groups, political currents or individuals the US government or its allies wished to confront. When in 2001 President George W Bush (George Bush Junior) declared for a War on Terror, now naming Hamas among target organisations, the US had been promoting state terror for over half a century.[7]

'Islamo-fascism'

The majority of targets on Bush's 2001 terror list were associated with Islamic activism. Fatah, now an American partner in the Oslo process, was not listed when Bush declared against 'a radical network' of Islamists who, he said, 'follow in the path of fascism':

> We have seen their kind before. They're the heirs of all the murderous ideologies of the 20th century. By sacrificing human life to serve their radical visions, by abandoning every value except the will to power, they follow in the path of fascism, Nazism and totalitarianism. And they will follow that path all the way to where it ends in history's unmarked grave of discarded lies.[8]

Bush began speaking of 'Islamo-fascism' – a development that was to have profound consequences for the Palestinians.[9] Stefan Wild describes the term as an example of 'word-gluing', like the Nazi Party's use of 'Judeo-Bolshevism' in the 1930s and 1940s and, he says, similar to equally hazy and dangerous slogans such as the War on Terror or the 'axis of evil'.[10] Wild identifies 'an amalgam of fear, rage, and hatred' associated with the term, rhetorically linking Islam with the genocidal slaughter in the mid-20th century of millions of European Jews:

> Once the diagnosis 'Islamofascism' is accepted, the speaker can count himself on the right side of history and feels morally unassailable. Everything becomes heartbreakingly black-and-white: Islam equals Nazism and Fascism; Gamal Abdelnasser and Yasir Arafat were Hitlers; and any attempt to come to terms with political Islam is a new Munich.[11]

In Israel political leaders had long compared Yasser Arafat to Adolf Hitler and the Palestinian Resistance to the Nazis. In 1982 then Prime Minister Menachem Begin proposed that Arafat was a contemporary Hitler, also comparing Beirut – then the PLO headquarters – to the Nazi capital Berlin.[12] In 1989, at the height of the first Palestinian intifada, Ariel Sharon declared that Palestinians had 'more Jewish blood on their hands than anyone since the Nazis'.[13] Begin, Sharon and others shared in the long-established practice of American and European politicians and mass media for whom perceived enemies of the West in the Middle East were 'fascist', their leaders seen as 'Hitlers'. In 1952, as the US and Britain prepared a coup against an Iranian government that had nationalised the Western-dominated oil industry, the *New York Times* declared Prime Minister Mohamed Mossadegh a dictator whose policy 'smacks of Hitler's technique'.[14] The following year, as the coup was enacted, *Time* magazine equated Mossadegh with both Hitler and Stalin.[15] In 1956 British Prime Minister Anthony Eden, supported by much of the national media, declared that Egyptian President Gamal Abdel-Nasser – who had nationalised the Suez Canal – was a 'new Hitler'. Eden told American President Eisenhower that Nasser was a 'Hitler' or 'Muslim Mussolini'.[16] These characterisations were used opportunistically: in the case of Egypt, both the US and Britain had initially attempted to recruit Nasser as an ally and collaborator against the Soviet Union. In the 1980s, the US attempted similarly to draw Iraq away from the influence of Moscow, treating Saddam Hussein as a potential ally. Later, when President George W Bush confected a case for invasion of Iraq, Saddam was a 'Hitler' and the offensive of 2003 directed to 'deNazification' of his Ba'th Party.[17] Ali Allawi, a minister in post-invasion Iraqi governments approved by the US, wrote:

> The planners of the [2003] war, especially those in the Pentagon and the vice-president's office, saw the Ba'th Party as an ideological block that had to be removed and its influence excised, a Nazi Party in all but name.[18]

In declaring against 'Islamo-fascism', George W Bush provided new opportunities for Israel to assault Palestinians in the West Bank and Gaza. On the afternoon of the 9/11 attacks in 2001 Ariel Sharon called for a global coalition against terror, to represent – he said – good versus evil, 'humanity' versus 'the blood-thirsty,' and 'the free world' against 'the forces of darkness' which were trying to destroy 'freedom' and our 'way of life', and offering Israel's support to the US.[19] Two days later, Israeli tanks entered towns on the West Bank. Palestinian leaders saw the attacks as evidence that, while world attention was focused on events in North America, the IDF was using ever-greater military force in the Occupied Territories. Saeb Erakat, then the PLO's chief negotiator with Israel and the US, said: 'Sharon has decided to enter the endgame against the Palestinians and is using what has happened in New York and Washington as a pretext. He is taking advantage of the fact that no one is watching.'[20] For Sharon, elimination of the Afghan Taliban – the Americans' key target following the 9/11 attacks – and elimination of the Palestinian Authority should be 'two parallel goals'.[21] If America was justified in its war on Al Qaida and the Taliban, said Sharon, Israel was justified in launching helicopter gunships against Hamas, Islamic Jihad and the Palestinian Authority.[22] He demanded of the US:

> Do not repeat the dreadful mistake of 1938 when enlightened European democracies decided to sacrifice Czechoslovakia for a convenient temporary solution. Do not try to appease the Arabs at our expense… This is unacceptable to us. Israel will not be Czechoslovakia. Israel will fight terrorism.[23]

Palestine in the 'war on terror'

The 9/11 attacks on the US, says Douglas Kellner, amounted to 'an extravagant terror spectacle' focused on symbolic targets representing global capital and American military power.[24] They were followed by a state-sponsored campaign in the mainstream American media based on the 'clash of civilizations' model, establishing 'a binary dualism between Islamic terrorism and civilization', and circulating war fever and calls for military intervention.[25] Broadcast media, says Kellner, 'oozed hatred and hysteria, calling for violence against Arabs and Muslims, nuclear retaliation, and global war':[26]

> Corporate television and radio in the United States allowed right-wing militarist zealots to vent and circulate the most aggressive, fanatic, and extremist views, creating a consensus around the need for immediate military action and all-out war.[27]

Bush's focus on 'Islamo-fascism' was pursued enthusiastically by neoconservatives in the US and by leading figures in Israel. Norman Podhoretz, a prominent American neocon, warned that the West would need to fight a 'fourth world war' against the Islamo-fascists.[28] The aim of radical Islam, he argued, was not merely 'to murder as many of us as possible and to conquer our land': like the Nazis and Communists before them, he said, Islamists were 'dedicated to the destruction of everything good for which America stands'.[29] The neocons launched a nationwide campaign: in 2007, conservative activist David Horowitz ran workshops on university campuses across the US under the banner 'Islamo-Fascism Awareness Week'. On scores of campuses leading neocons promoted ideas that critics said stimulated Islamophobia, discrimination and scapegoating.[30]

For Benjamin Netanyahu, the creation of 'Yasser Arafat's terror enclave' (the PA) had provided a 'safe haven' for Hamas and Islamic Jihad, both part of an international network seeking 'to roll back the West and install an extremist form of Islam as the dominant power in the world'.[31] Their key target was Israel, he said, 'the Middle East's only democracy and its purest manifestation of Western progress and freedom, [which] must be wiped off the face of the earth'.[32] The answer, declared Netanyahu, was to meet Islamic terrorism with implacable hostility, just as the Allies of World War Two had tackled Nazism in the 20th century.[33]

Muslim Brotherhood

Bush's War on Terror had long-term impacts among academics and media people, especially in states allied to the US and which supported American-led invasions of Afghanistan in 2001 and Iraq in 2003. A distinct current emerged among professional historians in North America, Europe and Israel, aiming to demonstrate that Islamist movements constituted 'neofascism'. Its key target was the Palestinian national movement: its central proposition was that the anti-colonial movement of the 1930s had been associated with European fascism and had passed key ideas to contemporary Islamists, notably Hamas. In *Nazi Propaganda for the Arab World*, Jeffrey Herf maintained that attempts by the Nazi regime in Germany to influence opinion in Palestine and the Arab region had their impact in the 1930s and 1940s, and later shaped 'Arab radicalism and Islamist politics'.[34] On this account, writes René Wildangel, events in Palestine during the Mandate period were not associated with conflict over land and the realities of colonial settlement but expressed Arab rejection of Jews 'because of anti-Semitism'.[35] He notes that although there were cases of Palestinian collaboration with Nazism, the Palestinian Arab community was 'far from embracing the Islamo-fascism paradigm and its ideological foundations'.[36] Identification of Palestinians with Nazism had nonetheless become an important element in 'inventing Islamo-fascism'.[37]

With Hamas a key target for Israel and its allies, the origin and development of its parent body, the Muslim Brotherhood, also came into focus. Hassan al-Banna, founder of the Brotherhood in Egypt in the late 1920s, was depicted in hostile accounts as strongly influenced by European fascism. For historian Matthias Küntzel, there was a direct connection between Nazi ideas and practices, the emergence of the Brotherhood, and the spread of contemporary 'Islamo-fascism'.[38] Banna and his co-thinkers were seen as cousins of Europe's fascists, handing on a hateful legacy to 21st century activists. Fascism of the mid-20th century, however, was an outcome of European capitalism in crisis. It did not emerge in states of the Global South under European control but in societies influenced by ultra-nationalism and by racism that had its roots in centuries of colonial rule. Joachim Scholtyseck observes:

> Fascism and National Socialism evolved in Europe, were shaped by the mood at the *fin de siècle*, became effective after the First World War in a unique political, social, economic and cultural atmosphere... They flourished in industrialized societies and aimed – in novel and twisted ways – at reversing the liberalization of 19th-century Europe. They emphasized power, national rebirth, military order and efficiency; and

> they were, in the case of Germany, driven by anti-Semitism and racism, resulting in totalitarian rule with genocidal consequences. National-socialist and fascist movements and regimes required the atmosphere and culture of liberal democracy as a foil – and liberal democracy was virtually non-existent in the Near and Middle East. The preconditions for fascism were thus lacking.[39]

In cases in which ultra-conservative currents such as the Kataeb in Lebanon consciously imitated European fascism they were aligned with the colonial powers: they were allies of imperialism. The Brotherhood that grew with spectacular speed in Egypt in the 1930s and 1940s was part of a surge of movements across the Global South that declared against imperialism, mobilising for liberation from colonialism. According to Richard Mitchell, author of the first focused study of the Brotherhood, it had four branches in 1929; five in 1930; ten in 1931; 15 in 1932; 300 in 1938; 500 in 1940; and 2,000 in 1949, when it was said to have 500,00 'active members'.[40] Its claim to be speaking in the name of a million Egyptians, says Mitchell, 'was not exaggerated'.[41] The organisation's increasing influence reflected intense hostility among the mass of Egyptians to the colonial state, to a corrupt and enfeebled monarchy, and to the failures of mainstream nationalist parties. Banna argued that the West was 'bankrupt and in decline':

> Its foundations are crumbling and its institutions and guiding principles are falling apart. Its political foundations are being destroyed by dictatorships, and its economic foundations are being swept away by crises. The millions of its wretched unemployed and hungry offer their testimony against it.[42]

The Brotherhood's key slogans were vague and encompassing: 'God is our King, the Quran is our constitution, the Prophet is our leader' and 'Islam is the solution'. They provided means of attaching people from all sectors of society, articulating widely felt grievances and rising anger. By the 1940s the Brotherhood was the largest mass organisation in the Middle East, capturing the aspiration of many Egyptians for independence and radical change. Its ideas and practices were laden with contradictions, however. Formally hostile to British rule, it attempted accommodation with the regime and even the monarchy. Banna was committed to the principles of early Islam and the *salaf* ('ancestors'/founding fathers of Islam), and to the teachings of the 19th-century activist Jamal al-Din-al-Afghani, who had declared for Muslim unity. 'Islamic society', said al-Afghani, 'stands witness to the fact that Muslims do not recognise unity on the basis of tribe, colour or race. It is only the religious brotherhood that counts.'[43] At the same time Banna focused upon establishment of an 'Islamic state', aiming to displace the British from Egypt and to establish an independent entity – in effect a nation-state that imitated the states of Europe. The organisation was elitist and authoritarian, its leaders drawn largely from the traditional commercial class, although many poor Egyptians including members of the working class were also affiliated. Far from aiming for radical change, its leaders hoped to establish an independent order in which they would enjoy enhanced status and economic influence, sharing much with nationalist movements under bourgeois or middle-class influence elsewhere in the Global South.

Notwithstanding these contradictions the Brotherhood was the largest and most active force contesting British colonial rule throughout the 1930s and 1940s. It mobilised public actions through demonstrations, rallies and strikes and eventually also created a 'Special Apparatus' prepared to take armed action against the colonial state. During the Palestinian intifada of the 1930s, the Brotherhood campaigned publicly for support, establishing solidarity committees across Egypt that embraced Muslims and Coptic Christians. A national network collected money for the Palestinian cause, circulated petitions, lobbied the British authorities to cease their support for Zionist settlement, and organised large demonstrations that sometimes clashed violently with British police and troops. These activities played a key role in the growth of the Brotherhood: Kramer suggests that it was the Palestine campaign 'that propelled them to prominence, attracting attention at home and abroad'.[44]

The case made against the Brotherhood as a 'fascist' movement is closely associated with this stance on Palestine. Wild comments that, 'Banna's movement was from the beginning anti-nationalist as well as anti-racist, and at the same time strongly critical of and violently opposed to Zionist settlement in Palestine'.[45] From the early 1930s the organisation highlighted British occupation and Zionist settlement of Palestine as a key part of its struggle against colonialism. Palestine, said Banna, 'was the knot of the Muslim peoples';[46] at the same time he insisted that Palestinian Muslims and Christians were equal participants in the national movement. Israel Gershoni writes that Banna and his colleagues succeeded in convincing many Egyptians that events in Palestine were both an organic element in the Egyptian national struggle for liberation from British imperialism and a vital stage in the historic battle between the West and the Islamic *umma* (the global community of Muslims).[47] In 1948 the Brotherhood sent units of volunteers to fight alongside Palestinians as Zionist militias undertook the ethnic cleansing of the Nakba.[48]

Banna was *murshid* ('guide', often translated as 'Supreme Guide') but far from emulating leaders of European fascism as what Patterson calls 'Führer of the Brotherhood', he was hostile to European fascism and its practices.[49] Gudrun Kramer writes that Banna 'openly repudiated fascist and Nazi racism', criticising European states for their focus on organised violence and declaring: 'Mussolini's Fascism, Hitler's Nazism and Stalin's Communism are based on pure militarism'.[50] Banna also rejected movements in the Arab world that focused on an exclusive national identity, including 'Pharaonicism' (in Egypt), 'Phoenicianism' (in Lebanon) and 'Syrianism' (in lands of the Fertile Crescent: Syria, Lebanon, Palestine and Iraq); he also opposed Arabism, 'when it became secularist and racist'.[51] It was these movements, including Young Egypt and in Lebanon the Maronite Kataeb, that were most strongly influenced by Europe's ultra-nationalism. In the case of the Kataeb, Israel was to find a ready ally.

Islamists and armed struggle

Proponents of the 'neofascism' thesis reached back into Palestinian history in attempts to demonstrate that the earliest guerrilla fighters of the national movement were also 'Nazis'. In the 1930s, armed struggle against the British and the settler movement had been initiated by the Muslim preacher Izz al-Din al-Qassam. When the Muslim Brotherhood in Palestine transformed into Hamas in 1987, it named its armed wing after the guerrilla leader.

There is no evidence of direct links between Banna in Egypt and Qassam in Palestine, but both set the project of resistance to colonialism in an Islamic context. Like Banna, Qassam referenced the *salaf* and the values of early Islam: in the 1920s, the mosque at which he preached as imam became 'a Salafi meeting ground'.[52] His audience was drawn from workers and the urban poor in Haifa, the destination for many peasants of northern Palestine dispossessed by Zionist settlement and where entry to the urban wage-labour force weakened divisions of clan, village and region. He set up a night school to combat illiteracy, encouraged establishment of co-operatives in nearby villages, and organised with railway workers who established PAWS, the country's first independent Arab trade union. Basheer Nafi comments that 'Al-Qassam encouraged, directed, and supported the pioneering group of Haifa workers, whose efforts were to change for ever the whole landscape of the Palestinian labour movement'.[53]

Qassam was a 'militant religious reformer', says Swedenburg,[54] an activist who called for moral regeneration, 'denouncing the factionalism and ineffectiveness of the elite politicians'.[55] His guerrilla campaign, launched in 1935, was quickly ended by the British but had a profound impact on Palestinian society, helping to launch mass action that in April 1936 became a national intifada. Following long-established practice in the face of resistance to colonial rule, the British labelled Qassam and his followers 'outlaws', 'brigands' and 'bandits': the colonial regime also called them 'bearded sheikhs' and 'fanatics'.[56] Within the Zionist movement they were 'terrorists'.[57] Qassam was an innovator, Swedenburg suggests. Like Banna, he 'refashioned Islamic traditions for use in the struggle against Zionism and British imperialism'.[58] Over several years he trained as many as 800 activists as guerrilla fighters and in 1935 prepared to raise a rural rebellion.[59] An accidental encounter with British troops led to his death and the dispersal of his followers, although they played a key role in armed struggles against the British and Zionist militias during the intifada of 1936-39. He 'touched a deep chord in the popular imagination', says Rashid Khalidi, and was 'much more closely in tune with Palestinian sentiment than was the elite leadership'.[60]

Qassam was the pioneer of militant armed action, his legacy later claimed by leaders of Fatah and by PLO radicals as well as by Hamas. Novelist and PFLP activist Ghassan Kanafani compared him to Che Guevara as 'the initiator of an advanced revolutionary focus', seeing parallels between the Palestinian resistance and Latin American uprisings a generation later.[61] British military historian Matthew Hughes also sees parallels with Guevara, viewing Qassam as 'a brave, magnetic operational leader', an innovator who combined 'populist Islamism' with 'rural-style socialism' – a form of radicalism that, says Hughes, was far more effective than the politics of the left in Palestine during this period (see Chapter 12).[62] Hughes draws comparisons with the Viet Minh resistance in Vietnam against French colonial control; Swedenburg sees parallels with the revolt led by Abd-al-Karim against Spanish occupation in Morocco in the 1920s.[63] The Qassamist movement, he suggests, combined 'nationalist, religious 'revivalist' and class-conscious components in a movement of anti-colonial struggle'.[64]

Early guerrilla initiatives in Palestine shared much with struggles worldwide against colonialism in which activists took up arms against the oppressor. Like the resistance of indigenous communities in Australasia, North America, Asia and Africa, they were dismissed as 'banditry' or 'terrorism'. In the case of Palestine, there was also the 'special disparagement' of Zionist accounts.[65] According to Israeli historian Shai Lachman, the Qassamists exhibited 'religious fanaticism', xenophobia and anti-Jewish hatred, and constituted 'the first Arab terrorist movement in Palestine'.[66] Swedenburg comments that in the 21st century, 'Given the West's ongoing panics about terrorism, such a designation is a potent means of disqualifying the Palestinian past.'[67]

Gaza under siege

In 2006, writes Avi Shlaim, Israel's leaders received 'an unpleasant surprise', as Palestinians elected Hamas with a majority in the Legislative Council.[68] After fierce conflict with Fatah, Hamas took control in Gaza: Israel responded with a complete lockdown. Sara Roy, who had been monitoring economic changes in the Occupied Territories for many years, observed:

> [T]he blockade has proven to be the single most damaging measure affecting Gaza's economy and society. The impact has been devastating. With the blockade the logical endpoint of de-development was arguably reached: an economy internally disabled, unable to function without external sources of support.[69]

Blockade – 'really an intensified military closure' – had begun in 1991 but was now imposed as 'economic deprivation', 'demographic isolation' and 'institutional destruction'.[70] Israeli leaders wished to minimise their problems in Gaza in order to facilitate annexation of the West Bank and bring to an end the prospect of a Palestinian state. Dov Weissglas, a member of Sharon's team that negotiated with the US, declared that Israel was now freezing the 'peace process':

> When you freeze that process you prevent the establishment of a Palestinian state and you prevent a discussion about refugees, the borders and Jerusalem. Effectively this whole package that is called the Palestinian state, with all that it entails, has been removed from our agenda indefinitely. And all this with authority and permission. All with [an American] presidential blessing and the ratification of both houses of Congress.[71]

Israeli strategists aimed to accelerate settlement of the West Bank while maintaining Gaza as a mass detention centre, what Ilan Pappé called 'the biggest prison on Earth'.[72] Denied the fruits of its electoral victory Hamas turned, says Avi Shlaim, to 'weapons of the weak' in the form of rocket attacks on southern Israel.[73] In 2008 Israel responded with a military offensive dubbed Operation Cast Lead. This was not war or even 'asymmetric warfare', says Shlaim, 'but a one-sided massacre' in which Israel killed 1,417 Gazans including 313 children in 'a deliberate and punitive war of aggression'.[74] This was followed by further Israeli attacks in 2012, 2014, 2018, 2021, 2022 and mid-2023 – before the genocidal offensive that began in October 2023.

For years Israeli generals spoke chillingly of 'mowing the grass' – routinely attacking Gaza from land, sea and air in efforts to weaken Hamas while assaulting what remained of civilian infrastructure. After the offensive of 2008, the United Nations established a commission to investigate: Israel refused to co-operate. The commission's report concluded that Israel had pursued a strategy of terror, attacking 'the foundations of civilian life in Gaza' by destroying industrial infrastructure, food production, water installations, sewage treatment plants and housing by means including 'unlawful and wanton destruction'.[75] Israeli forces destroyed Gaza's only flour mill, violating the right to adequate food and means of subsistence. Unjustified by military necessity, said the UN panel, this amounted to a war crime. Bulldozers systematically flattened buildings at a large chicken farm, killing all 31,000 birds inside, and destroyed the plant and material necessary to maintain the enterprise. Israeli forces struck a raw sewage lagoon of the Gaza wastewater treatment plant, caused the outflow of more than 200,000 cubic metres of raw sewage onto neighbouring farmland – part of 'deliberate' and 'systematic' targeting of industrial sites and water installations.[76] Houses were demolished and Palestinian civilians seized and subjected to 'continuous and systematic abuse, outrages on personal dignity, humiliating and degrading treatment' that amounted to collective punishment, 'intimidation and terror'.[77]

Gaza was no longer merely under occupation, said Ariella Azoulay and Adi Ophir: Israel had decided that it had no responsibility for the people confined there; in effect they had been abandoned.[78] When Israel imposed a state of siege, withdrawing its troops and civil administration from Gaza, it left the area to humanitarian organisations, retaining the option to invade, kill and destroy. '[Palestinians] have become fair game', said Azouley and Ophir: 'killing or hurting them is permissible and goes unpunished; those involved in injuring them enjoy immunity'.[79] Power supplies were limited and import of food strictly controlled, so that Israel could regulate household incomes and stimulate malnutrition. Gaza was enclosed 'like a holding pen', under remote-controlled surveillance so that Israeli forces could monitor daily activities, facilitating attacks including assassinations that removed key activists, notably members of Hamas. Azouley and Ophir describe 'governance through catastrophization'.[80]

Israel's military interventions were justified as part of the War on Terror. The Meir Amit Intelligence and Terrorism Information Center (ITIC) had been established in Israel in 2001 with a brief to monitor

'Palestinian terrorist organizations, their ideology, activities and military capabilities, their political activity, and their international battle for hearts and minds'.[81] Operating in effect as part of Israeli intelligence and in dissemination of *hasbara*, it designated Palestinian resistance across the board as 'terrorist', focusing in particular on Hamas. This covered the tracks of Israeli strategists who for 20 years after military occupation in 1967 cultivated the Muslim Brotherhood as if it was distinct from the national movement. Beverly Milton-Edwards writes that during the 1970s and 1980s Islamist organisations had been 'licensed' by Israel:

> When Islamic *dawa* organisations [linked to the Brotherhood] were licensed by Israel as a foil to the secularists in the PLO they were largely considered a temporary nuisance of no real capacity or legitimacy [and] dismissed as a 'here today gone tomorrow' Islamist phenomenon.[82]

Perhaps encouraged by the mild reformism of the Brotherhood in Egypt under the Sadat regime, Israel hoped to embed a conservative religious network in Gaza and the West Bank. Milton-Edwards quotes Israeli Brigadier-General Yossi Kuperwasser, who warned policy makers they risked 'catastrophe' in Gaza, where he knew the Islamists were growing fast.[83] Israel's policy of indulging the Brotherhood had been an error, he said: 'I think it was a mistake, yes.'[84] Kuperwasser had been director of intelligence analysis for the Israeli military apparatus: he and others knew well that historically the Brotherhood in Egypt had supported the Palestinian movement and had sent volunteer units to join armed struggle against the Zionist militias. They were also in full awareness of the ideas and practices of activist leader Izz al-Din al-Qassam and of his impact on those who contested the British regime of the 1930s and the settler militias. When, during the intifada of 1987, the Muslim Brotherhood/Hamas followed Fatah and PLO radicals in undertaking armed struggle, it marked a *historic continuity* in the Resistance, operating over the generations in the mode of anti-colonial movements worldwide.

In the 1980s Islamist currents in Palestine had grown rapidly, winning support for their clean credentials and ability 'to ideologically transform socio-economic discontent and nationalist longing' into action against Israel and later the PA.[85] Like the Brotherhood of the 1930s, in Egypt they declared that 'Islam is the solution', proposing that the Quran and its principles provided a basis to renew Palestinian struggles. Israeli politicians minimised their impact or even dismissed them as a significant force – an aspect of their denial of Palestinian agency. Israeli leaders, including then Prime Minister Menachem Begin, approved the strategy: 'they kept their eyes closed to the realities of what they were allowing to be created'.[86] The eventual outcome was an invigorated armed movement, leading to a belated discovery – that Islamists had for generations been associated with resistance. Like Fatah, the PFLP and DFLP – and like the National Liberation Front (NLF) of Vietnam, the Front de Libération Nationale (FLN) of Algeria, the ANC in South Africa, and other movements across the Global South – Hamas had emerged in the context of imperialism and the struggle for liberation from colonial rule. Rather than a 'temporary nuisance' it had become Israel's most energetic adversary, its popularity soaring as Israel froze 'peace' negotiations, continued savage attacks on Gaza, and built new settlements, roads and 'outposts' across the West Bank.

Colonisation and control

Israeli geographer Oren Yiftachel observes that from the early 1990s Israeli settlement policy entered a new era, what he calls 'oppressive consolidation'.[87] The state's priorities, he suggests, were: maximisation of settlement; security for 'Jewish space'; expansion of areas for new colonies; ethnicisation (exclusive spaces for the Jewish population and restriction of Palestinians to enclaves); control (keeping tight regulation in the hands of the state); and a drive to commercialisation by imposition of neoliberal policies.[88] Here the aim was fuelled by ethnocratic considerations of Jewish control from the Jordan to the Mediterranean, resulting in a process of 'creeping apartheid' – 'the solidification and institutionalizing of a situation of "separate and unequal" on the basis of ethnicity'.[89]

By 2010 Palestinian Arabs, numbering 46 percent of the population between the Jordan River and the Mediterranean, had been restricted to enclaves that covered over only 14 percent of the area.[90] Planning of settlements on the West Bank had been inspired by security-military thinking – concern over 'frontiers', 'threats', 'buffer zones', 'wedges' and 'strategic points', so that planning was 'part of the military system'.[91] This was advanced through connections between security forces and planning authorities including by participation of military officers on planning boards; constant surveillance of public spaces by security firms; and overall control exercised by the defence establishment. Landowners and developers were privileged by an agenda that prioritised the market in land and housing, speeding up the integration of Israel into a global economy in which neoliberal principles had become dominant.

The number of settlements in the West Bank increased relentlessly: by 2017 B'tselem recorded 131 settlements recognised by the government and 110 'outposts', plus a series of enclaves in predominantly Palestinian areas of major cities such as Jerusalem and Hebron.[92] Huge areas of land were seized by the state for settlements and local landholdings, and for infrastructure including roads for exclusive use of Israeli citizens and the military. B'tselem notes that much land declared state property had been under Palestinian ownership, having been seized by means of legal manoeuvres including categorisation as military zones off-limits to Palestinians: 'In contrast, Israeli citizens, Jews from around the world and tourists can enter them freely.'[93] Intensified colonial settlement was driven by the state and also by right-wing parties of the Revisionist tradition, which prospered in an environment of heightened ethnocentrism and life in militarised communities. In the 1970s Gush Emunim, linked to the National Religious Party (NRP), played a key role in establishing embryonic 'wildcat' settlements, declaring that the West Bank belonged to Israel and should be claimed by seizing land and challenging the government to recognise new colonies. Among its founders, Hanan Porat argued that 'fulfilment of the Zionist vision' was the route 'to complete redemption of the people of Israel and the entire world'.[94] Porat called for immediate annexation of territory occupied in 1967, declaring that 'alien minorities' should swear loyalty to Israel or must 'emigrate': the path to achieve every national goal, he said, was 'settlement throughout the Land'.[95]

Meir Kahane took a more strident position. Arriving in Israel from the US in 1971 he founded Kach ('Thus'), a party that argued aggressively for expulsion of the Palestinians. National redemption would follow annexation of the Occupied Territories, he said, together with expulsion of 'alien worship' (of Muslims) from the Temple Mount in Jerusalem, and eviction of all 'enemies of the Jews'.[96] In his book *They Must Go*, published in 1981, Kahane argued that 'no stranger' should live in Jerusalem and that non-Jews should be required to submit annually to an assessment that would determine whether they could remain in Israel.[97] Kahane created a 'terror group' that engaged in anti-Arab atrocities; Ehud Sprinzak describes him as 'exclusivist and nationalist to the point of racism' and Kach as a 'quasi-fascist movement'.[98] Kach was not fascist in the mode of 20th-century European ultra-nationalism, with its origins in socio-economic crisis and its aim to seize the state, assault the working class and systematically eliminate all perceived enemies.[99] It did, however, hold ideas of racial superiority common to dominant groups in colonial settings: there are parallels with political currents in European colonies in Africa and with communities closely tied to colonial powers, such as the Maronites of Lebanon. Kahane's vision of an expanded, purified Israel shared much with the most right-wing currents in Algeria under French colonial control. Here, the *Algérie française* of far-right elements among the pieds noirs was to be 'a territory dominated by European settlers, and from which its sworn enemies – Marxists, Jews and *indigènes* – were excluded, by violent means if necessary'.[100]

Kach drew upon and sharpened ideas present in Zionist ideology from the time of Herzl and the high era of European imperialism, later advanced by the Revisionist Right and eventually by the mainstream of the Zionist movement, with its plans for forceful exclusion of the Arab population. But Kahane was even more belligerent – setting out his strategy publicly in racist terms – too much even for the Israeli judiciary, which in 1988 banned Kach on the grounds of incitement to racial hatred. Kahane was assassinated in the US in 1990, but his followers established Kahane Chai (Kahane Lives), the New Kach Movement and later Otzma Jehudit (Jewish Power). Together with other elements of the Israeli Right, including Jewish Home, it formed a right-wing bloc that advanced steadily in Israel's national elections and exercised increasing influence on Israel's political culture.

Vigilantes

Settlements had become an important base for Israel's far right: locations in which ultra-nationalists pursued ideological initiatives through dedicated educational institutions and party rallies, and at which physical confrontation with Palestinians took place increasingly often. They had become a front line for the Right, including the most active Kahanists, sites at which to demonstrate commitment to the project of a Greater Israel, and places of danger for Palestinians from which armed activists threatened livestock, crops and property, and endangered life. Many settlements mounted vigilante actions against local Arab communities. Nir Gazit comments that, as part of Israel's official security doctrine, settlers had long been instructed by the Israeli government to establish paramilitary units, so that many settler males were constantly armed.[101] Gazit identifies a close relationship between local vigilantism and forces of the state – collusion that operated as 'an informal mechanism of political power'.[102] Turning its civilians into 'pseudo state agents', he says, the state made them not only objects of governmental control but also 'implanters of its practical sovereignty over territories and subordinated populations'.[103] Vigilantes and state officials, including the military command, operated with a shared agenda.

The PA – a military-bureaucratic apparatus led initially by Arafat – was at the service of Israeli officials. In the West Bank, as land grabs and settler violence increased, the PA stood aside while Israel demanded and received guarantees about its role in policing Hamas, deemed by Arafat to be 'terrorists' and 'fundamentalists'.[104] As the years passed, PA forces were seen as 'little more than security contractors for Israel'.[105] Islamists benefited from increased support, together with independent armed groups in West Bank cities such as Nablus and Jenin. Before the intifada of 1987, Israeli leaders had pursued a policy in the West Bank similar to their approach in Gaza, 'benignly supporting' the Muslim Brotherhood and using it 'as a convenient foil to the PLO'.[106] Milton-Edwards quotes an official in the Sharon government on its 'divide and conquer strategy', which aimed that the Islamists 'could serve a useful purpose in weakening the strength of Fatah on the street'.[107] As in Gaza, this backfired spectacularly: as the

PA lost support for both corruption and its attempts to suppress Palestinian resistance, 'blowback' produced wide support for Hamas. Khaled Hroub observed that with each new spate of killings and crackdowns the popular legitimacy of the organisation increased: 'The dilemma that has faced Israel', he said, '[and] the United States and even the PA is that the movement is deeply rooted in Palestinian society.'[108]

The War on Terror, says historian Robert Gildea, 'appeared very much a war on Islamism and even on Islam'.[109] It proposed a black-and-white division of the world in which the US and its allies would lead what President George W Bush called a 'crusade' that aimed to 'rid the world of evil-doers'.[110] Determined to demonstrate that Israel was an eager participant, Ariel Sharon declared 'a war that knows no borders', assaulting Gaza and the West Bank with new intensity. In the city of Jenin the refugee camp was reduced to a 'lunar landscape...a silent wasteland, permeated with the stench of rotting corpses and cordite':[111] Human Rights Watch charged Israel with multiple war crimes.[112] With the PA paralysed, Hroub observed, Hamas was increasingly viewed as 'the voice of Palestinian dignity and the symbol of defense of Palestinian rights'.[113] By 2004 polls in Gaza and the West Bank found that for the first time Hamas was the most popular organisation in the Territories.[114] The War on Terror had brought Palestine's Islamists unprecedented support. Traumatic confrontations were to come.

Chapter 11
Sumud – 'Steadfastness'

Sumud, repression and genocidal attacks. Settler colonialism and the Israeli Right

In October 2001 US forces launched the War on Terror with an assault on Afghanistan. Key decisions were taken by neoconservatives eager to demonstrate America's global status as 'the greatest power in history'.[1] They ordered Shock and Awe, also known as Rapid Dominance, an approach developed by US military strategists who aimed to 'destroy the adversary's will to resist', so that 'an adversary will have no alternative except to accept our strategic aims and military objectives'.[2] In Afghanistan and later in Iraq, US forces sought quick victories by mobilising overwhelming violence, installing military occupations and imposing regimes aligned with American interests:

> In Rapid Dominance it is an absolutely necessary and vital condition to be able to defeat, disarm or neutralize an adversary's military power [whilst maintaining] capacity for the physical and forceful occupation of territory.[3]

'Deep Strike' offensives also focused on political and economic resources in order to disable enemy leaderships and their 'national economic base'.[4] In 2003 the US not only struck the armed forces of Iraq and dismantled the Ba'thist state but also seized oilfields and pipelines, passing control to American corporations that proceeded to pillage the Iraqi economy. David Whyte describes the project as 'one of the most audacious and spectacular crimes of theft in modern history'.[5]

It was in this context that Israel, the US and their allies addressed the Al-Aqsa Intifada and the rise of Hamas. In *The Power of 'Shock and Awe': The Palestinian Authority and the Road to Reform* Mandy Turner shows how Israel combined intense military assaults with 'a unique and sophisticated web of control' that aimed to isolate and undermine Hamas in Gaza and ensure that the PA remained 'a (failed) quasi-state'.[6] Beginning with Operation Defensive Shield, launched in 2002, the IDF used unprecedented force. When it failed to suppress resistance, the attacks intensified. In 2008 the Cast Lead assault on Gaza drew directly on the strategy of Shock and Awe: according to Israeli media, 'IDF officers appear to have studied the doctrine closely'.[7] *Haaretz* reported that they pursued 'Israel's strategy of "shock and awe"...the closest thing there is to a war between Israel and Hamas'.[8] The *Jerusalem Post* reported on 'a doctrine formulated by the US military in the 1990s:

> [this] calls for use of overwhelming power, dominating maneuvers and spectacular displays of force to paralyse an adversary...that was the IDF's goal: to shock and awe Hamas with a blow the likes of which has not been seen in Gaza since the territory was conquered by Israel in 1967.[9]

Palestinian researchers concluded that the attack was 'the largest sustained offensive against the Palestinians since 1948'.[10] According to *Haaretz*, 'Like the U.S. assault on Iraq...little to no weight was apparently devoted to the question of harming innocent civilians'.[11]

A long series of assaults was accompanied by intensive efforts to bring the Palestinian ministate under close control. Restrictions on the PA created at the time of the Oslo Accords were reinforced, compelling Palestinian leaders to fall into line with a neoliberal agenda policed by Israel, the US and international financial organisations which controlled 'development' budgets and emergency aid. Naomi Klein identifies the role of 'shock doctors' in states such as Iraq which had been weakened by the traumas of war and occupation. They were charged to implement privatisation, deregulation and deep cuts to state spending with the aim of integration into US plans for the regional economy.[12] In the case of Palestine, 'doctors' included the World Bank, the IMF and a Palestine Investment Fund created in 2003 to receive assets previously owned by the PA, which became little more than a security apparatus linked to the Israeli state.

Neoliberal Palestine

The Oslo Process had specified that the World Bank would 'assume control over economic planning [and] Palestinian development'.[13] The Bank distributed funds for a 'mini-Marshall Plan' based on co-operation between Palestinian and Israeli partners and including free trade zones linked to the Israeli economy.[14] The agenda, writes Haddad, was shaped by the 'neoliberal euphoria of the 1990s': the Bank declared that Palestine was to be free of the problems of a centralised economy, a welfare state and an 'inflated public sector'; instead it would be led by 'the ability of the private sector to achieve miracles in adapting to the demands of a globalizing world economy'.[15]

Under Arafat, the PA had created trading monopolies and owned significant public assets, widely misused by the Fatah elite and encouraged by Israeli officials who also benefited from shady dealings.[16] Systemic corruption undermined Arafat's authority and there was a surge of hostility among Palestinians towards the '*abus*' (father-figures of the national movement), of whom many soon lived in expensive mansions constructed in an exclusive area of Ramallah. The World Bank worked with critics of the Authority to advance a 'reform' agenda. When Israeli forces assaulted the Occupied Territories with renewed force, the economy collapsed and Arafat was forced to accept a '100-Day Reform Plan' as Salam Fayyad, former IMF representative to the PA, became finance minister. American strategists had a long-term aim – that of integrating Israel and the Palestinian ministate into a much-changed Middle East economy. The region was to see market-driven change in which free ports and Qualified Industrial Zones (QIZs) would play a key role in facilitating trade, especially with the US and Europe. In 2003, as he pursued war in Iraq, George W Bush announced plans for a Middle East Free Trade Area (Mefta) to include states stretching from Morocco to Saudi Arabia. Investment from the Gulf was to be a key driver and was soon being channelled to Egypt, Syria, Jordan and Palestine.[17] Israel was to enter these arrangements as an economic partner, facilitating 'normalisation' – relations with Arab states that would become what former Secretary of State Christopher called 'a beautiful friendship'.[18]

The 'reform' plan amounted to a programme for the fragmentation of Palestinian society. It claimed to promote 'citizen empowerment', encouraging all manner of non-governmental organisations to 'create local leaders' and stimulate 'change-makers'.[19] Together with Israeli strategists the World Bank aimed to weaken collective identity and organisation – to undermine solidarities associated with decades of resistance. Adam Hanieh observes that in the post-Oslo years, Israel 'sharpened and rearticulated its control' so that Palestinian development was 'subject to Israeli power more than at any point in history'.[20] Much aid directed to local development went in practice to Israeli businesses, especially construction companies, while the use of the Israeli currency left the monetary system in the hands of Israel's central bank, draining wealth from the Palestinian population as the economy became 'a dependent adjunct to Israel'.[21] Arafat had declared: 'We will work to make Palestine economically the Singapore of the Middle East, and proud home of investment and successful businesses'.[22] Among the few Palestinian beneficiaries were capitalists who had survived within the Gulf economy and now exploited the limited opportunities available in the ministate. Hanieh shows that in banking and finance Gulf investors soon controlled 15 out of 17 banks in operation in the PA and dominated the telecommunications sector.[23] The mass of people had been impoverished. By 2008, under repeated assault from the IDF and intense pressure from the Bank, the Palestinian economy had shrunk and poverty rates had soared: based on household income, the poverty rate in Gaza had reached 79.4 percent and in the West Bank 45.7 percent.[24]

Fatah was in rapid decline. Arafat was long gone and it was Hamas that claimed the legacy of Palestinian resistance. Israel and its allies – architects of the strategy that had delivered both Shock and Awe and the neoliberal offensive – refused to accept this outcome, imposing an international boycott on the Islamists. Tony Blair, former British prime minister and key US ally in the invasion of Iraq, had been made Middle East envoy for The Quartet – the four-power group (the UN, the US, the EU and Russia) created in 2002 ostensibly to mediate the Israel–Palestine conflict. He insisted that action against Hamas would continue until the organisation ended violence, recognised Israel and abided by all international agreements. Visiting Israel in 2008 he was greeted by Foreign Minister Shimon Peres, who told him: 'Your success is our success. Your dreams are our dreams.'[25]

Imperial overreach

'Dreams' of a new world order dominated by the US and its allies had produced a nightmare scenario in Afghanistan and in Iraq, where invasion facilitated seizure of energy resources but also produced years of intense resistance, resulting in at least 300,000 deaths, most among civilians but including 15,000 American troops and civilian contractors.[26] The Iraq adventure was soon seen as 'a debacle…a defeat of historic proportions for US foreign policy'.[27] Among long-term outcomes the consolidation of Iran as a regional power seriously weakened US status in the region. Together with American difficulties in (and eventual retreat from) Afghanistan, the Iraq episode provided compelling evidence of imperial 'overreach':

> The United States…lost prestige; upset regional stability in the oil patch; set aside more important foreign policy priorities, such as responding to China's growing power; and lost credibility with both the international community and the American public.[28]

Alex Callinicos examines changes in the character of imperialism across the globe.[29] The end of the Cold War brought illusions of a 'unipolar moment', he observes, a period during which US power appeared to be overwhelming, feeding the ambitions of those who sought a New World Order. But the nature of imperialism, a system in which capitalist states compete for economic and political advantage, meant that US hegemony had always been contested and, at the end of the 20th century, was confronted by rising global and regional powers. The debacle in Iraq, followed by the world economic crash of 2008, accelerated developments under way for decades, as China's rulers became more confident and energetic, notably in the Middle East. These changes had their implications for relations between the US and Israel – and for the Palestinians.

The Gulf had long been a vital source for US energy supplies. After 2007, however, American energy imports declined and the US became a net exporter of oil and gas. The Gulf nonetheless remained a region of key strategic concern in Washington – not least because of inter-imperialist rivalries. China was now increasingly dependent on Gulf resources: it was soon the world's largest importer of oil, drawing over half its energy supplies from the region and importing three times more than the US and states of the EU combined.[30] In Beijing, the Gulf was viewed in the context of China's Belt and Road Initiative (BRI) – a partner in a 'two-way investment' and part of a global trade strategy.[31] China was making huge investments in construction and infrastructure in the Middle East – soon all 22 members of the Arab League had signed BRI agreements.[32] In the US, competition with China had become a key issue in strategic thinking about the region.[33] In 2023 the right-wing Cato Institute observed: 'The U.S. has come to view Chinese encroachment in the Middle East as a serious national security threat, part of a broader "Cold War 2.0" framing that has begun to dominate U.S. foreign policy in general.'[34]

Alarmed by China's inroads, write Christopher Preble and Will Smith, 'the United States has gone to great lengths to reassure partners of its commitment to their security'.[35] American leaders confirmed above all their commitment to Israel. Increasingly worried about Israel's links with China, especially in the field of high technology, successive US administrations restated their commitment to providing Israel with QME – a Qualitative Military Edge. When the Gaza war began in 2023, the US created a supply chain that provided unprecedented volumes of weaponry. Aipac, Israel's most important support organisation in the US, declared, 'Israel's QME is essential to its ability to defend its people, combat shared threats and promote American interests in a dangerous region… Israel is a capable partner on the frontlines against a shared enemy'.[36] Netanyahu asserted: 'Israel remains America's indispensable and strong ally in the Middle East.'[37] As bombardment of Gaza intensified, American researchers commented that despite mass protests worldwide, including in the US, 'Washington has exuded sympathy with Israel's declared intention to wipe out Hamas'.[38] In August 2024 Israeli media reported that since the start of the war the US had delivered more than 50,000 tons of military supplies.[39] Israel's defence ministry said the supply line had used 500 transport planes and 107 ships, declaring that American weaponry was 'crucial for sustaining the IDF's operational capabilities'.[40]

Sumud

In rare, dissident insights, leading officials in both Israel and the US declared that Hamas could not be defeated by military means. According to IDF spokesman Rear-Admiral Daniel Hagari, speaking in June 2024, 'Hamas is an idea. Anyone who thinks we can eliminate Hamas is wrong'.[41] Grace Wermenbol, of the US State Department, agreed: 'Israel's key identified aim for its Gaza offensive – the complete elimination of Hamas – remains an elusive prospect.'[42] She added:

> As Gaza lies in ruins, Hamas remains intractable, a deadly guerrilla force that is still in de facto control of large swaths of the Gaza Strip… Hamas is deeply rooted in Palestinian society and, through its political-societal dimensions and services, daily life. The reasons for Hamas' popularity, as Middle East policy analyst Khaled Hroub has argued, are not difficult to find. Hamas continues to be seen 'as the voice of Palestinian dignity and the symbol of defense of Palestinian rights, a force that refuses to capitulate'.[43]

Resistance in Gaza and the West Bank was not confined to armed action by Islamist organisations but had long been part of everyday practice in the face of occupation. Israeli researchers Ariella Azouley and Adi Ophir note continuous 'active, persistent and often painful Palestinian resistance'.[44] Confronted by the IDF, by settlers and by forces of the PA, resistance lay 'not just in their actions, but in their mere presence, their insistence on staying'.[45] Palestinian *persistence*, expressed in the idea of *sumud* ('steadfastness'/'fortitude') posed profound difficulties for the Israeli state and settler communities, which responded with greater violence and calls for Israel to annex much of the West Bank.

For centuries sustained violence had been at the heart of colonial projects worldwide. In the case of colonial settlement, writes Roxanne Dunbar-Ortiz, people do not hand over their land, resources, children and futures without a fight, and that fight is met with violence. 'In employing the force necessary to accomplish its expansionist goals,' she adds, 'a colonising regime institutionalises violence':

> The notion that settler-Indigenous conflict is an inevitable product of cultural differences and misunderstandings, or that the violence is committed equally by the colonised and the coloniser, blurs the nature of the historical process. Euro-American colonialism, as aspect of the capitalist economic globalisation, had from its beginnings a genocidal tendency.[46]

From its earliest phases industrial capitalism required resources – land, labour and materials – acquired from the Global South. In some regions the inhabitants were dispossessed – displaced, evicted, sometimes eliminated. Karl Marx observed that colonial ventures in the Americas had led to 'the extirpation, enslavement and entombment in mines of the aboriginal population'.[47] Later, the competitive drive among European powers to seize land and create colonies was associated with projects to clear the indigenous population, eliminating resistance and seizing resources that were claimed by the state, by commercial enterprises, or as individual private property. Where Europe implanted settler communities there was a compulsion to acquire land. In North America the land was seen as 'free' – open to settlers and slave owners who sought to expand their farms and plantations. As elsewhere in the Global South, violence was inherent in the project. Michael Grewock writes:

> Settler colonialism is characterized by the forcible occupation of land, the displacement of Indigenous populations and the construction of a new society on terms defined entirely by the settler population. To succeed, settler colonialism requires foundational and ongoing structural violence to be inflicted upon Indigenous peoples at an individual and communal level.[48]

Here sustained violence is associated with what Patrick Wolfe calls 'a logic of elimination' which 'strives for the dissolution of native societies, erecting a new colonial society on the expropriated land base'.[49]

Since the mid-20th century some processes of 'elimination' have been identified as genocide. During the 1930s Raphael Lemkin began formulating an approach to the focused use of violence against ethnic/national communities. In 1933 he developed a proposal on 'acts of persecution amounting to what is now called genocide'.[50] In 1944 his book *Axis Rule in Occupied Europe* introduced the term in the context of emerging evidence of the Nazi Holocaust. Genocide, he wrote, 'involves the destruction of a nation or of an ethnic group… Genocide is directed against the national group as an entity, and the actions involved are directed against individuals, not in their individual capacity but as members of the national group'.[51] Lemkin added that the objectives of genocidal plans included 'disintegration of the political and social institutions, of culture, language, national feelings, religion, and the economic existence of national groups'.[52] He participated in the commission that later formalised the Genocide Convention, agreed by the United Nations in 1948. This stated:

> In the present Convention, genocide means any of the following acts committed with intent to destroy, in whole or in part, a national, ethnical, racial or religious group, as such:
> (a) Killing members of the group;
> (b) Causing serious bodily or mental harm to members of the group;
> (c) Deliberately inflicting on the group conditions of life calculated to bring about its physical destruction in whole or in part;
> (d) Imposing measures intended to prevent births within the group;
> (e) Forcibly transferring children of the group to another group.[53]

It was not until the 1980s that colonialism came into view in international bodies as the context for genocide. Then the key regions under investigation were Australia, Africa and North America. When in 1998 Alison Palmer reviewed research on 'colonial and modern genocide', the issue of Palestine did not appear;[54] in 2009, however, an independent committee of lawyers and medical experts produced a report, *No Safe Place*, assessing the genocidal intent of the Cast Lead offensive on Gaza. It found that there was an arguable case against Israel: the charge of genocide was not proved, it concluded, although some members of Israel's armed forces may have acted with 'genocidal special intent'.[55]

'Genocidal ideology'

In 2010 Martin Shaw – one of the pioneer figures in Genocide Studies – made the case for colonial settlement and associated genocide perpetrated by Israel. He argued that developments in Palestine should be set within the history of colonial rule and of the 'genocidal mentality' present among nationalist elites in Eastern Europe – the milieu, he suggested, 'in which Zionism itself was formed', for '*it had become normal, in formulating a project for a nationally homogenous state, to envisage removing populations who did not fit*' (emphasis in original):

> The proposal here is therefore that we should view Israel's destruction of large parts of Arab society in Palestine in 1948 not simply through the perspective of settler-colonial genocide, but as an extension of the exclusivist nationalism which had recently brought about extensive genocidal violence in the European war.[56]

Shaw saw the widespread destruction of Arab society in Palestine in 1948 as 'partly genocidal', motivated by 'the genocidal ideology of "transfer"' but without an overarching plan. He called this 'a partly decentred, networked genocide'.[57] Debate intensified, with partisans of Israel expressing outrage that the Zionist movement should be viewed in this way but others asserting not only that the Nakba revealed genocidal intent but that, in the Palestinian case, genocide was an ongoing process.[58]

In 2024, during Israel's invasion and mass killings in Gaza, Raz Segal and Luigi Daniele declared that genocide in Palestine had been under way for generations. Rejection of this proposition, they said, amounted to denial of Palestinian history and to 'memoricide' – an attempt to marginalise, minimise and disavow the Palestinian experience.[59] In March 2024 Francesca Albanese, UN Special Rapporteur on the situation of human rights in the Occupied Palestinian Territories, declared: 'There are reasonable grounds to believe that the threshold indicating the commission of the crime of genocide…has been met'.[60] Israel had committed three acts of genocide, she said: causing serious bodily or mental harm to members of the group (Palestinians); deliberately inflicting on the group conditions of life calculated to bring about its physical destruction in whole or in part; and imposing measures intended to prevent births within the group. In a telling further observation, she declared: 'the genocide in Gaza is the most extreme stage of a long-standing settler colonial process of erasure of the native Palestinians':

> For over 76 years, this process has oppressed the Palestinians as a people in every way imaginable, crushing their inalienable right to self-determination demographically, economically, territorially, culturally and politically…the colonial amnesia of the West has condoned Israel's colonial settler project… [T]he world now sees the bitter fruit of the impunity afforded to Israel. This was a tragedy foretold.[61]

Israeli officials saw the report as 'an obscene inversion of reality', the charge of genocide against Israel as 'an outrageous distortion of the Genocide Convention'.[62] But for the first time in an international forum, Israel was not only faced by a formal charge of genocide but also held responsible for crimes committed as part of a colonial settler project. In May 2024 the International Court of Justice concluded that allegations of Israeli conduct in Gaza as genocide were 'plausible'. It ordered Israel to halt its military offensive and other actions which might inflict on the Palestinians in Gaza conditions of life 'that could bring about its physical destruction in whole or in part'.[63]

Zionism and exclusion

Settler colonialism 'destroys to replace', says Patrick Wolfe, quoting Theodor Herzl's manifesto-cum-novel *Altneuland* (Old/New Land), published in 1902: 'If I wish to substitute a new building for an old one,' wrote Herzl, 'I must demolish before I construct'.[64] In the case of Palestine, Herzl envisaged a Zionist state from which the indigenous population had been removed, proposing: 'We shall try to spirit the penniless population across the border' (see Chapter 1). Leaders of the settler project from Weizmann through Weitz and Ben-Gurion, together with leading figures of the Israeli state, had schemes for 'transfer' of the Palestinians, aiming to leave the land free for the Jewish population. Revisionist Zionists from Jabotinsky onwards were more confrontational, seeing decisive conflicts with the Palestinian Arabs and their expropriation as necessary and appropriate. Did this amount to a continuous effort to accomplish their elimination? Mark Levene warns against 'drawing a straight line from Herzl through Ben-Gurion to Ariel Sharon and beyond' and seeing a continuous commitment to removal of the Palestinians. This, he suggests, 'elides all manner of Zionist thinking and practice which has been more circumspect, cautious, and often energized by the potential for a Zionist–Arab relationship in which the two peoples might live together'.[65]

Some currents within Zionism sought such accommodations (see Chapter 3), but from 1948 Zionist militias/the Israeli state engaged in repeated efforts to target the Palestinians – first in the mass confrontations of the Nakba, later by attempts to induce 'migration' by deportation, by confinement, by repeated military assaults, and – in partnership with settler activists – by relentless exclusion from the land. Rather than a 'straight line' of Zionist ideologues and Israeli leaders working for elimination of the Palestinians, contemporary history records a process common to many projects of settler colonialism – that of 'slow-motion genocide'.[66] This has been marked by long periods of mass displacement, land seizures and intense repression – and attempts to exploit captive populations, to seek collaborators, and to project false visions of statehood.

To what extent did Israel's conquest of the West Bank and Gaza affect the process of colonial settlement and of 'slow-motion' genocide? Menachem Klein suggests that after 1967 'border conflict' became 'an ethnic struggle between Israeli Jews and Arab Palestinians within a one-state reality', where the single state was a Jewish ethnocracy.[67] It is at this point, he argues, that 'the ethnic foundation of Judaism is increasingly used to justify the system of Israeli control'.[68] In this view, it is not the colonial character of the Zionist project that is problematic but a specific expansion of territory, bringing millions of Palestinians under military occupation: here, the Israel of 1948 has legitimacy lacking in the case of territories seized in 1967. But, writes Lorenzo Veracini, 'settler colonial objectives have informed Zionist actions pre-1948, post-1948 and post-1967'.[69] There has been 'continuity of intent' among those who shaped the early strategies of the settler movement and later of the Israeli state.[70]

Israel's ability to pursue a successful settler colonial project based on comprehensive control of the indigenous population has declined because people of the West Bank and Gaza have repeatedly launched mass struggles. The more resistance, the more that Israel's offensives have been openly racist, championed in recent decades by parties embedded in Israel's settlements. In 2004 Avigdor Lieberman, leader of right-wing Yisrael Beiteinu (Israel Our Home), proposed a 'transfer' plan in which areas under settlement would become part of Israel in exchange for Arab villages within Israel's borders. Lieberman's agenda, says Yiftachel, was 'colonialist, racist', aiming to advance 'apartheid-like measures' and intensifying 'a race of ethnic outbidding', drawing mainstream Jewish parties in Israel towards more and more aggressive separatism.[71] As resistance continued, the Israeli Right successfully argued for regulations, laws and practices of militarism that entrenched ethnocentrism. Ronit Lentin comments that Israel became more 'blithely racist against its colonised subjects', including the Palestinian Arab minority within its borders.[72] In 2017 Lieberman, now in office as defence minister, declared that Palestinian Arab citizens had no place in Israeli society: 'They should understand that they are not wanted here, they are not part of us.'[73]

Max Blumenthal comments that by the time of the 50-day offensive on Gaza in 2014, calls for ethnic cleansing and incitements to genocide had become familiar features of mainstream Israeli discourse.[74] Religious nationalists and other parties of the Right dominated national debates, justifying brutal military actions with messianic pronouncements and fanning the flames of genocide in public discussion. Avigdor Lieberman was prominent among those demanding full reoccupation of Gaza: soon others with similar intentions entered government, appointed to ministerial positions under Benjamin Netanyahu.

In October 2023 they led efforts to transform 'slow-motion genocide' into erasure of the population of Gaza – assaults aimed not just to contain, control, or subordinate Gaza 'but to shatter and break up its social existence'.[75]

In 2024 Israel historian Arie Dubnov feared 'genocidal atrocities and ethnic cleansing' across the Occupied Territories: 'While everyone's attention would remain fixated on Gaza…local [Israeli] settlement guards or militias functioning as irregular or semi-regular units, akin to paramilitaries, could turn the West Bank into hell on earth'.[76] Belazel Smotrich of the Religious Zionism Party, Netanyahu's finance minister, called for 'establishment of new cities and settlements deep in the [West Bank]', housing hundreds of thousands of new settlers.[77] Palestinians who dissented should 'emigrate', he said.[78] In October 2024, at an event held close to Gaza and within sight and sound of the war, Israeli activists including government ministers called for re-occupation. Organised by Netanyahu's Likud Party and by Nachala, a settler group from the West Bank, the event, 'Planning to resettle Gaza', heard from Itamar Ben-Gvir, head of the Jewish Power party and minister for national security, propose that Israel should 'encourage emigration' of Palestinians from Gaza: 'We're giving you the option', he said, 'leave to other countries, the Land of Israel is ours.'[79]

Resistance in the 'mega-prison' of Gaza continued in ways that infuriated the Israeli state.[80] *Sumud* had become an aspect of everyday life – resistance expressed as resilience organised from below. Distinguished from armed struggle and high-profile public mobilisations, *sumud* marks refusal in daily life to accept occupation and subordination. An aspect of Palestinian life since the 1920s, *sumud* took on greater significance during the intifadas of 1987 and 2000 and then after full closure of the West Bank and Gaza. *Samidin* (those who are steadfast) included Palestinian prisoners, martyrs (those who have died in struggle), and all those living under pressure of occupation, especially families and close-knit communities. A focus of *sumud* is determination to stay on the land: as graffiti on Israel's apartheid wall declares, 'To exist is to resist'. Alexandra Rijke and Toine van Teeffelen comment:

> New prototypical examples of *sumud* entered popular consciousness: the peasant whose olive trees were uprooted by the Israeli army or settlers, but who replanted them; the family who rebuilt their house each time after it was demolished; the community surrounded by settlements but still hanging on; and in the different but also demanding context of Palestinians living in Israel, fighting for equality while keeping the link to the land, or rebuilding destroyed residential areas of the Bedouins in the Negev.[81]

Rijke and van Teeffelen quote a community organiser from Aida refugee camp in the West Bank: 'That I am here is *sumud*. To reclaim that you are a human being and defending your humanity is *sumud*.'[82] The word took on wider meanings, embracing Palestinians outside the historic homeland, those who 'stay steadfast in the diaspora', raising support and solidarity. *Sumud* challenged memoricide:

> To reclaim that I am Palestinian, wherever I am, is sumud. Sumud is preserving the identity, the memories, the customs and habits, the popular arts, the attachment to the land, the values that make us into human beings, across generations.[83]

If the aspiration of American strategists to enforce US hegemony worldwide had proved illusionary, so too was the aim of political leaders in Israel to suppress Palestinian resistance. In the face of *sumud*, zealous activists of the Israeli Right called for exclusionary measures. Mark Levene, a historian of genocide, wrote in the *Journal of Genocide Research*:

> From the very inception of the modern Zionist project, the notion that somehow the indigenous population might be whisked away, or, in later thought, formally transferred to somewhere outside Palestine has been a recurring motif. [Now] ultra-right calls for Palestinian removal from within Netanyahu's Government have become little short of deafening…the logic of what is happening now in Gaza *is* ethnic cleansing. A second Nakba [emphasis in original].[84]

The target of Israel's offensive could not realistically be Hamas, said Levene, for the organisation 'will redeploy from underneath the rubble at will'. Referencing the pioneering work of Rafael Lemkin, he saw Israel's war as 'a conscious, wilful effort to destroy the integrity of a society'. Levene concluded: 'The charge of genocide is legitimate.'[85]

'Global Palestine'

The assault on Gaza that began in October 2023 was carried out in plain sight. As Israel's allies endorsed mass killing and despatched arms and ammunition for the IDF, millions of people worldwide participated in demonstrations of protest. Changes that had been under way for decades, largely unobserved by media and academic researchers, had laid the basis for global solidarity.

The war of 1967, says historian Russell Rickford, was a 'watershed moment in African American–Palestinian relations'.[86] Young African Americans were grappling with the meaning of the Vietnam War and the relationship between their own struggles and those of oppressed people around the world. For the first time, 'Zionism's colonial subjects became potential comrades within the global circuits of liberation':

> [D]ispossessed African Americans, increasingly concentrated in deteriorating urban districts, faced circumstances akin to those of captive Palestinians. Both populations constituted internal or 'domestic' colonies – superexploited, sequestered, and subject to foreign authority. 'We are a kind of dispossessed people in exile,' the Black historian John Henrik Clarke asserted in 1973, 'so we have sympathy for the Arabs who were dispossessed of their land'.[87]

The radical mood of the late 1960s – 'Third World fellowship, the colonial thesis, and the imaginary of guerrilla warfare – evoked lines of affinity with Palestine', says Rickford.[88] Increasing evidence of links between Israel, the US and apartheid South Africa at a time of liberation struggles across the African continent solidified support for the Palestine cause.[89] In Europe both the 1967 war and an upsurge of struggles in France in 1968 brought heightened awareness of the Palestine issue. Students, including young French activists of

Arab heritage, played a key role in the establishment of Palestine Committees and later of the Arab Workers Movement.[90] Yoav Di-Capua describes how, in the context of war in Algeria and the mass struggles of 1968, 'the question of Palestine rapidly transformed into a global cause'.[91] In Britain, a first demonstration of solidarity took place in 1969, organised by Palestinian students and activists of the Israeli radical group Matzpen. The initiative began what Paul Kelemen calls a slow 'divorce' within the British left, long supportive of Israel.[92] Palestine activists remained isolated and few in number, however: for years 'the contrast with Britain's highly efficient and organised pro-Israel lobby could not have been greater'.[93]

In 2003 Edward Said noted an important change: 'solidarity here [in the US] and everywhere in Latin America, Africa, Europe, Asia and Australia…[for] a cause to which many people have committed themselves, difficulties and terrible obstacles notwithstanding'.[94] In 1999 an emerging anti-globalisation movement had challenged the World Trade Organisation (sibling of the IMF and the World Bank) at its conference in Seattle and in 2001 activists established a World Social Forum to debate strategies for global justice, with Palestine high on the agenda. The US-led invasion of Iraq produced huge protests worldwide: for the first time the issue of Palestine was widely linked to war in the Gulf, to imperialism and Israel's role in the Middle East. In the UK a mass movement co-ordinated by the Stop the War Coalition organised the largest protest in British history: opposing invasion of Iraq, it also headlined 'Freedom for Palestine'. By 2007 John Collins could write: 'The centrality of Palestine to the global struggle for justice and human dignity seems to grow larger by the day.'[95] A new slogan was being heard among activists across the continents, he noted: 'We are all Palestinians.'[96]

Chapter 12
Revolution

'Global Palestine' – movements of solidarity. Crisis of the left. Palestine as a catalyst for change – Egypt and the Tahrir Revolution

After decades of ignorance, misunderstanding and denial, Palestine was being integrated into agendas for change worldwide. In 2002 a conference in Cairo brought together anti-war activists from Egypt, the Arab region, Europe and North America. For the first time since the end of the colonial era, significant numbers of radical activists from the Middle East and the West met in common cause, welcoming speakers from Palestine and issuing a Cairo Declaration against US hegemony and war on Iraq, and in solidarity with the Palestinians.[1]

The conference met annually for the next seven years, as Palestine 'became a *cause célèbre* for global justice activists'.[2] Events in Cairo had already marked an important change – from passive identification of Egyptians with Palestinian struggles to active support. In 2000, as the Al-Aqsa Intifada gained momentum, school and university students in Cairo demonstrated against the Mubarak dictatorship and for Palestine – the first time since Egypt's 'Uprising of Bread' in 1977 that such numbers had taken to the streets.

Eyewitnesses in Giza, Egypt's third largest city, described an astonishing sight, as thousands of young women left their classrooms to demonstrate in the streets against Israeli repression.[3] A national solidarity organisation was soon established: the Egyptian Popular Committee in Solidarity with the Intifada (EPCSI), formed by ten leading NGOs. In September 2001 it successfully called a demonstration that marched through Tahrir Square in protest at US backing for Israel – an unprecedented defiance of the Mubarak regime. In 2002 the movement resumed with greater energy. Hossam el-Hamalawy later recollected:

> I recall the first time I heard protesters en masse chanting against the president [Mubarak] in April 2002, during the pro-Palestinian riots around Cairo University. Battling the notorious central security forces, protesters were chanting in Arabic: 'Hosni Mubarak is just like [Ariel] Sharon'.[4]

Other slogans included: 'We haven't forgotten you, Palestine: we are also occupied!'[5]

In 2003, as the US and its allies invaded Iraq, some 30,000 Egyptians fought the police in Cairo, taking over the centre of the city in what they called a 'Tahrir Intifada', often described by Egyptian activists as a breakthrough experience in their efforts to confront the dictatorship.[6] Demonstrators chanted: 'Mubarak, leave, leave' and 'Ala'a [Mubarak's son] tell your dad that millions hate him!'[7] One activist declared jubilantly: 'This is the first time we've made it out of the cage.'[8] Further protests became what Rabab El Mahdi calls a 'cycle of contestation' in which 'each phase of activity was related to earlier actions and to the responses of the state'.[9] These developments raised the confidence of activists who in 2004 initiated the Kifaya (Enough) movement, campaigning against the regime's aim to establish a hereditary presidency, for Egyptians' freedom of expression, and in solidarity with Palestine. A national democracy movement was under construction as rallies and marches that evaded Mubarak's riot police took place in working-class areas of Cairo and other cities[10]. At the same time, independent trade unions emerged – a response to years of neoliberal attacks on Egyptian workers. In 2008 there were over 600 strikes, sit-ins and demonstrations, and postal workers, health workers and teachers formed independent union groups.[11] Egypt moved towards the revolutionary confrontation of January 2011, when tens of millions mobilised against the regime. Scenes from Tahrir Square were broadcast worldwide, as demonstrators insisted: 'The people want to bring down the regime.' When, within days, mass strikes had paralysed key sectors of the economy, Mubarak fell. Working-class mobilisation was the key component of a movement that brought to an end three decades of dictatorship – an expression of the power of workplace action linked to the energies of the streets.

Palestine featured in many of the demonstrations, rallies and debates that continued for the next two and a half years. In 'The Road to Jerusalem through Tahrir Square', Reem Abou-el-Fadl writes that Egyptians connected their impoverishment to Mubarak's subservience to the US and Israel, and to his personal profiteering from such relationships:

> This subtle connection was made more explicit by banners, chants, and songs denouncing rising food prices, plummeting wages, and privatization, intermingled with slogans condemning foreign interference under Mubarak... The focus on Israel was particularly clear: images of Mubarak adorned with Israeli symbols appeared, along with banners in Hebrew asking him to leave and chants and signs saying that he would be welcome in Tel Aviv.[12]

Wassim Wagdy, an Egyptian revolutionary socialist, observed that Palestinians were mistreated and abused not only by Israel but also by all the Arab regimes because they were rightly considered to be carriers of a virus – 'that virus is called revolution'.[13] Palestinian resistance had long stimulated solidarity movements and opposition to the regimes:

> The link between the oppression and exploitation of the Egyptian masses and the dispossession and oppression of Palestinians is clear and direct. When people go on solidarity marches, they are beaten up by the same regimes that have made peace with Israel and abuse and mistreat the Palestinians.[14]

The revolution had begun with three main slogans, said Wagdy: '"Bread, Freedom and Social Justice" was the first. We borrowed the second one from the Tunisian revolution – "The people want the fall of the regime". But the third we learnt from the Palestinians – "Revolution until Victory"'.[15]

From Tahrir Square to the textile mills of the Nile Delta, among rail and bus workers, in hospitals and schools, on campuses and government offices, ideas and practices of radical change were in daily discussion. The movement that had deposed Mubarak took on the character of mass strikes. In the days following Mubarak's fall there were 40-60 disputes per day; by the end of February there had been almost 500 episodes of strike action or other forms of collective protest.[16] Here, mass action at the national and local levels combined economic, social and political issues. Demands over wages and conditions of work were made alongside opposition to the violence of the police and state security forces; calls for freedom of expression and organisation combined with insistent demands for provision of housing, clean water and sanitation, for *tathir* ('cleansing' of institutions associated with the Mubarak regime) and for rights to the land.[17] Palestine solidarity groups appeared in schools, universities, neighbourhoods and in workplace groups and networks, and in independent trade unions outside the control of the state. The newly formed Independent Egyptian Trade Union Federation declared: 'We affirm our complete support for the right of the Palestinian Arab people to create an independent state in the whole of Palestine, and their right to use whatever means of resistance to achieve their rights.'[18]

A week after Mubarak's fall in February 2011, 3 million people gathered in Tahrir Square: their demonstration, says Abou-el-Fadl, 'abounded in explicitly pro-Palestinian chants and statements, including "To Jerusalem we're going; martyrs in our millions!"'[19] Mass protests subsequently took place every Friday in Tahrir, ending with marches to the Israeli embassy. For months demonstrators besieged the embassy with slogans: 'Arm us, arm us, to Gaza, send us!'; 'The people want the liberation of Palestine!'; and 'Where is Israel? The Egyptian people are here!'[20] Nakba Day, 13 May, saw a demonstration of a million in Cairo, and during the summer months there were protests in provincial cities including Fayyum, Damanhur, Ismailiyya, Suez, Mansura and Luxor. In September 2011, tens of thousands marched to the embassy. *Al Jazeera* reported:

> Protesters demolished [an outer] wall, erected to protect the embassy which has become a focus for protests, with makeshift battering rams and hammers… Some protesters then scaled the wall of the building, replacing the Israeli flag with Egyptian and Palestinian flags… Hundreds of Egyptian soldiers backed by armoured cars were rushed to the embassy district and clashed with the protesters, who torched police vehicles and attacked regional police headquarters nearby.[21]

The Israeli ambassador and his staff were rescued by military police and flown out of Egypt to Tel Aviv. Egypt's interior ministry blamed 'foreign hands' – a routine explanation for protests that challenged institutions of the state.[22] Demonstrations continued and Egyptian activists travelled to Gaza in solidarity convoys involving delegates from women's organisations, youth, workers and representatives of the new trade unions.

'Surfing the tide'

The revolutionary movement demanded action on Palestine: most importantly abrogation of the peace treaty with Israel agreed by the Sadat regime in 1979. Politicians in Israel expressed their fears: 'The revolt against President Hosni Mubarak in Egypt', wrote Aluf Benn of *Haaretz*, 'invokes fear and anxiety among Israelis. Mubarak, Israel's oldest neighbor, is suddenly moving out, and Israelis are afraid of the consequences.'[23] Mubarak had been the key Arab ally of the US and Israel, apparently cemented into power and committed to neoliberal policies and to isolation and control of the Palestinians. His removal by a mass movement demanding social justice had implications for imperialist networks across the Middle East – arrangements that had sustained Israel for decades. Daniel Byman notes 'apocalyptic predictions' in Israel and fear of what was to come.[24] 'The biggest Israeli concern', he wrote, 'and the one that has gotten the most attention, is the replacement of the Mubarak regime in Egypt by, well, that's the question':

> For much of Israel's history, Egypt was its most dangerous foe, and the two countries fought bitter wars in 1948, 1956, 1967, 1969-1970, and 1973. Egyptian President Anwar Sadat upended this seemingly constant belligerency when he made peace with Israel, transforming Israel's greatest foe into a partner... [Mubarak] did maintain the peace treaty, cooperate on counterterrorism, oppose Iran, and otherwise share strategic objectives with the Jewish state. And he and his regime seemed immovable... Who comes to power next is of tremendous concern to Israel.[25]

The 'immovable' dictator had gone and 'tumult overturns all the certainties of past decades'.[26] Israeli leaders feared all manner of challenges: the spread of revolutionary contagion across the Arab states; the energisation of Palestinian resistance; weakened influence of the Fatah elite and the PA; and encouragement of Hamas and Palestine's homegrown Islamists. Most important, they feared ordinary Egyptians – those who had toppled Mubarak and aimed for social justice. The *Los Angeles Times* commented: 'Israel would rather have autocratic friends than democratic enemies.'[27] Its allies struggled to keep pace with events. The US had armed successive Egyptian regimes and trained Egypt's officer corps and security agencies – instruments of oppression. Now President Barack Obama attempted to stand publicly with the insurrection: 'There is something in the soul that cries out for freedom', said Obama – invoking civil rights leader Martin Luther King. 'Those were the cries that came from Tahrir Square, and the entire world has taken note.' Obama declared:

> The word Tahrir means liberation… And forevermore it will remind us of the Egyptian people – of what they did, of the things that they stood for, and how they changed their country, and in doing so changed the world.[28]

This was hollow praise: Sergio Fabbrini and Amr Yossef describe Obama's efforts to keep pace with events as 'surfing the tide'.[29] US strategists were confronted by mass participatory democracy – a striking contrast to decades of dictatorship that aimed to sow fear and suspicion among Egyptians on the basis of differences of religion, community and gender. Charles Hirschkind observes that millions of people organised together, notwithstanding religious affiliation or differences between secularists and religious believers: 'The entire mobilization unfolded without the question "secular or religious?" ever imposing itself on the expressions of popular sovereignty.'[30] Members of the large Christian minority were prominent in public mobilisations and in organisations that emerged in workplaces and neighbourhoods. Christian priests spoke alongside Muslim imams; both churches and mosques provided field hospitals and sanctuaries during conflicts with forces of the state. Many testimonies of women participants assert that the gender differences were minimised during the uprising. Women and men organised the protests, secured the squares, and gave speeches, said Nadia Tahir: 'No one sees you as a woman here; no one sees you as a man. We are all united in our desire for democracy and freedom.'[31] Women entered public political activity en masse, notably in workplaces and in the new independent trade unions.[32] After months of collective action the regime required a sinister initiative – in the form of public assaults on women and girls by military police – to introduce fear of harassment and abuse among protestors.[33] Here, there were parallels with the Palestinian intifadas – initiatives for direct democracy both drew strength from the mass movement and built local confidence to sustain it, overriding differences that those in power sought to sustain and deepen.

Laudatory comments from Obama and European leaders reflected their growing anxiety at the global impact of events. Within days of the Tahrir insurrection, activists in the US published calls for 'A million-man march on Wall Street: how to spark a people's revolt in the West'.[34] Soon, writes Sarah Kerton, they had initiated the Occupy Movement: 'a global protest form that borrow[ed] heavily from the strategic and tactical methodologies of the Egyptian revolution and gained widespread media coverage with the emergence of Occupy Wall Street'.[35] Jeffrey Alexander followed the explosive growth of the movement:

> The Egyptian Revolution captured the global imaginary: It became a neon-lit symbol of human courage, a flashing advertisement for the possibility of democratic social mobilization against the powers-that-be... Among massed demonstrators [worldwide] explicit references to 'Tahrir' frequently appeared.[36]

Occupy encampments were established in more than 150 cities in the US, declaring for the '99 percent' against inequality, corporate capital and corruption.[37] Within weeks, hundreds of cities worldwide had seen Occupy initiatives: in many encampments, tent-cities and demonstrations, Palestine featured as a key issue. Echoing events in Egypt, protestors raised Palestinian flags, demanded an end to Israeli occupation, and called for boycotts of Israeli products. Palestinians responded: the Boycott, Divestment and Sanctions National

Committee (BNC) declared that it was proud to stand in solidarity with 'movements struggling for a new world based on democracy, human rights and economic justice'. The BNC added:

> Palestinians, too, are part of the 99% around the world that suffer at the hands of the 1% whose greed and ruthless quest for hegemony have led to unspeakable suffering and endless war. Corporate power has not just profited from our suffering but has colluded in maintaining Israel's occupation and apartheid to perpetuate an unjust order that profits oil and military companies and multinational financial institutions.[38]

Such was the impact of the movement that in Israel protestors also established encampments to challenge 'social inequalities and wrongful national priorities'.[39] Encouraged by the power of the masses in Arab countries, demonstrators in cities including Tel Aviv, Haifa, Jerusalem, and Beer Sheva chanted: 'The People want Social Justice'. Hundreds of thousands participated, demanding an end to Israel's housing crisis and controls on consumer prices. Those who had initiated the movement, however, declined to address the Palestine issue and the occupation regime: 'social justice' remained justice for Israelis alone.[40] Eren Kaplan writes: 'When the social protests of 2011 began gaining steam, its leaders made a concerted effort to avoid questions regarding the Israeli occupation', seeking to present themselves as 'apolitical' and even welcoming leaders of the West Bank settlements.[41] The Egyptian movement, inspired by Palestinian struggles, sought change and an end to the occupation: there were implications for Israelis who questioned a Zionist future based on ethnic exclusivism and endless conflict, and who identified with the millions in Tahrir. But leaders of Occupy stood within the mainstream of Israeli politics – the issue of Palestine, says Kaplan, remained 'an elephant in the Israeli political "room"'.[42] Whether in ignorance of global solidarity with Palestine, or in denial, leading Israeli activists were prepared to disregard the most pressing issue in regional politics. Soon young participants from the tent camps were again in action with Israel's armed forces. Within a year the IDF had launched Operation Pillar of Defence, a new assault on Gaza, killing hundreds of Palestinians.

The Brotherhood retreats

On 21 August 2011, public figures from 13 Egyptian parties and organisations petitioned the Supreme Council of the Armed Forces (SCAF – an interim ruling body composed of senior officers) with demands including the suspension of diplomatic and economic ties with Israel. It was clear that, as Egypt moved towards its first democratic elections, Palestine would continue to be a key issue. In a general election held during December 2011 and January 2012, the Muslim Brotherhood (in the shape of its Freedom and Justice Party) won a clear majority; in June 2012 its candidate Mohamed Mursi was elected as president. He was empowered to take decisive action on Palestine – on Gaza, the peace treaty, trade with Israel, and a host of measures of 'normalisation'. Expectations were high that Mursi would bring change at home and act decisively on Palestine. He did neither. Busy appointing members of the Brotherhood to positions of authority and consolidating the organisation's business interests and international links, Mursi ignored the clamour for reform. In the past the Brotherhood had called on the regimes of Sadat and Mubarak 'to open the doors of *jihad* against Israel', invoking Islamic traditions of struggle (*jihad*: 'exertion'/'striving').[43] Now in government it was passive. The border with Gaza – viewed by millions as 'Egypt's shame' – remained closed. Following Israel's Pillar of Defence bombardment in November 2012, the Brotherhood called on Arab and Muslim leaders and rulers 'to champion the cause of their nation and apply all pressure to stop the shedding of Palestinian blood and put an end to Israeli arrogance'.[44] There were widespread demonstrations in support of Gaza but Mursi neither opened the border to solidarity initiatives nor accepted Palestinian victims of the assault. The contradiction became more glaring as the Brotherhood declared:

> [All] national political forces [should] consider all ways and procedures to support our Palestinian brothers, such as economic boycott, popular rejection, increasing public awareness of the truth about the Palestinian issue, and supporting the resistance alternative and the right of return of all Palestinian refugees.[45]

Mursi pursued none of these aims: as Ewan Stein points out, the Brotherhood behaved 'like a loyal opposition', maintaining most of the policies of the Mubarak regime. In foreign affairs, it wished 'to remain within the US-led security arrangement in the Middle East'.[46] Contradictions evident since the era of Hassan al-Banna had come to the fore: elitist and authoritarian, the Brotherhood was focused on acquiring influence in the state and prepared to compromise on issues that its formal politics once made matters of principle. The revolutionary upheaval – with its strikes, mass protests, independent unions, campaigns of cleansing, and millions of radical activists – had challenged Egyptian capitalism and destabilised the state. Expectations of radical change continued but Mursi, now residing in the presidential palace, ignored demands of the mass movement. One of the Brotherhood's leading youth activists declared:

> Our analysis is different and so is our vision. The Brotherhood [leadership] does not believe in revolutionary change only reform and to them the revolution so far has given them all they needed which is legal recognition. We want complete change from below...from the roots.[47]

Authority drained away from Mursi and his administration: by 2013 a petition campaign against the Brotherhood gained mass support, laying the ground for counter-revolution that in July 2013 brought a bloody military coup as General Abdel-Fattah al-Sisi seized control, targeting the Brotherhood in a series of massacres and jailing tens of thousands of its activists.[48] Israeli leaders were delighted: at a stroke, Sisi resolved many of their pressing problems. Hamas had celebrated the rise to influence in Egypt of its 'parent' organisation, the Muslim Brotherhood: in the event, the Brotherhood supervised an historic retreat, leaving Hamas isolated and consolidating the weakened status in Palestine of the Fatah-led PA. In Egypt, Sisi targeted activists who had played a key role in the revolutionary upsurge, including those who had launched and sustained the movement of solidarity with Palestine. The events of 2011 to 2013 had demonstrated the power of the masses and opportunities for profound change; they had also shown the importance of political agendas focused on change in the nature of the state, direct democracy and the fulfilment of promises, including commitments on Palestine. Egyptian activists were faced with profound questions. Why had their movement not fulfilled the expectations of millions? The Islamist movement had failed the test – but where was the left and the revolutionary socialist alternative?

The left – from Egypt to Palestine

The history of the left in Egypt is part of a story of uprisings, intifadas and revolutions made and unmade across the Arab region – and closely connected to the fate of the left in Palestine. Egypt's communists had played a leading role during workers' struggles and the emergence of a mass anti-colonial movement in the 1930s. They were part of a succession of strikes and demonstrations against British rule that, during the late 1940s, made Egypt ungovernable for the colonial regime. During this period revolutionary change seemed certain to remove the British and the Egyptian monarchy, and to sweep aside the ineffectual Wafd Party. Both communists and Islamists promised change and millions of Egyptians called for decisive action. But, writes historian Selma Botman, the communist movement 'was not set up to assume political power'.[49] Hampered by loyalties to the Soviet Union, and by twists and turns in policy pursued by the Communist International, Egypt's communist leaders retreated. The Communist International, or Comintern, had been born during the triumph of the Russian Revolution of 1917 but by the late 1920s had fallen under control of the Soviet Union's military-bureaucratic regime under Joseph Stalin. It directed Egypt's communists to find 'progressive forces' among the capitalist class with the aim of seeking reforms and positions in government. Joel Gordon comments that even as the colonial order disintegrated, the left was unable to take the initiative: 'Ideology, organisational deficiency, and a mind-set that remained reformist precluded serious thoughts of revolution.'[50] In 1952 the army seized power, suppressing the workers' movement and jailing leading activists.

Communists were disoriented, not least by policies advocated by Soviet leaders, for whom the army officers, under Colonel Gamal Abdel-Nasser, were alternately 'fascist' and 'progressive', depending upon their changing relationship with Moscow. After years of diminishing influence, leaders of the Egyptian Communist Party (ECP) liquidated their organisation on the basis that the military regime delivered everything that the party could hope to achieve.[51] The left never recovered, the few communists who remained later drawing close to the Mubarak regime. When revolution erupted in 2011, the traditional communist left was largely absent from the scene – a key reason why millions of people anticipating radical change focused expectations upon the Muslim Brotherhood, which for decades had grown in the political space vacated by a once-energetic communist movement. For 20 years, young Egyptians had sought to establish an independent left free of the constraints of Stalinism. In 2011 youth networks played a key role in the uprising; at the same time the Revolutionary Socialists emerged as an independent Marxist presence focused upon the workers' movement, a marker of possibilities for the left in the post-Stalinist era.[52] Playing their part in the events of 2011-2013, they were nonetheless challenged by the scale of the movement and by the increasing influence of the Muslim Brotherhood.

The story of Egypt's traditional left had earlier been repeated across the Middle East. Communist parties in Syria and Iraq had joined governments led by nationalist currents that proved hostile to the mass of people. In the 1960s and 1970s the Iraqi party, once the largest radical force in the Middle East, was ruthlessly attacked by Ba'thists with whom it sought to share power.[53] In Syria, communists joined Ba'thist officers who established the sectarian Assad dynasty, suppressing domestic opposition and the Palestinian resistance. In the search for 'progressive' allies and positions in government, the left was savaged by false friends and military regimes implacably opposed to the interests of the mass of people and to independent organisations of the working class.

'Yishuvism'

In the case of Palestine, communists had also been challenged by the agendas of settler colonialism. In the 1920s the Palestine Communist Party (PCP) was composed largely of Jewish socialists who had migrated to Palestine from Europe. Among its members were activists who aspired to solidarity with Palestinian Arabs in the face of British colonial rule. It was also, however, under the influence of left-Zionists for whom, writes Soliman Bashear, 'Socialism meant a Jewish socialism only':

> When left-wing Zionism happened to talk about a working class, a class struggle, production relations, trade unions, or similar concepts, only a Jewish context was meant. Consequently, it ignored the Arab rejection of Zionist 'socialism' and at best explained it by the backwardness or lack of development of class relations within the Arab camp. It could not perceive that this rejection was the outcome of the basic material contradiction between the colonialist economic and political aims of Zionism and the Palestinian Arab aspirations for independence... For, to realise this contradiction would mean to stop being a Zionist.[54]

Socialist-Zionists had developed the idea of the 'Conquest of Labour'. Settler institutions were to employ exclusively Jewish labour with the aim of developing a Jewish working class that, in theory, would advance socialist ideals. Warned repeatedly by the Comintern in its earliest years (before the organisation was seized by the regime of Stalin) of the dangers of an ethnocentric project, the party nonetheless embraced 'Yishuvism', seeing the Jewish community in Palestine as positively influencing prospects for revolutionary change.[55] After debilitating twists and turns that echoed changes in policy undertaken by communists worldwide, in 1937 the party set up a separate Jewish section; a year later the PCP split formally, with the Jewish group describing Palestinian armed struggles as 'a revolt organised by fascist agents' and asserting that the Jews in Palestine constituted 'a nation'.[56] In 1948, its support for foundation of a state of Israel and for the war that followed, notes Musa Budeiri, 'was total', and some members took active roles in displacement and dispossession of the Palestinian population.[57]

In 1947 the Soviet Union supported UN plans for the partition of Palestine – and its allies in Czechoslovakia supplied the new Israeli state with arms. Now communists were viewed among Palestinians with deep suspicion – discredited, writes Laure Guirguis, 'for having more or less blindly followed the USSR and accepted the United Nations partition plan of Palestine'.[58] When the national movement began to revive in the 1960s, the main influence on its activists – in the absence of an effective left – was that of Fatah's agenda, shaped within the proto-bourgeoisie of the Gulf states.

By the 1940s, collapse of the PCP consolidated support among radical Jewish activists for the Histadrut, integral to structures of the embryonic Zionist state. The organisation worked continuously to deny entry of Palestinian Arabs to mainstream occupations and for decades worked to subvert Palestinian struggles associated with the national movement. This was starkly clear during the intifada that began in December 1987, when most Palestinian workers in the Occupied Territories supported UNLU's call for strikes, so that Israeli agriculture, construction and services were all affected when migrant labour stayed at home. The Histadrut responded by rallying Jewish workers to the employers and to the state. Its general secretary, Israel Kessar, urged members to follow his example, declaring that he would work unpaid as part of an effort to bring in the harvest.[59] In the 1960s Israeli socialists had warned that when Arab activists asked if proletarian solidarity was compatible with calls for the creation of a Jewish state, no Zionist was able to answer: 'they cannot answer [the question] today, any more than they could answer it yesterday.'[60] Racist segregation ensured that their interests lay with the state. Palestinians could not expect solidarity: on the contrary, Israeli workers were part of the historic problem posed by settler colonialism.[61]

The radical left – 'loyal opposition'

It was not until the 1960s that Palestinian activists turned to the Marxist tradition to address the need for new theoretical insights and strategic perspectives. They were members of the Arab Nationalist Movement (ANM), founded in the early 1950s and which had initially rejected the left, viewing communism as 'a dangerous ideological threat to the concept of Arab nationalism'.[62] In the late 1960s they made a sharp turn, adopting radical ideas and practices, and becoming part of international networks that linked Palestinian struggles to anti-imperialist movements in South-East Asia, Africa and Latin America. Leading members of the ANM began to talk of class, imperialism and revolution, the need for 'scientific socialism' and 'a true Marxist-Leninist and internationalist stand'.[63] The DFLP for example sought 'to rally all the forces of national liberation, socialist revolution and the working-class movement' to the Palestinian cause, appealing to 'the world communist movement' for support.[64] But the embrace of Marxist ideas and practices was never wholehearted. In 1968 a delegate to the ANM conference warned: 'The Movement has accepted scientific socialism, but we do not know exactly what it means.'[65] Central to the revolutionary socialist tradition was the principle of independence of ideas and organisation, but the radical left was soon targeted by Arab regimes that sought to bring them under their own influence. Tabitha Petran comments:

> The growing popular appeal of the resistance movement after the 1967 war prompted each Arab regime to create its own 'Palestinian resistance'. Such organisations had little, if anything, to do with the Palestinian cause. They were intended to advance the aims of their patrons in inter-Arab conflicts and to contain and limit the local influence of the authentic resistance.[66]

Palestinian radicals called for 'revolution' but also courted the regimes, securing arms and finance variously from Syria, Algeria, Libya, Iraq and Yemen – each of which pursued its own agendas on the Palestine issue. Mustafa Omar writes that the PFLP made a false distinction between reactionary Arab regimes that accommodated to imperialism and 'progressive nationalist regimes that were forced to fight against it'.[67] The result was a series of alliances with states linked to the Soviet Union, which for decades had directed communists of the region to surrender independent organisation in the search for 'progressive' allies. The Fronts criticised Fatah for its links to the Gulf states but, argues Omar, they became 'a tool in the hands of Arab rulers' who wished to see Palestinian struggles contained and their contagious influence minimised.[68] Both the PFLP and DFLP also attempted to remain within institutions of the PLO where, says Yezid Sayigh, they became 'a loyal opposition' neutralised by Fateh and co-opted by the movement's leadership.[69]

The Syrian regime was particularly hostile to Palestinian struggles that affected its influence in the region. In 1970, Syrian forces watched passively as the Jordanian army assaulted the PLO, including the radical Fronts, during the Black September crisis. In 1976, the regime of President Hafez al-Assad joined with the Maronite Kataeb to attack Palestinian camps in Lebanon, and in 1983 again confronted what remained of PLO forces in northern Lebanon. During the Arab Spring of 2011–13, and in upheavals that followed, the regime of Bashar al-Assad maintained a two-year siege of Yarmouk, the largest Palestinian refugee camp in the diaspora. As tens of thousands of Palestinians crossed the border into Lebanon, the leader of the PLO in the Sabra and Shatila camps in Beirut asked: 'Why this is happening, we can't understand?... We did not interfere in the affairs of Syria and they shouldn't have interfered in ours.'[70]

'Lebanisation'

PFLP leader George Habash had declared: 'The road to Palestine passes through Amman, it passes through Beirut, it passes through Cairo, and it passes through Riyadh.'[71] The more that Palestinian organisations became entangled with regimes across the region, however, the more they faced existential challenges. Tracing the rise and decline of the left in the PLO, Francesco Leopardi observes that Syria 'succeeded to a large extent to limit the PFLP's independence and in some cases drove the Party [the Front] to adopt given stands inconsistent with its own goals'.[72] His comment could stand as an epitaph for the left: many activists were committed to radical change but their leaders aligned with regimes determined to inhibit the movement. The principle of 'non-interference' had shackled Arafat to Arab rulers who were hostile to the mass of Palestinians. When organisations of the left sought alliances with 'progressive' states, they too aligned with regimes disinterested in Palestinian liberation.

Problems intensified after Black September 1970 when Palestinian forces in retreat from Jordan were faced by 'Lebanisation'. The Lebanese state had collapsed and multiple organisations and militias were engaged in conflicts that soon became civil war. Palestinians faced not only the complexities of Lebanon's sectarian politics but also the efforts of Israel and of Arab states, often using agents provocateurs, to create instability by making and breaking alliances with the country's many factions. Syria's Sa'iqa ('Lightning') guerrillas and Iraq's Arab Liberation Front played particularly cynical roles: ostensibly Palestinian militias, they served the Ba'thist regimes in Damascus and Baghdad. During this period militarisation of the PLO advanced rapidly. Fatah constructed ever-larger military units, obtaining heavy weapons, artillery and tanks. The radical Fronts also focused on military means, competing for arms and for recruits. Rex Brynen comments that the project of liberation became increasingly vague and uncertain as 'military action became a veritable end in itself'.[73]

The left also underwent increasing bureaucratisation and institutionalisation.[74] As the focus of Palestinian struggles moved to the West Bank and Gaza, key activists were co-opted by Arafat and, after the Oslo Process of the 1990s, by the activities of a 'professional, elitist and depoliticised NGO sector' introduced by organisations in control of conditional aid to the Palestinian Authority.[75] The PFLP had initially opposed Arafat's initiative for a ministate, leaving the PLO and leading a Rejection Front of smaller radical groups. The organisation soon rejoined the PLO; however, its standing much reduced. Its members were particularly active in the intifada that began in 1987, but their influence declined: Tariq Dana describes a retreat from the initial focus on social justice, equality and socialism as activist practice 'dramatically faded'.[76]

Jamil Hilal, once a leading member of the DFLP, identifies a general crisis of the left as a key factor in these developments. Although organisations such as the PFLP and DFLP had avoided slavish subordination to Moscow, they had viewed the Soviet Communist Party as 'the authoritative reference in matters relating to organizational and intellectual issues'.[77] This not only shaped strategies of the left but also, when the Soviet Union collapsed, prompted an 'ideological retreat of revolutionary ideas and socialist alternatives'.[78] For decades, communist parties had encouraged accommodation with capitalist classes across the region, reducing the credibility of the left and providing opportunities for Islamists to extend their influence. The Soviet collapse accelerated this process: in the case of Palestine, confusion and retreat on the left was a contributory factor in the rise of Hamas and of Islamic Jihad. Dana observes:

> [T]he expansion of Hamas came at a moment when the PLO factions were in crisis amidst the failure to provide an effective liberation strategy. In particular, Hamas managed to fill the void left by the decline of the Palestinian left… As the multi-layered causes of the PFLP and wider left retreat from the political and social arenas intensified, the consequences were evident in the expansion of political Islam.[79]

Solidarity

By the time of the Al-Aqsa Intifada in 2000 the Palestinian movement was in deep crisis. At the same time, support for the Palestinians had grown worldwide, while active solidarity in the Arab states reached new levels of intensity. In Egypt, a process of radicalisation was under way that profoundly affected national politics. Hossam el-Hamalawy recalls:

> People immediately began drawing parallels between the oppression of the Palestinians at the hands of the Israeli apartheid regime and the repression Egyptians were facing under Mubarak's rule. They concluded that if those kids can take on the mighty Israeli tanks, we can take on Mubarak's armored vehicles.[80]

In 2002 there were mass street battles with Egypt's riot police: the following year, protests against the Iraq war and for Palestine led to the occupation of Tahrir Square. Activists independent of the country's tame mainstream parties – and also independent of remnants of the old left – were soon key participants in an emerging democracy movement and in support of strikes that, from 2004, brought a revival in workplace and trade union organisation. It is in this sense that mass protests in solidarity with the intifada were 'a dress rehearsal' for the revolution of 2011.[81]

The Egyptian uprising that began in January 2011, says historian John Chalcraft, showed 'astonishing co-ordination amid spontaneity'.[82] The Mubarak regime attempted to suppress protests in which young people – especially young workers – were most active in confronting the forces of repression. The Society of Heroes and Victims of the Revolution recorded 4,500 injured in early clashes with riot police in Cairo: 70 percent were workers without educational qualifications; 12 percent were workers with intermediate qualifications; 11 percent were school students; and 7 percent held higher qualifications.[83] Alexander and Bassiouney note clusters in traditional working-class quarters and in newer 'informal' housing areas that surround the city. They conclude that the presence of workers, urban poor and members of the lower middle class 'as insurgent citizens in the streets' dramatically shifted the balance of forces in the battle between the people and the regime in a host of Egyptian cities.[84] 'Insurgent citizens' also organised mass strikes in key industries, bringing immense pressure on Egypt's rulers and the swift fall of the dictator Mubarak.

Anne Alexander notes a similar pattern of participation in revolutionary upheavals in Tunisia, Syria and Sudan.[85] Years of neoliberal reform; a surge in informal, 'precarious' labour; declining access to decent healthcare, education and housing; and life in impoverished urban neighbourhoods produced common experiences that brought millions of people into sustained direct action. They shared much with Palestinians among whom for decades, 'the peaks of political mobilisation have expressed the anger of the poor majority at the combination of social injustice and national oppression which blight their lives'.[86] There was a key difference, however. In Egypt, workers' collective action had been intensifying for years before the 2011 revolution: between 2004 and 2010 there were over 3,400 strikes and other collective actions, involving up to four million workers.[87] In February 2011 there were almost 500 strikes affecting every area of the economy and bringing intense pressure on the regime to remove Mubarak.[88] When the dictator fell, the workers' movement – and notably the new independent unions – continued struggles for social justice and for solidarity with Palestine. The weight of workers' action was decisive, mobilising political resources denied to Palestinians by decades of repression and fragmentation of the Palestinian working class, and bringing onto the agenda the issue of revolutionary change, challenging regimes complicit in Israel's colonial project.

For several years after the counter-revolution of 2013, workers' struggles continued. Despite renewed repression, in 2019 cities across Egypt saw demonstrations against the regime of Abdel-Fatah al-Sisi. Slogans raised by thousands of overwhelmingly young participants included: 'Leave, Sisi'; 'Rise up, fear not, Sisi must go'; and once again, 'The people want to bring down the regime.'[89] Increasing problems of unemployment, inflation, corruption and growing inequality make renewed struggles likely, especially among millions of young people who face a deepening jobs crisis – 'a ticking timebomb' according to Egyptian researcher Adel Abdel Ghafar.[90] In 2023 Israel's assault on

Gaza brought renewed solidarity with Palestine. Recalling the date when revolution began in 2011, tens of thousands joined rallies with the slogan: 'We are the youth of January 25, and we will not abandon you, Palestine!'[91] Fearful of pressure from below Sisi lifted restrictions on public protest. Masses filled the streets: in Cairo, their demonstration, says Hesham Sallam, evoked the spirit of the 2011 and 'the subversive energy' that had animated the revolutionary upheaval.[92] Sisi was appalled, ordering a crackdown that carried risks for the regime but, he hoped, would contain radicalisation once more associated with the Palestinian cause. Hundreds were arrested but within months Egyptian students had established a new campaign as campus protests called for Boycott, Divestment and Sanctions (BDS), including action against corporations with investments in Egypt and Israel – key agents of 'normalisation' between the two states. Beneath the surface of a police state, solidarity continued to swirl, linking with struggles across the border in Gaza.

The fate of Egypt is of special concern to Sisi's allies in the US and Israel. The dictator praises young people as 'the hope that lit the flames of change' in 2011.[93] He knows that the fire next time could remove his regime and ignite much wider change. Western analysts warn that Egypt is on a knife-edge. Typical is an assessment of the International Crisis Group that public outrage about the Gaza war may be a catalyst for protest directed at the regime:

> The generation that has come of age since Sisi rose to power in 2013 could lead the way [in mass protests]: these young people did not suffer the bitter disappointment that has coloured the views of their elders, who led the uprising against Mubarak and then watched as the country's democratic experiment collapsed.[94]

Egypt is central to developments across the region. With a population of almost 120 million, the region's largest working class, and more than a century of mass action against colonial powers, home-grown capitalists, and Israel's settler colonialism, Egypt is a focal point for anti-imperialist struggles. A revolutionary activist in Cairo explains: 'Palestine has always brought Egyptians into conflict with the state':

> Israel's crimes, and those of its allies, highlight the history of imperialism in our region, especially the corruption and repression of our own regime. Palestinians' struggle is our own struggle. It played a vital role in events that finally brought revolution in 2011. A great upheaval will come again.
>
> Tens of millions of Egyptians are in poverty and a police state invades our lives. Events in Palestine – Israel's attacks and its attempts at genocide, and the bravery of our sisters and brothers in Gaza and the West Bank – may again be part of a move to insurrection.
>
> We learned much from our revolution in 2011 – the successes and the failures. Next time we want to bring lasting change and to make Egypt a society that stands in solidarity with Palestine: no peace treaties, no deals with the murderer Netanyahu, no troops at the border with Gaza. We owe much to the Palestinians and we'll aim to match their courage and resolve.[95]

In October 2024 revolutionary activists in Cairo recognised the remarkable character of Palestinian resistance in Gaza and the West Bank against overwhelming odds: 'Amid the ruins,' they said, 'fighters and their vast network of supporters continue to stand firm with remarkable courage.'[96] But the resistance could not single-handedly liberate Jerusalem or topple Zionism – 'the very tool of imperialism in our region'.[97] The road to liberating Palestine must include liberation of countries in which regimes have long aligned with imperialism. 'If we are to free Jerusalem,' they insisted, 'we must first free Egypt.'[98] This declaration from the independent left embraced solidarity with a Palestinian people under genocidal threat, recognising their fortitude and the energies of resistance. It also looked forward to further mass struggles in the Arab states – part of a long story of intifadas and revolutions that is far from over.

Endnotes

Preface

1 Miki Zohar in Sokol, Sam (2025) "Ben Gvir says he'll return to government if PM implements Trump's Gaza transfer plan", *Times of Israel*, 5 February. See Introduction to this book on Israel's discourse of 'miracles'.

Introduction

1 Confino, Alon (2012) "Miracles and snow in Palestine and Israel: Tantura, a history of 1948", *Israel Studies*, Vol 17, No 2, pp25–61, p26.

2 Confino, 2012, p26.

3 Confino, 2012, p26.

4 Masalha, Nur (1992) *Expulsion of the Palestinians: The Concept of 'Transfer' in Zionist Political Thought, 1892–1948* (Washington, DC: Institute for Palestine Studies), p175.

5 Rackman, Emanuel (1954) *Israel's Emerging Constitution 1948–51* (Columbia University Press), pix.

6 Quoted in Adelman, Jonathan (2008) *The Rise of Israel: A History of a Revolutionary State* (Routledge), p14.

7 Shlaim, Avi (1995) "The debate about 1948", *International Journal of Middle East Studies*, Vol 27, No 3, pp287–304, p293.

8 Trouillot. Michel-Rolph (1995) *Silencing the Past: Power and the Production of History* (Boston: Beacon Press), pxix.

9 Trouillot, 1995, pxix.

10 Masalha, Nur (2018) "Decolonising methodology, reclaiming history: Palestinian oral histories and memories of the Nakba", in Abdo, Nahla and Masalha, Nur (eds) *An Oral History of the Palestinian Nakba* (London: Zed), p7.

11 Khalidi, Rashid I. (2021) "The Journal of Palestine Studies in the twenty-first century: An editor's reflections", *Journal of Palestine studies*, Vol 50, No 3, pp5–17, p7.

12 Khalidi, 2021, p7.

13 Kaplan, Amy (2018) *Our American Israel: The Story of an Entangled Alliance* (Cambridge, MA: Harvard University Press).

14 Kaplan, 2018, front matter.

15 Finlay, Thomas (1878) "The centenary of Voltaire", *The Irish Monthly*, Vol 6, pp397–411, p406.

16 Masalha, 2018, p9.

17 Masalha, 2018, p10.

18 Euro-Mediterranean Human Rights Monitor (2023) "Israel hits Gaza Strip with the equivalent of two nuclear bombs", 2 November.

19 Office of the High Commissioner for Human Rights (United Nations) (2024) "UN Report: Israel use of heavy bombs in Gaza raises serious concerns under the laws of war", 19 June.

20 Office of the High Commissioner for Human Rights, 2024.

21 United States Congress (2012) "Public Law 112–150" [United States–Israel Enhanced Security Cooperation Act of 2012]: https://www.congress.gov/112/statute/STATUTE-126/STATUTE-126-Pg1146.pdf

22 Masters, Jonathan and Merrow, Will (2024) "U.S. aid to Israel in four charts", (New York: Council on Foreign Relations): https://www.cfr.org/article/us-aid-israel-four-charts

23 Wenger, Martha (1990) "US aid to Israel: From handshake to embrace", *Merip* No164/165: https://merip.org/1990/05/us-aid-to-israel/

24 Masters and Merrow, 2024.

25 Little, Douglas (1993) "The making of a special relationship: The United States and Israel, 1957–68", *International Journal of Middle East Studies*, Vol 25, No 4, pp563–585, p563.

26 "U.S. floods arms into Israel despite mounting alarm over war's conduct", *Washington Post*, 6 March. https://www.washingtonpost.com/national-security/2024/03/06/us-weapons-israel-gaza/

27 Singh, Kanishka and Stoner, Mike (2014) "US approves sale to Israel of $20 billion weapons package", *Reuters*, 13 August.

28 Pappé, Ilan (2014) *The Idea of Israel: A History of Power and Knowledge* (London: Verso), p32.

29 Pappé, 2014, p32.

30 Pappé, 2014, p33.

31 Lockman, Zachary (1996) *Comrades and Enemies: Arab and Jewish Workers in Palestine, 1906–1948* (Berkeley: University of California Press), p64.

32 Veracini, Lorenzo (2010) *Settler Colonialism: A Theoretical Overview* (London: Palgrave Macmillan), p25.

33 Pappé, 2014, p35.

34 Lockman, 1996, p64.

35 Herzl, Theodor (1988) [1986] *The Jewish State* (New York: Dover Publications), p85. See also Chapter II: https://www.jewishvirtuallibrary.org/quot-the-jewish-state-quot-theodor-herzl

36 Gordon, Neve (2011) "A villa in the jungle: The Arab awakening through the lens of the Israeli media", *Middle East Law and Governance*, Vol 3, Nos 1/2, pp105–117, p106.

37 Baroud, Ramzy (2021) "From the 'iron wall' to the 'villa in the jungle': Palestinians demolish Israel's security myths", *Counterpunch*, 17 September.

38 Baroud, 2021.

39 Berman, Lazar (2023) "Netanyahu to Dutch leader: This war is civilization vs. barbarism", *Times of Israel*, 23 October.

40 Bishara, Marwan (2022) "Why Israel hates the Palestinians so much", *Al Jazeera*, 8 August: https://www.aljazeera.com/opinions/2022/8/8/why-israel-hates-the-palestinians-so-much

41 Barghouti, Omar (2011), *Boycott, Divestment, Sanctions: The Global Struggle for Palestinian Rights* (Chicago: Haymarket), p56.

42 BDS National Committee (2005) "Palestinian civil society call for BDS": https://bdsmovement.net/call

43 Cosatu (2006) "South African Trade Union Congress supports CUPE boycott of Israel", www.connexions.org/CxLibrary/Docs/CX5270-COSATU.htm

44 Reut Institute (2010) *The Delegitimisation Challenge: Creating a Political Firewall*: https://www.reutgroup.org/Publications/building-a-political-firewall--against-israel's-delegitimization-

45 Reut Institute, 2010.

46 Tessier, Yann (2023) "Hundreds of thousands rally across cities to support Palestinians", *Reuters*, 29 October: https://www.reuters.com/world/uk/thousands-join-pro-palestinian-protest-london-demand-gaza-ceasefire-2023-10-28/

47 Socialist Worker (2023) "Biggest ever Palestine solidarity demo in British history", *Socialist Worker*, 11 November: https://socialistworker.co.uk/palestine-2023/palestine-march-london-national-4/

48 Hilal, Jamil (2016) "Reflections on identity and youth in historical Palestine and the diaspora", in Hilal, Jamil (ed) *Palestinian Youth: Studies on Identity, Space and Community Participation* (Bir Zeit: Bir Zeit University): https://shorturl.at/mWLmk

49 Hilal, 2016.

50 Pappé Ilan (2021) "Palestinian youth: A silver lining and a ray of hope", *International Socialism*, No 161, pp89-102.

51 Pappé, 2021, p91.

52 Pappé, 2021, p94.

53 Author's interview with Mohamed, Cairo, April 2024.

54 Rabbani, Mouin (2024) "All shook up", in Stein-Weiner (ed), *Deluge: Gaza and Israel from Crisis to Cataclysm* (New York: OR Books), pp157–170.

55 Barghouti, Omar (2024) "A secular democratic state in historic Palestine: Self-determination through ethical decolonisation", in Loewenstein, Anthony and Moor, Ahmed (2024), *After Zionism: One State for Israel and Palestine* (London: Saqi), pp174–189, p175.

56 Lynch, Marc (2021) "The Arab uprisings never ended: The enduring struggle to remake the Middle East", *Foreign Affairs*, No 100.

57 Lynch, 2021.

58 Message to subscribers from *Foreign Affairs*, December 2024.

59 Message to subscribers from *Foreign Affairs*, December 2024.

Chapter 1
Imperialism, racism, Zionism

1 Graham-Harrison, Emma and Kierszenbaum, Quique (2024) "'It is a time of witch hunts in Israel': Teacher held in solitary confinement for posting concern about Gaza deaths", *Observer*, 13 January. https://www.theguardian.com/world/2024/jan/13/it-is-a-time-of-witch-hunts-in-israel-teacher-held-in-solitary-confinement-for-posting-concern-about-gaza-deaths

2 Graham-Harrison and Kierszenbaum, 2024.

3 Yiftachel, Oren (2013) "Liberal colonialism? Israel's 2013 elections and the 'Ethnocratic Bubble'", *Journal of Palestine Studies*, Vol 42, No 3, pp48–67, p49.

4 Khalili, Laleh (2010) "Palestinians: The politics of control, invisibility and the spectacle", in Khalidi, Muhammed (ed) *Manifestations of Identity* (Institute of Palestine Studies: Beirut), pp125–145, p130.

5 Khalili, 2010, p140.

6 On images of Palestinians in Israeli media during the intifada that began in 2000, see Liebes, Tamar, and Zohar, Kampf (2009) "Black and white and shades of gray: Palestinians in the Israeli media during the 2nd intifada", *The International Journal of Press/Politics*, Vol 14, No 4, pp434–453.

7 Nadeau, Mary-Jo, and Sears, Alan (2010) "The Palestine test: Countering the silencing campaign", *Studies in Political Economy*, Vol 85, No 1, pp7–33, p7.

8 Nadeau and Sears, 2010, p7.

9 Said, Edward (1980) *The Question of Palestine* (London: Routledge & Kegan Paul), p75.

10 Said, 1980, p75.

11 Cromer [Earl of, Evelyn Baring] (1908) *Modern Egypt* (New York: Macmillan), p130.

12 Cromer [Earl of, Evelyn Baring] (1913), "The government of subject races", *Political and Literary Essays, 1908-1913* (London: Macmillan, 1913), p13.

13 Milner asserted: "We had gone to Egypt professedly with no other object than to 'restore order', nor can there be the smallest doubt of the absolute *bona fides* of that profession". Milner, Alfred (1892) *England in Egypt* (London: Arnold), p14.

14 Milner, 1892, p14.

15 Milner, 1892, p178.

16 Milner, 1892, p4, p12.

17 Conder, Claude (1879) "The Present Condition of Palestine", *Palestine Exploration Quarterly*, Vol 11, No 1, pp6–15, p9

18 Conder, 1879, p9.

19 Macalister, Robert (1912) *A History of Civilisation in Palestine* (Cambridge, Cambridge University Press), p32, p34; Internet Archive: https://archive.org/details/historyofciviliz00macauoft/page/n5/mode/2up

20 Macalister, 1912, p34.

21 Macalister, 1912, p79, p80.

22 Macalister, 1912, p32.

23 Ghandour, Zeina (2010) *A Discourse on Domination in Mandate Palestine: Imperialism, Property and Insurgency* (London: Routledge), p2.

24 Ghandour, 2010, p3.

25 Ghandour, 2010, p3.

26 Ghandour, 2010, p3.

27 Thompson, Gardner (2021) *Legacy of Empire: Britain, Zionism and the Creation of Empire* (London: Saqi), p132.

28 Thompson, 2021, p132.

29 Penslar, Derek (2005) "Herzl and the Palestinian Arabs: Myth and counter-myth", *The Journal of Israeli History*, Vol 24, No 1, pp65-77, p69.

30 Penslar, 2005, p67.

31 Penslar, 2005, p67.

32 Herzl, Theodor (1960) *Complete Diaries Vol 1*, (ed Patai, Raphael) (New York: Herzl Press), p88.

33 Khalidi, Rashid (2020) *The Hundred Years War on Palestine* (London: Profile Books), p7.

34 Khalidi, 2020, p5.

35 Khalidi's letter to Herzl, from the Central Zionist Archives, quoted by Khalidi, 2020, p5.

36 Khalidi, 2020, p7.

37 Khalidi, 2020, p7.

38 Khalidi, 2020, p7-8.

39 Gutwein, Danny (2016) "The politics of the Balfour Declaration: Nationalism, imperialism and the limits of Zionist-British cooperation", *Journal of Israeli History*, Vol 35, No 2, pp 117–152, p120.

40 Theodor Herzl (1946) *The Jewish State: An Attempt at a Modern Solution of the Jewish Question* (New York: American Zionist Emergency Council), p15. For an assessment of Herzl's attitude towards racial difference and colonial conquest, see Penslar, Derek (2020) "Theodor Herzl, race, and empire", in Maciejko, Paweł and Ury, Scott (eds) *Making History Jewish: The Dialectics of Jewish History in Eastern Europe and the Middle East. Essays in Honor of Israel Bartal* (Leiden: Brill), pp185–209.

41 Gutwein, 2016, p10.

42 Yergin, Daniel (2017) *The Prize: The Epic Quest for Oil, Money, and Power* (New York, The Free Press), p183.

43 Cabinet minutes quoted in Cronin, 2017, p7.

44 Shlaim, Avi (2005) "The Balfour Declaration and its consequences" in Louis, William (ed) *Yet More Adventures with Britannia: Personalities, Politics and Culture in Britain* (London: I. B. Tauris), pp251–270, p252.

45 Balfour Declation (2016) [1917] House of Commons Library, Briefing Paper CPB 7766, 14 November, p4: https://researchbriefings.files.parliament.uk/documents/CBP-7766/CBP-7766.pdf

46 Chatty, Dawn (2013) "Refugees, exiles, and other forced migrants in the late Ottoman Empire", *Refugee Survey Quarterly*, Vol 32, No 2, pp35–52.

47 The term had been adopted at a conference of the Zionist movement in 1897. Herzl's colleague Max Nordau wrote that, 'It was equivocal but we all knew what it meant. To us it signified *Judenstaat*… [State of the Jews/Jewish State]'. Quoted in Ingrams, Doreen

(1972), *Palestine Papers 1917–1922: Seeds of Conflict* (London: John Murray), p5.

48 Shlaim, 2005, p253.

49 Shlaim, 2005, p253.

50 Tom Segev (2000) *One Palestine, Complete: Jews and Arabs under the British Mandate* (London: Abacus), p33.

51 David Fromkin (1989) *A Peace to End All Peace: The Fall of the Ottoman Empire and the Creation of the Modern Middle East* (New York: Avon Books), p181.

52 Segev, 2000, p111.

53 Diary entry by Colonel Edward House, Chief Aide to Woodrow Wilson, quoted in Segev, 2000, p119.

54 Klug, Brian (2003), "The collective Jew: Israel and the new antisemitism", *Patterns of Prejudice*, Vol 37, No 2 pp117–138, p124.

55 Cronin, 2015, p15.

56 Ingrams, 1972, p31.

57 Ingrams, 1972, p32.

58 Ingrams, 1972, p32.

59 Said, 1980, p28.

60 Said, 1980, p28.

61 Katz, Ethan (2018) "An Imperial entanglement: Anti-semitism, islamophobia, and colonialism", *The American Historical Review*, Vol 123, No 4, pp1190–1209, p1191.

62 Segev, 2000, p109.

63 Segev, 2000, p110.

64 Massad, Joseph (2004) "The persistence of the Palestinian Question", in Aretxaga, Begoña, Dworkin, Dennis, Gabilondo, Joseba and Joseba Zulaika (eds) *Empire & Terror: Nationalism/ Postnationalism in the New Millennium* (Reno: University of Nevada), p69.

65 Herzl, 1988, p93.

66 Herzl, 1988, p122.

67 Herzl, 1988, p112

68 Cronin, 2017, p18.

69 Colonial Office files cited in Cronin, 2017, p19.

70 Deeb, Marius (1979) *Party Politics in Egypt: The Wafd and Its Rivals, 1919–38* (London: Ithaca), p42.

71 Seth, Ronald (1966) *Russell Pasha* (London: William Kimber), p130.

72 Fahmy, Ziad (2011) *Ordinary Egyptians* (Stanford: Stanford University Press), p138–9.

73 Fahmy, 2011, p140–148.

74 Burns, Eleanor (1928) *British Imperialism in India* (London: Labour Research Department).

75 Al-Rifi' quoted in Brown, Nathan (1990) *Peasant Politics in Modern Egypt* (New Haven: Yale University Press), p205, p251n60.

76 Colonel C. E. Yate, addressing the House of Commons, 22 March 1916, quoted in Townshend, Charles (2010) *When God Made Hell: The British Invasion of Mesopotamia and the Creation of Iraq, 1914–1921* (London: Faber & Faber), p369.

77 An RAF officer leading the bombing, quoted in Grosscup, Beau (2006) *Strategic Terror: The Politics and Ethics of Aerial Bombardment* (London: Zed Books), p55.

78 Grosscup, 2006, p55.

79 Segev, 2000, p183.

80 Cahill, Richard (2009) "'Going Beserk': 'Black and Tans' in Palestine", *Jerusalem Quarterly*, Vol 38

81 Cahill, 2009.

82 Cronin, 2017, p22-23.

83 Cronin, 2017, p23.

84 Khalidi, 2020, p42.

85 Khalidi, 2020, p39.

86 League of Nations (1922) "Question of Palestine: Text of Mandate", p4. https://digitallibrary.un.org/record/829707?ln=en&v=pdf

87 League of Nations, 1922.

88 Khalidi, 2020, p40.

89 Smith, Barbara J. (1993) *The Roots of Separatism in Palestine: British Economic Policy, 1920–1929* (London: IB Tauris).

90 Smith, B., 1993, p97–98.

91 Stein, Kenneth (1980) "Legal Protection and circumvention of rights for cultivators in Mandatory Palestine", *Palestinian Society and Politics* (Princeton: Princeton University Press), pp233–61, p246.

92 Alff, Kristen (2018) "Levantine joint-stock companies, trans-Mediterranean partnerships, and nineteenth-century capitalist development", *Comparative Studies in Society and History*, Vol 60, No 1, pp150–177, p154.

93 Ruedy, John (1971) "Dynamics of land alienation" in Abu-Lughod, Ibrahim (ed), *The Transformation of Palestine: Essays on the Origin and Development of the Arab–Israeli Conflict* (Evanston [Ill.] Northwestern University Press) pp119–138, p131.

94 *Report of the Committee Assigned to Study the Economic Conditions of Agriculturalists in Palestine*, in Smith, Pamela-Ann (1984) *Palestine and the Palestinians, 1976–1983* (London: Croom Helm), p52.

95 Anderson, Charles (2015) *Will the Real Palestinian Peasantry Please Sit Down? Towards a New History of British Rule in Palestine, 1917–1936* (LSE Middle East Paper No 10), p6.

96 Anderson, 2015, p9.

97 Sherman, Taylor (2010) *State Violence and Punishment in India* (London: Routledge), p139.

98 *Manual of Military Law* and *Notes on Imperial Policing*, quoted in Hughes, Matthew (2009) "The banality of brutality: British armed forces and the repression of the Arab revolt in Palestine, 1936–39", *The English Historical Review*, Vol 124, No 507, pp313–354

99 Hughes, 2009.

100 Segev, 2000, p195.

101 Hughes notes: 'Prisoners jumped to their deaths from high windows to escape their captors, had their testicles tied with cord, were tortured with strips of wood with nails in, had wire tightened around their big toes, hair was torn from their faces and heads, special instruments were used to pull out fingernails, red hot skewers were used on detainees, prisoners were sodomized, boiling oil was used on prisoners as were intoxicants (morphine, cocaine and heroin), there were electric shocks, water was funnelled into suspects' stomachs and there were mock executions'. Hughes, Matthew (2013) "A British 'Foreign Legion'? The British Police in Mandate Palestine", *Middle Eastern Studies*, Vol 49, No 5, pp696–711

102 Segev, 2000, p194.

103 Segev, 2000, p381.

104 Glaser, Amelia (2021) "Localizing the pogrom: Jewish leftist poets on Palestine, 1929", *Dibur Literary Journal* (Peripheral Modernisms), Vol 9/10, p192.

105 Smith, P-A., 1984, p216, n65.

106 Smith, P-A., 1984, p54.

107 Smith, P-A., 1984, p54.

108 Lockman, Zachary (1996) *Comrades and Enemies: Arab and Jewish Workers in Palestine, 1906–1948* (Berkeley: University of California Press), p68.

109 Lockman, 1996, p68.

110 Hanegbi, Haim, Machover, Moshe and Orr, Akiva (1971) *The Class Nature of Israeli Society* (Pluto: London), p15.

111 Smith, B., 1993, p146.

112 Smith, B., 1993, p147.

113 Smith, B, 1993, p147.

114 Lockman, 1996, p56.

115 Piterberg, Gabriel (2008) *The Returns of Zionism: Myth, Politics and Scholarship in Israel* (London: Verso), pp51–92, p74. See also Shafir, Gershon (1989) *Land, Labor and the Origins of the Israeli-Palestinian Conflict, 1882–1914* (Cambridge: Cambridge University Press), and Lockman, Zachary (2012) "Land, labor and the logic of Zionism: A critical engagement with Gershon Shafir", *Settler Colonial Studies*, Vol 2, No 1, p9–38.

116 Hanegbi, Machover and Orr, 1971, p15.

Chapter 2
Land, crisis, conflict

1 Segev, 2000, p381.

2 Smith, B., 1993, p65.

3 Smith, B., 1993, p77.

4 Segev, 2000, p286.

5 Bentwich, Norman and Bentwich, Helen (1965) *Mandate Memories, 1918–1948: From the Balfour Declaration to the Establishment of Israel* (London, Hogarth Press), p53.

6 Kidron, Anat (2016) "Separatism, coexistence and the landscape: Jews and Palestinian-Arabs in mandatory Haifa", *Middle Eastern Studies*, Vol 52, No 1, pp79–101, p79.

7 Masalha, Nur (1992) *Expulsion of the Palestinians: The Concept of 'Transfer' in Zionist Political Thought, 1882–1948* (Beirut: Institute of Palestine Studies).

8 Smith, B., 1993, p181.

9 Segev, 2000, p284.

10 Shamir, Ronen (2013) *Current Flow: The Electrification of Palestine* (Stanford Stanford University Press), p17.

11 Segev, 2000, p284.

12 Thompson, 2019, p181.

13 Pappé, Ilan (2010) "Zionizing the Palestinian space: Historical and historiographical perspectives", in Hanaa Hamdan-Saliba (ed) "The right to a spatial narrative", *Makan*, Vol 2 (Haifa: Adalah), pp9–21, p11.

14 Masalha, Nur (2020) *Imperial Israel and the Palestinians: The Politics of Expansion* (London: Pluto), p56.

15 Jabotinsky, Ze'ev (1923) *The Iron Wall*: https://en.jabotinsky.org/media/9747/the-iron-wall.pdf

16 Jabotinsky, 1923.

17 Masalha, 2000, p57.

18 Masalha, 2000, p57.

19 Masalha, 2000, p57.

20 Edelman, Maurice (1964) *Ben Gurion: A Political Biography* (London: Hodder & Stoughton), p95.

21 Shabtai, Teveth, (1997) *The Burning Ground* (Tel Aviv: Schocken), p412.

22 Madeleine Tress addresses claims that Jabotinsky was a fascist in the European mode, concluding that although he drew extensively on ideas and practices of fascist currents in Europe, conditions in Palestine during the Mandate period make the label inappropriate: Tress, Madeleine (1984) "Fascist components in the political thought of Vladimir Jabotinsky", *Arab Studies Quarterly*, Vol 6, No 4, pp304–324.

23 Edelman, 1964, p95.

24 Khalaf, Issa (1997) "The effect of socioeconomic change on Arab societal collapse in Mandate Palestine", *International Journal of Middle East Studies*, Vol 29, No 1, pp93–112, pp97-98.

25 Khalaf, 1997, p98.

26 Lockman, 1996, p212.

27 Lockman, 1996, p104.

28 Steven Glazer (2001) "Picketing for Hebrew labor: A window on Histadrut

tactics and strategy", *Journal of Palestine Studies*, Vol 30, No 4, pp39–54.

29 Report of pickets organised from the settlement of Kfar Saba in the *Jewish Chronicle*: Kelemen, Paul (2012) *The British Left and Zionism: History of a Divorce* (Manchester: Manchester University Press), p41n87.

30 Bernstein, Deborah (2000) *Constructing Boundaries: Jewish and Arab Workers in Mandatory Palestine* (Albany: State University of New York Press), p101–2.

31 Bernstein, 2000, p101.

32 Nathan Weinstock (1979) *Zionism: False Messiah* (London: Ink Links), p133.

33 Chatty, Dawn (2010) *Displacement and Dispossession in the Modern Middle East* (Cambridge, Cambridge University Press), p75.

34 Bernstein, 2000, p64.

35 Bernstein, 2000, p64.

36 Haiduc-Dale, N. (2013) *Arab Christians in British Mandate Palestine, Communalism and Nationalism 1917–1948* (Edinburgh: Edinburgh University Press), p4.

37 Haiduc-Dale, 2013, p3.

38 Laura Robson notes the importance of an evangelical 'Restorationist' movement that promoted the idea of the return of the Jews to their biblical homeland. Protestant missions to Palestine, initially aimed at Jews but expanding to target Muslims and Orthodox Christians, helped found a British consulate in Jerusalem and promoted the idea of 'a Protestant stake in Palestine'. During the Mandate period 'Protestantism was inextricably woven into the conditions of British rule over what evangelicals viewed as the Christian "Holy Land".' Robson, Laura (2011) "Church, state, and the Holy Land: British Protestant approaches to imperial policy in Palestine, 1917–1948", *Journal of Imperial & Commonwealth History*, Vol 39, No 3, pp457–477, p459.

39 Lockman, 1996, ch 5, describes in detail continuing, unsuccessful efforts at class unity across communal divides.

40 Winder, Alex (2012) "The 'Western Wall' riots of 1929: Religious boundaries and communal violence", *Journal of Palestine Studies*, Vol 42, No 1, pp6–23, p6. Israeli historian Ouzi Elyada suggests that Jabotinsky and colleagues of the Revisionist movement campaigned for months to provoke confrontations at the Western Wall and carried much responsibility for the conflicts that eventually erupted: Elyada, Ouzi (2019) "A nexus of sensationalism and politics: Doar Ha-Yom and the 1929 Western Wall crisis", *Israel Studies Review*, Vol 34, No 2, pp114–133.

41 Segev notes the testimony of Jews in Hebron that most of the city's Jews survived because Arabs hid them in their homes. Segev, 2000, p325.

42 The official casualty count listed 133 Jews killed and 339 wounded, and 116 Arabs killed and 232 wounded. Among those killed by British security forces, most were Arabs: *Report of the Commission on the Palestine Disturbances of August, 1929* [The Shaw Report] (1930) (London: His Majesty's Stationery Office), p65.

43 Gagnon, George (1993) "British Air Control from 1922 to 1936", (Maxwell Air Force Base, Alabama: Air University Press): http://www.jstor.com/stable/resrep13755.9

44 Anderson, 2018, p173.

45 Saposnik, Arieh (2015) "Wailing walls and iron walls: The Western Wall as sacred symbol in Zionist national iconography", *The American Historical Review*, Vol 120, No 5, pp1653–1681, p1653.

46 *Report of the Commission on the Palestine Disturbances of August, 1929* [The Shaw Report], p163.

47 Segev, 2000, p337.

48 Kelemen, 2012, p23.

49 Segev, 2000, p337.

50 Segev, 2000, p337.

51 Storrs, Ronald (1937) *Orientations* [Memoirs of Sir Ronald Storrs], (Newton Abbott: Readers Union), p364.

52 *Report of the Commission on the Palestine Disturbances of August 1929* [The Shaw Report] (1930), p66–67.

53 Anderson, Charles (2013) *From Petition to Confrontation: The Palestinian National Movement and the Rise of Mass Politics, 1929–1939*, PhD thesis, New York University, p518.

54 Smith, P-A., 1984, p44.

55 Fahmy, 2011, p143.

56 For an account of party and class in the Egyptian revolution see Marfleet, Philip (2022) "From nationalism to Islamism: Revolution, the Wafd and the rise of the Muslim Brotherhood" in Hellyer, H. A. and Springborg, Robert (eds) *The Egyptian Revolution of 1919: Legacies and Consequences of the Fight for Independence* (London: Bloomsbury).

57 Porath, Yehoshua (1977) *The Emergence of the Palestinian National Movement: From Riots to Rebellion Vol 2, 1929–1939* (London: Frank Cass), p86.

58 Anderson, 2013, p79.

59 Tamura, Yukie (2009) "A study of the influence of the Young Men's Muslim Associations in Palestine through their charitable activities in the late 1920s", *Kyoto Bulletin of Islamic Area Studies*, Vol 3, No 1, pp237–248

60 Matthews, Weldon (2006) *Confronting an Empire, Constructing a Nation: Arab Nationalists and Popular Politics in Mandate Palestine*, (London: IB Tauris), p62.

61 Anderson, 2013, p89.

62 Anderson, 2013, p117.

63 Cronin, 2017, pp35–36.

64 Grenville, Anthony (2010) *Jewish Refugees from Germany and Austria in Britain, 1933–1970: Their Image in AJR Information* (London: Vallentine Mitchell), p4.

65 Sherman, A. J. (1994) *Island Refuge: Britain and the Refugees from the Third Reich, 1933–1939* (London: Frank Cass), p32.

66 Sherman, 1994, p32.

67 Schuster, Lisa and Solomos, John (1999) "The politics of refugee and asylum policies in Britain: Historical patterns and contemporary realities", in Bloch, Alice and Levy, Carl (eds) *Refugees, Citizenship and Social Policy and in Europe* (Basingstoke, Macmillan), p56.

68 Litvinoff, Barnet (1989) *The Burning Bush: Anti-Semitism and World History* (London: William Collins), p297.

69 Litvinoff, 1989, p297.

70 Litvinoff, 1989, p297.

71 Marfleet, Philip (2006) *Refugees in a Global Era* (Basingstoke: Macmillan): see ch 6 on Britain and the Jewish refugees.

72 Grenville, 2010, p5.

73 Grenville, 2010, p10.

74 Thompson, 2019, p207.

75 Cesarani, David (1989) "The anti-Jewish career of Sir William Joynson-Hicks, Cabinet Minister", *Journal of Contemporary History*, Vol 24, No 3, pp461–482.

76 London, Louise (2000) *Whitehall and the Jews, 1933–1948* (Cambridge, Cambridge University Press), pp32–33.

77 London, 2000, p33.

78 London, 2000, p44.

79 London, 2000, p38.

80 London, 2000, p38.

81 London, 2000, p42.

82 Morris, Benny (1999) "Response of the Jewish Daily Press in Palestine to the accession of Hitler, 1933", *Yad Vashem Studies*, Vol 27, pp363–407, p406

83 Segev, 2000, p393.

84 Segev, 2000, p393.

85 Segev, 2000, p393.

86 Thompson, 2019, p206.

87 Shepherd, Naomi (1999) *Ploughing Sand: The British in Palestine* (London: John Murray), p96.

88 Anderson, 2013, p222.

89 Reports by British police: Anderson, 2013, p231.

90 Anderson, 2013, p222.

91 Anderson, 2013, p223.

92 Anderson, 2013, p224.

93 Kolinsky, Martin (1993) *Law, Order and Riots in Mandatory Palestine, 1928-35* (New York: Springer), p174.

94 Anderson, 2013, p226.

95 Colonial Office records, in Anderson, 2013, p238.

96 Anderson, 2013, p238.

97 In typical attacks in Iraq the RAF dropped hundreds of gallons of petrol followed by incendiary bombs, laying waste to settlements and large areas of land. In reports to London British commanders boasted: 'any village which gave shelter to assistance to the rebels was immediately bombed'. Tanaka, Yukie (2009) "British 'human bombing' in Iraq during the interwar era", in Tanaka, Yukie and Young, Marylin, *Bombing Civilians: A Twentieth-Century History* (New York, The New Press), p22–23.

98 Cronin, 2017, p37.

99 Cronin, 2017, p37.

100 Anderson, 2013, p148.

101 Knight, John (2011) "Securing Zion? Policing in British Palestine, 1917–39", *European Review of History/Revue Européenne d'Histoire*, Vol 18, No 4, pp523–543; Segev, 2013, p383.

Chapter 3
Intifada

1 Ben-Gurion later admitted that the arms, carried on a Belgian ship, were to go to the Zionist militia. Anderson, 2013, p591.

2 Anderson, 2013, p602.

3 Anderson, 2013, p517.

4 Anderson, 2013, p582.

5 Lockman, 1996, p236.

6 Lockman, 1996, p239.

7 Hansard [House of Commons] (1936) "Jaffa disturbances", HC Deb 05 May 1936, Vol 311, cc1546-7W: https://api.parliament.uk/historic-hansard/written-answers/1936/may/05/jaffa-disturbances

8 Smith, P-A. 1984, p64.

9 Swedenburg, 1988, p182.

10 Smith, P-A, 1984, p55.

11 Anderson, 2013, pp592-593.

12 Thomas Hodgkin (1986) "Letter to RHH" (23 April 1936) *Thomas Hodgkin: Letters from Palestine 1932-36* (London: Quartet), p160.

13 As part of an agreement with the Wafd, British troops were to remain in the Suez Canal Zone for at least twenty years. Britain retained overall control in Egypt until 1952.

14 Beinin, Joel and Lockman, Zachary (1987) *Workers on the Nile: Nationalism, Communism, Islam and the Egyptian Working Class, 1882–1954* (Princeton: Princeton University Press), p220.

15 Lockman, 1996, p235.

16 Kramer, Gudrun (2010) *Hasan al-Banna*, (London: Oneworld), pp45-46.

17 Chalcraft, John (2016) *Popular Politics in the Making of the Modern Middle East*, (Cambridge, Cambridge University Press), p248.

18 Hodgkin, 1986, p164.

19 Fleischmann, Ellen (1996) *The Nation and its 'New' Women: Feminism, Nationalism, Colonialism, and the Palestinian Women's Movement, 1920–1948* (PhD Thesis, Georgetown University), p205.

20 Swedenburg, Ted (2003) *Memories of Revolt: The 1936–1939 Rebellion and the Palestinian National Past* (Fayetteville: University of Arkansas Press), p176. During the 1919 revolution in Egypt, Muslim and Coptic Christian women joined crowds at mosques and churches where they "preached for a general strike": Fahmy, Ziad (2011) *Ordinary Egyptians: Creating the Modern Nation Through Popular Culture* (Stanford: Stanford University Press), pp147–148.

21 Swedenburg, 2003, p176.

22 Fleischmann, 1996, p205

23 Fleischmann, 1996, p214.

24 Hughes, Matthew (2019) "Women, violence, and the Arab Revolt in Palestine, 1936–39", *The Journal of Military History*, Vol 83, pp487–507, p490.

25 Fleischmann, 1996, p126.

26 Hughes, 2019, p500.

27 Fleischmann, 1996, p216.

28 Fleischmann, 1996, p216n86.

29 Fleischmann, 1996, p208.

30 Ian Black (1986) *Zionism and the Arabs, 1936–1939* (London: Routledge), p25.

31 Anderson, Charles (2017) "State formation from below and the great revolt in Palestine", *Journal of Palestine Studies*, Vol 47, No 1, pp39–55, p42.

32 Anderson, 2017, p43.

33 Anderson, 2017, p43.

34 Anderson, 2013, p478.

35 Cronin, 2017, p47.

36 Cronin, 2017, p46.

37 Cronin, 2017, p47.

38 Secretary of State for the Colonies (1937) *Palestine Royal Commission Report* [Peel Commission] (London: His Majesty's Stationery Office), vi: https://unispal.un.org/pdfs/Cmd5479.pdf

39 Segev, 2000, p401.

40 The Royal Warrant listed commissioners as: '[O]ur Right Trusty and Right Well-beloved Cousin and Counsellor William Robert Wellesley, Earl Peel, Knight Grand Commander of Our Most Exalted Order of the Star of India, Knight Grand Cross of Our Most Excellent Order of the British Empire, Our Right Trusty and Well-beloved Counsellor Sir Horace George Montage Rumbold, Baronet, Knight Grand Cross of Our Most Honourable Order of the Bath, Knight Grand Cross of Our Most Distinguished Order of St. Michael and St. George, Member of Our Royal Victorian Order, Our Trusty and Well-beloved Sir Egbert Laurie Lucas Hammond, Knight Commander of Our Most Exalted Order of the Star of India, Commander of Our Most Excellent Order of the British Empire, Our Trusty and Well-beloved Sir William Morris Carter Knight, Commander of Our Most Excellent Order of the British Empire, Our Trusty and Well-beloved Sir Harold Morris, Knight, Member of Our Most Excellent Order of the British Empire, One of Our Counsel Learned in the Law, and Our Trusty and Well-beloved Reginald Coupland, Companion of Our Most Eminent Order of the Indian Empire.' Secretary of State for the Colonies [Peel Commission Report] 1937, pvi.

41 Peel Commission Report, 1937, p374.

42 Peel Commission Report, 1937, p370.

43 Peel Commission Report, 1937, p370.

44 Hodgkin, Thomas (1988) "The events in Palestine" (Letter published in *Labour*

Monthly, July 1936), in *Letters from Palestine 1932–36* (London: Quartet), p192.

45 Hodgkin, 1988, p192.

46 Hodgkin, 1988, p201.

47 Peel Commission Report, 1937, p374.

48 London, 2000, p131.

49 Thompson, 2019, p227

50 Sinanoglu, Penny (2019) *Partitioning Palestine: British Policymaking at the End of Empire*, (Chicago: University of Chicago Press), p127.

51 Parsons, Laila (2019) "The secret testimony of the Peel Commission (Part I): Underbelly of Empire", *Journal of Palestine Studies*, Vol 49, No 1, pp7–24, p10.

52 Parsons, 2019, p12.

53 Parsons, 2019, p16.

54 Shepherd, 1999, p98.

55 Secretary of State for the Colonies (1939) *Palestine: Statement of Policy* (MacDonald White Paper), (London: His Majesty's Stationery Office): https://www.palquest.org/en/historictext/6722/macdonald-white-paper

56 Hodgkin, 1988, p193.

57 Segev, 2000, p404.

58 Morris. Benny (1999) *Righteous Victims: A History of the Arab-Zionist Conflict, 1881–1999* (New York: Alfred Knopf), p142.

59 Masalha, Nur, 1992, p32.

60 Flapan, Simha (1979) *Zionism and the Palestinians* (London: Croom Helm), p93 n65.

61 Masalha, 1992, p35.

62 Masalha, 1992, p37.

63 Masalha, 1992, p37.

64 Segev, 2000, p407.

65 Masalha, 1992, p96.

66 Masalha, 1992, p107.

67 Masalha, 1992, p108

68 Anderson, 2013, p615.

69 Here Jabotinsky apparently references demands from Nazi Germany in 1939 to relocate Lithuanians and ethnic Germans. Melman, Yossi and Raviv, Dan (1988) "Expelling Palestinians", *Washington Post*, 6 February: https://www.washingtonpost.com/archive/opinions/1988/02/07/expelling-palestinians/a54c4262-ec35-4f20-a705-f47aa18d72db/

70 Masalha, 1992, p30.

71 Masalha, 1992, p30.

72 Matthews, Weldon (2006) *Confronting an Empire, Constructing a Nation: Arab Nationalists and Popular Politics in Mandate Palestine* (New York: I.B Tauris),p162.

73 Anderson, 2013, p888.

74 Shepherd, 2013, p204.

75 Cronin, 2017, p49.

76 Cronin, 2017, p49.

77 Cronin, 2017, p52.

78 Hughes, Matthew (2009) "The Banality of Brutality: British Armed Forces and the Repression of the Arab Revolt in Palestine, 1936-39", *The English Historical Review*, Vol. 124, No. 507, pp313-354, p320.

79 Hughes, 2009, p321.

80 Hughes, 2009, p322.

81 Hughes, 2009.

82 Shepherd, 1999, p202.

83 Cronin, 2017, p53.

84 Allon, Yigal (2009) *The Making of Israel's Army*, (London: Vallentine, Mitchell), p9.

85 Segev, 2000, p430.

86 Segev, 2000, p431.

87 Cahill, Richard (2018) "The Tegart Police Fortresses in British Mandate

Palestine: A reconsideration of their strategic location and purpose", *Jerusalem Quarterly*, Vol 75, No 48

88 Cahill, 2018.

89 El Rifai, Yasid, Dima Yaser, and Jarrar, Adele (2017) "Tegart's modern legacy: The reproduction of power, a timeless paradox", *Jerusalem Quarterly*, Vol 69, p79

90 Shepherd, 1999, p209.

91 Shepherd, 1999, p210.

92 Anderson, 2013, p1017.

93 Anderson, 2013, p1065.

94 Anderson, 2013, p1092.

95 Secretary of State for the Colonies, 1939.

96 Segev, 2000, p440.

97 Segev, 2000, p440.

98 Segev, 2000, p441.

99 Segev, 2000, p441.

100 Khalidi, 2020, p49.

101 Khalidi, 2000, p49.

Chapter 4
Displacement and dispossession

1 Segev, 2000, p460.

2 Masalha, 1992, p131.

3 Masalha, 1992, p131.

4 Masalha, 1992, p131.

5 Masalha, 1992, p135.

6 Masalha, 1992, p138.

7 Begin envisaged a state that encompassed 'the biblical land of Israel', extending from the Nile in the west to the Euphrates in the east and including most of Syria and much of Iraq. He '"urged redemption of the land", convinced that it would be accomplished by force': Segev, 2000, p456.

8 Hernon, Ian (2007) *Assassin! 200 years of British political murder* (London: Pluto Press), p161.

9 Pappé, 2006, p19.

10 Sela, Rona (2013) "Scouting Palestinian territory, 1940–1948: Haganah Village Files, aerial photos, and surveys", *Jerusalem Quarterly*, Vol 52, p40.

11 Davis, Caitlin (2016) "Archiving governance in Palestine", *Journal of Contemporary Archival Studies*, Vol 3, No 1, pp1–15, p7.

12 Segev, 2000, p493.

13 All figures from the *Report of the Anglo-American Committee of Enquiry Regarding the Problems of European Jewry and Palestine*: Sayigh, 1979, pp72–73.

14 Shlaim, 1995, 293.

15 Hughes, Matthew (2019) *Britain's Pacification of Palestine* (Cambridge, Cambridge University Press), p244.

16 Hughes, 2019, p247.

17 Hughes, 2019, p247.

18 Hughes, 2019, p247.

19 Hughes, 2019, p248.

20 Hughes, 2019, p350.

21 Hughes, 2019, p260.

22 Segev, 2000, p494.

23 Report of UNSCOP to the United Nations Special Assembly, , September 1947: https://digitallibrary.un.org/record/703295?ln=en&v=pdf#files (English: *A_364-EN* - PDF)

24 Edelman, 1964, p144.

25 Pappé, 2006, p70.

26 Pappé, 2006, p74.

27 Khalidi, Walid (1988) "Plan Dalet: Master plan for the conquest of Palestine", *Journal of Palestine Studies*, Vol 18, No 1, pp4–19

28 Khalidi, 1988, pp24–29.

29 Pappé, 2006, p87.

30 Pappé, 2006, p88.

31 Pappé, 2006, p88.

32 Pappé, 2006, p89.

33 Pappé, 2006, p90.

34 Sacher, Harry (1952) *Israel: The Establishment of a State* (New York: British Book Centre), p217.

35 Various figures are provided for the number of those murdered, Pappé settles upon ninety-three. Pappé, 2006, pp90-91.

36 Ilan Pappé notes that a British commander intervened to prevent demolitions in Shaikh Jarrah, Jerusalem. He comments: 'British inaction was the rule, however.' Pappé, 2006, p98.

37 Pappé, 2006, p103.

38 Morris's early findings challenged official Zionist narratives: he later revised his approach, falling into line with key principles of Zionist historiography. See Masalha, Nur (1991) "A critique of Benny Morris", *Journal of Palestine Studies*, Vol 21, No 1, pp90–97.

39 Morris, Benny (1994) *1948 and After: Israel and the Palestinians* (Oxford: Clarendon Press), p22.

40 See for example, Harkabi, Yehoshua (1972) *Arab Attitudes to Israel* (Jerusalem: Israel Universities Press), pp37–38.

41 Shlaim, Avi (2012) "Israel and the Arab Coalition in 1948", in Rogan, Eugene and Shlaim Avi (eds) *The War for Palestine: Rewriting the United States and the Israeli-Palestinian Conflict History of 1948*, pp79–103

42 Shlaim, p2001.

43 Shlaim, p2001.

44 Shlaim, p2001.

45 Shlaim, p2001.

46 Irfan, Anne (2023) *Refuge and Resistance: Palestinians and the International Refugee System* (New York: Colombia University Press), p26.

47 Pappé, 2006, p182.

48 Manna, Adel (2019) "Resistance and survival in Central Galilee, July 1948–July 1951", *Jerusalem Quarterly*, Vol 79, pp28–37, p29.

49 Hallaj, Muhammed (2008) "Recollections of the Nakba through a teenager's eyes", *Journal of Palestine Studies*, Vol 38, No 1

50 Chatty, Dawn (2010) *Displacement and Dispossession in the Modern Middle East* (Cambridge: Cambridge University Press), p223.

51 Sayigh, Rosemary (1979) *Palestinians: From Peasants to Revolutionaries* (London: Zed), p80.

52 Sayigh, 1979, p89.

53 Sayigh, 1979, p92.

54 Pappé, 2006, pp195–197.

55 Chatty, 2010, p203.

56 Said, 1979, p5.

57 See Zurayk, Constantine (1956) *The Meaning of the Disaster* (Beirut: Khayat) and in Arabic, al-'Arif, 'Arif (2013) *Al-Nakba: The Catastrophe of Jerusalem and the Lost Paradise* (Beirut and Sidon, Lebanon: Al-Maktaba al-'Asriyya).

58 Sayigh, 1979.

59 Sayigh, 1979, p5.

60 Sayigh, 1979, p64.

61 Khalidi, Walid (ed) (1992) *All That Remains: The Palestinian Villages Occupied and Depopulated by Israel in 1948* (Beirut: Institute for Palestine Studies).

62 Hirsch, Michal Ben-Josef (2007) "From taboo to the negotiable: The Israeli new historians and the changing representation of the Palestinian refugee problem", *Perspectives on Politics*, Vol 5, No 2, pp241–258.

63 Pappé, Ilan (2006) *The Ethnic Cleansing of Palestine* (Oxford: OneWorld), p8.

64 Flapan, Simha (1987) "The Palestinian exodus of 1948", *Journal of Palestine Studies*, Vol 16, No 4, pp3–26, p4.

65 Flapan, 1987, p5.

66 Flapan, 1987, pp5-6.

67 Khalidi, Walid (2005) "Why did the Palestinians leave, revisited", *Journal of Palestine Studies*, Vol 34, No 2, pp42–54, p44.

68 Childers, Erskine (1961) "The other exodus", *The Spectator*, 12 May, pp8–11: https://archive.spectator.co.uk/article/12th-may-1961/8/the-other-exodus

69 Childers, 1961.

70 Childers, 1961.

71 Khalidi identifies pamphlets published in 1949 as the source of these stories, placing responsibility with one of the leading Revisionist activists: Khalidi, 2005, pp43–44.

72 Khalidi, 2005, p43.

73 Edelman, 1964, p164.

74 Renan, Ernest (1992) "What is a nation?" (text of a conference delivered at the Sorbonne on 11 March, 1882,) in Ernest Renan, *Qu'est-ce qu'une nation?* (Paris: Presses-Pocket): http://ucparis.fr/files/9313/6549/9943/What_is_a_Nation.pdf

75 Shlaim, Avi (2004) "The war of the Israeli historians", *Annales*, Vol 59, No 1, pp161–67

76 Shlaim, 2004.

77 Shlaim, 2004.

78 Hirsch, 2007, p245.

79 Hirsch, 2007, p255n33.

80 Shlaim, 2004.

81 Hirsch, 2007, p253.

82 Beker, Avi (2010) "When history is flexible", *Jerusalem Post*, 26 June: https://www.jpost.com/Christian-In-Israel/Features/When-history-is-flexible

83 Anderson, 2013, p1122.

84 The total may have been higher, notes Weinstock, as those arriving by 'irregular' routes were not counted in official figures: Weinstock, 1979, p232.

85 Cronin, 2017, p53.

86 Hughes, Matthew (2015) "Terror in Galilee: British-Jewish collaboration and the Special Night Squads in Palestine during the Arab Revolt, 1938–39", *The Journal of Imperial and Commonwealth History*, Vol 43, No 4, pp590–610, p592.

87 Shepherd, 1999, p202.

88 Hughes, 2015, p593.

89 Allon, 1970, p10.

90 Hughes, 2015, pp604–605.

91 Shepherd, 1999, pp216–217.

92 Shepherd, 1999, pp215–216; see also Cox, Stephen (2015) "Britain and the origin of Israeli Special Operations: SOE and PALMACH during the Second World War", *Dynamics of Asymmetric Conflict*, Vol 8, No 1, pp60–78.

93 Pappé, 2006, p45.

94 Shepherd, 1999, p216.

95 Shepherd, 1999, p217.

96 Shepherd, 1999, p218.

97 Shepherd, 1999, p218.

98 Shepherd, 1999, p219.

99 Shepherd, 1999, p220.

100 Morris, Benny (1982) *The Birth of the Palestinian Refugee Problem, 1947–1949* (Cambridge: Cambridge University Press), p22.

101 Segev, 2000, p509.

102 Hughes, 2019, p348.

103 Comments made by Palestinian judge Anwar Nusseibah, an observer of events in 1948, quoted in Segev, 2000, p510.

104 Cronin, 2017, p64.

105 Cronin, 2017, p74.

Chapter 5
Palestine in a new era

1 Unrwa (the United Nations Relief and Works Agency) recognised sixteen camps in Lebanon, twelve in Syria, ten in Jordan, nineteen in the West Bank, and eight in the Gaza Strip. Full list in Irfan, 2023, pp207–209.

2 United Nations (1949) *First Interim Report of the United Nations Economic Survey Mission for the Middle East* (the Clapp Report), 6 November: https://www.un.org/unispal/document/auto-insert-210462/

3 United Nations, 1949.

4 Sayigh, 1979, p104.

5 Marfleet, 2006, ch7.

6 Neff, Donald (1988) "US policy and the Palestinian refugees", *Journal of Palestine Studies*, Vol 18, No 1, pp96–111, p99.

7 Neff, 1988, p99.

8 Neff, 1988, p99.

9 Segev, Tom (1985) *1949: The First Israelis* (New York: The Free Press), p30.

10 Segev, 1985, p30.

11 US State Department (1949), "Presidential message to the prime minister of Israel", 28 May: https://www.jewishvirtuallibrary.org/truman-letter-to-ben-gurion-expresses-displeasure-regarding-territory-refugees#1

12 US State Department, 1949.

13 Neff, 1988, p107.

14 Sayigh, 1979, p108.

15 The UN did not come into existence formally until November 1945.

16 Marfleet, 2006, pp141–142.

17 Loescher, Gil (1993) *Beyond Charity: International Cooperation and the Global Refugee Crisis* (Oxford: Oxford University Press), p48.

18 Irfan, 2023, p43.

19 Irfan, 2023, p43.

20 Irfan, 2023, p45.

21 Turki, Fawaz (1972) *The Disinherited* (New York: Monthly Review Press), p8, p58.

22 Klare, Michael (2007) *Blood and Oil* (New York: Henry Holt), p33.

23 "Truman Doctrine" (1947) *US National Archives*, March 12: https://www.archives.gov/milestone-documents/truman-doctrine

24 "Truman Doctrine", 1947.

25 Kennan, George [anonymous, as 'X'] (1947) "The sources of Soviet conduct", *Foreign Affairs*, 1 July: https://www.academia.edu/69959208/The_Sources_of_Soviet_Conduct_by_X_George_Kennan_Foreign_Affairs_July_1947

26 Kennan, 1947.

27 Jablonsky, David (1995) *Paradigm Lost?: Transitions and the Search for a New World Order* (New York: Praeger/Bloomsbury Publishing USA).

28 Jones, Toby (2012) "America, oil and war in the Middle East", *Journal of American History*, Vol 99, No 1, pp208-218, p208.

29 Jones, 2012, p208.

30 Irfan, 2023, p47.

31 Irfan, 2023, p47.

32 Irfan 2023, pp93–94.

33 Smith, P-A, 1984, p147.

34 King-Irani, Laurie (2006) "Exiled to a liminal legal zone: Are we all Palestinians now?", *Third World Quarterly*, Vol 27, No 5, pp923–936, p926.

35 Peretz, Don (1993) *Palestinians, Refugees and the Middle East Peace Process* (Washington DC: United States Institute of Peace Press), p61.

36 Turki, Fawaz (1988) *Soul in Exile: Lives of a Palestinian Revolutionary* (New York: Monthly Review Press) p41.

37 Sayigh notes that in Lebanon average annual family incomes for all refugees (including middle class and more prosperous households) fell from £Palestinian41 in 1944 to £P8.9 in 1951–52: Sayigh, 1979, p115.

38 Peretz, 1993, p62.

39 Sayigh, 1979, p120.

40 Smith, Pamela-Ann (1975) "Aspects of class structure in Palestinian society", in Davis, Uri, Mack, Andrew and Yuval-Davis, Nira (eds) *Israel and the Palestinians* (London: Ithaca Press), pp98–117, p103.

41 Owen, Roger (1981) *The Middle East in the World Economy* (London: Methuen).

42 Seikaly, Sherine (2016) *Men of Capital: Scarcity and Economy in Mandate Palestine* (Stanford: Stanford University Press), p14.

43 Seikaly, 2016.

44 Smith, P-A, 1984, pp124–125.

45 Kechichian, Joseph (2010) "Abdul Hamid Shoman, the visionary entrepreneur", *Gulf News*, 8 January: https://gulfnews.com/general/abdul-hamid-shoman-the-visionary-entrepreneur-1.563057

46 Mason, Victoria (2009) "Revenge and terror: The destruction of the Palestinian community in Kuwait", in Jackson, Richard, Murphy, Eamon and Poynting, Scott (eds) *Contemporary State Terrorism*, pp138–154 (London: Routledge), p125.

47 See Smith, P-A, 1984, pp112–143, for a detailed account of these developments.

48 Smith, P-A, 1984, p115.

49 Smith, P-A, 1984, p115.

50 Korn, Alina (2003) "From refugees to infiltrators: Constructing political crime in Israel in the 1950s", *International Journal of the Sociology of Law*, Vol 31, No 1, pp1–22, p20.

51 Korn, 2003, p9.

52 Morris, cited in Shlaim, Avi (1994) "Israel's dirty war", *London Review of Books*, 8 August.

53 Morris, cited in Korn, 2003, p12.

54 Shalhoub-Kevorkian, Nadera (2016) "Infiltrated intimacies: The case of Palestinian returnees," *Feminist Studies*, Vol 42, No 1, pp166–193, p167.

55 Morris, Benny (1997) *Israel's Border Wars, 1949–1956: Arab Infiltration, Israeli Retaliation, and the Countdown to the Suez War* (Oxford: Clarendon Press), p38.

56 Morris, 1997, p37.

57 *Oleh* (Hebrew) – one who ascends or "goes up", engaging in *aliyah* ("ascent"). The term had been in use by the Zionist movement for migration to Palestine since the end of the nineteenth century. See "Law of Return": https://www.jewishvirtuallibrary.org/israel-s-law-of-return

58 Segev, 1986, p97.

59 Segev, 1986, p115.

60 Yiftachel, Oren (1996) "Nation-building or ethnic fragmentation? Frontier settlement and collective identities in Israel", *UCLA Working Paper Series*: https://escholarship.org/content/qt0t48n0zb/qt0t48n0zb.pdf

61 Rozin, Orit (2016) "Infiltration and the making of Israel's emotional regime in the state's early years", *Middle Eastern Studies*, Vol 52, No 3, pp448–472, p452.

62 Greenstein, Ran (2015) *Jadaliyya*, August 15: https://www.jadaliyya.com/Details/32396/Israel-Where-do-the-Mizrahim-fit-in-Part-1

63 Van Creveld, Martin (1998) *The Sword and the Olive* (New York: Public Affairs), p130.

64 Bracha, Oren (1998) "Questionably unfortunate, questionably dangerous: The infiltrators, the law, and the Supreme Court, 1948-1954", *Iyunei Mishpat* [Tel Aviv University Law Review], Vol 21, No 2, pp345–369, p338.

65 Van Creveld, 1998, p130.

66 Van Creveld, 1998, p130.

67 Van Crefeld, 1998, p130.

68 Shalhoub-Kevorkian, Nadera (2016). “Infiltrated intimacies: The case of Palestinian returnees”, *Feminist Studies*, Vol 42, No 1, pp166–193, p172.

69 Muslih, Muhammed (1988) *The Origins of Palestinian Nationalism* (New York: Colombia University Press).

70 Crafts, Nicholas, and Toniolo, Gianni (2008) “European economic growth, 1950–2005: An overview” (London: Centre for Economic Policy Research), p32.

71 Crafts and Toniolo, 2008, p32.

72 Graf, Rüdiger (2014) “Expert estimates of oil-reserves and the transformation of ‘petroknowledge’ in the Western world from the 1950s to the 1970s”, *Managing the Unknown. Essays on Environmental Ignorance*, pp140–167, p154.

73 Mitchell, Timothy (2009) “Carbon democracy,” *Economy and Society*, Vol 38, No 3, pp399–432.

74 Painter, David (2012) “Oil and the American century”, *The Journal of American History*, Vol 99, No 1, pp24–39, p29.

75 Painter, 2012, p29.

76 Engels, Frederick, 1968 [1884] “Origins of the family, private property and the state”, in Marx, Karl and Engels, Frederick, *Collected Works* (London: Lawrence and Wishart), p577.

77 Goldsmith, Daniel (2005) “Confronting threats before they materialize: The United States and the overthrow of the Iranian government”, *McGill Journal of Middle East Studies*, Vol 8, pp 81–99, p83.

78 Goldsmith, 2005, p85.

79 Goldsmith, 2005, p86.

80 Office of the Historian (nd) “Memorandum of Discussion at the 135th Meeting of the National Security Council, Washington, March 4, 1953”: https://history.state.gov/historicaldocuments/frus1952-54v10/d312#:~:text=Dulles%20pointed%20out%2C%20if%20Iran,would%20fall%20into%20Communist%20control

81 Gordon, Robert (1992) *Nasser’s Blessed Movement: Egypt’s Free Officers and the July Revolution* (Oxford: Oxford University Press).

82 Stork, Joe (1980) “The Carter doctrine and US bases in the Middle East”, *MERIP Reports*, No. 90 (September), p10.

83 Schoken, Gershon (1951) “The prostitutes of the seaports and ourselves: Meditations on the eve of the new year”, *Ha’aretz*,30 September, in Hanegbi *et al*, 1971, p9.

84 Machover, Moshe (1978) “Israel and the new order in the Middle East”, *Matzpen*, 10 October: https://matzpen.org/english/1978-10-10/israel-and-the-new-order-in-the-middle-east/

85 Tal, David (2020) “United States-Israel relations (1953–1957) revisited”, *Israel Studies*, Vol 26, No 1, pp24–46, p37.

86 Little, Douglas (1993) “The making of a special relationship: The United States and Israel, 1957–68”, *International Journal of Middle East Studies*, Vol 25, No 4, pp563–585, p563.

87 Masalha, Nur (1996) “The 1956–57 occupation of the Gaza strip: Israeli proposals to resettle the Palestinian refugees”, *British Journal of Middle Eastern Studies*, Vol 23, No 1, pp55–68, p56, p59.

88 Masalha, 1996, p57, quoting Israeli sources. See also Masalha, 2000, pp12–13.

89 Little, 1993, p564.

90 Little, 1993, p565.

91 For a full account of the rise and fall of the revolutionary movement and of the Iraqi Communist Party, see:

Batatu, Hanna (1978) *The Old Social Classes and the Revolutionary Movements of Iraq: A Study of Iraq's Old Landed and Commercial Classes and of its Communists, Ba'thists and Free Officers* (London: Saqi Books).

92 Schmidt, Dana (1959) "CIA head warns of danger in Iraq", *New York Times*, 29 April, p1.

93 Little, 1993, p566.

94 Little, 1993, p575.

95 Chair of the Knesset Finance Committee introducing a bill for financing the war on 5 June 1967: in Gorenberg, Gershom (2007) *Occupied Territories: The Untold Story of Israel's Settlements* (London: I.B. Tauris), p35.

96 Gorenberg, 2007, p37.

97 Gorenberg, 2007, p37.

98 Economist (1967), "They did it", *Economist*, 10 June.

99 Economist, 1967.

100 Donovan, Robert and the staff of the Los Angeles Times (1967) *Six Days in June: Israel's Fight for Survival* (New York: Signet), p155.

101 Rubenberg, Cheryl (1986) *Israel and the American National Interest: A Critical Examination* (Urbana: University of Illinois Press), p10.

102 Rubenberg, 1986, p11.

103 Goldstein, Yossi (2018) "The Six Day War: the war that no one wanted", *Israel Affairs*, Vol 24, No 5, pp767–784, p779.

104 Rubenberg, 1986, p11.

105 Masalha, 2000, p21.

106 Smith, Pamela-Ann (1986) "The exile bourgeoisie of Palestine", *MERIP Reports*, No 142: https://merip.org/1986/09/the-exile-bourgeoisie-of-palestine/

Chapter 6
'Our American Israel'

1 Little, 1993, p569.

2 Wenger, Martha (1990) "US aid to Israel: From handshake to embrace", *Merip*, pp164–165: https://merip.org/1990/05/us-aid-to-israel/

3 Wenger, 1990.

4 Little, 1993, p564, p580.

5 *New York Times*, quoted in Aruri, Nasser (1995), *The Obstruction of Peace* (Monroe, Maine: Common Courage Press), p45.

6 Carter, Jimmy (1977) "News conference of May 12", *The Department of State Bulletin*, Vol 76, Issues 1971–1983, 7 June (Washington DC: Department of State), p605.

7 Wenger, 1990.

8 Wenger, 1990.

9 Kaplan, Amy (2018) *Our American Israel: The Story of an Entangled Alliance* (Cambridge, Mass: Harvard University Press), p22.

10 Office of the Historian (1972) "Intelligence Memorandum ER IM 72–79": https://history.state.gov/historicaldocuments/frus1969-76ve04/d181#:~:text=The%20United%20States%20has%20provided%20Iran%20with%20about%20%241.4%20billion,)%20(see%20Table%202)

11 Parsi, Triti (2007) *Treacherous Alliance: The Secret Dealings of Israel, Iran, and the United States* (New Haven: Yale University Press), p36.

12 The US both rewarded Israel for the 1979 peace agreement with Egypt and massively boosted its military hardware in the context of Iran's collapse as an ally. Council on Foreign Relations (CFR) (2024) "US aid to Israel in four charts:" (Washington DC: CFR) https://www.cfr.org/article/us-aid-israel-four-charts

13 Decalo, Samuel (1976) "Afro-Israeli technical co-operation", in Curtis, Michael and Gitelson, Susan (eds) *Israel in the Third World* (New Jersey), p93.

14 Hanegbi *et al*, 1971, pp10-11.

15 'The Jews' had not taken Palestine from the Arab population: Verwoerd interpreted the aims and practices of the Zionist movement in 'racial' terms. Henrik Verwoerd, speaking to the *Rand Daily Mail* (1961), Johannesburg, 23 November, in Stevens, Richard (1971), "Zionism, South Africa and Apartheid: The paradoxical triangle", *Phylon,* Vol 32, No 2, pp123–142, p134.

16 See Stevens, 1971, for an account of relations between South Africa's Nationalist Party, which formalised the apartheid state, and the Zionist movement.

17 Polakow-Suransky, Sasha (2010) *The Unspoken Alliance: Israel's Secret Relationship with Apartheid South Africa* (New York: Pantheon), p210.

18 Peled addressing the Knesset, *Ha'aretz*, 4 August 1985, in Thomas, Baylis, (2009) *The Dark Side of Zionism: The Quest for Security Through Dominance* (Lanham, MD: Lexington Books), p85.

19 Bourdon, Jérôme, (2017) "The export of Zionism: Global images of Israel in the 1960s" in Chaplin, Tamara and Mooney, Jadwiga, *The Global 1960s: Convention, Contest and Counterculture* (London: Routledge), p237. Kaplan, Amy (2018) *Our American Israel: The Story of an Entangled Alliance* (Cambridge, Mass: Harvard University Press), p3.

20 Knowledge of the Holocaust and implications for support of the Israeli state and for understandings of the Palestinian *nakba* are addressed in Rose, John (2004) *The Myths of Zionism* (London: Pluto), ch8.

21 Cummings, Jonathan (2016) *Israel's Public Diplomacy: The Problems of Hasbara, 1966–1975* (Lanham, MD: Rowman and Littlefield), p52.

22 Bourdon, 2017, p237.

23 Pappé, Ilan (2015) *The Idea of Israel: A History of Power and Knowledge* (London: Verso), p50.

24 Pappé, 2015, p50.

25 Pappé, 2015, p51.

26 Bourdon, 2017, p250.

27 Jensehaugen, Jørgen (2023) "Photographing 1948: Robert Capa's absent Palestinians", *Journal of Palestine Studies*, Vol 52, No 2, pp5–23

28 Jensehaugen, 2023.

29 Jensehaugen, 2023.

30 Kaplan, 2018, p3.

31 Kaplan, 2018, p94.

32 Llewellyn, Tim (2023) "The crafting of the news: The British media and the Israel-Palestine Question", (2023) in Parker, Ian (ed) *For Palestine: Essays from the Tim Hurndall Memorial Group Lecture* (London: Open Books), pp229–244, p229.

33 From the Head of the BBC Secretariat, in Llewellyn, 2023, p234.

34 Llewellyn, 2023, p231.

35 Segev, 1986, p37.

36 Pappé, 2006, p226.

37 Pappé, 2006, p228.

38 See JNF official website on 'turning the desert green': Jewish National Fund (nd) https://www.kkl-jnf.org/forestry-and-ecology/afforestation-in-israel/turning-the-desert-green/?_gl=1*jxfq05*_up*MQ..*_ga*MzM0NTgwNjUwLjE3MTY4MzAxNzg.*_ga_2CHBB0KSME*MTcxNjgzMDE3OC4xLjEuMTcxNjgzMDIxMi4yNi4wLjA

39 Shahak, Israel (1976) "Arab villages destroyed in Israel", in Davis Uri and Mevlinsky, Norton, *Documents from Israel, 1967–1973: Readings for a Critique of Zionism* (London: Ithaca Press), pp44–45.

40 Shahak, 1975, p44.

41 Shahak, 1975, p44. Almost twenty years later, after painstaking work, Walid Khalidi and others provided detailed information on 418 villages that had been occupied and depopulated: Khalidi *et al*, 1992.

42 Pappé, Ilan (2016) *The Idea of Israel: A History of Power and Knowledge* (London: Verso), p19.

43 Podeh, E. (2000) "History and memory in the Israeli educational system: The portrayal of the Arab–Israeli conflict in history textbooks (1948–2000)", *History and Memory*, Vol 12, No 1 (Spring/Summer 2000), pp65–100, p72.

44 Podeh, 2000, p72. Podeh notes that the 'national' approach was challenged by Israeli scholars who embraced an 'academic' perspective, quoting one of its proponents, Zvi Adar, to the effect that: 'students should not be taught to revere the nation's history uncritically or worship its heroes blindly'. But such views were marginal to mainstream efforts to establish for Israeli society a positive narrative of the events of 1948 and of their outcomes.

45 Ram, Uri (2009) "Ways of forgetting: Israel and the obliterated memory of the Palestinian Nakba", *Journal of Historical Sociology*, Vol 22, No 3, pp366–395, p368.

46 Dayan in *Ha'aretz*, 4 April 1969, quoted in Said, 1980, p14.

47 Golda Meir in an interview with the *Sunday Times*, 15 June 1969.

48 Said, 1980, p5.

49 Stephens, Robert (1971) *Nasser: A Political Biography* (London: Penguin), p448.

50 Hirst, David (2010) *Beware of Small States: Lebanon, Battleground of the Middle East* (New York: Nation Books), pp80–81.

51 Sayigh, 1979, p149.

52 The League of Arab States, or Arab League, was formed in 1945, initially with seven states and headquartered in Cairo.

53 Stephens, 1971, pp450–451.

54 Cobban, Helena (1984) *The Palestinian Liberation Organisation: People, Power and Politics* (Cambridge: Cambridge University Press), p31.

55 Stephens, 1971, p452.

56 Sayigh, 1979, p144.

57 Stephens, 1971, p453.

58 The full name in Arabic is *Harakat al-Taḥrīr al-Waṭanī al-Filasṭīnī*, the Palestinian National Liberation Movement. The reverse acronym spells "Fath" – a term with historic Islamic associations meaning victory, conquered, or the opening.

59 Hart, Alan (1989) *Arafat: A Political Biography*, (Bloomington, IN: Indiana University Press), p127.

60 Hart, 1989, p127.

61 Among Arafat's collaborators were Salah Khalaf, Khalid al-Hassan and Khalil al-Wazir, activists who also became historic figures in the Palestinian movement. They were widely known by their *kunya* – the name given for a first-born son or daughter and which could also be a non-de-guerre or nickname. Arafat was known as Abu [father of] Ammar, Khalaf as Abu Iyad, Hassan as Abu Said, and Wazir as Abu Jihad.

62 Iyad Abu [Salah Khalaf] (1981) *My Home, My Land* (New York: Times Books), p20.

63 Harris, Lillian Craig (1977) "China's relations with the PLO", *Journal of Palestine Studies*, Vol 7, No 1, pp123–154, p123.

64 Iyad, 1981, p42.

65 Cobban, 1984, p33.

66 Cobban, 1984, p42.

67 Chamberlin, Paul Thomas (2012) *The Global Offensive: The United States, the Palestine Liberation Organization, and the Making of the Post-Cold War Order* (Oxford: Oxford University Press), p20.

68 Chamberlin, 2012, p27.

69 Directed against senior army officers granted clemency despite their performance in the 1967 war with Israel.

70 Hussein, Mahmoud (1973) *Class Conflict in Egypt: 1945–1970* (New York: Monthly Review Press), p293.

71 Hussein, 1973, p303.

72 Ajami, Fouad (1992) *The Arab Predicament: Arab Political Thought and Practice Since 1967* (Cambridge: Cambridge University Press), pp105–106.

73 Ajami, 1992, p105.

74 Ajami, 1992, p100.

75 Stephens, 1971, p537.

76 Said, 1980, p7; Sayigh, 1979, p150.

77 Irfan, Anne (2020) *An Unusual Revolution: The Palestinian* Thawra *in Lebanon, c1969–82*, Durham Middle East Paper 103 (Durham: Durham University), p17.

78 Sayigh, 1979, p166.

79 Sayigh, 1979, pp165–166.

80 Peteet, Julie (1991) *Gender in Crisis: Women and the Palestinian Resistance Movement* (New York: Colombia University Press), p3.

81 Peteet, 1991, p6.

82 Meier, Daniel (2014) "The Palestinian *fiday'i* as an icon of transnational struggle: The Lebanese experience", *British Journal of Middle Eastern Studies*, Vol 41, No 3, pp322–334, p327.

83 Rouleau, Eric (1985) "The Palestinian diaspora of the Gulf", *Merip*, 132: https://merip.org/1985/05/the-palestinian-diaspora-of-the-gulf/

84 Iyad, Abu [Salah Khalaf, with Eric Rouleau] (1981) *My Home, My Land* (New York: Times Books), p38.

85 Smith, Pamela-Ann (1986) "The exile bourgeoisie of Palestine", *Merip*, 142: https://merip.org/1986/09/the-exile-bourgeoisie-of-palestine/

86 Seikaly, 2016.

87 Smith, P-A, 1984, p196.

88 Khalidi, Raja (2018) "Nation and class: Generations of Palestinian liberation", *Rethinking Marxism*, Vol 30, No 3, pp368-392, p378.

89 Abu-Sharif, Bassam (2009) *Arafat and the Dream of Palestine: An Insider's Account* (Basingstoke: Palgrave Macmillan), p13.

90 PLO (1964) *Palestine Liberation Organisation: The Original Palestine National Charter 1964*: Internet Archive: https://archive.org/details/palestine-liberation-organization-the-original-palestine-national-charter-1964

91 Smith, P-A, 1986.

92 *Time* (1966) "Middle East: How they broke the bank", *Time* Magazine, 25 November.

93 Smith, P-A, 1984, p142.

94 Rouleau, p1985.

95 Rouleau, p1985.

96 Rouleau, p1985.

97 Hart, 1989, p286.

98 Smith, P-A, 1984, pp172–173.

99 Sayigh, Yusuf (1999) *Armed Struggle and the Search for State: The Palestinian National Movement, 1949–1993* (Oxford: Oxford University Press), p603.

100 Hart, 1989, p288.

Chapter 7
Guerrilla strategy

1 Smith, 1984, pp192–193. Disoriented by the military coup that brought Egypt's Free Officers to power under Gamal Abdel-Nasser, the Brotherhood split - with leadership factions of support and of opposition to the new regime. In 1954 the Brotherhood was banned and underwent severe repression. Mitchell, 1969, ch 5.

2 Baumgarten, Helga (2005) "The three faces/phases of Palestinian nationalism, 1948–2005", *Journal of Palestine Studies*, Vol 34, No 4, pp25–48, p34.

3 Article in *Our Palestine*, November 1960, in Baumgaten, 2005, p33.

4 Hart, Alan (1984) *Arafat: Terrorist or Peacemaker?* (London: Sidgwick and Jackson), p157.

5 Iyad, 1981, p55.

6 Hart, 1984, p236.

7 Hart, 1984, p153.

8 Hart, 1984, p153.

9 El-Hamalawy, Hossam (2001) "January 18 and 19, 1977. 'Uprising of Thieves' or an aborted revolution?" Unpublished MA thesis, The American University in Cairo, 65: https://arabawy.org/wp-content/uploads//2020/12/MA-Thesis-Hossam-el-Hamalawy.pdf

10 Hussein, 1973, p308.

11 Said, 1980, p158.

12 Gresh, Alain (1988), *The PLO: The Struggle Within* (London: Zed), p15.

13 Kazziha, Walid (1975) *Revolutionary Transformation in the Arab World: Habash and his Comrades from Nationalism to Marxism* (London: Charles Knight), p20.

14 Kazziha, 1975, p84.

15 Kazziha, 1975, p87.

16 Cobban, 1984, p33.

17 Sayigh, Y., 1997, p244.

18 Ashton, Nigel (2006) "Pulling the strings: King Hussein's role during the crisis of 1970 in Jordan", *International History* Review, Vol 28, No 1, pp94–118, p100.

19 Cooley, John (1973) *Green March, Black September* (London: Frank Cass), p112.

20 Sayigh, Y., 1997, p245.

21 Sayigh, Y., 1997, p244.

22 Sayigh Y., 1997, p244.

23 Sayigh, Y., 1997, p248.

24 Sayigh, Y., 1997, p248.

25 Chamberlin, 2012, p5.

26 As recorded in state papers published in 2008 by the Office of the Historian: United States Government (2008) "Middle East Region and Arabian Peninsula, 1969–1972"; Vol XXIV [Jordan, September 1970] (Washington: US Government Printing Office).

27 Chamberlin, 2012, p124.

28 Chamberlin, 2012, p2.

29 Chamberlin, 2012, p5.

30 Sayigh, Y., 1997, p252.

31 Sayigh, Y., 1997, p255.

32 Sayigh, Y.,1997, p255.

33 Hart, 1984, p268.

34 Chamberlin, 2012, p109.

35 Chamberlin, 2012, p110.

36 United States Government, 2008, p686.

37 United States Government, 2008, p630.

38 United States Government, 2008, p629.

39 United States Government, 2008, pp630–631.

40 United States Government, 2008, p644.

41 United States Government, 2008, p650.

42 Chamberlin, 2012, p125.

43 Odeh, B. J. (1985), *Lebanon: Dynamics of Conflict* (London: Zed), p10.

44 Kazziha, 1975, p87.

45 Khalidi, Rashid (1997) *Palestinian Identity: The Construction of Modern National Consciousness* (New York: Colombia University Press), p197.

46 Khalidi, 1997, p197.

47 Hart, 1984, p294.

48 Hart, 1984, p294.

49 Abu-Odeh, Adnan (1999) *Jordanians, Palestinians, and the Hashemite Kingdom in the Middle East Peace Process* (Washington: United States Institute of Peace), p188.

50 Abu-Sharif, Bassam and Mahnaimi, Uzi (1995) *Tried by Fire* (London: Little, Brown), p89.

51 Hudson, Michael (1972) "Developments and setbacks in the Palestinian Resistance Movement 1967–1971", *Journal of Palestine Studies*, Vol 1, No 3, pp64–84, p64

52 Hudson, 1971, p66.

53 Hudson, 1971, p82.

54 Chalcraft, 2016, pp375–376.

55 Popular Front for the Liberation of Palestine (1973) *Tasks of the New Stage* (Beirut: Foreign Relations Committee, PFLP), p23.

56 PFLP, 1973, p25.

57 PFLP, 1973, pp37–38.

58 PFLP, 1973, p38.

59 Hasso, Frances (2005) *Resistance, Repression, and Gender Politics in Occupied Palestine and Jordan* (Syracuse, NY: Syracuse University Press) https://muse.jhu.edu/pub/204/oa_monograph/chapter/2842481

60 Hasso, 2005.

61 Hudson, 1971, p83.

62 Hudson, 1971, p83.

63 PFLP, 1973, p39.

64 Hart, 1984, p294.

65 Brynen, Rex (2019) *Sanctuary and Survival: The PLO in Lebanon* (London: Routledge), p11.

66 Brynen, 2019, p11.

67 In 1960, half the population was below the poverty line: Kukrety, Nupur (2016) *Poverty, inequality and social protection in Lebanon* (Oxfam International/American University of Beirut), p38.

68 Chalcraft, 2016, p381.

69 Brynen, 2019, p65.

70 Khalidi, Walid (1979) *Violence and Conflict in Lebanon* (Cambridge, Mass: Harvard Centre for International Studies), p124.

71 Sayigh, Rosemary (2015) *Too Many Enemies: The Palestinian Experience in Lebanon* (Beirut: Al Mashriq).

72 Allon, Yigal (1976) "Israel: the case for defensible borders", *Foreign Affairs*, Vol 55 (October), pp38–53, p42.

73 Gorenberg (2007) p124.

74 Gorenberg, 2007, p84.

75 Allon Plan (1967) *Allon Plan*: https://www.jewishvirtuallibrary.org/s

76 Gorenberg, 2007, pp97–98; Lesch, Anne (1975) "Israeli Settlements the Occupied Territories, 1967–1977", *Journal of Palestine Studies*, Vol 7, No 1, pp26–47, p24.

77 Gorenberg, 2007, pp99–100. *The Geneva Convention Relative to the Protection of Civilian Persons in Time of War*, 1949, Article 49, "The Occupying Power shall not deport or transfer parts of its own civilian population into the territory it occupies": https://ihl-databases.icrc.org/en/ihl-treaties/gciv-1949/article-49?activeTab=undefined

78 All figures from Tenenbaum, Karen, and Eiran, Ehud (2005) "Israeli settlement activity in the West Bank and Gaza: A brief history." *Negotiations Journal*, Vol 21, pp171–175 pp173-174.

79 Tenenbaum and Eiran, 2005, p174.

80 Tenenbaum and Eiran, 2005, p175.

81 Lesch, 1975, p27.

82 Bisharat, George E (1993) "Land, law, and legitimacy in Israel and the occupied territories", *American University Law* Review, Vol 43, pp467-561, pp527–528.

83 Lesch, 1975, p2

84 Gorenberg, 2007, p132.

85 Gorenberg, 2007, p79.

86 Gazit, Shlomo (1995) *The Carrot and the Stick: Israel's Policy in Judea and Samaria, 1967–68* (Washington DC: B'nai B'rith Books).

87 Pappé, Ilan (2024) *Gaza: The Biggest Prison on Earth: A History of Gaza and the Occupied Territories* (London: One World), pxxii.

88 Pappé, 2024, pxxv.

89 Abu-Lughod, Janet (1984) "The demographic consequences of the occupation" in Aruri, Naseer (ed) *Occupation: Israel Over Palestine* (London: Zed), p258.

90 Raviv, Omri (2021) "Israeli emigration policies in the Gaza Strip: Crafting demography and forming control in the aftermath of the 1967 War", *Middle Eastern Studies*, Vol 57, No 2, pp342–356, p344.

91 Raviv, 2021, p344.

92 Raviv, 2021, p345.

93 Raviv, 2021, p346.

94 Gorenberg, 2007, p142.

95 Raviv, 2021, p348.

96 Segev, Tom (2007) *1967: Israel, the War and the Year that Transformed the Middle East* (London: Abacus), p646.

97 Segev, 2007, p646.

98 Raviv, 2021, p352.

99 Gabriel, Stuart, and Sabatello, Eitan (1986) "Palestinian migration from the West Bank and Gaza: Economic and demographic analyses", *Economic Development and Cultural Change*, Vol 34, No 2, pp245–262, p251.

100 Rabbani, Mouin and Hajjar, Lisa (1988) "Israel and the Palestinians, 1948–1988", *Merip Reports*, No 52, p22.

101 Hever, Shir (2012) "Exploitation of Palestinian labour in contemporary Zionist colonialism", *Settler Colonial Studies*, Vol 2, No 1, pp124–132, p127.

102 Roy, Sara (2001) *The Gaza Strip: The Political Economy of De-Development*, 2nd ed. (Washington: Institute for Palestine Studies).

103 Gabriel and Sabatello, 1986, p255.

104 *Financial Times* (1988) 13 January.

105 Farsakh, Leila (2002) "Palestinian labour flows to the Israeli economy: A finished story?" *Journal of Palestine Studies*, Vol 32, No 1, pp13–27, p14.

106 Bishara, Azmi (1995) "Bantustanisation or binationalism?" in Usher, Graham, *Dispatches from Palestine*, pp59–66.

107 Middle East Report (1979), No 74 (January), p7.

108 Middle East Report, 1988, p36.

109 West Bank Data Base Project (1986) *The Middle East Magazine*, August (London: IC Publications).

110 Hever, 2012, p124.

111 Middle East Report, 1988, p35.

112 Middle East Report, 1988, p35.

113 Raviv, 2021, p350.

114 Raviv, 2021, p350.

115 Raviv, 2021, p350.

116 Middle East Report, 1988, p35.

117 Middle East Report, 1988, p37.

118 Middle East Report (1987), No 152, p19.

Chapter 8
Intifada renewed

1 Mideast Mirror, 1987, 11 December.

2 Middle East Report, 1988a, p9.

3 Middle East Report, 1988a, p9.

4 Jerusalem Post, 1988 (international edition), 23 January.

5 Bishara, Ghassan (1989) "Impotence in the face of adversity: Arab regimes and the Palestine Question", *Arab Studies Quarterly*, Vol 11, No 2/3, pp303–314, p311.

6 Mideast Mirror, 1988, 14 January.

7 Bargouti, Husain (1990) "Jeep versus bare feet: The villages in the Intifada", in Nassar and Heacock, p108.

8 Farsoun, Samih and Landis, Jean (1990) "The sociology of an uprising", in Nassar and Heacock, p23.

9 Rosenhek, Zeev (2003) "The political dynamics of a segmented labour market: Palestinian citizens, Palestinians from the Occupied Territories and migrant workers in Israel", *Acta Sociologica*, Vol 46, No 3, pp231–249, p241.

10 Farsoun and Landis, 1990, p27.

11 Farsoun and Landis, 1990, p27.

12 Naser-Najjab, Nadia (2020) "Palestinian leadership and the contemporary significance of the First Intifada", *Race and Class*, Vol 62, No 2, pp61–79, p71.

13 Naser-Najjab, 2020, p71.

14 Middle East Report (1988b), No 155, p39.

15 Darweish, Marwan (1989) "The intifada: Social change", *Race and Class*, Vol 39, No 2, pp47–61, p54.

16 *Ha'aretz* (1988) (Tel Aviv), 5 December.

17 Mideast Mirror, 1989, 27 February.

18 Tamari, Salim (1983) "In league with Zion: Israel's search for a native pillar", *Journal of Palestine Studies,* Vol 12, No 4, pp41–56, p42.

19 Tamari, 1983, p43.

20 Tamari, 1983, p43.

21 Tamari, 1983, p49.

22 Gorenberg, 2007, p360.

23 Farsoun and Landis, 1988, p22.

24 Farsoun and Landis, p22.

25 Moughrabi, Fouad (1992) "Israeli control and Palestinian resistance", *Social Justice*, Vol 19, No 3, pp46–62, p55.

26 Mougrabi, 1992, p55.

27 Reich, Bernard (1984) *The United States and Israel: Influences in the Special Relationship* (New York: Praeger), p181.

28 Schiff, Ze'ev and Ya'ari, Yehud (1985) *Israel's Lebanon War* (London: Touchstone), p75.

29 According to the *Financial Times*, within weeks the force amounted to 90,000 troops; 1,300 tanks and an equal number of armoured personnel carriers; 12,000 troop and supply trucks; 3,500 ambulances and 300 buses; and hundreds of heavy artillery pieces. Paul, James and Stork, Joe (1982) "The War in Lebanon", *Merip Reports*, No 108: https://merip.org/1982/09/the-war-in-lebanon/

30 James and Stork, 1982.

31 Fisk, Robert (1990) *Pity the Nation: Lebanon at War* (London: André Deutsch), p256.

32 Kapeliouk, Amnon (1984) *Sabra and Shatila: Inquiry into a Massacre* (Belmont, MA: Association of Arab-American University Graduates), p45. See also: Shahid, Leila (2002) "The Sabra and Shatila Massacres: Eye-witness reports", *Journal of Palestine Studies*, Vol 32, No 1, pp36–58.

33 Hirst, 2010, p153.

34 Friedman, Thomas (2006) *From Beirut to Jerusalem* (New York: Anchor Books), p157.

35 *Guardian*, 1988, 9 December.

36 Qassem, Khalid (1988) "Repercussions in the Middle East", *Middle East Report*, No 152, p47..

37 Qassem, 1988.

38 Middle East Report, 1988, p47.

39 Middle East Report, 1988, p47.

40 Middle East Report, 1988, p51.

41 Mideast Mirror, 1988, 10 February.

42 Mideast Mirror, 1988, 10 February.

43 Middle East Report, 1988, p52.

44 ElMahdi, Rabab and Marfleet, Philip (2009) *Egypt: The Moment of Change* (London: Zed); Marfleet, Philip (2016) *Egypt: Contested Revolution* (London: Pluto).

45 Hirst, David and Beeson Irene (1982) *Sadat* (London: Faber and Faber).

46 Yahia, Karem (1987) "The image of the Palestinians in Egypt, 1982-85", *Journal of Palestine Studies*, Vol 16, No 2, pp45–63, p46.

47 Ross, Michael (1988) "Violence in Gaza echoes in Egypt: Like Lebanon invasion, unrest strains 2 neighbors' ties", *Los Angeles Times*, 12 January.

48 Personal account of an Egyptian journalist given to the author, September 1988, and Middle East Report, 1988, p45.

49 In February 1986 Egypt's riot police, the core of the repressive state, had launched their own uprising, eventually suppressed by the army.

50 Mideast Mirror, 1988, 4 January; Brynen, Rex (1991) "Palestine and the Arab State System: Permeability, state consolidation and the *Intifada*", *Canadian Journal of Political Science/Revue Canadienne de Science Politique*, Vol XXIV, No 3, pp596–621, p613.

51 Mideast Mirror, 1988, 4 January.

52 Mideast Mirror, 1988, 5 January.

53 Mideast Mirror, 1988, 11 January.

54 Mideast Mirror, 1988, 12 January.

55 Mideast Mirror, 1988, 4 January.

56 Middle East Report, 1988, p52.

57 UPI (1990) "Former Egyptian minister calls for expulsion of Palestinians", 6 November.

58 Mideast Mirror, 1988, 1 February.

59 United Nations (1988) Palestine question/ Mideast situation, Final Declaration of the Arab Summit, letter from Algeria: https://www.un.org/unispal/document/auto-insert-187887/

60 Cobban, Helena (1990) "The PLO and the 'Intifada'", *Middle East Journal*, Vol 44, No 2, pp207–233, p229.

61 Cobban, 1990, p227.

62 Cobban, 1990, p227.

63 Cobban, 1990, p232.

64 Farah, Randa (2013) "Palestinian refugees, the nation, and the shifting political landscape", *Social Alternatives*, Vol 32, No 3, pp41–47, p44.

65 Hart, Alan (1985) "Don't blame Arafat", *Journal of Palestine Studies*, Vol 14, No 3, pp187–190, p188.

66 Muslih, Muhammed (1976) "Moderates and rejectionists within the Palestine Liberation Organization", *Middle East Journal*, Vol 30, No 2, pp127–140, p130.

67 Hart, 1985, p188.

68 Hart, 1985, p379.

69 Iyad, 1981, p142.

70 United Nations (1974) "PLO sole legitimate representative of the Palestinian people – LAS Rabat Summit – resolution", Seventh Arab League Summit Conference "Resolution on Palestine" (Rabat, Morocco, 28 October 1974): https://www.un.org/unispal/document/auto-insert-194621/

71 Hirst, David (1977) *The Gun and the Olive Branch* (London: Faber and Faber), p333.

72 Iyad, 1981, p147.

73 'Abid, Ibrahim (1969) *A Handbook to the Palestinian Question* (Beirut: Palestine Liberation Organisation), p184.

74 'Abid, 1969, p188.

75 Hart, 1985, p188.

76 Hart, 1985, p188.

77 Muslih, 1976, p130.

78 Muslih, 1976, p132.

79 Musli, 1976, p132.

80 Said, 1980, p161.

81 Said, 1980, p162.

82 Said, 1980, p162.

83 Said, 1980, p170.

84 Said, 1980, pp162–163.

85 Mideast Mirror, 1988, 10 October.

86 Roberts, Hugh (2017) *The Battlefield: Algeria 1988-2002: Studies in a Broken Polity* (London: Verso), p83.

87 Roberts, Hugh (2002) "Moral economy or moral polity? The political anthropology of Algerian riots", London School of Economics and Political Science, Crisis States Programme Working Paper, No 1, p9.

88 Roberts, 2002, p10.

89 Mideast Mirror, 1988, 7 October.

90 Mideast Mirror, 1988, 7 October.

91 Mideast Mirror, 1988, 10 October.

92 Mideast Mirror, 1988, 11 October.

93 Mideast Mirror, 1988, 10 October.

94 Christison, Kathleen (1998) "Bound by a frame of reference, Part II: US policy and the Palestinians, 1948–88", *Journal of Palestine Studies*, Vol 27, No 3, pp20–34, p32.

Chapter 9
Hamas intervenes

1 Walton, John and Seddon, David (2011) *Free Markets and Food Riots: The Politics of Global Adjustment* (London: Wiley-Blackwell).

2 Aarts, Paul (1992) Democracy, oil and the Gulf War, *Third World Quarterly*, Vol 13, No 3, pp525–538, p526.

3 Aarts, 1992, p527.

4 Aarts, 1992, p527.

5 Bush, George H. W. (1990) "Out of these troubled times...a new world order", *Washington Post (speech to Congress, September 11)* https://www.washingtonpost.com/archive/politics/1990/09/12/bush-out-of-these-troubled-times-a-new-world-order/b93b5cf1-e389-4e6a-84b0-85f71bf4c946/

6 Shlaim, Avi (1994) "Israel and the Conflict", in Danchev, Alex and Keohane, Dan (eds) *International Perspectives on the Gulf Conflict, 1990–91* (London, St Martin's Press), pp59–79, p59.

7 Shlaim, 1994, p62.

8 Human Rights Watch (1990) "The Israeli Army and the intifada policies that contribute to the killings" (New York: Human Rights Watch): https://www.hrw.org/legacy/campaigns/israel/intifada-intro.htm

9 Mattar, Philip (1994) "The PLO and the Gulf Crisis", *Middle East Journal*, Vol 48, No 1 pp31–46, 37.

10 Mattar, 1994, p43.

11 Usher, Graham (1995) *Palestine in Crisis: The Struggle for Peace and Political Independence after Oslo* (London: Pluto), p2.

12 Usher, 1995, p2.

13 Mattar, 1994, p43.

14 Sabella, Bernard (1993) "Russian Jewish immigration and the future of the Israeli-Palestinian conflict" *Middle East Report*, No 182

15 Sabella, 1993.

16 Sabella, 1993.

17 Lochery, Neil (2005) "Israel's Soviet immigrants", *British Academy Review*, No 8, pp4–7.

18 Rovner, Joshua (2014) "Delusion of defeat: The United States and Iraq, 1990–1998", *The Journal of Strategic Studies*, Vol 37, No 4, pp482–507, p491.

19 Fukuyama, Francis (1991) *The End of History and the Last Man* (New York: Free Press).

20 Project for a New American Century (1997) "Statement of Principles": https://web.archive.org/web/20130112235337/http://www.newamericancentury.org/statementofprinciples.htm

21 Peleg, Ian and Scham, Paul (2007) "Israeli neo-revisionism and American neoconservatism: The unexplored parallels, *The Middle East Journal*, Vol 61, No1, pp73–94.

22 Peleg and Scham, 2007, p76. The authors emphasise that there was no conspiratorial alliance between the two currents; rather, they shared key developmental and ideological preoccupations.

23 Fuller, Adam (2020) *Israel and the Neoconservatives: Zionism and American Interests* (Lexington Books, Lanham MD), p1.

24 Fuller, 2020, p2.

25 Usher, 1995, p3.

26 Silber, Efrat (2011) "Israel's policy of house demolitions during the First Intifada, 1987–1993", *Terrorism and Political Violence*, Vol 23, pp89–107.

27 Usher, 1995, p6.

28 Israeli historian Efrat Silber's chilling analysis includes the assertion that 'No rule, military or otherwise, can accept a situation in which a governed populace tries to attack it and its representatives. Thus the IDF cannot be expected to sit idly by when an attack is carried out. In such a situation, the question is not whether the IDF must take steps to ensure its control of the region, but rather what means it is entitled to use and how effective they are.' Silber, 2011, p100.

29 Silber, 2011, p100.

30 Usher, 1995, p5.

31 Usher, 1995, p5.

32 Usher, 1995, p4.

33 Abu-Amr, Ziad (1994) *Islamic Fundamentalism in the West Bank and Gaza* (Bloomington: Indiana University Press), p63–64.

34 Abu-Amr, Ziad (1993) "Hamas: A historical and political background", *Journal of Palestine Studies*, Vol 22, No 4, pp5–19, p6.

35 Filiu, Jean-Pierre (2012) "The origins of Hamas: Militant legacy or Israeli tool?" *Journal of Palestine Studies*, Vol 41, No 3, pp54–70, p64.

36 Knudsen, Are (2005) "Crescent and sword: The Hamas enigma," *Third World Quarterly*, Vol 26, No 8, pp1373–1388, p1376.

37 Kimmerling, Baruch (2003) *Politicide: Ariel Sharon's War Against the Palestinians* (London: Verso), p76.

38 Filiu, p64.

39 Robinson, Glenn (2003) "Hamas as social movement", in Wiktorowicz, Quintan (ed) *Islamic Activism: A Social Movement Theory Approach* (Bloomington: Indiana University Press), pp112–139, p120.

40 Abu-Amr, 1994, p77.

41 Zuhur, Sharifa (2008) *Hamas and Israel: Conflicting Strategies of Group-Based Politics* (Washington: Strategic Studies Institute), p27.

42 Robinson, 2003, p123.

43 Robinson, 2003, p123.

44 Abu-Amr, 1994, pp17–18.

45 Abu-Amr, 1994, p66.

46 Robinson, 2003, p124.

47 Higgins, Andrew (2009) "How Israel helped to spawn Hamas", *Wall Street Journal*, 24 January: http://www.wsj.com/articles/SB123275572295011847

48 Knudsen, 2005, p1382.

49 Peace Agreements (1993) "Israel–PLO Recognition – exchange of letters" (9 September 1993) https://www.peaceagreements.org/viewmasterdocument/34

50 Beinin, Joel (2003) "Is terrorism a useful term in understanding the Middle East and the Palestinian-Israeli conflict?" *Radical History Review*, Vol 85, No 1, pp12–23, p18.

51 Pappé, 2103, p35.

52 Abu-Amr, Ziad (1993) "Hamas: A historical and political background", *Journal of Palestine Studies*, Vol 22, No 4, pp5–19, p14.

53 Hroub, Khaled (2004) "Hamas after Shaykh Yasin and Rantisi", *Journal of Palestine Studies*, Vol 33, No 4, pp21-38, pp21–22.

54 See for example, Lerner, Daniel (1958) *The Passing of Traditional Society: Modernising the Middle East* (New York: Free Press).

55 Lewis, Bernard (1990) "The roots of Muslim rage", *The Atlantic*, Vol 266, No 3. See also Patai, Raphael (1973) *The Arab Mind* (New York: Scribner). Fouad Mougrabi notes that Patai's book was reprinted and distributed by the Pentagon to US Army officers teach them how to understand 'the Arab mind' and Arab culture: Moughrabi, Fouad (2009) "Moving towards a knowledge society in the Arab world", *Arab Studies Quarterly*, Vol 31, No 4, pp17–31, p19.

56 Huntington, Samuel (1993) "The clash of civilizations?", *Foreign Affairs*, Vol 72, No 3, pp22–49.

57 Huntington, Samuel (1996) *The Clash of Civilizations and the Remaking of World Order* (New York: Simon & Schuster), p21.

58 Said, Edward (1998) *The Myth of 'The Clash of Civilizations'* (transcript from the Media Information Foundation): https://www.mediaed.org/transcripts/Edward-Said-The-Myth-of-Clash-Civilizations-Transcript.pdf

59 Cook, Jonathan (2008) *Israel and the Clash of Civilisations* (London: Pluto), p106.

60 Shahak, Israel (1997) *Open Secrets: Israeli Nuclear and Foreign Policies* (London: Pluto), pp41–43.

61 Said, Edward (1993) "The morning after", *London Review of Books*, 21 October.

62 Said, 1993.

63 Ismael, Tareq, "Arafat's Palestine National Authority", *Durham Middle East Papers*, No 71 (Durham: University of Durham), p19.

64 Ismael, 2022, p19.

65 Ismael, 2002, p21.

66 Farsakh, Leila (2000) "Under siege: Closure, separation and the Palestinian economy", *Merip*, No 217: https://merip.org/2000/12/under-siege/

67 Hass, A. (2002) "Israel's closure policy: An ineffective strategy of containment and repression", *Journal of Palestine Studies*, Vol 31, No 3, pp5–20, p8.

68 Hass, 2002, p8.

69 Hass, 2002, p15.

70 Hass, 2002, p9.

71 Ismael, 2002, p22.

72 Andoni, Lamis (1996) "The Palestinian elections: Moving toward democracy or one-party rule?", *Journal of Palestine Studies*, Vol 25, No 3, pp5–16.

73 Andoni, 1996, p8.

74 Andoni, 1996, p13.

75 Shpiro, Shlomo (2003) "The CIA as Middle East peace broker?" *Survival*, Vol 32, No 2, pp91–112, p99.

76 Shpiro, 2003, p100.

77 Amnesty International (1999) "Palestinian Authority: Defying the rule of law: Political detainees held without charge or trial": https://www.amnesty.org/en/documents/mde21/003/1999/en/

78 Usher, 1995, p68.

79 Rubenberg, Cheryl (2003) *The Palestinians: In Search of a Just Peace* (Boulder, CO: Lynne Reiner), p255.

80 Rubenberg, 2003, pp260–261.

81 Human Rights Watch (1999) "The Palestinian Security Forces": https://www.hrw.org/reports/1997/palestina/Israel-03.htm

82 Pappé, Ilan (2017) *The Biggest Prison on Earth* (London: Oneworld), p194.

83 Hass, 2002, p12.

84 Hass, 2002, p15.

85 Hass, 2002, p19.

86 According to Brym and Araj, while 26 percent of the Palestinian population expressed support for suicide bombing in 1999, a year later the figure had ballooned to 66 percent, as 'increasing support for suicide bombing was associated with falling support for Fatah and rising support for Hamas': Brym, Robert and Araj, Bader (2008) "Palestinian suicide bombing revisited: A critique of the outbidding thesis," *Political Science Quarterly*, No 123, pp485–500, p497.

87 Hass, 2002, p20.

88 Farsakh, 2000.

89 Farsakh, 2000.

90 Farsakh, 2000.

91 Roy, Sara (2004) "The Palestinian–Israeli conflict and Palestinian socioeconomic decline: A place denied", *International Journal of Politics, Culture and Society*, Vol 17, No 3, pp365–403, p365.

92 UN OCHA, 2002.

93 Roy, 2004, p373.

94 'The right of the Jewish people to the Land of Israel is an eternal right that is not subject to question, and it is combined with a right to security and peace; thus, Judea and Samaria [the West Bank] will not be transferred to any foreign rule; there will be only Israeli sovereignty applied between the Mediterranean Sea and the Jordan River.' The Likud platform for the seventh Knesset elections in Naor, Arye (2015) "'A simple historical truth': Judea, Samaria and the Gaza Strip in Menachem Begin's ideology", *Israel Affairs*, Vol 21, No 3, pp462–481, p471.

95 Kimmerling, Baruch (2003) "From Barak to Road Map", *New Left Review*, September, pp134–44, p136.

96 Whitson, Sarah (2014) "Ariel Sharon's Legacy is Deeply Disturbing", *Human Rights Watch*, 13 January: https://www.hrw.org/news/2014/01/13/ariel-sharons-legacy-deeply-disturbing

97 Kimmerling, 2003, p141.

98 United Nations (2004) "ICJ advisory opinion on the legal consequences of the construction of a wall in the OPT": https://www.un.org/unispal/document/auto-insert-178825/#:~:text=Settlements%20established%20by%20Israel%20in,of%20the%20wall%20severely%20impedes

99 Israel Central Bureau of Statistics (2020) "Number of Settlers in the Israeli Settlements in the West Bank by Region, 1986–2019", Palestinian Central Bureau of Statistics: https://www.pcbs.gov.ps/Portals/_Rainbow/Documents/SETTTime%20SeriesE-2019.html

100 Outposts data from Peace Now in Tilley, Virginia (2007) "A two-state solution, or smoke and mirrors? Looking awry at Israel's state-building agenda", in Farouk-Alli, Aslan (ed) *The Future of Palestine and Israel: From Colonial Roots to Postcolonial Realities* (Midrand, South Africa: Institute for Global Dialogue/Friedrich Ebert Stiftung), p241.

Chapter 10
'War on Terror'

1 Kimmerling, Baruch (2003) *Politicide: Ariel Sharon's War Against the Palestinians* (London: Verso), p4.

2 Kimmerling, 2003, p4.

3 US Department of State, Bureau of Counterterrorism (2001) "Executive Order 13224": https://www.state.gov/executive-order-13224/

4 US Office of the Vice-President (1989) "Terrorist Group Profiles" [Washington DC: Superintendent of Documents]: https://apps.dtic.mil/sti/tr/pdf/ADA204627.pdf

5 In 1985 the School of the Americas was transferred to Fort Benning, Georgia, USA; in 2001, as the US announced a War on Terror, it was renamed the Western Hemisphere Institute for Security Cooperation (WHINSEC).

6 Gill, Lesley (2004) *The School of the Americas: Military Training and Political Violence in the Americas* (Durham, NC: Duke University Press), p3.

7 Monbiot, George (2001) "Backyard terrorism", *Guardian*, 31 October.

8 Washington Post (2001) "Text: President Bush Addresses the Nation", 20 September.

9 Bush, George W. (2005) "President discusses war on terror at National Endowment for Democracy", 6 October, (Washington, DC: The White House) https://georgewbush-whitehouse.archives.gov/news/releases/2005/10/20051006-3.html

10 Wild, Stefan (2012) "'Islamofascism'? Introduction", *Die Welt des Islams*, Vol 52, No 3/4, pp225–24, pp228–229, p234.

11 Wild, 2012, p234.

12 UPI (1982) "Begin compares Arafat to Hitler", *UPI*, 5 August: https://www.upi.com/Archives/1982/08/05/Begin-compares-Arafat-to-Hitler/2671397368000/

13 Gart, Murray (1989) "Interview with Israel's Ariel Sharon: Never! Never! Never!", *Time*, 17 April: https://time.com/archive/6702324/interview-with-israels-ariel-sharon-never-never-never/

14 *New York Times* (1952) "A bid for dictatorship", 15 July.

15 *Time* Magazine (1953) "99.93% pure", 17 August.

16 Henderson, Jon (1976) "Leadership personality and war: The cases of Richard Nixon and Anthony Eden", *Political Science*, Vol 28, No 2, pp141–164, p156.

17 Bremer, Paul (2006) *My Year in Iraq: The Struggle to Build a Future of Hope* (New York: Simon and Schuster), p38.

18 Allawi, Ali (2007) *The Occupation of Iraq: Winning the War, Losing the Peace* (New Haven: Yale University Press), p152. See also: Marfleet, Philip (2015) "Iraq: what happened next...", *International Socialism*, No 161.

19 Sharon, Ariel (2001) *CNN*, 11 September.

20 Goldberg, Suzanne (2001) "Israeli tanks invade two West Bank towns", *Guardian*, 13 September.

21 Gregory, Derek (2004) "Palestine and the 'War on Terror'", *Comparative Studies of South Asia, Africa and the Middle East*, Vol 24, No 1, pp183–195, p184.

22 Gregory, 2004, p184.

23 Reeves, Phil (2001) "Sharon appeals to America not to 'appease' Arabs", *Independent*, 5 October.

24 Kellner, Douglas (2004) "9/11, spectacles of terror, and media manipulation", *Critical Discourse Studies*, Vol 1, No 1, pp41–64, p43.

25 Kellner, 2004, p44.

26 Kellner, 2004, p49.

27 Kellner, Douglas (2007) "Bushspeak and the politics of lying: Presidential rhetoric in the 'War on Terror'", *Presidential Studies Quarterly*, Vol 37, No 4, pp577–792, p625.

28 Podhoretz, Norman (2004) "World War IV: How it started, what it means, and why we have to win", *Commentary*, September, pp17–54, p18.

29 Podhoretz, 2004, p18.

30 Political Research Associates (2014) *Antisemitism and Islamophobia on US College Campuses, 2007–2011* (Somerville, MA: Political Research Associates).

31 Netanyahu, Benjamin (2001) "The strategy to end terrorism", *New Perspectives Quarterly*, No 18, pp58–65, p60.

32 Netanyahu, 2001, p60.

33 Netanyahu, 2001, p60.

34 Herf, Jeffrey (2009) *Nazi Propaganda for the Arab World* (New Haven, Yale University Press), pix. A series of publications elaborated aspects of this thesis, including: Mallman, Klaus-Michael and Cüppers, Martin (2010) *Nazi Palestine: The Plans for the Extermination of the Jews in Palestine* (New York: Enigma Books); Gensicke, Klaus (2011) *The Mufti of Jerusalem and the Nazis: The Berlin* Years, (London: Vallentine Mitchell); and Rubin, Barry and Schwanitz, Wolfgang (2014) *Nazis, Islamists, and the Making of the Modern Middle East* (New Haven: Yale University Press).

35 Wildangel, Rene (2012) "The invention of "Islamofascism": Nazi propaganda to the Arab World and perceptions from Palestine", *Die Welt des Islams*, Vol 52, No 3/4, pp526–543, p527.

36 Wildangel, 2012, p526. Here a key figure was Muhammed Amin al-Husseini, Chief Mufti of Jerusalem and a key figure in the HAC. Fleeing Palestine in 1937 after the British regime sought his arrest, he claimed protection in Arab states and later in Italy and Germany, both under fascist governments, and where he sought support against the British in Palestine. See Gensicke, 2011, and Spoerl, Joseph (2020) "Parallels between Nazi and Islamist Anti-Semitism", *Jewish Political Studies Review*, Vol 31, No1/2, pp210–244, for the alleged impact Husseini's views on later expressions of Palestinian nationalism.

37 Wildangel, 2012, p527.

38 Küntzel, Matthias (2007) *Jihad and Jew Hatred: Islamism, Nazism and the Roots of 9/11*, (New York: Telos Press). See the assessment of this and similar accounts by Mia Lee: Lee, Mia (2018) "Nazis in the Middle East: Assessing links between Nazism and Islam", *Contemporary European History*, Vol 27, No 1, 125–135.

39 Scholtyseck, Joachim (2012) "Fascism – National Socialism – Arab 'Fascism': Terminologies, definitions and distinctions", *Die Welt des Islams*, No 52, pp242–289, p242.

40 Mitchell, Richard (1969) *The Society of the Muslim Brothers* (London: Oxford University Press), p328.

41 Mitchell, 1969, p328.

42 Wendell, Charles (1978) *Five tracts of Hasan Al-Banna (1906–1949): A selection from the Majmuat rasail al-Imam al-Shahid Hasan al-Banna* [translation and annotation of Arabic originals] (Berkeley, University of California Press), p106.

43 Moazzam, Anwar (1984) *Jamā⊠ al-Dīn al-Afghāni: A Muslim Intellectual* (New Delhi: Concept Publishing), p25. Afghani referred continuously to a Quranic verse, "*innama al-mu'minuma ikhwatun*" ("all Muslims are brethren"), insisting: "*La jinsiya li 'lmuslimin illa fi dinahim*" ("There is no nationality of Muslims except Islam").

44 Kramer, 2010, p48.

45 Wild, 2012, p240.

46 Mitchell, 1969, p267.

47 Gershoni, Israel (1986) "The Muslim Brothers and the Arab Revolt in Palestine, 1936–39", *Middle Eastern Studies* Vol 22, No 3, pp 367–397, p390.

48 Kramer, 2010, p78.

49 Patterson, David (2011) *A Genealogy of Evil: Anti-Semitism from Nazism to Islamic Jihad* (Cambridge: Cambridge University Press), p125.

50 Kramer, 2010, p100, p104.

51 Mitchell, 1969, p266.

52 Nafi, Basheer (1997) "Shaykh 'Izz Al-Dīn Al-Qassām: A reformist and a rebel leader", *Journal of Islamic Studies*, Vol 8, No 2, pp185–215, p198.

53 Nafi, 1997, p195.

54 Swedenburg, 1988, p183.

55 Lockman, 1996, p235.

56 Swedenburg, Ted (1987) "Al-Qassam remembered", *Alif: Journal of Comparative Poetics*, No 7, pp9–24, p12, and Hughes, 2019, p8.

57 As evidenced in Lachman, Shai (1982) "Arab rebellion and terrorism in Palestine 1929-39: The case of Sheikh Izz al-Din al-Qassam and his Movement", in Kedourie, Elie and Haim, Sylvia (eds) *Zionism and Arabism in Palestine and Israel* (London: Frank Cass), pp52–99.

58 Swedenburg, 1987, p10.

59 Swedenburg, 1988, p190.

60 Khalidi, 1997, p189.

61 Kanafani, Ghassan (1980) [1972] *The 1936–39 Revolt in Palestine* (London: Tricontinental Society), p38.

62 Hughes, 2019, p10.

63 Swedenburg, 1988, p189.

64 Swedenburg, 1988, p190.

65 Swedenbvurg, 2003, p13.

66 Lachman, 1982, 62, pp86–87.

67 Swedenburg, 2003, p13.

68 Shlaim, Avi (2024) "Israel's war on Gaza", in Stern-Weiner, Jamie (ed) *Deluge: Gaza and Israel: From Crisis to Cataclysm* (OR Books: New York), pp13–34, p18.

69 Roy, Sara (2024) "Econocide in Gaza", in Stern-Weiner (ed), pp37–55, p38.

70 Roy, 2024, 39, p42.

71 Shevit, Ari (2004) "Top PM aide: Gaza plan aims to freeze the peace process", *Haaretz*, 6 October.

72 Pappé, 2024, p224.

73 Shlaim, 2024, p20.

74 Shlaim, Avi (2019) "Ten years after the first war on Gaza, Israel still plans endless brute force", *Guardian*, 7 January.

75 United Nations (2009) *Human Rights in Palestine and Other Occupied Arab Territories: Report of the United Nations Fact Finding Mission on the Gaza Conflict* (Executive Summary) [The Goldstone Report], p10.

76 United Nations, 2009, p10, p11.

77 United Nations, 2009, p12. Under intense pressure, including allegations of 'blood libel' against Israel and its forces, Richard Goldstone – who had chaired the UN commission – retreated from some findings: Urquhart, Conor (2001) "Judge Goldstone expresses regrets about his report into Gaza war", *Guardian*, 3 April. Goldstone's three co-investigators defended the report and all its findings: Horowitz, Adam, Ratner Lizzy and Philip Weiss (2011) "The Goldstone Affair", *The Nation*, 2 May.

78 Azoulay, Ariella and Ophir, Adi (2008) *The One-State Condition: Occupation and Democracy in Israel/Palestine* (Stanford: Stanford University Press), p168.

79 Azoulay and Ophir 2008, p168.

80 Azoulay and Ophir, 2008, p175.

81 Meir Amit Intelligence and Terrorism Information Center (ITIC): https://www.terrorism-info.org.il/en/about/

82 Milton-Edwards, Beverley (2014) "Islamist versus Islamist: Rising challenge in Gaza", *Terrorism and Political Violence*, Vol 26, No 2, pp259–276, p260.

83 Milton-Edwards, Beverley and Farrell, Stephen (2024) *Hamas: The Quest for Power* (Cambridge: Polity), p41.

84 Milton-Edwards, 2024, p41.

85 Milton-Edwards, 2014, p262.

86 Palestinian academic Riad al-Agha in Milton-Edwards, 2014, p42.

87 Yiftachel, Oren (2010) "From Sharon to Sharon: Spatial planning and separation regime in Israel/Palestine", *HAGAR Studies in Culture, Polity and Identities*, Vol 10, No 1, pp.73–106, p79.

88 Yiftachel, 2010, p79.

89 Yiftachel, 2010, p79.

90 Yiftachel, 2010, p88.

91 Yiftachel, 2010, p91.

92 B'tselem (2017) "Settlements": https://www.btselem.org/settlements

93 B'tselem, 2017.

94 Gorenberg, 2007, p267.

95 Gorenberg, 2007, p267.

96 Sprinzak, Ehud (1985) "Kach and Meir Kahane: The emergence of Jewish quasi-fascism II: Ideology and politics", *Patterns of Prejudice*, Vol 19, No 4, pp3–13, p7.

97 Kahane, Meir (1981) *They Must Go* (New York: Grosset and Dunlap); Sprinzak, 1985, p7.

98 Sprinzak, 1985, p7.

99 Suzannah Heschel makes the case for Kahane as 'fascist' in Heschel, Suzannah (2022) "Meir Kahane and race as incarnational theology", *Journal of Religious Ethics*, Vol 50, No 2, pp293–302.

100 Kalman, Samuel (2013) *French Colonial Fascism: The Extreme Right in Algeria, 1919–1939* (Basingstoke: Palgrave MacMillan), p4.

101 Gazit, Nir (2015) "State-sponsored vigilantism: Jewish settlers' violence in the occupied Palestinian territories", *Sociology*, Vol 49, No 3, pp438–454.

102 Gazit, 2015, p440.

103 Gazit, 2015, p251–252.

104 Said, 1993.

105 Milton-Edwards, 2024, p110.

106 Milton-Edwards, 2024, p52.

107 Milton-Edwards, 2024, p54.

108 Hroub, 2004, p22.

109 Gildea, Robert (2019) *Empires of the Mind: The Colonial Past and the Politics of the Present* (Cambridge: Cambridge University Press), p184.

110 Waldman, Peter and Pope, Hugh (2001) "'Crusade' reference reinforces fears war on terrorism is against Muslims", *Wall Street Journal*, 21 September.

111 Goldenberg, Suzanne (2002) "The lunar landscape that was the Jenin refugee camp", *Guardian*, 16 April.

112 Human Rights Watch (2002) "Israel/Occupied Territories: Jenin war crimes investigation needed", 2 May: https://www.hrw.org/news/2002/05/02/israel/occupied-territories-jenin-war-crimes-investigation-needed

113 Hroub, 2004, p22.

114 Hroub, 2004, p21.

Chapter 11
Sumud – 'Steadfastness'

1 Hoffman, Stanley and Bozo, Frédéric (2004) *Gulliver Unbound: America's Imperial Temptation and the War in Iraq* (Lanham, MD: Rowman and Littlefield), p41.

2 Ullman, Harman and Wade, James (1996) *Shock and Awe: Achieving Rapid Dominance* (Washington, DC: National Defense University), px.

3 Ullman and Wade, 1996, pxii.

4 Ullman and Wade, 1996, p129.

5 Whyte, D. (2007) "The crimes of neo-liberal rule in occupied Iraq", *British Journal of Criminology*, Vol 47, No 2, pp177–195, p185.

6 Turner, Mandy (2009) "The power of 'Shock and Awe': The Palestinian Authority and the road to reform", *International Peacekeeping*, Vol 16, No 4, pp562–577, p562.

7 Fogelman, Shay (2010) "Shock and Awe", *Haaretz*, 31 December.

8 Harel, Amos (2008) "ANALYSIS IAF: Strike on Gaza is Israel's version of 'Shock and Awe'", *Haaretz*, 27 December.

9 Katz, Yaakov (2008) "Shock, awe…and deception", *Jerusalem Post*, 28 December.

10 Journal of Palestine Studies (2009) "Prelude to operation Cast Lead: Israel's unilateral disengagement tthe eve of war", *Journal of Palestine Studies*, Vol 38, No 3, pp 139–168, p168.

11 Harel, 2008.

12 Klein, Naomi (2008) *The Shock Doctrine: The Rise of Disaster Capitalism* (London: Penguin).

13 Haddad, Toufic (2018), *Palestine Ltd: Neoliberalism and Nationalism in the Occupied Territory* (London: I.B. Tauris), p84.

14 The idea of a Marshall Plan for Palestine is attributed to billionaire Israeli businessman Stef Wertheimer: Goldberg, Ari (2002) "Israeli tycoon urges help for Palestinians", *BBC News*, 17 July.

15 Haddad, 2018, p87.

16 Cheryl Rubenberg examines relations between the PA and the occupation regime, noting Israel's benign approach to a corrupt bureaucracy. Rubenberg, 2003, ch6.

17 Between 2003 and 2010 Gulf investments made up 75 percent of total foreign investment into Lebanon, 69 percent to Jordan, 61 percent to Syria, 59 percent to Egypt, and 46 percent to Iraq; from 2003 to 2008, more than two-thirds of foreign investment areas under control of the PA originated in the Gulf region. Hanieh, Adam (2021) "The political economy of state formation in Palestine", in Farsakh, Laila (ed) *Rethinking Statehood in Palestine: Self-Determination and Decolonization Beyond Partition* (Oakland, CA: University of California Press), p42.

18 Hanieh, 2021, p40.

19 Hanieh, 2016, p34.

20 Hanieh, 2016, p37.

21 Hanieh, 2016, p38.

22 Haddad, 2018, p88.

23 Hanieh, 2021, p43.

24 Turner, 2009, p573.

25 Black, Ian (2008) "Blair firm on boycott of Hamas", *Guardian*, 6 June.

26 Crawford, Neta and Lutz, Catherine (2019) "Human cost of post-9/11 wars", Watson Institute Public and International Affairs, Brown University: https://watson.brown.edu/costsofwar/files/cow/imce/papers/2019/Direct%20War%20Deaths%20COW%20Estimate%20November%2013%202019%20FINAL.pdf

27 Dodge, Tony (2007) "The causes of US failure in Iraq", *Survival*, Vol 49, No 1, pp81–106, p87.

28 Macdonald, Michael (2014) *Overreach: Delusions of Regime Change in Iraq* (Cambridge, MASS: Harvard University Press), p8.

29 Callinicos, Alex (2014) 'Imperial delusions", *International Socialism*, Series 2, No 142.

30 Reale, Hannah, Bingham, Emma and Greenberg, Kara (2020) "Where does China get its oil?", Centre on Global Energy Policy, Colombia University, 12 July. See also Baabood, Abdallah (2023) "Why China is emerging as a main promoter of stability in the Strait of Hormuz", Carnnegie Middle East Centre: https://carnegieendowment.org/research/2023/05/why-china-is-emerging-as-a-main-promoter-of-stability-in-the-strait-of-hormuz?lang=en&center=middle-east

31 Qian, Xuming, and Fulton, Jonathan (2017) "China-Gulf economic relationship under the 'Belt and Road' Initiative", *Asian Journal of Middle Eastern and Islamic Studies*, Vol 11, No 3, pp12–21, p20.

32 Preble, Christopher and Smith, Will (2024) "Great power competition shouldn't drive US policy in the Middle East", 31 October, (Washington, DC: Stimson Center).

33 Evron, Yoram (2017) "The economic dimension of China–Israel relations: political implications, roles and limitations", *Israel Affairs*, Vol 23, No 5, pp828–847.

34 Hoffman, Jon (2023) "The U.S. has nothing to fear from China in the Middle East", Cato Institute, 6 December: https://www.cato.org/commentary/us-has-nothing-fear-china-middle-east

35 Preble, Christopher and Smith, Will, 2024.

36 AIPAC [American Israeli Public Affairs Committee] (2024) "Preserving Israel's QME Promotes America's Interests": https://www.aipac.org/resources/qualitative-military-edge-qme

37 Mackenzie, James (2024) "Netanyahu says Israel will be a key US ally whoever replaces Biden", Reuters, 22 July.

38 Simon, Steven and Stevenson, Jonathan (2023) "The Gaza horror and US policy", *Survival*, Vol 65, No 6, pp37–56, p42.

39 Fabian, Emanuel (2024) "Israel says US shipments of arms and equipment during war exceed 50,000 tons", *Times of Israel*, 26 August.

40 Fabian, 2024.

41 Shalev, Tal (2024) "IDF spokesperson Hagari: 'Hamas is an idea. You can't destroy an idea'", *Jerusalem Post*, 19 June.

42 Wermenbol, Grace (2024) "Why Hamas cannot be destroyed", *Cairo Review of Global Affairs*, Summer.

43 Wermenbal, 2024.

44 Azoulay and Ophir, 2008, p168.

45 Azoulay and Ophir, 2008, p148.

46 Dunbar-Ortiz, 2014, p8.

47 Marx, Karl (1957) [1885] *Capital*, Vol 2, Chapter 31 (London: J.M. Dent), p832.

48 Grewcock, Michael (2018) "Settler-colonial violence, primitive accumulation and Australia's genocide", *State Crime Journal*, Vol 7, No 2, pp222–250, p229.

49 Wolfe, Patrick (2006) "Settler colonialism and the elimination of the native, *Journal of Genocide Research*, Vol 8, No 4, pp387–409, p388.

50 Bachman, Jeffrey (2022) *The Politics of Genocide: From the Genocide Convention to the Responsibility to Protect* (New Brunswick: Rutgers University Press), p48.

51 Bachman, 2022, p48.

52 Bachman, 2022, p48.

53 United Nations (1951) *Convention on the Prevention and Punishment of the Crime of Genocide*: https://www.un.org/en/genocideprevention/documents/atrocity-crimes/Doc.1_Convention%20on%20the%20Prevention%20and%20Punishment%20of%20the%20Crime%20of%20Genocide.pdf

54 Palmer, Alison (1998) "Colonial and modern genocide: explanations and categories", *Ethnic and Racial Studies*, Vol 21, No 1, pp89–115.

55 Independent-Fact Finding Committee On Gaza (2009) *No Safe Place*, para 564: https://www.tromso-gaza.no/090501ReportGaza.pdf para 564.

56 Shaw, Martin (2010) "Palestine in an international historical perspective on genocide" *Holy Land Studies*, Vol 9, No 1, pp1–24, p8.

57 Shaw, 2010, p13.

58 See, for example, the exchange between Shaw and Omer Bartov: Shaw, Martin and Bartov, Omer (2010) "The question of genocide in Palestine, 1948: A debate

between Martin Shaw and Omer Bartov", *Journal of Genocide Research*, Vol 12, Nos 3/4, pp243–259; also Rashed, Haifa, Short, Damien and Docker, John (2014) "Nakba memoricide: Genocide studies and the Zionist/Israeli genocide of Palestine", *Holy Land Studies*, Vol 13, No 1, pp1–23.

59 Segal, Raz and Daniele, Luigi (2024) "Gaza as twilight of Israel exceptionalism: Holocaust and genocide studies from unprecedented crisis to unprecedented change", *Journal of Genocide Research* (published online), 5 March: https://www.tandfonline.com/doi/epdf/10.1080/14623528.2024.2325804?needAccess=true

60 UN News (2024) "Human Rights", 26 March: https://news.un.org/en/story/2024/03/1147976

61 UN News, 2024.

62 UN News, 2024.

63 United Nations (2024) "The Question of Palestine" (Summary of ICJ's Order of 24 May 2024): https://www.un.org/unispal/document/summary-of-icjs-order-24may24/#:~:text=The%20Court%20recalls%20that%2C%20on,as%20at%2018%20May%202024

64 Wolfe, 2006, p388. See Herzl, Theodor (1941) [1902]) *Altneuland* (New York: M. Wiener), p38. *Altneuland*, observes Herzl's biographer, Desmond Stewart, 'has the distinction of being the only Utopia fashioned by a man whose ideas have also led directly to the construction of a state': Stewart, Desmond (1981) *Theodor Herzl, Artist and Politician* (London: Quartet), p293.

65 Levene, Mark (2007) "Review: Ilan Pappé's The Ethnic Cleansing of Palestine", *Journal of Genocide Research*, Vol 9, No 4, December: pp675–81, p676.

66 Lendman, Steve (2010) "Israel's slow-motion genocide in occupied Palestine", in Cook, W. (ed) *The Plight of the Palestinians: A Long History of Destruction*, pp29–38 (New York: Palgrave Macmillan US).

67 Klein, Menachem (2008) "One state in the Holy Land? A dream or a nightmare?", *The International Spectator*, Vol 43, No 4, pp89–101, p94.

68 Klein, 2008, p94.

69 Veracini, Lorenzo (2013) "The other shift: Settler colonialism, Israel and the occupation", *Journal of Palestine Studies*, Vol 42, No 2, pp26–42, p28.

70 Veracini, 2013, p28.

71 Yiftachel, 2009, p75.

72 Lentin, Ronit (2018) *Traces of Racial Exception: Racializing Israeli Settler Colonialism* (London: Bloomsbury) p12.

73 Lentin, 2018, p169.

74 Blumenthal, Max (2014) "Politicide in Gaza: How Israel's far right won the war", *Journal of Palestine Studies*, Vol 44, No 1, pp14–28, p15.

75 Shaw, 2010, p13.

76 Dubnov, Arie (2024) "Where do we go from here?" in Dubnov, Arie, Reinhold, Jonathan, Klein, Menachem and Shafir, Gershon, *Governing Gaza After the War: The Israeli Perspectives* (Washington: Carnegie Endowment for International Peace).

77 Sokol, Sam (2024) "Smotrich urges ramping up West Bank, Gaza settlements, pushing Palestinians out", *Times of Israel*, 28 October.

78 Sokol, 2024.

79 Laizans, Janis and Itzhaki, Michal (2024) "On the edge of Gaza, Israeli settlers want back in", *Reuters*, 21 October.

80 Pappé, 2024, p229.

81 Rijke, Alexandra and van Teeffelen, Toine (2014) "To exist is to resist: Sumud, heroism, and the everyday", *Jerusalem Quarterly*, Vol 59, pp86–98, p88.

82 Rijke and van Teeffelen, 2014, p90.

83 Community activists in 'Aida camp, Rijke and van Teeffelen, 2014, p90.

84 Levene, Mark (2024) "Gaza 2023: Words matter, lives matter more", *Journal of Genocide Research*: https://www.tandfonline.com/doi/full/10.1080/14623528.2024.2301866

85 Levene, 2024.

86 Rickford, Russell (2019) "'To build a New World': Black American internationalism and Palestine solidarity", *Journal of Palestine Studies*, Vol 48, No 4, pp52–68, p55.

87 Rickford, 2019, p57.

88 Rickford, 2019, p57.

89 Some leading Black activists such as civil rights veteran Bayard Rustin were supporters of Israel; others, including historic figures such as Stokely Carmichael and Huey Newton of the Black Panther Party were among its strongest American critics. Rickford, 2019, p58.

90 Hajjat, Abdelalli (2022) "Comités Palestine (1970–72): On the origins of solidarity with the Palestinian cause in France", in Maasri, Zeina, Bergin, Cathy and Burke, Francesca (eds) *Transnational solidarity: Anticolonialism in the global sixties* (Manchester: Manchester University Press), pp55–77.

91 Di-Capua, Yoav (2020) "Palestine comes to Paris: The global sixties and the making of a universal cause", *Journal of Palestine Studies*, Vol 50, No 1, pp19–50, p24.

92 Keleman, Paul (2012) *The British Left and Zionism: History of a Divorce* (Manchester: Manchester University Press).

93 Keleman, 2012, p160.

94 Said, Edward (2003) "Dignity, solidarity and the penal colony", *Counterpunch*, 25 September: https://www.counterpunch.org/2003/09/25/dignity-solidarity-and-the-penal-colony/

95 Collins, John (2007) "Global Palestine: A collision for our time", *Critique: Critical Middle Eastern Studies*, Vol 16, No 1, pp3–18, p3.

96 Collins, 2007, p3.

Chapter 12
Revolution

1 Cairo Conference (2002) "The Cairo Declaration": https://web.archive.org/web/20050226210148/http://www.stopwar.org.uk/Resources/cairo.pdf During the 1960s the PLO organised a series of solidarity conferences, notably at Cairo, Algiers, Amman, and Beirut, largely under the auspices of Arab governments. There were small numbers of participants from Europe: see Thomson, Sorcha, Olsen, Pelle and Haugbolle, Sunne (2022) "Palestine solidarity conferences in the global sixties", *Journal of Palestine Studies*, Vol 51, No 1, pp27–49.

2 Collins, John (2011) *Global Palestine* (London: Hurst), p134.

3 Eyewitness testimony shared with the author, Cairo April 2002.

4 El-Hamalawy, Hossam (2011) "Egypt's revolution has been 10 years in the making", *Guardian*, 2 March.

5 Abou-el-Fadl, Reem (2012) "The Road to Jerusalem through Tahrir Square: Anti-Zionism and Palestine in the 2011 Egyptian Revolution", *Journal of Palestine Studies*, Vol 41, No 2, pp6–26, p11.

6 Numerous participants who were later leading activists in the democracy movement and in the revolutionary upheaval of 2011 testified to the liberating experience of mass public protest in 2003. 'It was our rehearsal for the revolution that's coming', said Ahmed Hassan, interviewed by the author in Cairo in April 2004.

7 Schemm, Paul (2003) "Egypt Struggles to Control Anti-War Protests", *Merip*, 31 March.

8 Schemm, 2003.

9 El-Mahdi, Rabab (2009) in El-Mahdi, Rabab and Marfleet, Philip (eds) *Egypt: The Moment of Change* (London: Zed), p98.

10 A detailed account of these developments has yet to be produced. Among demonstrations that challenged the regime's ban on all forms of public protest was a march of hundreds in Shubra, Cairo – an old working-class quarter – that evaded police and astonished local residents, among whom most had never seen collective action against the regime, some joining the participants. Author's eyewitness observations.

11 Alexander, Anne and Bassiouny, Mustafa (2014) *Bread, Freedom, Social Justice: Workers and the Egyptian Revolution* (London: Zed), p108.

12 Abou-el-Fadl, 2012, p13.

13 Wagdy, Wassim (2014) "Palestinian liberation is ingrained into the Egyptian revolution" *Socialist Worker*, 15 July: https://socialistworker.co.uk/comment/palestinian-liberation-is-ingrained-into-the-egyptian-revolution/

14 Wagdy, 2014.

15 Wagdy, 2014.

16 Figures compiled by Awlad al-Ard in Beinin and Duboc, 2015, p144. See also Marfleet, 2016, ch 3.

17 The events had much in common with historic revolutionary movements, notably that described by the German revolutionary activist Rosa Luxemburg, observing events in Russia in 1905: "Political and economic strikes, mass strikes and partial strikes, demonstrative strikes and fighting strikes, general strikes of individual branches of industry and general strikes in individual towns, peaceful wage struggles and street massacres, barricade fighting – all these run through one another, run side by side, cross one another, flow in and over one another – it is a ceaselessly moving, changing sea of phenomena." Luxemburg, Rosa (2021) [1906] *The Mass Strike – The Political Party and the Trade Unions* (Paris: Foreign Languages Press), p37.

18 Abou-el-Fadl, 2012, p15.

19 Abou-el-Fadl, 2012, p13.

20 Abou-el-Fadl, 2012, p16.

21 Al Jazeera News (2011) "Crowds attack Israel embassy in Cairo", *Al Jazeera*, 10 September: https://www.aljazeera.com/news/2011/9/10/crowds-attack-israel-embassy-in-cairo

22 Al Jazeera News, 2011.

23 Benn, Aluf (2011) "Overcoming fear and anxiety in Tel Aviv", *Foreign Affairs*, 8 February.

24 Byman, Daniel (2011) "Israel's pessimistic view of the Arab Spring", *The Washington Quarterly*, Vol 34, No 3, pp123–136, p123.

25 Byman, 2011, p124.

26 Byman, 2011, p126.

27 Sanders, Edmund (2011) "Israel fears regional regime change", *Los Angeles Times*, 4 February.

28 Obama, Barack (2011) "Remarks by the President on Egypt", The White House, Washington, 11 February: https://obamawhitehouse.archives.gov/the-press-office/2011/02/11/remarks-president-egypt

29 Fabbrini, Sergio and Yossef, Amr (2015) "Obama's wavering: US foreign policy on the Egyptian crisis, 2011–13", *Contemporary Arab Affairs*, Vol 8, No 1, pp65–80, p67.

30 Hirschkind, Charles (2012) "Beyond secular and religious: An intellectual genealogy of Tahrir Square", *American Ethnologist*, Vol 39, No 1, pp49–53, p49. See also Dina al-Sharnouby on ideas and practices pursued in Tahrir Square and in city centres across Egypt, expressing 'discontent with all the binaries that define and contribute to exclusionary practices of social groups (young versus old, man versus woman,

Christian versus Muslim) and, at the same time, offered an inclusive space according to the popular imagination and aspirations': El-Sharnouby, Dina (2015) "From state exclusionary politics to youth inclusionary practices: The Tahrir Square experience", *International Journal of Sociology*, Vol 45, No 3, pp176–189, p183.

31 Taher, Nadia (2012) "'We are not women, we are Egyptians'. Spaces of protest and representation." *City*, Vol 16, No 3, pp369–376, p369.

32 When teachers took national strike action thousands of women travelled to Cairo to join demonstrations in which they successfully challenged control by male leaders of their organisations (author's observations, April and September 2011).

33 In a defining incident in December 2011, uniformed soldiers attacked a young woman in Tahrir Square. Sherine Hafez describes "the case of the woman in the blue bra, in which the body of a woman is rendered vulnerable, debilitated, feminized, objectified and sexualized". Hafez, Sherine (2014) "Bodies that protest: The girl in the blue bra, sexuality, and state violence in revolutionary Egypt", *Signs: Journal of Women in Culture and Society*, Vol 40, No 1, pp20-28, p22.

34 Initiated in the anti-capitalist magazine *Adbusters*: Kerton, Sarah (2012) "Tahrir, here? The influence of the Arab Uprisings on the emergence of Occupy", *Social Movement Studies*, Vol 11, Nos 3/4, pp302–308, p302.

35 Kerton, 2012, p302.

36 Alexander, Jeffrey (2013) "The arc of civil liberation: Obama-Tahrir-Occupy", *Philosophy and Social Criticism*, Vol 39, Nos 4/5, pp341–347, p344.

37 Alexander, 2013, p345.

38 BDS National Committee (2011) "Occupy Wall Street not Palestine!", 14 October: https://bdsmovement.net/news/occupy-wall-street-not-palestine

39 Eitan, Alimi (2012) "'Occupy Israel': A tale of startling success and hopeful failure", *Social Movement Studies*, Vol 11, Nos 3/4, pp402–407, p404.

40 Anderson, Sophie (2021) "The 2011 Israeli housing protests: The occupation of public space and the decentered state", *On Politics*, Vol 14, No 2, pp77–86.

41 Kaplan, Eren (2019) "Watching Fight Club in Tel Aviv: or the 2011 social protests in Israel, a political postmortem", *Comparative Literature and Culture*, Vol 21, No 2, pp6–16, p10.

42 Kaplan, 2019, p11.

43 Stein, Ewan (2015) "Jihad discourse in Egypt under Muhammad Mursi", in Kendall, Elizabeth and Stein, Ewan *Twenty-First Century Jihad: Law, Society and Military Action* (London: I.B. Tauris), pp176–200, p182.

44 Stein, 2015, p182.

45 Stein, 2015, p182.

46 Stein, 2015, p191.

47 Shukrallah, Hani (2011) "How divided is Egypt's Muslim Brotherhood?", *Ahram Online*, 4 April. Online at: http://english.ahram.org.eg/NewsContent/1/64/8949/Egypt/Politics-/How-divided-is-Egypts-Muslim-Brotherhood.aspx; accessed 2 June 2015

48 Amnesty International (2013) "People were dying all around me": https://www.amnesty.org.uk/files/2013_-_08_-_people_were_dying_all_around_me_english_0.pdf

49 Botman, Sela (1988) *The Rise of Egyptian Communism, 1939–70* (Syracuse, NY: Syracuse University Press), p115.

50 Gordon, Joel (1992) *Nasser's Blessed Movement: Egypt's Free Officers and the July Revolution* (Oxford: Oxford University Press), p32.

51 Ismael, Tareq and El-Sa'id, Rifa'at (1990) *The Communist Movement in Egypt, 1920–1988* (Syracuse: Syracuse University Press), p124.

52 The Revolutionary Socialists of Egypt were active successively in initiatives for Palestine, in the democracy movement and in the rejuvenated workers movement of the early 2000s. They were prominent in activities of the left throughout the revolutionary events of 2011-2013. See Abdelrahman, Maha (2009) " 'With the Islamists?—Sometimes. With the State?—Never!' Cooperation between the Left and Islamists in Egypt", *British Journal of Middle Eastern Studies* Vol 36, No 1, pp:37–54. See also Hafez, Bassem (2013) "New social movements and the Egyptian Spring: a comparative analysis between the April 6 Movement and the Revolutionary Socialists", *Perspectives on Global Development and Technology*, Vol 12, Nos 1-2, pp98-113; and Zohdi, Helena (2024) "Contemporary fellow travellers: Egyptian Revolutionary Socialists and the theory and political practice of Marxism", *Third World Quarterly*, 21 October: https://www.tandfonline.com/doi/pdf/10.1080/01436597.2024.2412649

53 Batatu, 1978; Ismael, Tareq (2009) *The Rise and Fall of the Communist Party of Iraq* (Cambridge: Cambridge University Press).

54 Bashear, Suliman (1980) *Communism in the Arab East, 1918–1928* (London: Ithaca), p35.

55 Frantzen, Johan (2007) "Communism versus Zionism: The Comintern, Yishuvism and the Palestine Communist Party", *Journal of Palestine Studies*, Vol36, No 2, pp6–24.

56 Budeiri, 1979, p110.

57 Budeiri, 1979, p143.

58 Guirguis, Laure (2019) "The New Left in 1960s and 1970s Lebanon and 1917 as model and foil", in Feliu and Izquierdo-Brichs, *Communist Parties in the Middle East*, pp258–267, p259.

59 *Jerusalem Post* (1988), 30 January.

60 Hanegbi *et al*, 1971, p16.

61 For analysis of the rise and fall of the communist movement in Palestine and the Arab East see Marfleet, Philip, "The Arab Left and Palestine", *International Socialism*, forthcoming 2025.

62 Kazziha, 1975, p22.

63 DFLP, 1969, p23.

64 DFLP, 1969, p22.

65 Kazziha, 1975, p90.

66 Petran, Tabitha (1987) *The Struggle over Lebanon* (New York: Monthly Review Press), p93.

67 Mustafa, Omar (2020) [2002] "The national liberation struggle: a socialist analysis", in Awad, Sumaya and Bean, Brian, *Palestine: A Socialist Introduction* (Chicago: Haymarket), pp53–78, p65.

68 Mustafa, p65.

69 Sayigh, Yezid (1989) "Struggle within, struggle without: The transformation of PLO politics since 1982", *International* Affairs, Vol 65, No 2, pp247–27, p248.

70 Chulov, Martin (2012) "Palestinians flee to Lebanon after jet bombs Syria's largest refugee camp" *Guardian*, 18 December.

71 Attributed initially to the first chairman of the PLO, the conservative lawyer Ahmed Shuqueri, referencing the aims of Arab nationalism in the 1960s. On this view Palestinian liberation required support from governments 'in all or most of the Arab states'. Buck, Terry (2013) *The Decline of the Popular Front for the Liberation of Palestine: A Historical Analysis* (Amherst: Hampshire College), p4: https://yplus.ps/wp-content/uploads/2021/01/Buck-Terry-James-The-Decline-of-the-Popular-Front-for-the-Liberation-of-Palestine.pdf

72 Leopardi, Francesco (2013) *After Beirut: History and Narrative of the Popular Front for the Liberation of Palestine in the Mid-eighties* (Venice: Università Ca'Foscari Venezia), p104.

73 Brynen, Rex (1989) "PLO policy in Lebanon: Legacies and lessons", *Journal of Palestine Studies*, Vol 18, No 2, pp48–70, p60.

74 See Kilani, Ramsis (2024) "Strategies for liberation: Old and new arguments in the Palestinian left", *International Socialism*, No 183 (NS), pp29–50.

75 Dana, Tariq (2017) "The prolonged decay of the Palestinian National Movement", *National Identities*, Vol 21, No 1, pp39–55, p51.

76 Dana, 2017, p51.

77 Hilal, Jamil (2010) "The Palestinian Left and the multi-layered challenges ahead" (Birzeit: Rosa Luxemburg Foundation in Palestine): https://www.rosalux.de/fileadmin/rls_uploads/pdfs/Standpunkte/Standpunkte_international/RLS_PAL_-_Hilal_Palestinian_Left.pdf

78 Dana, Tariq (2010) "Social struggle and the crisis of the Palestinian Left parties" (Birzeit: Rosa Luxemburg Foundation in Palestine) http://www.rosaluxemburg.ps/wp-content/uploads/2016/04/RLS-Articles-English-Tariq-Dana-Paper_20160330.pdf

79 Dana, 2017, p48.

80 El-Hamalawy, Hossam (2024) "From Palestine to Tahrir Square: What Egyptians owe Palestinians", *Spectre*, 1 May: https://spectrejournal.com/from-palestine-to-tahrir-square/

81 El-Hamalawy, 2024.

82 Chalcraft, John (2012) "Horizontalism in the Egyptian revolutionary process, *Merip*, No 261, pp6–11, p6.

83 Alexander and Bassiouny, 2014, p198.

84 Alexander and Bassiouny, 2014, p199.

85 Alexander, Anne (2022) *'Revolution is the Choice of the People': Crisis and Revolt in the Middle East and North Africa* (London: Bookmarks), pp213–220.

86 Alexander, 2022, p220.

87 Beinin, Joe and Duboc, Marie (2015) "The Egyptian workers' movement before and after the 2011 popular uprising", *Socialist Register*, Vol 51, pp1–22, p3.

88 Beinin and Duboc, 2015, p9.

89 Al Jazeera News (2019) "'Leave, Sisi!': All you need to know about the protests in Egypt", *Al Jazeera*, 21 September.

90 Abdel-Ghafar, Adel (2016) "Youth unemployment in Egypt: A ticking timebomb"(Doha: Brookings Institution).

91 Sallam, Hesham (2023) "The Egyptian public and the war on Gaza", *Merip*, No 309: https://merip.org/2024/01/sisi-the-egyptian-public-and-the-war-on-gaza/

92 Sallam, 2023.

93 Amnesty International (2015) "Egypt: Beware al-Sisi's claims of freedoms", 3 June: https://www.amnesty.org/en/latest/news/2015/06/egypt-beware-al-sisis-claims-of-freedoms/

94 International Crisis Group (2024) *Egypt's Gaza Dilemmas*, Briefing No 91, 16 May, p15: https://www.crisisgroup.org/sites/default/files/2024-05/b091-egypt-gaza-dilemmas_1.pdf See also: Abou-El-Fadl, Reem (2023), "The war on Gaza has sharpened Egyptian popular grievances – both on Palestine and at home", *Guardian*, 29 November.

95 Communication from Egyptian revolutionary activist, April 2024. For an analysis of Palestine in the context of wider revolutionary upheavals in the Middle East, see: Alexander, Anne (2024) "Palestine between permanent war and permanent revolution", *International Socialism* (NS), No 181, pp41–64.

96 Revolutionary Socialists of Egypt (2024) "The most important lesson from October 6th and 7th: Liberating Jerusalem starts with liberating Cairo", 7 October: https://global.revsoc.me/2024/10/the-most-important-lesson-from-october-6th-and-7th-liberating-jerusalem-starts-with-liberating-cairo/

97 Revolutionary Socialists of Egypt, 2024.

98 Revolutionary Socialists of Egypt, 2024.

Bibliography

Aarts, Paul (1992) "Democracy, oil and the Gulf War", *Third World Quarterly*, Vol 13, No 3, pp525–538.

'Abid, Ibrahim (1969) *A Handbook to the Palestinian Question* (Beirut: Palestine Liberation Organisation).

Abdel-Ghafar, Adel (2016) "Youth unemployment in Egypt: A ticking timebomb" (Doha: Brookings Institution).

Abdelrahman, Maha (2009) "'With the Islamists? – Sometimes. With the State? – Never!' Cooperation between the Left and Islamists in Egypt", *British Journal of Middle Eastern Studies*, Vol 36, No 1, pp37–54.

Abou-el-Fadl, Reem (2012) "The road to Jerusalem through Tahrir Square: Anti-Zionism and Palestine in the 2011 Egyptian Revolution", *Journal of Palestine Studies*, Vol 41, No 2, pp6–26.

Abou-El-Fadl, Reem (2023), "The war on Gaza has sharpened Egyptian popular grievances – both on Palestine and at home", *Guardian*, 29 November.

Abu-Amr, Ziad (1993) "Hamas: A historical and political background", *Journal of Palestine Studies*, Vol 22, No 4, pp5–19.

Abu-Amr, Ziad (1994) *Islamic Fundamentalism in the West Bank and Gaza* (Bloomington: Indiana University Press).

Abu-Lughod, Janet (1984) "The demographic consequences of the occupation" in Aruri, Naseer (ed) *Occupation: Israel Over Palestine* (London: Zed).

Abu-Odeh, Adnan (1999) *Jordanians, Palestinians, and the Hashemite Kingdom in the Middle East Peace Process* (Washington: United States Institute of Peace).

Abu-Sharif, Bassam (2009) *Arafat and the Dream of Palestine: An Insider's Account* (Basingstoke: Palgrave Macmillan).

Abu-Sharif, Bassam and Mahnaimi, Uzi (1995) *Tried by Fire* (London: Little, Brown).

Adelman, Jonathan (2008) *The Rise of Israel: A History of a Revolutionary State* (London: Routledge).

AIPAC [American Israeli Public Affairs Committee] (2024) "Preserving Israel's QME Promotes America's Interests": https://www.aipac.org/resources/qualitative-military-edge-qme

Ajami, Fouad (1992) *The Arab Predicament: Arab Political Thought and Practice Since 1967* (Cambridge: Cambridge University Press).

al-'Arif, 'Arif (2013) *Al-Nakba: The Catastrophe of Jerusalem and the Lost Paradise* (Beirut and Sidon, Lebanon: Al-Maktaba al-'Asriyya) [Arabic].

Alexander, Anne (2022) *'Revolution is the Choice of the People': Crisis and Revolt in the Middle East and North Africa* (London: Bookmarks).

Alexander, Anne (2024) "Palestine between permanent war and permanent revolution", *International Socialism* (NS), No 181, pp41–64.

Alexander, Anne and Bassiouny, Mustafa (2014) *Bread, Freedom, Social Justice: Workers and the Egyptian Revolution* (London: Zed).

Alexander, Jeffrey (2013) "The arc of civil liberation: Obama-Tahrir-Occupy", *Philosophy and Social Criticism*, Vol 39, Nos 4/5, pp341–347.

Alff, Kristen (2018) "Levantine joint-stock companies, trans-Mediterranean partnerships, and nineteenth-century capitalist development", *Comparative Studies in Society and History*, Vol 60, No 1, pp150–177.

Al Jazeera News (2011) "Crowds attack Israel embassy in Cairo", *Al Jazeera*, 10 September: https://www.aljazeera.com/news/2011/9/10/crowds-attack-israel-embassy-in-cairo

Al Jazeera News (2019) "'Leave, Sisi!': All you need to know about the protests in Egypt", *Al Jazeera*, 21 September.

Allawi, Ali (2007) *The Occupation of Iraq: Winning the War, Losing the Peace* (New Haven: Yale University Press).

Allon, Yigal (1976) "Israel: The case for defensible borders", *Foreign Affairs*, Vol 55 (October), pp38–53.

Allon, Yigal (2009) *The Making of Israel's Army* (London: Vallentine, Mitchell).

Amnesty International (1999) "Palestinian Authority: Defying the rule of law: Political detainees held without charge or trial": https://www.amnesty.org/en/documents/mde21/003/1999/en/

Amnesty International (2013) "People were dying all around me": https://www.amnesty.org.uk/files/2013_-_08_-_people_were_dying_all_around_me_english_0.pdf

Amnesty International (2015) "Egypt: Beware al-Sisi's claims of freedoms", 3 June: https://www.amnesty.org/en/latest/news/2015/06/egypt-beware-al-sisis-claims-of-freedoms/

Anderson, Charles (2013) *From Petition to Confrontation: The Palestinian National Movement and the Rise of Mass Politics, 1929–1939*, PhD thesis (unpublished), New York University.

Anderson, Charles (2015) *Will the Real Palestinian Peasantry Please Sit Down? Towards a New History of British Rule in Palestine, 1917–1936* (LSE Middle East Paper No 10).

Anderson, Charles (2017) "State formation from below and the great revolt in Palestine", *Journal of Palestine Studies*, Vol 47, No 1, pp39–55.

Anderson, Sophie (2021) "The 2011 Israeli Housing Protests: The occupation of public space and the decentered state", *On Politics*, Vol 14, No 2, pp77–86.

Andoni, Lamis (1996) "The Palestinian elections: Moving toward democracy or one-party rule?", *Journal of Palestine Studies*, Vol 25, No 3, pp5–16.

Aruri, Nasser (1995), *The Obstruction of Peace* (Monroe, Maine: Common Courage Press).

Ashton, Nigel (2006) "Pulling the strings: King Hussein's role during the crisis of 1970 in Jordan", *International History* Review, Vol 28, No 1, pp94–118.

Azoulay, Ariella and Ophir, Adi (2008) *The One-State Condition: Occupation and Democracy in Israel/Palestine* (Stanford: Stanford University Press).

Baabood, Abdallah (2023) "Why China Is emerging as a main promoter of stability in the Strait of Hormuz", Carnnegie Middle East Center: https://carnegieendowment.org/research/2023/05/why-china-is-emerging-as-a-main-promoter-of-stability-in-the-strait-of-hormuz?lang=en&center=middle-east

Bachman, Jeffrey (2022) *The Politics of Genocide: From the Genocide Convention to the Responsibility to Protect* (New Brunswick: Rutgers University Press).

Barari, Hassan (2003) "The Al-Aqsa Intifada as seen in Egypt", *Civil Wars*, Vol 6, No 3, pp86–106.

Bargouti, Husain (1990) "Jeep versus bare feet: The villages in the Intifada", in Nassar, Jamal and Heacock, Roger (eds) *Intifada: Palestine at the Crossroads* (New York: Praeger).

Barghouti, Omar (2011), *Boycott, Divestment, Sanctions: The Global Struggle for Palestinian Rights* (Chicago: Haymarket).

Barghouti, Omar (2024) "A secular democratic state in historic Palestine: Self-determination through ethical decolonisation", in Loewenstein, Anthony and Moor, Ahmed (2024), *After Zionism: One State for Israel and Palestine* (London: Saqi), pp174–189.

Baroud, Ramzy (2021) "From the 'iron wall' to the 'villa in the jungle': Palestinians demolish Israel's security myths", *Counterpunch*, 17 September.

Bashear, Suliman (1980) *Communism in the Arab East, 1918–1928* (London: Ithaca).

Batatu, Hanna (1978) *The Old Social Classes and the Revolutionary Movements of Iraq: A Study of Iraq's Old Landed and Commercial Classes and of its Communists, Ba'thists and Free Officers* (London: Saqi Books).

Baumgarten, Helga (2005) "The three faces/ phases of Palestinian nationalism, 1948–2005", *Journal of Palestine Studies*, Vol 34, No 4, pp25–48.

BDS National Committee (2005) "Palestinian civil society call for BDS": https://bdsmovement.net/call

BDS National Committee (2011) "Occupy Wall Street not Palestine!", 14 October: https://bdsmovement.net/news/occupy-wall-street-not-palestine

Beker, Avi (2010) "When history is flexible", *Jerusalem Post*, 26 June: https://www.jpost.com/Christian-In-Israel/Features/When-history-is-flexible

Beinin, Joel (2003) "Is terrorism a useful term in understanding the Middle East and the Palestinian-Israeli conflict?", *Radical History Review*, Vol 85, No 1, pp12–23.

Beinin, Joe and Duboc, Marie (2015) "The Egyptian workers' movement before and after the 2011 popular uprising", *Socialist Register*, Vol 51, pp136–156.

Beinin, Joel and Lockman, Zachary (1987) *Workers on the Nile: Nationalism, Communism, Islam and the Egyptian Working Class, 1882–1954* (Princeton: Princeton University Press).

Benn, Aluf (2011) "Overcoming fear and anxiety in Tel Aviv", *Foreign Affairs*, 8 February.

Bentwich, Norman and Bentwich, Helen (1965) *Mandate Memories, 1918–1948: From the Balfour Declaration to the Establishment of Israel* (London, Hogarth Press).

Berman, Lazar (2023) "Netanyahu to Dutch leader: This war is civilization vs. barbarism", *Times of Israel*, 23 October.

Bernstein, Deborah (2000) *Constructing Boundaries: Jewish and Arab Workers in Mandatory Palestine* (Albany: State University of New York Press).

Bishara, Azmi (1995) "Bantustanisation or binationalism?" in Usher, Graham, *Dispatches from Palestine*, pp59–66.

Bishara, Ghassan (1989) "Impotence in the face of adversity: Arab regimes and the Palestine Question", *Arab Studies Quarterly*, Vol 11, No 2/3, pp303–314.

Bishara, Marwan (2022) "Why Israel hates the Palestinians so much", *Al Jazeera*, 8 August: https://www.aljazeera.com/opinions/2022/8/8/why-israel-hates-the-palestinians-so-much

Bisharat, George E (1993) "Land, law, and legitimacy in Israel and the occupied territories", *American Universirty Law Review*, Vol 43, pp467–561.

Black, Ian (1986) *Zionism and the Arabs, 1936–1939* (London: Routledge).

Black, Ian (2008) "Blair firm on boycott of Hamas", *Guardian*, 6 June.

Blumenthal, Max (2014) "Politicide in Gaza: How Israel's far right won the war", *Journal of Palestine Studies*, Vol 44, No 1, pp14–28.

Botman, Sela (1988) *The Rise of Egyptian Communism, 1939–70* (Syracuse, NY: Syracuse University Press).

Bourdon, Jérôme, (2017) "The export of Zionism: Global images of Israel in the 1960s" in Chaplin, Tamara and Mooney, Jadwiga, *The Global 1960s: Convention, Contest and Counterculture* (London: Routledge).

Bracha, Oren (1998) "Questionably unfortunate, questionably dangerous: The infiltrators, the law, and the supreme court, 1948–1954," *Iyunei Mishpat* [Tel Aviv University Law Review], Vol 21, No 2, pp345–369.

Bremer, Paul (2006) *My Year in Iraq: The Struggle to Build a Future of Hope* (New York: Simon and Schuster).

Brown, Nathan (1990) *Peasant Politics in Modern Egypt* (New Haven: Yale University Press).

Brym, Robert and Araj, Bader (2008) "Palestinian suicide bombing revisited: A critique of the outbidding thesis," *Political Science Quarterly*, No 123, pp485–500.

Brynen, Rex (1989) "PLO policy in Lebanon: Legacies and lessons", *Journal of Palestine Studies*, Vol 18, No 2, pp48–70.

Brynen, Rex (1991) "Palestine and the Arab state system: Permeability, state consolidation and the *Intifada*", *Canadian Journal of Political Science/Revue canadienne de science politique*, Vol XXIV, No 3, pp596–621.

Brynen, Rex (2019) *Sanctuary and Survival: The PLO in Lebanon* (London: Routledge).

B'tselem (2017) "Settlements": https://www.btselem.org/settlements

Buck, Terry (2013) *The Decline of the Popular Front for the Liberation of Palestine: A Historical Analysis* (Amherst: Hampshire College), p4: https://yplus.ps/wp-content/uploads/2021/01/Buck-Terry-James-The-Decline-of-the-Popular-Front-for-the-Liberation-of-Palestine.pdf

Burns, Eleanor (1928) *British Imperialism in India* (London: Labour Research Department).

Bush, George H. W. (1990) "Out of these troubled times…a new world order", *Washington Post* (speech to Congress, 11 September) https://www.washingtonpost.com/archive/politics/1990/09/12/bush-out-of-these-troubled-times-a-new-world-order/b93b5cf1-e389-4e6a-84b0-85f71bf4c946/

Bush, George W. (2005) "President discusses war on terror at National Endowment for Democracy", 6 October, (Washington, DC: The White House) https://georgewbush-whitehouse.archives.gov/news/releases/2005/10/20051006-3.html

Byman, Daniel (2011) "Israel's pessimistic view of the Arab Spring", *The Washington Quarterly*, Vol 34, No 3, pp123–136.

Cahill, Richard (2009) "'Going Beserk': 'Black and Tans' in Palestine", *Jerusalem Quarterly*, Vol 38: https://www.palestine-studies.org/sites/default/files/jq-articles/38_Going_Beserk_2_0.pdf

Cahill, Richard (2018) "The Tegart Police Fortresses in British Mandate Palestine: A reconsideration of their strategic location and purpose", *Jerusalem Quarterly*, Vol 75, No 48: https://www.palestine-studies.org/sites/default/files/jq-articles/Pages_from_JQ_75_-_Cahill.pdf

Callinicos, Alex (2014) "Imperial delusions", *International Socialism*, Series 2, No 142, pp3–12.

Carter, Jimmy (1977) "New conference of May 12", *The Department of State Bulletin*, Vol 76, Issues 1971–1983, 7 June (Washington DC: Department of State).

Cesarani, David (1989) "The anti-Jewish career of Sir William Joynson-Hicks, Cabinet Minister", *Journal of Contemporary History*, Vol 24, No 3, pp461–482.

Chalcraft, John (2012) "Horizontalism in the Egyptian revolutionary process, *Merip*, No 261, pp6–11.

Chalcraft, John (2016) *Popular Politics in the Making of the Modern Middle East* (Cambridge, Cambridge University Press).

Chamberlin, Paul Thomas (2012) *The GlobaOffensive: The United States, the Palestine Liberation Organization, and the Making of the Post-Cold War Order* (Oxford: Oxford University Press).

Chatty, Dawn (2010) *Displacement and Dispossession in the Modern Middle East* (Cambridge, Cambridge University Press).

Chatty, Dawn (2013) "Refugees, exiles, and other forced migrants in the late Ottoman Empire", *Refugee Survey Quarterly*, Vol 32, No 2, pp35–52.

Childers, Erskine (1961) "The other exodus", *The Spectator*, 12 May, pp8–11: https://archive.spectator.co.uk/article/12th-may-1961/8/the-other-exodus

Christison, Kathleen (1998) "Bound by a frame of reference, part II: US policy and the Palestinians, 1948–88", *Journal of Palestine Studies*, Vol 27, No 3, pp20–34.

Chulov, Martin (2012) "Palestinians flee to Lebanon after jet bombs Syria's largest refugee camp", *Guardian*, 18 December.

Cobban, Helena (1984) *The Palestinian Liberation Organisation: People, Power and Politics* (Cambridge: Cambridge University Press).

Cobban, Helena (1990) "The PLO and the 'Intifada'", *Middle East Journal*, Vol 44, No 2, pp207–233.

Collins, John (2007) "Global Palestine: A collision for our time", *Critique: Critical Middle Eastern Studies*, Vol 16, No 1, pp3–18.

Collins, John (2011) *Global Palestine* (London: Hurst).

Conder, Claude (1879) "The present condition of Palestine", *Palestine Exploration Quarterly*, Vol 11, No 1, pp6–15, p9

Confino, Alon (2012) "Miracles and snow in Palestine and Israel: Tantura, a history of 1948", *Israel Studies*, Vol 17, No 2, pp25–61.

Cook, Jonathan (2008) *Israel and the Clash of Civilisations* (London: Pluto).

Cooley, John (1973) *Green March, Black September* (London: Frank Cass).

Cosatu (2006) "South African Trade Union Congress supports CUPE boycott of Israel": www.connexions.org/CxLibrary/Docs/CX5270-COSATU.htm

Council on Foreign Relations (CFR) (2024) "US aid to Israel in four charts" (Washington DC: CFR) https://www.cfr.org/article/us-aid-israel-four-charts

Cox, Stephen (2015) "Britain and the origin of Israeli Special Operations: SOE and PALMACH during the Second World War", *Dynamics of Asymmetric Conflict*, Vol 8, No 1, pp60–78.

Crafts, Nicholas, and Toniolo, Gianni (2008) "European economic growth, 1950–2005: An overview" (London: Centre for Economic Policy Research).

Crawford, Neta and Lutz, Catherine (2019) "Human cost of post-9/11 wars", Watson Institute Public and International Affairs, Brown University: https://watson.brown.edu/costsofwar/files/cow/imce/papers/2019/Direct%20War%20Deaths%20COW%20Estimate%20November%2013%202019%20FINAL.pdf

Cromer [Earl of, Evelyn Baring] (1908) *Modern Egypt* (New York: Macmillan).

Cromer [Earl of, Evelyn Baring] (1913), "The government of subject races", *Political and Literary Essays, 1908–1913* (London: Macmillan).

Cummings, Jonathan (2016) *Israel's Public Diplomacy: The Problems of Hasbara, 1966–1975* (Lanham, MD: Rowman and Littlefield).

Dana, Tariq (2017) "The prolonged decay of the Palestinian National Movement", *National Identities*, Vol 21, No 1, pp39–55.

Darweish, Marwan (1989) "The intifada: Social change", *Race and Class*, Vol 39, No 2, pp47–61.

Davis, Caitlin (2016) "Archiving governance in Palestine", *Journal of Contemporary Archival Studies*, Vol 3, No 1, pp1–15.

Decalo, Samuel (1976) "Afro-Israeli technical co-operation", in Curtis, Michael and Gitelson, Susan (eds) *Israel in the Third World* (New Jersey).

Deeb, Marius (1979) *Party Politics in Egypt: The Wafd and Its Rivals, 1919–38* (London: Ithaca).

Di-Capua, Yoav (2020 "Palestine comes to Paris: The global sixties and the making of a universal cause", *Journal of Palestine Studies*, Vol 50, No 1, pp19–50, p24.

Dodge, Tony (2007) "The causes of US failure in Iraq", *Survival*, Vol 49, No 1, pp81–106.

Donovan, Robert and the staff of the *Los Angeles Times* (1967) *Six Days in June: Israel's Fight for Survival* (New York: Signet).

Dubnov, Arie (2024) "Where do we go from here?" in Dubnov, Arie, Reinhold, Jonathan, Klein, Menachem and Shafir, Gershon, *Governing Gaza After the War: The Israeli Perspectives* (Washington: Carnegie Endowment for International Peace).

Edelman, Maurice (1964) *Ben Gurion: A Political Biography* (London: Hodder & Stoughton).

Economist (1967), "They did it", *Economist*, 10 June.

Eitan, Alimi (2012) "'Occupy Israel': A tale of startling success and hopeful failure", *Social Movement Studies*, Vol 11, Nos 3/4, pp402–407.

El-Hamalawy, Hossam (2001) "January 18 and 19, 1977. 'Uprising of Thieves' or an aborted revolution?" Unpublished MA thesis, The American University in Cairo: https://arabawy.org/wp-content/uploads//2020/12/MA-Thesis-Hossam-el-Hamalawy.pdf

El-Hamalawy, Hossam (2011) "Egypt's revolution has been 10 years in the making", *Guardian*, 2 March.

El-Hamalawy, Hossam (2024) "From Palestine to Tahrir Square: What Egyptians owe Palestinians", *Spectre*, 1 May: https://spectrejournal.com/from-palestine-to-tahrir-square/

El-Mahdi, Rabab and Marfleet, Philip (2009) *Egypt: The Moment of Change* (London: Zed).

El Rifai, Yasid, Dima Yaser, and Jarrar, Adele (2017) "Tegart's modern legacy: The reproduction of power, a timeless paradox", *Jerusalem Quarterly*, Vol 69, p79

El-Sharnouby, Dina (2015) "From state exclusionary politics to youth inclusionary practices: The Tahrir Square experience", *International Journal of Sociology*, Vol 45, No 3, pp176–189.

Elyada, Ouzi (2019) "A nexus of sensationalism and politics: Doar Ha-Yom and the 1929 Western Wall Crisis", *Israel Studies Review*, Vol 34, No 2, pp114–133.

Engels, Frederick, 1968 [1884] "Origins of the family, private property and the state", in Marx, Karl and Engels, Frederick, *Collected Works* (London: Lawrence and Wishart).

Euro-Mediterranean Human Rights Monitor (2023) "Israel hits Gaza Strip with the equivalent of two nuclear bombs", 2 November.

Evron, Yoram (2017) "The economic dimension of China–Israel relations: political implications, roles and limitations", *Israel Affairs*, Vol 23, No 5, pp828–847.

Fabian, Emanuel (2024) "Israel says US shipments of arms and equipment during war exceed 50,000 tons", *Times of Israel*, 26 August.

Fabbrini, Sergio and Yossef, Amr (2015) "Obama's wavering: US foreign policy on the Egyptian crisis, 2011–13", *Contemporary Arab Affairs*, Vol 8, No 1, pp65–80.

Farah, Randa (2013) "Palestinian refugees, the nation, and the shifting political landscape", *Social Alternatives*, Vol 32, No 3, pp41–47.

Farsoun, Samih and Landis, Jean (1990) "The sociology of an uprising", in Nassar, Jamal and Heacock, Roger (eds) *Palestine at the Crossroads* (New York: Praeger).

Fahmy, Ziad (2011) *Ordinary Egyptians: Creating the Modern Nation Through Popular Culture* (Stanford: Stanford University Press).

Farsakh, Leila (2000) "Under siege: Closure, separation and the Palestinian economy", *Merip*, No 217: https://merip.org/2000/12/under-siege/

Farsakh, Leila (2002) "Palestinian labour flows to the Israeli economy: A finished story?" *Journal of Palestine Studies*, Vol 32, No 1, pp13–27.

Filiu, Jean-Pierre (2012) "The origins of Hamas: Militant legacy or Israeli tool?", *Journal of Palestine Studies*, Vol 41, No 3, pp54–70.

Finlay, Thomas (1878) "The centenary of Voltaire", *The Irish Monthly*, Vol 6, pp397–411.

Fisk, Robert (1990) *Pity the Nation: Lebanon at War* (London: Andre ⊠ Deutsch).

Flapan, Simha (1979) *Zionism and the Palestinians* (London: Croom Helm).

Flapan, Simha (1987) "The Palestinian exodus of 1948", *Journal of Palestine Studies*, Vol 16, No 4, pp3–26.

Fleischmann, Ellen (1996) *The Nation and its 'New' Women: Feminism, Nationalism, Colonialism, and the Palestinian Women's Movement, 1920–1948* (PhD Thesis, Georgetown University), p205.

Fogelman, Shay (2010) "Shock and awe", *Haaretz*, 31 December.

Frantzen, Johan (2007) "Communism versus Zionism: The Comintern, Yishuvism and the Palestine Communist Party", *Journal of Palestine Studies*, Vol XXXVI, No 2, pp6–24.

Friedman, Thomas (2006) *From Beirut to Jerusalem* (New York: Anchor Books).

Frisch, Hillel (2004) "Jordan and the Palestinian Authority: Did better fences make better neighbours?", *Middle East Journal*, Vol 58, No 1, pp52–71.

Fromkin, David (1989) *A Peace to End All Peace: The Fall of the Ottoman Empire and the Creation of the Modern Middle East* (New York: Avon Books).

Fukuyama, Francis (1991) *The End of History and the Last Man* (New York: Free Press).

Fuller, Adam (2020) *Israel and the Neoconservatives: Zionism and American Interests* (Lexington Books, Lanham MD).

Gabriel, Stuart, and Sabatello, Eitan (1986) "Palestinian migration from the West Bank and Gaza: Economic and demographic analyses", *Economic Development and Cultural Change*, Vol 34, No 2, pp245–262.

Gagnon, George (1993) "British Air Control from 1922 to 1936" (Maxwell Air Force Base, Alabama: Air University Press): http://www.jstor.com/stable/resrep13755.9

Gart, Murray (1989) "Interview with Israel's Ariel Sharon: Never! Never! Never!", *Time*, 17 April: https://time.com/archive/6702324/interview-with-israels-ariel-sharon-never-never-never/

Gazit, Nir (2015) "State-sponsored vigilantism: Jewish settlers' violence in the occupied Palestinian territories", *Sociology*, Vol 49, No 3, pp438–454,

Gazit, Shlomo (1995) *The Carrot and the Stick: Israel's Policy in Judea and Samaria, 1967–68* (Washington DC: B'nai B'rith Books).

Gensicke, Klaus (2011) *The Mufti of Jerusalem and the Nazis: The Berlin* Years, (London: Vallentine Mitchell).

Gershoni, Israel (1986) "The Muslim Brothers and the Arab Revolt in Palestine, 1936–39", *Middle Eastern Studies*, Vol 22, No 3, pp367–397.

Ghandour, Zeina (2010) *A Discourse on Domination in Mandate Palestine: Imperialism, Property and Insurgency* (London: Routledge).

Gildea, Robert (2019) *Empires of the Mind: The Colonial Past and the Politics of the Present* (Cambridge: Cambridge University Press).

Gill, Lesley, (2004) *The School of the Americas: Military Training and Political Violence in the Americas* (Durham, NC: Duke University Press).

Glaser, Amelia (2021) "Localizing the pogrom: Jewish Leftist poets on Palestine, 1929", *Dibur Literary Journal* (Peripheral Modernisms), Vol 9/10.

Glazer, Steven (2001) "Picketing for Hebrew labor: A window on Histadrut tactics and strategy", *Journal of Palestine Studies*, Vol 30, no 4, pp39–54.

Goldberg, Ari (2020 "Israeli tycoon urges help for Palestinians", *BBC News*, 17 July.

Goldenberg, Suzanne (2001) "Israeli tanks invade two West Bank towns", *Guardian*, 13 September.

Goldenberg, Suzanne (2002) "The lunar landscape that was the Jenin refugee camp", *Guardian*, 16 April.

Goldsmith, Daniel (2005) "Confronting threats before they materialize: The United States and the overthrow of the Iranian government", *McGill Journal of Middle East Studies*, Vol 8, pp81–99.

Goldstein, Yossi (2018) "The Six Day War: The war that no one wanted", *Israel Affairs*, Vol 24, No 5, pp767–784.

Gordon, Neve (2011) "A Villa in the Jungle: The Arab Awakening through the lens of the Israeli media", *Middle East Law and Governance*, Vol 3, Nos1/2, pp105–117.

Gordon, Robert (1992) *Nasser's Blessed Movement: Egypt's Free Officers and the July Revolution* (Oxford: Oxford University Press).

Gorenberg, Gershom (2007) *Occupied Territories: The Untold Story of Israel's Settlements* (London: I.B. Tauris).

Graf, Rüdiger (2014) "Expert estimates of oil-reserves and the transformation of 'petroknowledge' in the Western world from the 1950s to the 1970s", *Managing the Unknown: Essays on Environmental Ignorance*, pp140–167.

Graham-Harrison, Emma and Kierszenbaum, Quique (2024) "'It is a time of witch hunts in Israel': Teacher held in solitary confinement for posting concern about Gaza deaths", *Observer*, 13 January

Gregory, Derek (2004) "Palestine and the 'War on Terror'", *Comparative Studies of South Asia, Africa and the Middle East*, Vol 24, No 1, pp183–195.

Greenstein, Ran (2015) *Jadaliyya*, 15 August: https://www.jadaliyya.com/Details/32396/Israel-Where-do-the-Mizrahim-fit-in-Part-1

Grenville, Anthony (2010) *Jewish Refugees from Germany and Austria in Britain, 1933–1970: Their Image in AJR Information* (London: Vallentine Mitchell.

Gresh, Alain (1988), *The PLO: The Struggle Within* (London: Zed).

Grewcock, Michael (2018) "Settler-colonial violence, primitive accumulation and Australia's genocide", *State Crime Journal*, Vol 7, No 2, pp222–250.

Grosscup, Beau (2006) *Strategic Terror: The Politics and Ethics of Aerial Bombardment* (London: Zed Books).

Guirguis, Laure (2019) "The New Left in 1960s and 1970s Lebanon and 1917 as model and foil", in Feliu and Izquierdo-Brichs, *Communist Parties in the Middle East*, pp258–267.

Gutwein, Danny (2016) "The politics of the Balfour Declaration: Nationalism, imperialism and the limits of Zionist-British cooperation", *Journal of Israeli History*, Vol 35, No 2, pp117–152.

Haddad, Toufic (2018) *Palestine Ltd: Neoliberalism and Nationalism in the Occupied Territory* (London: I.B. Tauris).

Hafez, Bassem (2013) "New social movements and the Egyptian Spring: a comparative analysis between the April 6 Movement and the Revolutionary Socialists", *Perspectives on Global Development and Technology*, Vol 12, Nos 1-2, pp98-113.

Hafez, Sherine (2014) "Bodies that protest: The girl in the blue bra, sexuality, and state violence in revolutionary Egypt", *Signs: Journal of Women in Culture and Society*, Vol 40, No 1, pp20-28.

Haiduc-Dale, N. (2013) *Arab Christians in British Mandate Palestine, Communalism and Nationalism 1917–1948* (Edinburgh: Edinburgh University Press.

Hajjat, Abdelalli (2022) "Comités Palestine (1970–72): On the origins of solidarity with the Palestinian cause in France", in Maasri, Zeina, Bergin, Cathy and Burke, Francesca (eds) *Transnational solidarity: Anticolonialism in the global sixties* (Manchester: Manchester University Press), pp55–77.

Hallaj, Muhammed (2008) "Recollections of the Nakba through a teenager's eyes", *Journal of Palestine Studies*, Vol 38, No 1: https://www.palestine-studies.org/en/node/42079

Hanegbi, Haim, Machover, Moshe and Orr, Akiva (1971) *The Class Nature of Israeli Society* (Pluto: London).

Hanieh, Adam (2021) "The political economy of state formation in Palestine", in Farsakh, Laila (ed) *Rethinking Statehood in Palestine: Self-Determination and Decolonization Beyond Partition* (Oakland, CA: University of California Press).

Harel, Amos (2008) "ANALYSIS IAF: Strike on Gaza is Israel's version of 'shock and awe'", *Haaretz*, 27 December.

Harkabi, Yehoshafat (1972) *Arab Attitudes to Israel* (Jerusalem: Israel Universities Press).

Harris, Lillian Craig (1977) "China's relations with the PLO", *Journal of Palestine Studies*, Vol 7, No 1, pp123–154.

Hart, Alan (1984) *Arafat: Terrorist or Peacemaker?* (London: Sidgwick and Jackson).

Hart, Alan (1985) "Don't blame Arafat", *Journal of Palestine Studies*, Vol 14, No 3, pp187–190.

Hart, Alan (1989) *Arafat: A Political Biography* (Bloomington, IN: Indiana University Press).

Hass, A. (2002) "Israel's closure policy: An ineffective strategy of containment and repression", *Journal of Palestine Studies*, Vol 31, No 3, pp5–20.

Hasso, Frances, Susan (2005) *Resistance, Repression, and Gender Politics in Occupied Palestine and Jordan* (Syracuse, NY: Syracuse University Press).

Henderson, Jon (1976) "Leadership personality and war: The cases of Richard Nixon and Anthony Eden", *Political Science*, Vol 28, No 2, pp141–164.

Herf, Jeffrey (2009) *Nazi Propaganda for the Arab World* (New Haven, Yale University Press).

Hernon, Ian (2007) *Assassin! 200 years of British Political Murder* (London: Pluto Press).

Herzl, Theodor (1941) [1902]) *Altneuland* (New York: M. Wiener).

Herzl, Theodor (1946) *The Jewish State: An Attempt at a Modern Solution of the Jewish Question* (New York: American Zionist Emergency Council).

Herzl, Theodor (1960) *Complete Diaries Vol 1* (ed Patai, Raphael) (New York: Herzl Press), p88.

Herzl, Theodor (1988) [1896] *The Jewish State* (New York: Dover Publications).

Heschel, Suzannah (2022) "Meir Kahane and race as incarnational theology", *Journal of Religious Ethics*, Vol 50, No 2, pp293–302.

Hever, Shir (2012) "Exploitation of Palestinian labour in contemporary Zionist colonialism", *Settler Colonial Studies*, Vol 2, No 1, pp124–132.

Higgins, Andrew (2009) "How Israel helped to spawn Hamas", *Wall Street Journal*, 24 January: http://www.wsj.com/articles/SB123275572295011847

Hilal, Jamil (2010) "The Palestinian Left and the multi-layered challenges ahead" (Birzeit: Rosa Luxemburg Foundation in Palestine): https://www.rosalux.de/fileadmin/rls_uploads/pdfs/Standpunkte/Standpunkte_international/RLS_PAL_-_Hilal_Palestinian_Left.pdf

Hilal, Jamil (2016) "Reflections on identity and youth in historical Palestine and the diaspora", in Hilal, Jamil (ed) *Palestinian Youth: Studies on Identity, Space and Community Participation* (Birzeit: Birzeit University): https://shorturl.at/mWLmk

Hirsch, Michal Ben-Josef (2007) "From taboo to the negotiable: The Israeli new historians and the changing representation of the Palestinian refugee problem", *Perspectives on Politics*, Vol 5, No 2, pp241–258.

Hirschkind, Charles (2012) "Beyond secular and religious: An intellectual genealogy of Tahrir Square", *American Ethnologist*, Vol 39, No 1, pp49–53.

Hirst, David (1977) *The Gun and the Olive Branch* (London: Faber and Faber).

Hirst, David and Beeson Irene (1982) *Sadat* (London: Faber and Faber).

Hirst, David (2010) *Beware of Small States: Lebanon, Battleground of the Middle East* (New York: Nation Books).

Hodgkin, Thomas (1986) "Letter to RHH" (23 April 1936) *Thomas Hodgkin: Letters from Palestine 1932–36* (London: Quartet).

Hoffman, Jon (2023) "The U.S. has nothing to fear from China in the Middle East", Cato Institute, 6 December: https://www.cato.org/commentary/us-has-nothing-fear-china-middle-east

Hoffman, Stanley and Bozo, Frédéric (2004) *Gulliver Unbound: America's Imperial Temptation and the War in Iraq* (Lanham, MD: Rowman and Littlefield).

Horowitz, Adam, Ratner Lizzy and Philip Weiss (2011) "The Goldstone Affair", *The Nation*, 2 May.

Hroub, Khaled (2004) "Hamas after Shaykh Yasin and Rantisi", *Journal of Palestine Studies*, Vol 33, No 4, pp21–38.

Hudson, Michael (1972) "Developments and setbacks in the Palestinian Resistance Movement 1967–1971", *Journal of Palestine Studies*, Vol 1, No 3, pp64–8.

Hughes, Matthew (2009) "The banality of brutality: British armed forces and the repression of the Arab revolt in Palestine, 1936–39", *The English Historical Review*, Vol 124, No 507, pp313–354

Hughes, Matthew (2013) "A British 'Foreign Legion'? The British police in Mandate Palestine", *Middle Eastern Studies*, Vol 49, No 5, pp696–711: https://bura.brunel.ac.uk/bitstream/2438/9798/2/Fulltext.pdf

Hughes, Matthew (2015) "Terror in Galilee: British-Jewish collaboration and the Special Night Squads in Palestine during the Arab Revolt, 1938–39", *The Journal of Imperial and Commonwealth History*, Vol 43, No 4, pp590–610.

Hughes, Matthew (2019) *Britain's Pacification of Palestine* (Cambridge, Cambridge University Press).

Hughes, Matthew (2019) "Women, violence, and the Arab Revolt in Palestine, 1936–39", *The Journal of Military History*, Vol 83, pp487–507.

Human Rights Watch (1990) "The Israeli army and the Intifada policies that contribute to the killings" (New York: Human Rights Watch): https://www.hrw.org/legacy/campaigns/israel/intifada-intro.htm

Human Rights Watch (1999) "The Palestinian security forces": https://www.hrw.org/reports/1997/palestina/Israel-03.htm

Human Rights Watch (2002): "Israel/Occupied Territories: Jenin war crimes investigation needed", 2 May: https://www.hrw.org/news/2002/05/02/israel/occupied-territories-jenin-war-crimes-investigation-needed

Huntington, Samuel (1993) "The clash of civilizations?", *Foreign Affairs*, Vol 72, No 3, pp22–49.

Huntington, Samuel (1996) *The Clash of Civilizations and the Remaking of World Order* (New York: Simon & Schuster).

Hussein, Mahmoud (1973) *Class Conflict in Egypt: 1945–1970* (New York: Monthy Review Press).

Independent Fact-Finding Committee on Gaza (2009) *No Safe Place*: https://www.tromso-gaza.no/090501ReportGaza.pdf

Irfan, Anne (2020) *An Unusual Revolution: The Palestinian* Thawra *in Lebanon, c1969–82*, Durham Middle East Paper 103 (Durham: Durham University).

Irfan, Anne (2023) *Refuge and Resistance: Palestinians and the International Refugee System* (New York: Colombia University Press).

Ismael, Tareq (2006) "Arafat's Palestine National Authority", *Durham Middle East Papers*, No 71 (Durham: University of Durham).

Ismael, Tareq and El-Sa'id, Rifa'at (1990) *The Communist Movement in Egypt, 1920–1988* (Syracuse: Syracuse University Press),

Israel Central Bureau of Statistics (2020) "Number of settlers in the Israeli settlements in the West Bank by region, 1986–2019", Palestinian Central Bureau of Statistics: https://www.pcbs.gov.ps/Portals/_Rainbow/Documents/SETTTime%20SeriesE-2019.html

Iyad Abu [Salah Khalaf] (1981) *My Home, My Land* (New York: Times Books).

Jablonsky, David. (1995) *Paradigm Lost?: Transitions and the Search for a New World Order* (New York: Praeger/Bloomsbury Publishing USA).

Jabotinsky, Ze'ev (1923) *The Iron Wall*: https://en.jabotinsky.org/media/9747/the-iron-wall.pdf

Jensehaugen, Jørgen (2023) "Photographing 1948: Robert Capa's absent Palestinians", *Journal of Palestine Studies*, Vol 52, No 2, pp5–23: https://www.tandfonline.com/doi/full/10.1080/0377919X.2023.2219031

Jewish National Fund (nd) https://www.kkl-jnf.org/forestry-and-ecology/afforestation-in-israel/turning-the-desert-green/?_gl=1*-jxfq05*_up*MQ..*_ga*MzM0NTgwNjU-wLjE3MTY4MzAxNzg.*_ga_2CHBB0KS-ME*MTcxNjgzMDE3OC4xLjEuMTcxN-jgzMDIxMi4yNi4wLjA

Jones, Toby (2012) "America, oil and war in the Middle East", *Journal of American History*, Vol 99, No 1, pp208–218.

Journal of Palestine Studies (2009) "Prelude to operation Cast Lead: Israel's unilateral disengagement to the eve of war", *Journal of Palestine Studies*, Vol 38, No 3, pp139–168.

Kahane, Meir (1981) *They Must Go* (New York: Grosset and Dunlap).

Kalman, Samuel (2013) *French Colonial Fascism: The Extreme Right in Algeria, 1919–1939* (Basingstoke: Palgrave MacMillan).

Kanafani, Ghassan (1980) [1972] *The 1936–39 Revolt in Palestine* (London: Tricontinental Society).

Kapeliouk, Amnon (1984) *Sabra and Shatila: Inquiry into a Massacre* (Belmont, MA: Association of Arab-American University Graduates).

Kaplan, Amy (2018) *Our American Israel: The Story of an Entangled Alliance* (Cambridge, MA: Harvard University Press).

Kaplan, Eren (2019) "Watching Fight Club in Tel Aviv: Or the 2011 social protests in Israel: A political postmortem", *Comparative Literature and Culture*, Vol 21, No 2, pp6–16.

Katz, Ethan (2018) "An Imperial entanglement: Anti-semitism, islamophobia, and colonialism", *The American Historical Review*, Vol 123, No 4, pp1190–1209.

Katz, Yaakov (2008) "Shock, awe…and deception", *Jerusalem Post*, 28 December.

Kazziha, Walid (1975) *Revolutionary Transformation in the Arab World: Habash and His Comrades from Nationalism to Marxism* (London: Charles Knight).

Kechichian, Joseph (2010) "Abdul Hamid Shoman: The visionary entrepreneur", *Gulf News*, 8 January: https://gulfnews.com/general/abdul-hamid-shoman-the-visionary-entrepreneur-1.563057

Kelemen, Paul (2012) *The British Left and Zionism: History of a Divorce* (Manchester: Manchester University Press).

Kellner, Douglas (2004) "9/11, spectacles of terror, and media manipulation", *Critical Discourse Studies*, Vol 1, No 1, pp41–64.

Kellner, Douglas (2007) "Bushspeak and the politics of lying: Presidential rhetoric in the 'War on Terror'", *Presidential Studies Quarterly*, Vol 37, No 4, pp577–792.

Kennan, George [anonymous, as 'X'] (1947) "The sources of Soviet conduct", *Foreign Affairs*, 1 July: https://www.academia.edu/69959208/The_Sources_of_Soviet_Conduct_by_X_George_Kennan_Foreign_Affairs_July_1947

Kerton, Sarah (2012) "Tahrir, here? The influence of the Arab Uprisings on the emergence of Occupy", *Social Movement Studies*, Vol 11, Nos 3/4, pp302–308.

Khalaf, Issa (1997) "The effect of socioeconomic change on Arab societal collapse in Mandate Palestine", *International Journal of Middle East Studies*, Vol 29, No 1, pp93–112.

Khalidi, Raja (2018) "Nation and class: Generations of Palestinian liberation", *Rethinking Marxism*, Vol 30, No 3, pp368–392.

Khalidi, Rashid (1997) *Palestinian Identity: The Construction of Modern National Consciousness* (New York: Colombia University Press).

Khalidi, Rashid (2021) "The Journal of Palestine Studies in the twenty-first century: An editor's reflections", *Journal of Palestine Studies*, Vol 50, No 3, pp5–17.

Khalidi, Rashid (2020) *The Hundred Years War on Palestine* (London: Profile Books).

Khalidi, Walid (1979) *Violence and Conflict in Lebanon* (Cambridge, Mass: Harvard Centre for International Studies).

Khalidi, Walid (1988) "Plan Dalet: Master plan for the conquest of Palestine", *Journal of Palestine Studies*, Vol 18, No 1, pp4–19: https://www.palestine-studies.org/sites/default/files/attachments/jps-articles/Plan%20dalet.pdf

Khalidi, Walid (ed) (1992) *All That Remains: The Palestinian Villages Occupied and Depopulated by Israel in 1948* (Beirut: Institute for Palestine Studies).

Khalidi, Walid (2005) "Why did the Palestinians leave, revisited", *Journal of Palestine Studies*, Vol 34, No 2, pp42–54.

Khalili, Laleh (2010) "Palestinians: The politics of control, invisibility and the spectacle", in Khalidi, Muhammed (ed) *Manifestations of Identity* (Institute of Palestine Studies: Beirut), pp125–145.

Kidron, Anat (2016) "Separatism, coexistence and the landscape: Jews and Palestinian-Arabs in mandatory Haifa", *Middle Eastern Studies*, Vol 52, No 1, pp79–101.

Kilani, Ramsis (2024) "Strategies for liberation: Old and new arguments in the Palestinian left", *International Socialism*, No 183 (NS), pp29–50.

Kimmerling, Baruch (2003) "From Barak to Road Map", *New Left Review*, September, pp134–44.

Kimmerling, Baruch (2003) *Politicide: Ariel Sharon's War Against the Palestinians* (London: Verso).

King-Irani, Laurie (2006) "Exiled to a liminal legal zone: Are we all Palestinians now?", *Third World Quarterly*, Vol 27, No 5, pp923–936.

Klare, Michael (2007) *Blood and Oil* (New York: Henry Holt).

Klein, Naomi (2008) *The Shock Doctrine: The Rise of Disaster Capitalism* (London: Penguin).

Klein, Menachem (2008) "One state in the Holy Land? A dream or a nightmare?", *The International Spectator*, Vol 43, No 4, pp89–101.

Klug, Brian (2003), "The collective Jew: Israel and the new antisemitism", *Patterns of prejudice*, Vol 37, No 2, pp117–138.

Knight, John (2011) "Securing Zion? Policing in British Palestine, 1917–39, *European Review of History/ Revue Européenne d'Histoire*, Vol 18, No 4, pp523–543.

Knudsen, Are (2005) "Crescent and sword: The Hamas enigma," *Third World Quarterly*, Vol 26, No 8, pp1373–1388.

Kolinsky, Martin (1993) *Law, Order and Riots in Mandatory Palestine, 1928–35* (New York: Springer).

Korn, Alina (2003) "From refugees to infiltrators: Constructing political crime in Israel in the 1950s", *International Journal of the Sociology of Law*, Vol 31, No 1, pp1–22.

Kramer, Gudrun (2010) *Hasan al-Banna*, (London: Oneworld), pp45–46.

Kukrety, Nupur (2016) *Poverty, Inequality and Social Protection in Lebanon* (Oxfam International/American University of Beirut).

Küntzel, Matthias (2007) *Jihad and Jew Hatred: Islamism, Nazism and the Roots of 9/11*, (New York: Telos Press).

Lachman, Shai (1982) "Arab rebellion and terrorism in Palestine 1929–39: The case of Sheikh Izz al-Din al-Qassam and his movement", in Kedourie, Elie and Haim, Sylvia (eds) *Zionism and Arabism in Palestine and Israel* (London: Frank Cass), pp52–99.

Laizans, Janis and Itzhaki, Michal (2024) "On the edge of Gaza, Israeli settlers want back in", *Reuters*, 21 October.

League of Nations (1922) "Question of Palestine: Text of Mandate", p4: https://digitallibrary.un.org/record/829707?ln=en&v=pdf

Lee, Mia (2018) "Nazis in the Middle East: Assessing links between Nazism and Islam", *Contemporary European History*, Vol 27, No 1, pp125–135.

Lendman, Steve (2010) "Israel's slow-motion genocide in occupied Palestine", in Cook, W. (ed) *The Plight of the Palestinians: A Long History of Destruction* (New York: Palgrave Macmillan US), pp29–38.

Lentin, Ronit (2018) *Traces of Racial Exception: Racializing Israeli Settler Colonialism* (London: Bloomsbury).

Leopardi, Francesco (2013) *After Beirut: History and Narrative of the Popular Front for the Liberation of Palestine in the Mid-eighties* (Venice: Università Ca'Foscari Venezia).

Lerner, Daniel (1958) *The Passing of Traditional Society: Modernising the Middle East* (New York: Free Press).

Lesch, Anne (1975) "Israeli settlements in the Occupied Territories, 1967–1977", *Journal of Palestine Studies*, Vol 7, No 1, pp26–47.

Levene, Mark (2007) "Review: Ilan Pappé's The Ethnic Cleansing of Palestine", *Journal of Genocide Research*, Vol 9, No 4, December: pp675–81.

Levene, Mark (2024) "Gaza 2023: Words matter, lives matter more", *Journal of Genocide Research*: https://www.tandfonline.com/doi/full/10.1080/14623528.2024.2301866

Lewis, Bernard (1990) "The roots of Muslim rage", *The Atlantic*, Vol 266, No 3.

Liebes, Tamar, and Zohar, Kampf (2009) "Black and white and shades of gray: Palestinians in the Israeli media during the 2nd intifada", *The International Journal of Press/Politics*, Vol 14, No 4, pp434–453.

Little, Douglas (1993) "The making of a special relationship: The United States and Israel, 1957–68", *International Journal of Middle East Studies*, Vol 25, No 4, pp563–585.

Litvinoff, Barnet (1989) *The Burning Bush: Anti-Semitism and World History* (London: William Collins).

Llewellyn, Tim (2023) "The crafting of the news: The British media and the Israel–Palestine Question", in Parker, Ian (ed) *For Palestine: Essays from the Tim Hurndall Memorial Group Lecture* (London: Open Books), pp229–244.

Lochery, Neil (2005) "Israel's Soviet immigrants", *British Academy Review*, No 8, pp4–7.

Lockman, Zachary (1996) *Comrades and Enemies: Arab and Jewish Workers in Palestine, 1906–1948* (Berkeley: University of California Press).

Lockman, Zachary (2012) "Land, labor and the logic of Zionism: A critical engagement with Gershon Shafir", *Settler Colonial Studies*, Vol 2, No 1, pp9–38.

Loescher, Gil (1993) *Beyond Charity: International Cooperation and the Global Refugee Crisis* (Oxford: Oxford University Press.

London, Louise (2000) *Whitehall and the Jews, 1933–1948* (Cambridge, Cambridge University Press).

Luxemburg, Rosa (2021) [1906] *The Mass Strike: The Political Party and the Trade Unions* (Paris: Foreign Languages Press).

Macalister, Robert (1912) *A History of Civilisation in Palestine* (Cambridge, Cambridge University Press), p32, p34; Internet Archive: https://archive.org/details/historyofciviliz00macauoft/page/n5/mode/2up

MacDonald, Michael (2014) *Overreach: Delusions of Regime Change in Iraq* (Cambridge, MASS: Harvard University Press).

Mackenzie, James (2024) "Netanyahu says Israel will be a key US ally whoever replaces Biden", Reuters, 22 July.

Machover, Moshe (1978) "Israel and the new order in the Middle East", *Matzpen*, 10 October: https://matzpen.org/english/1978-10-10/israel-and-the-new-order-in-the-middle-east/

Mallman, Klaus-Michael and Cüppers, Martin (2010) *Nazi Palestine: The Plans for the Extermination of the Jews in Palestine* (New York: Enigma Books).

Manna, Adel (2019) "Resistance and survival in central Galilee, July 1948–July 1951", *Jerusalem Quarterly*, Vol 79, pp28–37.

Marfleet, Philip (2006) *Refugees in a Global Era* (Basingstoke: Macmillan).

Marfleet, Philip (2015) "Iraq: What happened next…", *International Socialism*, No 161, pp83–105.

Marfleet, Philip (2016) *Egypt: Contested Revolution* (London: Pluto).

Marfleet, Philip (2022) "From nationalism to Islamism: Revolution, the Wafd and the rise of the Muslim Brotherhood" in Hellyer, H. A. and Springborg, Robert (eds) *The Egyptian Revolution of 1919: Legacies and Consequences of the Fight for Independence* (London: Bloomsbury).

Marx, Karl (1957) [1885] *Capital*, Vol 2, Ch 31 (London: J.M. Dent).

Masalha, Nur (1991) "A critique of Benny Morris", *Journal of Palestine Studies*, Vol 21, No 1, pp90–97.

Masalha, Nur (1992) *Expulsion of the Palestinians: The Concept of 'Transfer' in Zionist Political Thought, 1892–1948* (Washington, DC: Institute for Palestine Studies).

Masalha, Nur (1996) "The 1956–57 occupation of the Gaza strip: Israeli proposals to resettle the Palestinian refugees", *British Journal of Middle Eastern Studies*, Vol 23, No 1, pp55–68.

Masalha, Nur (2018) "Decolonising methodology, reclaiming history: Palestinian oral histories and memories of the Nakba", in Abdo, N. and Masalha,

N. (eds) *An Oral History of the Palestinian Nakba* (London: Zed).

Mason, Victoria (2009) "Revenge and terror: The destruction of the Palestinian community in Kuwait", in Jackson, Richard, Murphy, Eamon and Poynting, Scott (eds) *Contemporary State Terrorism* (London: Routledge), pp138–154.

Massad, Joseph (2004) "The persistence of the Palestinian Question", in Aretxaga, Begoña, Dworkin, Dennis, Gabilondo, Joseba and Joseba Zulaika (eds) *Empire & Terror: Nationalism/ Postnationalism in the New Millennium* (Reno: University of Nevada).

Masters, Jonathan and Merrow, Will (2024) "U.S. aid to Israel in four charts" (New York: Council on Foreign Relations): https://www.cfr.org/article/us-aid-israel-four-charts

Mattar, Philip (1994) "The PLO and the Gulf crisis", *Middle East Journal*, Vol 48, No 1, pp31–46.

Matthews, Weldon (2006) *Confronting an Empire, Constructing a Nation: Arab Nationalists and Popular Politics in Mandate Palestine*, (London: IB Tauris).

Meier, Daniel (2014) "The Palestinian *fiday'i* as an icon of transnational struggle: The Lebanese experience", *British Journal of Middle Eastern Studies*, Vol 41, No 3, pp322–334.

Meir Amit Intelligence and Terrorism Information Center (ITIC): https://www.terrorism-info.org.il/en/about/

Melman, Yossi and Raviv, Dan (1988) "Expelling Palestinians", *Washington Post*, 6 February: https://www.washingtonpost.com/archive/opinions/1988/02/07/expelling-palestinians/a54c4262-ec35-4f20-a705-f47aa18d72db/

Milton-Edwards, Beverley (2014) "Islamist versus Islamist: Rising challenge in Gaza", *Terrorism and Political Violence*, Vol 26, No 2, pp259–276.

Milton-Edwards, Beverley and Farrell, Stephen (2024) *Hamas: The Quest for Power* (Cambridge: Polity).

Mitchell, Richard (1969) *The Society of the Muslim Brothers* (London: Oxford University Press).

Mitchell, Timothy (2009) "Carbon democracy", *Economy and Society*, Vol 38, No 3, pp399–432.

Moazzam, Anwar (1984) *Jamā⊠ al-Dīn al-Afghāni: A Muslim intellectual* (New Delhi: Concept Publishing).

Monbiot, George (2001) "Backyard terrorism", *Guardian*, 31 October.

Morris, Benny (1982) *The Birth of the Palestinian Refugee Problem, 1947–1949* (Cambridge: Cambridge University Press).

Morris, Benny (1994) *1948 and After: Israel and the Palestinians* (Oxford: Clarendon Press).

Morris, Benny (1997) *Israel's Border Wars, 1949–1956: Arab Infiltration, Israeli Retaliation, and the Countdown to the Suez War* (Oxford: Clarendon Press).

Morris, Benny (1999) "Response of the Jewish daily press in Palestine to the accession of Hitler, 1933", *Yad Vashem Studies*, Vol 27, pp363–407: https://www.yadvashem.org/odot_pdf/Microsoft%20Word%20-%203221.pdf

Morris, Benny (1999) *Righteous Victims: A History of the Arab-Zionist Conflict, 1881–1999* (New York: Alfred Knopf).

Moughrabi, Fouad (1992) "Israeli control and Palestinian resistance", *Social Justice*, Vol 19, No 3, pp46–62.

Moughrabi, Fouad (2009) "Moving towards a knowledge society in the Arab world", *Arab Studies Quarterly*, Vol 31, No 4, pp17–31.

Muslih, Muhammed (1976) "Moderates and rejectionists within the Palestine Liberation Organization", *Middle East Journal*, Vol 30, No 2, pp127–140.

Muslih, Muhammed (1988) *The Origins of Palestinian Nationalism* (New York: Colombia University Press).

Mustafa, Omar (2020) [2002] "The national liberation struggle: a socialist analysis", in Awad, Sumaya and Bean, Brian, *Palestine: A Socialist Introduction* (Chicago: Haymarket), pp53–78.

Nadeau, Mary-Jo, and Sears, Alan (2010) "The Palestine test: Countering the silencing campaign", *Studies in Political Economy*, Vol 85, No 1, pp7–33.

Nafi, Basheer (1997) "Shaykh 'Izz Al-Dīn Al-Qassām: A reformist and a rebel leader", *Journal of Islamic Studies*, Vol 8, No 2, pp185–215.

Naor, Arye (2015) "'A simple historical truth': Judea, Samaria and the Gaza Strip in Menachem Begin's ideology", *Israel Affairs*, Vol 21, No 3, pp462–481.

Naser-Najjab, Nadia (2020) "Palestinian leadership and the contemporary significance of the First Intifada", *Race and Class*, Vol 62, No 2, pp61–79.

Neff, Donald (1988) "US policy and the Palestinian refugees", *Journal of Palestine Studies*, Vol 18, No 1, pp96–111.

Netanyahu, Benjamin (2001) "The strategy to end terrorism", *New Perspectives Quarterly*, No 18, pp58–65.

New York Times (1952) "A bid for dictatorship" (15 July).

Aruri, Nasser (1995), *The Obstruction of Peace* (Monroe, Maine: Common Courage Press).

Odeh, B. J. (1985), *Lebanon: Dynamics of Conflict* (London: Zed).

Office of the High Commissioner for Human Rights (United Nations) (2024) "UN Report: Israel use of heavy bombs in Gaza raises serious concerns under the laws of war", 19 June.

Office of the Historian [United States Government] (1972) "Intelligence Memorandum ER IM 72–79": https://history.state.gov/historicaldocuments/frus1969-76ve04/d181#:~:text=The%20United%20States%20has%20provided%20Iran%20with%20about%20%241.4%20billion,)%20(see%20Table%202).

Office of the Historian [United States Government] (2008) "Middle East Region and Arabian Peninsula, 1969–1972"; Vol XXIV [Jordan, September 1970] (Washington: US Government Printing Office).

Office of the Historian (nd) "Memorandum of Discussion at the 135th Meeting of the National Security Council, Washington, March 4, 1953": https://history.state.gov/historicaldocuments/frus1952-54v10/d312#:~:text=Dulles%20pointed%20out%2C%20if%20Iran,would%20fall%20into%20Communist%20control

Owen, Roger (1981) *The Middle East in the World Economy* (London: Methuen).

Painter, David (2012) "Oil and the American century", *The Journal of American History*, Vol 99, No 1, pp24–39.

Palestine Royal Commission Report (1937) [Peel Commission] (London: His Majesty's Stationery Office), pvi: https://unispal.un.org/pdfs/Cmd5479.pdf

Palmer, Alison (1998) "Colonial and modern genocide: explanations and categories", *Ethnic and Racial Studies*, Vol 21, No 1, pp89–115.

Pappé, Ilan (2006) *The Ethnic Cleansing of Palestine* (Oxford: OneWorld).

Pappé, Ilan (2010) "Zionizing the Palestinian space: Historical and historiographical perspectives", in Hamdan-Saliba, Hanaa (ed) "The right to a spatial narrative", *Makan*, Vol 2 (Haifa: Adalah), pp9–21.

Pappé, Ilan (2014) *The Idea of Israel: A History of Power and Knowledge* (London: Verso).

Pappé, Ilan (2017) *Gaza: The Biggest Prison on Earth: A History of Gaza and the Occupied Territories* (London: One World).

Pappé, Ilan (2021) "Palestinian youth: A silver lining and a ray of hope", *International Socialism*, No 161, pp89–102.

Parsi, Triti (2007) *Treacherous Alliance: The Secret Dealings of Israel, Iran, and the United States* (New Haven: Yale University Press).

Parsons, Laila (2019) "The secret testimony of the Peel Commission (Part I): Underbelly of Empire", *Journal of Palestine Studies*, Vol 49, No 1, pp7–24.

Patai, Raphael (1973) *The Arab Mind* (New York: Scribner).

Patterson, David (2011) *A Genealogy of Evil: Anti-Semitism from Nazism to Islamic Jihad* (Cambridge: Cambridge University Press).

Paul, James and Stork, Joe (1982) "The War in Lebanon", *Merip Reports*, No 108: https://merip.org/1982/09/the-war-in-lebanon/

Peace Agreements (1993) "Israel–PLO recognition: Exchange of letters", 9 September 1993: https://www.peaceagreements.org/viewmasterdocument/34

Peleg, Ian and Scham, Paul (2007) "Israeli neo-revisionism and American neoconservatism: The unexplored parallels, *The Middle East Journal*, Vol 61, No1, pp73–94.

Penslar, Derek (2005) "Herzl and the Palestinian Arabs: Myth and counter-myth", *The Journal of Israeli History*, Vol 24, No 1, pp65–77.

Penslar, Derek (2020) "Theodor Herzl, Race, and Empire," in Maciejko, Paweł and Ury, Scott (eds) *Making History Jewish: The Dialectics of Jewish History in Eastern Europe and the Middle East. Essays in Honor of Israel Bartal* (Leiden: Brill).

Peretz, Don (1993) *Palestinians, Refugees and the Middle East Peace Process* (Washington DC: United States Institute of Peace Press.

Peteet, Julie (1991) *Gender in Crisis: Women and the Palestinian Resistance Movement* (New York: Colombia University Press).

Petran, Tabitha (1987) *The Struggle over Lebanon* (New York: Monthly Review Press).

Piterberg, Gabriel (2008) *The Returns of Zionism: Myth, Politics and Scholarship in Israel* (London: Verso).

PLO (1964) *Palestine Liberation Organisation: The Original Palestine National Charter 1964*, Internet Archive: https://archive.org/details/palestine-liberation-organization-the-original-palestine-national-charter-1964

Podeh, E. (2000) "History and memory in the Israeli educational system: The portrayal of the Arab–Israeli conflict in history textbooks (1948–2000)", *History and Memory*, Vol 12, No 1, pp 65–100.

Podhoretz, Norman (2004) "World War IV: How it started, what it means, and why we have to win", *Commentary*, September, pp17–54.

Polakow-Suransky, Sasha (2010) *The Unspoken Alliance: Israel's Secret Relationship with Apartheid South Africa* (New York: Pantheon).

Political Research Associates (2014) *Antisemitism and Islamophobia on US College Campuses, 2007–2011* (Somerville, MA: Political Research Associates).

Popular Front for the Liberation of Palestine (1973) *Tasks of the New Stage* (Beirut: Foreign Relations Committee, PFLP).

Porath, Yehoshua (1977) *The Emergence of the Palestinian National Movement: From riots to rebellion Volume 2, 1929–1939* (London: Frank Cass).

Preble, Christopher and Smith, Will (2024) "Great power competition shouldn't drive US policy in the Middle East", 31 October (Washington, DC: Stimson Center).

Project for a New American Century (1997) "Statement of Principles": https://web.archive.org/web/20130112235337/http://www.newamericancentury.org/statementofprinciples.htm

Qassem, Khalid (1988) "Repercussions in the Middle East", *Middle East Report*, p152.

Qian, Xuming, and Fulton, Jonathan (2017) "China–Gulf economic relationship under the 'Belt and Road' Initiative", *Asian Journal of Middle Eastern and Islamic Studies*, Vol 11, No 3, pp12–21.

Rabbani, Mouin (2024) "All shook up", in Stein-Weiner (ed), *Deluge: Gaza and Israel from Crisis to Cataclysm* (New York: OR Books), pp157–170.

Rabbani, Mouin and Hajjar, Lisa (1988) "Israel and the Palestinians, 1948–1988", *Merip Reports*, No 52.

Rackman, Emanuel (1954) *Israel's Emerging Constitution 1948–51* (New York: Columbia University Press).

Ram, Uri (2009) "Ways of forgetting: Israel and the obliterated memory of the Palestinian Nakba", *Journal of Historical Sociology*, Vol 22, No 3, pp366–395.

Rashed, Haifa, Short, Damien and Docker, John (2014) "Nakba memoricide: Genocide studies and the Zionist/Israeli genocide of Palestine", *Holy Land Studies*, Vol 13, No 1, pp1–23.

Raviv, Omri (2021) "Israeli emigration policies in the Gaza Strip: Crafting demography and forming control in the aftermath of the 1967 War", *Middle Eastern Studies*, Vol 57, No 2, pp342–356.

Reale, Hannah, Bingham, Emma and Greenberg, Kara (2020) "Where does China get its oil?" Centre on Global Energy Policy, Colombia University, 12 July.

Reeves, Phil (2001) "Sharon appeals to America not to 'appease' Arabs", *Independent*, 5 October.

Reich, Bernard (1984) *The United States and Israel: Influences in the Special Relationship* (New York: Praeger).

Renan, Ernest (1992) "What is a nation?" (text of a conference delivered at the Sorbonne on 11 March, 1882,) in Ernest Renan, *Qu'est-ce qu'une nation?* (Paris: Presses-Pocket): http://ucparis.fr/files/9313/6549/9943/What_is_a_Nation.pdf

Report of the Commission on the Palestine disturbances of August, 1929 (1930) [The Shaw Report] (London: His Majesty's Stationery Office).

Reut Institute (2010) *The Delegitimisation Challenge: Creating a Political Firewall*: https://www.reutgroup.org/Publications/building-a-political-firewall--against-israel's-delegitimization-

Revolutionary Socialists of Egypt (2024) "The most important lesson from October 6th and 7th: Liberating Jerusalem starts with liberating Cairo", 7 October: https://global.revsoc.me/2024/10/the-most-important-lesson-from-october-6th-and-7th-liberating-jerusalem-starts-with-liberating-cairo/

Rickford, Russell (2019) "'To build a new world': Black American internationalism and Palestine solidarity", *Journal of Palestine Studies*, Vol 48, No 4, pp52–68.

Rijke, Alexandra and van Teeffelen, Toine (2014) "To exist is to resist: Sumud, heroism, and the everyday", *Jerusalem Quarterly*, Vol 59, pp86–98.

Roberts, Hugh (2002) "Moral economy or moral polity? The political anthropology of Algerian riots", London School of Economics and Political Science, Crisis States Programme Working Paper, No 1.

Roberts, Hugh (2017) *The Battlefield: Algeria 1988–2002: Studies in a Broken Polity* (London: Verso).

Robinson, Glenn (2003) "Hamas as social movement", in Wiktorowicz, Quintan (ed) *Islamic Activism: A Social Movement Theory Approach* (Bloomington: Indiana University Press), pp112–139.

Robson, Laura (2011) "Church, state, and the Holy Land: British Protestant approaches to imperial policy in Palestine, 1917–1948", *Journal of Imperial & Commonwealth History*, Vol 39, No3, pp457–477.

Rose, John (2004) *The Myths of Zionism* (London: Pluto).

Rosenhek, Zeev (2003) "The political dynamics of a segmented labour market: Palestinian citizens, Palestinians from the Occupied Territories and migrant workers in Israel", *Acta Sociologica*, Vol 46, No 3, pp231–249.

Ross, Michael (1988) "Violence in Gaza echoes in Egypt: Like Lebanon invasion, unrest strains 2 neighbors' ties", *Los Angeles Times*, 12 January.

Rouleau, Eric (1985) "The Palestinian diaspora of the Gulf", *Merip*, 132

Rovner, Joshua (2014) "Delusion of defeat: The United States and Iraq, 1990–1998", *The Journal of Strategic Studies*, Vol 37, No 4, pp482–507.

Roy, Sara (2001) *The Gaza Strip: The Political Economy of De-Development*, 2nd ed. (Washington: Institute for Palestine Studies).

Roy, Sara (2004) "The Palestinian–Israeli Conflict and Palestinian socioeconomic decline: A place denied", *International Journal of Politics, Culture and Society*, Vol 17, No 3, pp365–403.

Roy, Sara (2024) "Econocide in Gaza", in Stern-Weiner (ed) *Deluge: Gaza and Israel from Crisis to Cataclysm* (New York: OR Books), pp37–55.

Rozin, Orit (2016) "Infiltration and the making of Israel's emotional regime in the state's early years", *Middle Eastern Studies*, Vol 52, No 3, pp448–472.

Rubenberg, Cheryl (1986) *Israel and the American National Interest: A Critical Examination* (Urbana: University of Illinois Press).

Rubenberg, Cheryl (2003) *The Palestinians: In Search of a Just Peace* (Boulder, CO: Lynne Reiner).

Rubin, Barry and Schwanitz, Wolfgang (2014) *Nazis, Islamists, and the Making of the Modern Middle East* (New Haven: Yale University Press).

Ruedy, John "Dynamics of land alienation" (1971) in Abu-Lughod, Ibrahim (ed), *The Transformation of Palestine: Essays on the Origin and Development of the Arab–Israeli Conflict* (Evanston [Ill.] Northwestern University Press), pp119–138.

Sabella, Bernard (1993) "Russian Jewish immigration and the future of the Israeli–Palestinian conflict"

Middle East Report, No 182: https://merip.org/1993/05/russian-jewish-immigration-and-the-future-of-the-israeli-palestinian-conflict/

Sacher, Harry (1952) *Israel: The Establishment of a State* (New York: British Book Centre).

Said, Edward (1980) *The Question of Palestine* (London: Routledge & Kegan Paul).

Said, Edward (1993) "The morning after", *London Review of Books*, 21 October.

Said, Edward (1998) *The Myth of 'The Clash of Civilizations'* (transcript from the Media Information Foundation): https://www.mediaed.org/transcripts/Edward-Said-The-Myth-of-Clash-Civilizations-Transcript.pdf

Said, Edward (2003) "Dignity, solidarity and the penal colony", *Counterpunch*, 25 September: https://www.counterpunch.org/2003/09/25/dignity-solidarity-and-the-penal-colony/

Sallam, Hesham (2023) "The Egyptian public and the war on Gaza", *Merip*, No 309

Sanders, Edmund (2011) "Israel fears regional regime change", *Los Angeles Times*, 4 February.

Saposnik, Arieh (2015) "Wailing walls and iron walls: The Western Wall as sacred symbol in Zionist national iconography", *The American Historical Review*, Vol 120, No 5, pp1653–1681.

Sayigh, Rosemary (1979) *Palestinians: From Peasants to Revolutionaries* (London: Zed).

Sayigh, Rosemary (2015) *Too Many Enemies: The Palestinian Experience in Lebanon* (Beirut: Al Mashriq).

Sayigh, Yusuf (1999) *Armed Struggle and the Search for State: The Palestinian National Movement, 1949–1993* (Oxford: Oxford University Press).

Schemm, Paul (2003) "Egypt Struggles to Control Anti-War Protests", *Merip*, 31 March

Schiff, Ze'ev and Ya'ari, Yehud (1985) *Israel's Lebanon War* (London: Touchstone).

Schmidt, Dana (1959) "CIA head warns of danger in Iraq," *New York Times*, 29 April.

Schoken, Gershon (1951) "The prostitutes of the seaports and ourselves: Meditations on the eve of the new year", *Ha'aretz* (30 September) in Hanegbi *et al*, 1971.

Scholtyseck, Joachim (2012) "Fascism – National Socialism – Arab 'Fascism': Terminologies, definitions and distinctions", *Die Welt des Islams*, No 52, pp242–289.

Schuster, Lisa and Solomos, John (1999) "The politics of refugee and asylum policies in Britain: Historical patterns and contemporary realities", in Bloch, Alice and Levy, Carl (eds) *Refugees, Citizenship and Social Policy in Europe* (Basingstoke, Macmillan).

Secretary of State for the Colonies (1939) *Palestine: Statement of Policy* (MacDonald White Paper), (London: His Majesty's Stationery Office): https://www.palquest.org/en/historictext/6722/macdonald-white-paper

Segal, Raz and Daniele, Luigi (2024) "Gaza as twilight of Israel exceptionalism: Holocaust and genocide studies from unprecedented crisis to unprecedented change", *Journal of Genocide Research*, 5 March: https://www.tandfonline.com/doi/epdf/10.1080/14623528.2024.2325804?needAccess=true

UN News (2024) "Human rights", 26 March: https://news.un.org/en/story/2024/03/1147976

Segev, Tom (1985) *1949: The First Israelis* (New York: The Free Press).

Segev, Tom (2000) *One Palestine, Complete: Jews and Arabs under the British Mandate* (London: Abacus).

Segev, Tom (2007) *1967: Israel, the War and the Year that Transformed the Middle East* (London: Abacus).

Seikaly, Sherine (2016) *Men of Capital: Scarcity and Economy in. Mandate Palestine* (Stanford: Stanford University Press).

Sela, Rona (2013) "Scouting Palestinian territory, 1940–1948: Haganah Village Files, aerial photos, and surveys", *Jerusalem Quarterly*, Vol 52.

Seth, Ronald (1966) *Russell Pasha* (London: William Kimber).

Shafir, Gershon (1989) *Land, Labor and the Origins of the Israeli–Palestinian Conflict, 1882–1914* (Cambridge: Cambridge University Press).

Shabtai, Teveth, (1997) *The Burning Ground* (Tel Aviv: Schocken).

Shahak, Israel (1976) "Arab villages destroyed in Israel", in Davis Uri and Mevlinsky, Norton, *Documents from Israel, 1967–1973: Readings for a Critique of Zionism* (London: Ithaca Press).

Shahak, Israel (1997) *Open Secrets: Israeli Nuclear and Foreign Policies* (London: Pluto), pp41–43.

Shahid, Leila (2002) "The Sabra and Shatila massacres: Eye-witness reports", *Journal of Palestine Studies*, Vol 32, No 1, pp36–58.

Shalev, Tal (2024) "IDF spokesperson Hagari: 'Hamas is an idea. You can't destroy an idea'", *Jerusalem Post*, 19 June.

Shalhoub-Kevorkian, Nadera (2016) "Infiltrated intimacies: The case of Palestinian returnees", *Feminist Studies*, Vol 42, No 1, pp166–193.

Shamir, Ronen (2013) *Current Flow: The Electrification of Palestine* (Stanford: Stanford University Press).

Sharon, Ariel (2001) *CNN*, 11 September.

Shaw, Martin (2010) "Palestine in an international historical perspective on genocide", *Holy Land Studies*, Vol 9, No 1, pp1–24.

Shaw, Martin and Bartov, Omer (2010) "The question of genocide in Palestine, 1948: A debate between Martin Shaw and Omer Bartov", *Journal of Genocide Res*earch, Vol 12, Nos 3/4, pp243–259.

Shepherd, Naomi (1999) *Ploughing Sand: The British in Palestine* (London: John Murray).

Sherman, A. J. (1994) *Island Refuge: Britain and the Refugees from the Third Reich, 1933–1939* (London: Frank Cass).

Shevit, Ari (2004) "Top PM aide: Gaza plan aims to freeze the peace process", *Haaretz*, 6 October.

Sherman, Taylor (2010) *State Violence and Punishment in India* (London: Routledge).

Shlaim, Avi (1994) "Israel and the conflict", in Danchev, Alex and Keohane, Dan (eds) *International Perspectives on the Gulf Conflict, 1990–91* (London, St Martin's Press), pp59–79.

Shlaim, Avi (1994) "Israel's Dirty War", *London Review of Books*, 8 August.

Shlaim, Avi (1995) "The debate about 1948", *International Journal of Middle East Studies*, Vol 27, No 3, pp 287–304.

Shlaim, Avi (2005) "The Balfour Declaration and its consequences" in Louis, William (ed) *Yet More Adventures with Britannia: Personalities, Politics and Culture in Britain* (London: I. B. Tauris), pp251–270.

Shlaim, Avi (2004) "The war of the Israeli historians", *Annales*, Vol 59, No 1, pp161–67

Shlaim, Avi (2012) "Israel and the Arab Coalition in 1948", in Rogan, Eugene and Shlaim Avi (eds) *The War for Palestine: Rewriting the United States and the Israeli–Palestinian Conflict History of 1948*, pp79–103

Shlaim, Avi (2019) "Ten years after the first war on Gaza, Israel still plans endless brute force", *Guardian*, 7 January.

Shlaim, Avi (2024) "Israel's War on Gaza", in Stern-Weiner, Jamie (ed) *Deluge: Gaza and Israel: From Crisis to Cataclysm* (OR Books: New York), pp13–34.

Shpiro, Shlomo (2003) "The CIA as Middle East peace broker?" *Survival*, Vol 32, No 2, pp91–112.

Shukrallah, Hani (2011) "How divided is Egypt's Muslim Brotherhood?", *Ahram Online*, 4 April: http://english.ahram.org.eg/NewsContent/1/64/8949/Egypt/Politics-/How-divided-is-Egypts-Muslim-Brotherhood.aspx; accessed 2 June 2015

Silber, Efrat (2011) "Israel's policy of house demolitions during the First Intifada, 1987–1993", *Terrorism and Political Violence*, Vol 23, pp89–107.

Simon, Steven and Stevenson, Jonathan (2023) "The Gaza horror and US Policy", *Survival*, Vol 65, No 6, pp37–56.

Sinanoglu, Penny (2019) *Partitioning Palestine: British Policymaking at the End of Empire* (Chicago: University of Chicago Press).

Singh, Kanishka and Stoner, Mike (2014) "US approves sale to Israel of $20 billion weapons package", *Reuters*, 13 August.

Smith, Barbara J. (1993) *The Roots of Separatism in Palestine: British Economic Policy, 1920–1929* (London: IB Tauris).

Smith, Pamela-Ann (1975) "Aspects of class structure in Palestinian society", in Davis, Uri, Mack, Andrew and Yuval-Davis, Nira (eds) *Israel and the Palestinians* (London: Ithaca Press), pp98–117.

Smith, Pamela-Ann (1984) *Palestine and the Palestinians, 1976–1983* (London: Croom Helm).

Smith, Pamela-Ann (1986) "The exile bourgeoisie of Palestine", *Merip Reports*, No 142

Socialist Worker (2023) "Biggest ever Palestine solidarity demo in British history", *Socialist Worker*, 11 November: https://socialistworker.co.uk/palestine-2023/palestine-march-london-national-4/

Sokol, Sam (2024) "Smotrich urges ramping up West Bank, Gaza settlements, pushing Palestinians out", *Times of Israel*, 28 October.

Sokol, Sam (2025) "Ben Gvir says he'll return to government if PM implements Trump's Gaza transfer plan", *Times of Israel*, 5 February.

Spoerl, Joseph (2020) "Parallels between Nazi and Islamist Anti-Semitism", *Jewish Political Studies Review*, Vol 31, No1/2, pp210–244.

Sprinzak, Ehud (1985) "Kach and Meir Kahane: The emergence of Jewish quasi-fascism II: Ideology and politics", *Patterns of Prejudice*, Vol 19, No4, pp3–13.

Stein, Ewan (2015) "Jihad discourse in Egypt under Muhammad Mursi", in Kendall, Elizabeth and Stein, Ewan (eds) *Twenty-First Century Jihad: Law, Society and Military Action* (London: I.B. Tauris), pp176–200.

Stein, Kenneth (1980) "Legal protection and circumvention of rights for cultivators in Mandatory Palestine", *Palestinian Society and Politics* (Princeton: Princeton University Press), pp233–61.

Stephens, Robert (1971) *Nasser: A Political Biography* (London: Penguin).

Stevens, Richard (1971) "Zionism, South Africa and Apartheid: The Paradoxical Triangle", *Phylon*, Vol 32, No 2, pp123–142.

Stewart, Desmond (1981) *Theodor Herzl, Artist and Politician* (London: Quartet).

Stork, Joe (1980) "The Carter Doctrine and US bases in the Middle East", *Merip Reports*, No 90, September.

Storrs, Ronald (1937) *Orientations* [Memoirs of Sir Ronald Storrs], (Newton Abbott: Readers Union).

Swedenburg, Ted (1987) "Al-Qassam remembered", *Alif: Journal of Comparative Poetics*, No 7, pp9–24.

Swedenburg, Ted (2003) *Memories of Revolt: The 1936–1939 Rebellion and the Palestinian National Past* (Fayetteville: University of Arkansas Press).

Taher, Nadia (2012) "'We are not women, we are Egyptians': Spaces of protest and representation", *City*, Vol 16, No 3, pp369–376.

Tal, David (2020) "United States–Israel Relations (1953–1957) revisited", *Israel Studies*, Vol 26, No 1, pp24–46.

Tamari, Salim (1983) "In league with Zion: Israel's search for a native pillar", *Journal of Palestine Studies*, Vol 12, No 4, pp41–56.

Tamura, Yukie (2009) "A study of the influence of the Young Men's Muslim Associations in Palestine through their charitable activities in the late 1920s", *Kyoto Bulletin of Islamic Area Studies*, Vol 3, No 1, pp237–248

Tanaka, Yukie (2009) "British 'human bombing' in Iraq during the interwar era", in Tanaka, Yukie and Young, Marylin, *Bombing Civilians: A Twentieth-Century History* (New York, The New Press).

Tenenbaum, Karen, and Eiran, Ehud (2005) "Israeli settlement activity in the West Bank and Gaza: A brief history", *Negotiations Journal*, Vol 21, pp171–175.

Thomas, Baylis, (2009) *The Dark Side of Zionism: The Quest for Security Through Dominance* (Lanham, MD: Lexington Books).

Time Magazine (1953) "99.93% pure," 17 August.

Harry S. Truman (1947) *US National Archives*, 12 March: https://www.archives.gov/milestone-documents/truman-doctrine

Tessier, Yann (2023) "Hundreds of thousands rally across cities to support Palestinians", *Reuters*, 29 October: https://www.reuters.com/world/uk/thousands-join-pro-palestinian-protest-london-demand-gaza-ceasefire-2023-10-28/

Thomson, Sorcha, Olsen, Pelle and Haugbolle, Sunne (2022) "Palestine solidarity conferences in the global sixties", *Journal of Palestine Studies*, Vol 51, No 1, pp27–49.

Thompson, Gardner (2021) *Legacy of Empire: Britain, Zionism and the Creation of Empire* (London: Saqi).

Tilley, Virginia (2007) "A two-state solution, or smoke and mirrors? Looking awry at Israel's state-building agenda", in Farouk-Alli, Aslan (ed) *The Future of Palestine and Israel: From Colonial Roots to Postcolonial Realities* (Midrand, South Africa: Institute for Global Dialogue/Friedrich Ebert Stiftung).

Time (1966) "Middle East: How they broke the bank", *Time* Magazine, 25 November.

Townshend, Charles (2010) *When God Made Hell: The British Invasion of Mesopotamia and the Creation of Iraq, 1914–1921* (London: Faber & Faber).

Tress, Madeleine (1984) "Fascist components in the political thought of Vladimir Jabotinsky", *Arab Studies Quarterly*, Vol 6, No 4, pp304–324.

Trouillot. Michel-Rolph (1995) *Silencing the Past: Power and the Production of History* (Boston: Beacon Press).

Turki, Fawaz (1972) *The Disinherited* (New York: Monthly Review Press).

Turki, Fawaz (1988) *Soul in Exile: Lives of a Palestinian Revolutionary* (New York: Monthly Review Press).

Turner, Mandy (2009) "The power of 'shock and awe': The Palestinian Authority and the road to reform" *International Peacekeeping*, Vol 16, No 4, pp562–577.

Ullman, Harman and Wade, James (1996) *Shock and Awe: Achieving Rapid Dominance* (Washington, DC: National Defense University).

United Nations (1947) "United Nations Special Committee on Palestine, September 1947": https://web.archive.org/web/20120603150222/http://domino.un.org/unispal.nsf/9a798adbf322aff38525617b006d88d7/07175de9fa2de563852568d3006e10f3?OpenDocument

United Nations (1949) *First Interim Report of the United Nations Economic Survey Mission for the Middle East* (the Clapp Report), 6 November: https://www.un.org/unispal/document/auto-insert-210462/

United Nations (1951) *Convention on the Prevention and Punishment of the Crime of Genocide*: https://www.un.org/en/genocideprevention/documents/atrocity-crimes/Doc.1_Convention%20on%20the%20Prevention%20and%20Punishment%20of%20the%20Crime%20of%20Genocide.pdf

United Nations (1974) "PLO sole legitimate representative of the Palestinian people – LAS Rabat Summit – resolution", Seventh Arab League Summit Conference "Resolution on Palestine" (Rabat, Morocco, 28 October 1974): https://www.un.org/unispal/document/auto-insert-194621/

United Nations (1988) Palestine question/Mideast situation, Final Declaration of the Arab Summit, letter from Algeria: https://www.un.org/unispal/document/auto-insert-187887/

United Nations (2004) "ICJ advisory opinion on the legal consequences of the construction of a wall in the OPT": https://www.un.org/unispal/document/auto-insert-178825/#:~:text=Settlements%20established%20by%20Israel%20in,of%20the%20wall%20severely%20impedes

United Nations (2009) *Human Rights in Palestine and Other Occupied Arab Territories: Report of the United Nations Fact Finding Mission on the Gaza Conflict* (Executive Summary) [The Goldstone Report].

United Nations (2024) "The Question of Palestine" (Summary of ICJ's Order of 24 May 2024): https://www.un.org/unispal/document/summary-of-icjs-order-24may24/#:~:text=The%20Court%20recalls%20that%2C%20on,as%20at%2018%20May%202024

United States Congress (2012) "Public Law 112–150" [United States-Israel Enhanced Security Cooperation Act of 2012]: https://www.congress.gov/112/statute/STATUTE-126/STATUTE-126-Pg1146.pdf

UPI (1982) "Begin compares Arafat to Hitler", *UPI*, 5 August: https://www.upi.com/Archives/1982/08/05/Begin-compares-Arafat-to-Hitler/2671397368000/

UPI (1990) "Former Egyptian minister calls for expulsion of Palestinians", 6 November.

Urquhart, Conor (2001) "Judge Goldstone expresses regrets about his report into Gaza war", *Guardian*, 3 April.

US Department of State (1949), "Presidential message to the prime minister of Israel", 28 May: https://www.jewishvirtuallibrary.org/truman-letter-to-ben-gurion-expresses-displeasure-regarding-territory-refugees#1

US Department of State, Bureau of Counterterrorism (2001) "Executive Order 13224": https://www.state.gov/executive-order-13224/

US Office of the Vice-President (1989) "Terrorist Group Profiles" [Washington DC: Superintendent of Documents]: https://apps.dtic.mil/sti/tr/pdf/ADA204627.pdf

Usher, Graham (1995) *Palestine in Crisis: The Struggle for Peace and Political Independence after Oslo* (London: Pluto).

US Department of State, Bureau of Counterterrorism (2001) "Executive Order 13224": https://www.state.gov/executive-order-13224/

Van Creveld, Martin (1998) *The Sword and the Olive* (New York: Public Affairs).

Veracini, Lorenzo (2010) *Settler Colonialism: A Theoretical Overview* (London: Palgrave Macmillan).

Veracini, Lorenzo (2013) "The other shift: Settler colonialism, Israel and the Occupation", *Journal of Palestine Studies*, Vol 42, No 2, pp26–42.

Wagdy, Wassim (2014) "Palestinian liberation is ingrained into the Egyptian revolution"

Socialist Worker, 15 July: https://socialistworker.co.uk/comment/palestinian-liberation-is-ingrained-into-the-egyptian-revolution/

Waldman, Peter and Pope, Hugh (2001) "'Crusade' reference reinforces fears War on Terrorism is against Muslims", *Wall Street Journal*, 21 September.

Walton, John and Seddon, David (2011) *Free Markets and Food Riots: The Politics of Global Adjustment* (London: Wiley-Blackwell).

Washington Post (2001) "Text: President Bush addresses the nation", 20 September.

Washington Post (2024) "U.S. floods arms into Israel despite mounting alarm over war's conduct", *Washington Post*, 6 March: https://www.washingtonpost.com/national-security/2024/03/06/us-weapons-israel-gaza/

Weinstock, Nathan (1979) *Zionism: False Messiah* (London: Ink Links).

Wendell, Charles (1978) *Five Tracts of Hasan Al-Banna (1906–1949): A Selection from the Majmuat Rasail al-Imam al-Shahid Hasan al-Banna* [translation and annotation of Arabic originals] (Berkeley, University of California Press).

Wenger, Martha (1990) "US aid to Israel: From handshake to embrace", *Merip*, pp164–165, May/June: https://merip.org/1990/05/us-aid-to-israel/

Wermenbol, Grace (2024) "Why Hamas cannot be destroyed", *Cairo Review of Global Affairs*, Summer.

Whitson, Sarah (2014) "Ariel Sharon's legacy is deeply disturbing", *Human Rights Watch*, 13 January: https://www.hrw.org/news/2014/01/13/ariel-sharons-legacy-deeply-disturbing

Whyte, D. (2007) "The crimes of Neo-Liberal rule in occupied Iraq", *British Journal of Criminology*, Vol 47, No 2, pp177–195.

Wild, Stefan (2012) "'Islamofascism'? Introduction", *Die Welt des Islams*, Vol 52, No 3/4, pp225–24, pp228–229.

Wildangel, Rene (2012) "The invention of 'Islamofascism': Nazi propaganda to the Arab World and perceptions from Palestine", *Die Welt des Islams*, Vol 52, No 3/4, pp526–543.

Winder, Alex (2012) "The 'Western Wall' Riots of 1929: Religious boundaries and communal violence", *Journal of Palestine Studies*, Vol 42, No 1, pp6–23.

Yahia, Karem (1987) "The image of the Palestinians in Egypt, 1982–85", *Journal of Palestine Studies*, Vol 16, No 2, pp45–63.

Yergin, Daniel (2017) *The Prize: The Epic Quest for Oil, Money, and Power* (New York, The Free Press).

Yiftachel, Oren (1996) "Nation-building or ethnic fragmentation? Frontier settlement and collective identities in Israel", *UCLA Working Paper Series*: https://escholarship.org/content/qt0t48n0zb/qt0t48n0zb.pdf

Yiftachel, Oren (2010) "From Sharon to Sharon: Spatial planning and separation regime in Israel/Palestine", *HAGAR Studies in Culture, Polity and Identities*, Vol 10, No 1, pp73–106.

Yiftachel, Oren (2013) "Liberal colonialism? Israel's 2013 elections and the 'Ethnocratic Bubble'", *Journal of Palestine Studies*, Vol 42, No 3, pp48–67.

Zohdi, Helena (2024) "Contemporary fellow travellers: Egyptian Revolutionary Socialists and the theory and political practice of Marxism", *Third World Quarterly*, 21 October: https://www.tandfonline.com/doi/pdf/10.1080/01436597.2024.2412649

Zuhur, Sharifa (2008) *Hamas and Israel: Conflicting Strategies of Group-Based Politics* (Washington: Strategic Studies Institute).

Zurayk, Constantine (1956) *The Meaning of the Disaster* (Beirut: Khayat),

Index